RUSSIA IN THE
NEW CENTURY

RUSSIA IN THE NEW CENTURY

Stability or Disorder?

Edited by

VICTORIA E. BONNELL
GEORGE W. BRESLAUER

A Member of the Perseus Books Group

Copyright © 2001 by Westview Press, A Member of the Perseus Books Group

Published in 2001 in the United States of America by Westview Press, 5500 Central Avenue, Boulder, Colorado 80301-2877, and in the United Kingdom by Westview Press, 12 Hid's Copse Road, Cumnor Hill, Oxford OX2 9JJ

Visit us on the World Wide Web at www.westviewpress.com

Library of Congress Cataloging-in-Publication Data
    Russia in the new century : stability or disorder? / edited by Victoria E. Bonnell and George W. Breslauer
        p.   cm.
    Includes bibliographical references and index.
    ISBN 0-8133-9041-9
    1. Russia (Federation)—Politics and government—1991–.   2. Russia (Federation)—Economic conditions—1991–.   3. Russia (Federation)—Social conditions—1991–.   4. Nationalism—Russia (Federation).   5. Post-communism—Russia (Federation).   I. Bonnell, Victoria E.   II. Breslauer, George W.

DK510.763 .R859 2000
947.086—dc21   00-043310

The paper used in this publication meets the requirements of the American National Standard for Permanence of Paper for Printed Library Materials Z39.48-1984.

10   9   8   7   6   5   4   3   2   1

Contents

PART III: SOCIETY

PART IV: THE NATION

Tables and Figures

Acknowledgments

This project was initiated with the encouragement and support of Astrid Tuminez and David Speedie at the Carnegie Corporation of New York. We are grateful to the Carnegie Corporation for funding the broad, ambitious research effort launched by our group in 1998. Many of the ideas and research findings included in this volume were first presented at Carnegie-funded seminars conducted over a two-year period at the Center for Slavic and East European Studies, of the University of California at Berkeley.

We also would like to acknowledge and thank the many UC, Berkeley faculty members, graduate students, visiting scholars, and invited guests whose participation in the seminar series and in the subsequent conference in May 1999 helped make the discussions both lively and informative.

We owe a considerable debt to Edward Walker, executive director of the Berkeley Program in Soviet and Post-Soviet Studies (BPS), whose contributions to the design and implementation of the project and to the preparation of this book were invaluable. We are grateful also for substantial assistance rendered by other BPS staff members, including Sasha Radovich and Denise Monczewski. We appreciate Jane Zavisca's help with the page proofs. Matthew Bencke made important contributions to the project as rapporteur during the Carnegie seminars, and later, during the preparation of the manuscript, as editorial and research assistant.

Victoria E. Bonnell
George W. Breslauer

Acronyms

ASSR	autonomous Soviet socialist republic
CIS	Commonwealth of Independent States (of the former Soviet Union)
CPCD	Congress of Peoples of Chechnya and Dagestan
CPRF	Communist Party of the Russian Federation (also KPRF)
CP RSFSR	Communist Party of the RSFSR
CPSU	Communist Party of the Soviet Union
DEMOS	a commercial electronic communication network, the Russian equivalent of UNIX
FBIS-SOV	Foreign Broadcast Information Service, report on the Soviet/post-Soviet states
FBIS-UMA	Foreign Broadcast Information Service, report on military affairs
FDR	Franklin Delano Roosevelt
FIG	financial-industrial group
FNS	National Salvation Front
Gazprom	the Russian natural gas monopoly
GDP	gross domestic product
GKO	short-term government bond
GUUAM	the alliance among Georgia, Ukraine, Uzbekistan, Azerbaijan, and Moldova
IDP	internally displaced person
IMEMO	Institute of the World Economy and International Relations (at the Russian Academy of Sciences)
IP	Internet protocol
ISP	Internet service provider
ITAR-TASS	Independent Telegraph Agency of Russia–Telegraph Agency of the Soviet Union
Komsomol	Young Communist League
KPRF	Communist Party of the Russian Federation (also CPRF)
KRO	Congress of Russian Communities
LDPR	Liberal Democratic Party of Russia
Mbps	millibytes per second
MDR	multiple-drug-resistant (adj.)

Menatep	one of the first Soviet banking ventures; the acronym stands for Inter-Branch Center for Scientific and Technological Program
MGIMO	Moscow State Institute of International Relations
MVO	Russian Interior Ministry
MZhK	Soviet housing complex for youth
NATO	North Atlantic Treaty Organization
NDR	Our Home Is Russia (political party)
NG	Nezavisimaia Gazeta
NPSR	Narodno-Patrioticheskii Soiuz Rossii (Popular-Patriotic Union of Russia)
NTTM	Center for Scientific-Technical Creativity of Youth
NVO	*Nezavisimoe voennoe obozrenie* (Russian armed forces newspaper)
R&D	research and development
RAN	Rossiiskaia Akademiia Nauk (Russian Academy of Sciences)
RCC	Russian Constitutional Court
RELCOM	Reliable Communication (Russia's first electronic communication network)
RF	Russian Federation
RFE/RL	Radio Free Europe/Radio Liberty
RNE	Russian National Unity party
RNS	Russkii Natsional'nyi Sobor (Russian National Union)
ROCIT	Russian Public Center for Information Technologies
ROS	Russian All-People's Union
RSFSR	Russian Soviet Federated Socialist Republic
RUIE	Russian Union of Industrialists and Entrepreneurs
SBS-Agro	Stolichny Bank of Savings–Agroprombank
SFOR	Stabilization Force (peacekeeping operation in Bosnia)
SMZ	Syktyvkar Machine Building Factory
TB	tuberculosis
TsK KPSS	Russian acronym for the Central Committee of the CPSU
USIA	United States Information Agency
VTsIOM	Russian Center for Public Opinion Research

Introduction

1

Informal Networks, Collective Action, and Sources of (In)stability in Russia

A Brief Overview

Victoria E. Bonnell

George W. Breslauer

University of California, Berkeley

Almost a decade has passed since the collapse of communism in the USSR and the dismemberment of the country. In the immediate aftermath of the monumental events of 1991, Western scholars offered widely divergent assessments of the country's trajectory. Whereas some anticipated progress toward democratization and marketization, many others made ominous predictions that Russia might not survive the coming winter.[1] At the same time, Western politicians justified their support for economic and other assistance to Russia by stressing the potentially apocalyptic consequences of "losing" Russia and allowing that country to fall victim to chaos, communist restoration, or fascist reaction.[2] Russian leaders, eager to secure loans and grants from the West, consciously reinforced these fears with their own rhetoric.[3]

Neither apocalyptic fears nor optimistic hopes have been realized. Russia has in fact survived many winters since the demise of the USSR, but there has also been widespread human suffering. Russia possesses a minimalist electoral democracy with extensive civil liberties but has made little progress in building the many other strong, autonomous institutions needed to consolidate liberal democracy and civil society. Similarly, Russia has a market economy of sorts—but one that more closely resembles Third World economies, with their crony capitalism and racketeering, than it does economies in the West. Russia has descended into the ranks of "failed states" whose distinguishing feature is the diminished power and authority of the central government to enforce the law; collect taxes; enforce conscription; ensure a minimum standard of living; provide basic health, education, and welfare service; and maintain public order.

As this project comes to completion at the end of March 2000, Russia's future prospects remain uncertain. Although that country has escaped widespread social disorder or political collapse, few observers would argue that the situation has truly stabilized. The financial crisis of August 1998 underscored the continuing fragility and vulnerability of major institutions. The renewed warfare in Chechnya holds out the prospect of an extended guerrilla war and increased domestic terrorism.

Nevertheless, the reactions of most Russians have thus far been adaptive rather than defiant. Yearnings for stabilization and predictability have steadily grown stronger as the visible enfeeblement and corruption of the central government have increased. That Yevgenii Primakov was the most popular politician in the country throughout most of 1999 provided a telling indicator of the centrist orientation of most Russians and their desire for stability. The results of parliamentary elections in December 1999 also reflected a preference for political parties that would maintain order and avoid transformative policies of both the "left" and the "right."

The groundswell of support for presidential candidate Vladimir Putin, due in large part to the renewed Chechen war, reflected the craving of many citizens for a decisive and dependable leader capable of preserving order, fighting domestic terrorism, and sustaining the national integrity of the Russian state. At his election on March 26, 2000, this former KGB intelligence officer had yet to articulate a clear set of policies for domestic and foreign affairs. Nevertheless, Putin's bland but diligent demeanor, and the popularity of his "get tough" rhetoric, enabled him to attract a broad and motley coalition of political leaders and parties, ranging from communists to liberal reformers. But in order to deliver on his promise to restore Kremlin power at home and abroad he will have to contend with Russia's conflicting historical legacies and with a formidable set of contemporary problems.

What path will Russia take in the new century? Is the current balance between authoritarian and democratic elements in the political order likely to persist? Will the combination of racketeering and free-marketization eventually lead to a stable economy? Does the weakness of the Russian state portend greater or lesser public unrest and defiance of that state by regional elites? Will Russia's passage from imperial core to independent nation-state bring with it the consolidation of liberal nationalism, or the reemergence of a revanchist, imperialist mentality? Will the current situation, so laced with contradictions, soon give way to an alternative, such as an authoritarian regime, military rule, growing political violence, civil war, or an accelerating "Ottomanization" of the country?

These questions are addressed by the contributors to this volume—seventeen distinguished scholars from the United States, Russia, and Europe—with the aim of identifying the institutions, social forces, and ideas that are transforming Russia and are in turn being transformed. There is abundant evidence that Russia is in crisis. Far less is known about popular and elite reactions to that crisis. We have asked the authors to map Russia's postcommunist experience during the Yeltsin era with an eye to the country's prospects for stability and disorder in the coming century.

We address the issues without a preconceived theoretical or political agenda. Russia today shows features suggestive of a revolutionary situation—such as splits among elites, widespread alienation, and a state fiscal crisis. The current situation in Russia somewhat resembles that in Germany before the rise of Hitler, and in Italy before the rise of Mussolini. But neither social revolution nor fascism provides an adequate basis for assessing the trajectory of contemporary Russia, given the vast differences among these nations with respect to their history, international context, sociopolitical organization, and patterns of economic development.[4]

Were we testing specific propositions, we might have narrowed our focus significantly. One could, for example, envision a project that would combine theory with empirical observation in order to test specific hypotheses about the relationship, say, between frustration and aggression. Alternatively, one might devote a volume to reexamining the evidence about Russian political culture and public orientations to authority in order to test various theories about the prerequisites for democratic consolidation.[5] Our approach is broader, more eclectic, and less disciplined, as we have sought to give attention to a multiplicity of actual and potential challenges to stability, both from above and from below.

We begin with the assumption that there can be many paths to systemic breakdown. Violent challenges to the existing order could come from within the political establishment, from social forces, or from some combination of the two. Economic shocks or internal or international incidents could trigger such challenges. Political and social forces can be mobilized by restricted cabals, by electoral victories (whether rigged or not), or by popular movements united by compelling ideas that congeal into a credible alternative ideology. A collectivity may suffer from widespread deprivation and disaffection and yet find itself incapable of organizing for collective action to improve conditions. In a single volume, we could not explore all these possibilities. What we have tried to do instead is to analyze major features of postcommunist Russia with an eye to specifying the factors that brought about the current situation, the tensions that create pressures for change, and the circumstances that are likely to promote or inhibit stability.

Inevitably, as in any general discussion about this vast and varied nation, there are gaps in coverage—most notably, that of Russia's regions (other than the North Caucasus and Dagestan); of relations between Moscow and the regions; and of the rural population. A truly comprehensive, equitable discussion of the regions would have required many more pages than could be accommodated in this volume. Moreover, as regards rural areas in particular, we concluded early on that the peasantry is much less likely to challenge political stability than is the urban working class. These particular omissions notwithstanding, we believe that our contributors' informed observations and empirical findings will generate new insights among scholars, students, and other readers making their way through the complex and variegated landscape of Russia today.

A Brief Outline of Chapters

The chapters in the first part of the volume analyze political institutions. M. Steven Fish discusses the formation of the system of "superpresidentialism," which accords vast legislative, fiscal, and judicial powers to the executive even as it emasculates other branches of government. Utilizing political theory as well as the experiences of other postcommunist countries, Fish argues that such a concentration of authority has "pernicious effects" on Russia by interfering with both democratization and the emergence of a vibrant civil society. More specifically, he finds that superpresidentialism "has impaired the legitimacy of the post-Soviet regime and helped to discredit democracy itself, arrested the development of political-societal organizations, enfeebled state agencies and undermined state capacity, and diminished the accountability of officialdom to the citizenry" in Russia.

George W. Breslauer, who also focuses on the Russian presidency, makes a complementary argument. He examines the evolution of Boris Yeltsin's personalistic and patriarchal leadership style since 1991. His chapter emphasizes the negative consequences of these arrangements, which have undermined the "rational distribution of formal power," fostered an "individualized, anti-procedural and anti-institutional" approach to governance, widespread corruption, and "crony capitalism." By frustrating the construction of institutions based on stable procedures, Boris Yeltsin has bequeathed a legacy of institutions that are highly personalized and fragile. Both Fish and Breslauer emphasize the importance of future measures to halt further devolution of power and to promote the development of institutions capable of buttressing civil society and democratization.

The Constitutional Court, which is modeled on the U.S. Supreme Court, is the subject of Robert Sharlet's contribution. In contrast to the institutional weaknesses discerned in the executive branch by Fish and Breslauer, Sharlet sees subtle but steady progress over time in the Court's ability to influence both the legal agenda and elite opinion concerning issues such as the separation of powers, individual rights, and federalism. To be sure, Russia's fledgling judicial order remains fragile. The key to judicial influence, according to Sharlet, lies in avoiding too sharp a break with those in power, and in adopting a pragmatic, cautious approach to judicial innovation. Sharlet avoids prognostications on whether the Court will gain greater freedom from political intervention in coming years, but he clearly believes that an expansion of the Court's discretion would have a salutary effect on political stabilization.

Kimberly Zisk analyzes the condition of Russian military forces and the prospects for a military coup in response to widespread disaffection both in the military and in the population at large. Zisk reaches the conclusion that the risk of such a coup is very low. She finds that although disaffection is high, the deterioration of collective solidarity within and among the ranks, the erosion of military resources and discipline, and the spread of corruption and demoralization at all levels have robbed potential coup plotters of both the ideological and the organizational means necessary for a successful military coup.

In Part II, the authors address issues relating to the Russian economy. Clifford Gaddy and Barry Ickes find that the Russian economy is trapped in a condition that they describe as the "virtual economy." The virtual economy combines elements of the old Soviet system and of macroeconomic policies followed since 1992 with the defensive, adaptive behavior of enterprises and management in response to the dislocations and uncertainties they face. The economy is only partially monetized, for barter remains widespread; and many enterprises find themselves in the anomalous situation of producing goods but destroying value. All this and much else is hidden from public view.

The virtual economy is a continuation of Soviet welfarism, aimed at staving off social dislocations that could cause workers to take to the streets en masse. It may purchase near-term political stability, but how long can it last? There are limits to the International Monetary Fund's willingness to subsidize this economy as well as to the Russian government's ability to subsidize loss-making enterprises. Furthermore, the entire arrangement impedes the industrial restructuring that is so necessary if Russia is to become competitive in international markets for manufactured goods. In short, the temporary stability eventually may be followed by a day of reckoning.

Another source of social inequality is explored by Emma Kiselyova and Manuel Castells, whose analysis focuses on the role of technological innovation and the diffusion of information technology in Russia. Since 1991, Russia has witnessed the demise of microelectronics and the traditional computer industry as well as the retardation of the public telecommunications network. As a consequence of these developments, Kiselyova and Castells conclude that a process of "dualization" has been accelerating within Russia. This process separates the minority of the population that is plugged into the Internet (whom they call "netizens") from the vast majority of the population, which remains outside the new technology and the global economy more generally. Netizens do not necessarily coincide as a social group with wealthy industrialists and bankers. Their ranks also include many young, urban professionals who are seeking to establish their own small businesses, as well as many urban intellectuals who are seeking to plug into the global information highway. Kiselyova and Castells see this group as the country's best hope for the future.

Victor M. Sergeyev addresses the issue of organized crime, another source of mass indignation, extreme social inequality, and remonopolization of the economy. In a complement to Gaddy and Ickes's "virtual economy," Sergeyev employs spatial metaphors to explain the circumstances that allow organized crime to flourish in Russia. He argues that much of the economy has been transformed into enormous "gray zones"—the space that exists between formal rules, on the one hand, and informal understanding and patterns of behavior that survived the collapse of the Soviet Union, on the other. The "alternative state" that has arisen within these gray zones provides the terrain for a wide array of criminal activities. In the worst cases, gray zones have become black holes in which the state has almost entirely lost its power to enforce the law. But in most of Russian society, gray zones predominate as a result of the paucity of legal development, the weakness of judicial organs, and the corruption of political and economic elites. Organized crime now performs some of the regulatory functions that are usually performed by a strong state, such as contract enforcement.

Part III is devoted to an exploration of social groups, specifically entrepreneurs and workers. Victoria Bonnell's analysis of the evolution of the entrepreneurial class reinforces the image of Russia's dualization described by Kiselyova and Castells. Forged in the crucible of the *perestroika* era, this highly variegated group stratified rapidly into an oligarchy (made up of a small number of wealthy and influential businessmen who preside over vast resources) and a much larger group of middle-level and small-scale entrepreneurs struggling to survive. Personal ties, political connections, crime, and corruption have been major formative elements in the creation of this social stratum. A "circulation of elites" at the top has taken place, bringing regional tycoons and former Soviet bureaucrats into positions of vast wealth and power, together with a handful of self-made men. The deep lines of stratification within the business community and the predatory relationship between business and state present major obstacles to the organizational consolidation and public recognition of the new entrepreneurial stratum.

Victor Zaslavsky examines the working class—coal workers, in particular. The number of Russian strikes and striking workers has grown steadily since the Soviet collapse, but the working class has yet to coalesce into a stable formation and has proven unable to engage in effective and sustained collective action. Rather than organize for long-term gain, the working class remains generally atomized, with individuals and small groups struggling among themselves for limited resources.

Zaslavsky finds that the working class has been a force for stability due to the symbiotic relationship between management and workers—a relationship focused on preserving employment and generating "informal" income. But even as workers cushioned the transition to a market economy, they also hindered this transition, contributing to widespread disillusionment about economic reform and democracy. Zaslavsky concludes that despite this disillusionment, the still growing mass of un- and underemployed workers, and workers' relative disempowerment, Russian society shows little sign of polarizing along class lines.

How do ordinary people cope with the deprivations that have been their lot in recent years? This question was the subject of ethnographic research conducted by Michael Burawoy, Pavel Krotov, and Tatyana Lytkina. The authors report two kinds of coping strategies—defensive and entrepreneurial—developed by ordinary people in Syktyvkar, the capital of Komi, in northern Russia. Their ethnographic research brings to light several key factors shaping the lives of ordinary people. Like other contributors to this volume, Burawoy, Krotov, and Lytkina find a dualistic pattern: (1) The vast majority of people react defensively to their conditions and engage in an unremitting struggle for survival; and (2) a small minority, often for a lack of alternatives, embrace proactive, entrepreneurial strategies for finding and exploiting opportunities for survival and advancement.

The key to defensive (survivalist) strategies is a combination of public welfare and social networks, whereas the keys to entrepreneurial coping strategies are one's ability and willingness to combine material, skill, and social and citizenship assets to venture into economic exchange. Most Komi residents seem to have chosen their strategy for coping with "economic involution" by 1994–1995, and their choice has proven remarkably stable despite ongoing environmental challenges and uncertainty. The authors' findings highlight the continuing role of the state in providing minimal but essential transfer payments, and the critical role of social (particularly kin-based) networks in keeping people afloat.

Part IV includes three chapters on the theme of the nation. As the imperial center is being transformed into an independent nation-state, Russian nationalism is undergoing a re-formation. The search for a national identity may have many outcomes. A liberal, inclusive, and tolerant variant would provide an ideational buttress for stabilization, whereas a reactionary, exclusive, and intolerant variant would surely facilitate an authoritarian or fascist ascendancy.

Igor Zevelev surveys Russian political parties and their positions on issues of nation-building, national security, and Russia's relations with the so-called near abroad. He presents a typology of five major perspectives on Russia's post-Soviet role in the former Soviet space, and more generally, in its international relations: those of "state-builders," "restorationists," "ethnonationalists," "dominators," and "integrationalists." Zevelev develops this typology in reviewing the referents, goals, threats, and instruments of the major post-Soviet Russian factions and deploying this framework in a case study of Russian-Ukrainian relations. He finds that coalitions formed by political actors are based in large part on particular concerns about nation-building and security policies. In other words, Zevelev asserts that foreign policy, to a large extent, determines the identity of domestic political actors. He concludes that a common preoccupation with the pursuit of stability has provided grounds for compromise among key Russian factions, producing a relatively cautious foreign policy and a measure of domestic political collaboration. This common ground has tended to marginalize extreme viewpoints, and Zevelev speculates that it may prove a force for future stability.

The historical and contemporary context of Russian national identity is further explored by Veljko Vujacic. His chapter focuses on the strange union between the Communist "left" and the Russian "right," dating from the perestroika era if not earlier. Through a close analysis of the rhetoric and actions of nationalist and neocommunist groups, Vujacic analyzes the circumstances that have given rise to ideologies and organizations whose celebration of the ideal of the corporatist state is reminiscent of interwar right-wing authoritarianism and fascism in Western Europe.

The early success of the Liberal Democratic Party of Russia (LDPR) was no accident, Vujacic argues, but a product of Vladimir Zhirinovsky's unsurpassed ability to tap into the sentiment of national humiliation. Yet the LDPR's achievements faded by the end of the decade, and the Communist Party of the Russian Federation (CPRF) proved the most enduring and influential of national-revanchist organizations. By the middle of the decade, the Communist party had co-opted nationalistic policy and rhetoric, purveying a distinctive brand of patriotism. The left, the right, and the left-right coalition all failed to mobilize the people for a successful seizure of power during the Yeltsin era. Like other contributors to this volume, Vujacic discerns a weak variety of stability to date, with a weak foundation for the future.

The final chapter in the volume examines the problem of stability through a case study of the most violence-prone region in Russia, the North Caucasus. Edward W. Walker's investigation of the Republic of Dagestan seeks to explain Dagestan's avoidance of large-scale political violence since 1991, notwithstanding the republic's deep economic and social crisis. Walker's chapter addresses a question that has preoccupied foreign policy experts and policymakers in Moscow: Will Russia's conflict in Chechnya spread beyond Chechnya's borders, prompting a region-wide Islamic or pan-highlander uprising that drives Russia from the region and limits Russia's participation in the new "Great Game" unfolding in the South Caucasus and Caspian region?

Walker argues that the nature of Dagestan's social structure, which encompasses numerous religious and national identities, has created a "classic balance-of-power system" that makes it quite unlikely that Dagestan will follow Chechnya in waging a long-term, armed struggle against Moscow. Walker highlights the potentially stabilizing consequences of localized solidarities, particularistic concerns, and social atomization in a society in which broader allegiances and networks for collective action and identity have been undermined. On the other side, he notes that economic and social conditions in the republic are unlikely to improve significantly for the foreseeable future. As a result, Dagestan's "stable instability," as Walker puts it, is very likely to persist.

Common Themes

Several unifying themes cut across the contributions to this volume. Over the past decade, Russia has witnessed a variety of new social, economic, and political formations, ranging from entrepreneurial groups to netizens to political parties. At the same time, preexisting elements at all levels of society and polity have regrouped and reconfigured. What all of these have in common is a persistent tendency toward fragmentation or dualization and a relatively low level of institutionalization.

Weak legal traditions, combined with personalism, corruption, privatization of violence, economic deprivation, and nationalistic (not to speak of anti-Western) rhetoric, reinforce the lines of cleavage among groups and create new forms of stratification. In this connection, Soviet legacies are particularly potent and lasting. The absence of a genuine civil society and truly voluntary associations for so many decades has been difficult to overcome, and there is considerable evidence that Russians remain trapped in the residue of their Soviet experience. The net result is a society and a polity in which the capacity for *antisystemic* collective action remains low.

These circumstances have proved conducive to the flourishing of ad hoc informal networks and groups, formed under adverse conditions, by people trying to cope with crisis rather than to overthrow the system. Some networks informally unite the reform-minded; others, the backward-looking. But all unite people in ways that reinforce the particularistic concerns that are dominant in Russia today. Thus, informal networks have congealed among segments within the military (Zisk); among value-subtractors (Gaddy and Ickes); netizens (Kiselyova and Castells); organized criminals (Sergeyev); entrepreneurs (Bonnell); workers (Zaslavsky); lower-class groups (Burawoy, Krotov, and Lytkina); coalitions organized around foreign policy concerns (Zevelev); "patriotic" political factions (Vujacic); and localized solidarities in Dagestan (Walker).

The imposition of superpresidentialism and the corresponding underdevelopment of political parties and groups have further contributed to fragmentation. Yeltsin's personalistic and arbitrary leadership, along with the corruption it fostered, helped keep the military and other possible contenders for power divided and off-balance, thereby diminishing the near-term prospects for antisystemic actions. Similarly, the underdevelopment of political parties in Russia, largely traceable to Yeltsin's leadership style, reduced the capacity of oppositional elites to mobilize the citizenry. At the same time, both democracy and stability hinge on the creation of reliable venues into which collective action may be channeled. But personalistic leadership, which divides organized collectivities by buying off key members or leaders of those groupings, can blunt various forms of collective action.

Moreover, the country's political leaders have exercised power in ways that reinforce this sociopolitical fragmentation (Fish, Breslauer) and that force the protean formal-procedural institutions (Sharlet) to exercise their powers with utmost caution. Socioeconomic and sociopolitical networks, and the strategies and tactics they deployed, provided interim stability in Russia during the 1990s. They are but a fragile basis for long-term stability, however. Although the current pattern could conceivably endure well into the new century, there is no way to predict how long the "near term" will last. President Putin is banking on near-term stability; but the test of his leadership will come when he confronts the need to build institutions that will buttress long-term stability.

Notes

1. See, for example, Keith Bradsher, "Forecasting the Hungriest Soviet Winter in Years," *New York Times,* November 10, 1991, section 4, p. 4; and Fred Kaplan, "Muscovites Chilled by Thoughts of a Another Lean Russian Winter," *Journal of Commerce,* October 20, 1992, p. 3A.

2. See, for example, Amy Kaslow, "Bush Aid Plan Aims to Bolster Yeltsin Reforms," *Christian Science Monitor,* April 3, 1992, p. 1; and "Might We Lose Russia? Nixon Dares to Ask the Question," *Los Angeles Times,* March 13, 1992, part B, p. 6.

3. See, for example, "Yeltsin Warns of Threat to His Rule," *Daily Telegraph,* February 7, 1992, p. 9; and Fred Hiatt, "A-Arms Chief Says Russia Needs Help," *Washington Post,* February 5, 1992, p. A22.

4. Stephen E. Hanson and Jeffrey S. Kopstein, "The Weimar/Russia Comparison," *Post-Soviet Affairs,* 13, 3, July–September 1997, pp. 252–283; but see, for a counter-argument, Stephen D. Shenfield, "The Weimar/Russia Comparison: Reflections on Hanson and Kopstein," 14, 4, October–December 1997, pp. 355–368; and the reply by Kopstein and Hanson, in ibid., pp. 369–375.

5. Harry Eckstein, Frederic J. Fleron, Jr., Erik P. Hoffmann, and William M. Reisinger, *Can Democracy Take Root in Post-Soviet Russia?* (Lanham, Md.: Rowman & Littlefield, 1999).

PART I

Politics

2

When More Is Less

Superexecutive Power and Political Underdevelopment in Russia

M. Steven Fish

University of California, Berkeley

When legislative power is united with executive power in a single person or in a single body of the magistracy, there is not liberty, because one can fear that the same monarch or senate that makes tyrannical laws will execute them tyrannically.

Nor is there liberty if the power of judging is not separate from legislative power and from executive power. If it were joined to legislative power, the power over the life and liberty of the citizens would be arbitrary, for the judge would be the legislator. If it were joined to executive power, the judge could have the force of an oppressor.

All would be lost if the same man or the same body of principal men, either of nobles, or of the people, exercised these three powers: that of making the laws, that of executing public resolutions, and that of judging the crimes or the disputes of individuals.

—**Montesquieu**[1]

Among citizens and students of postcommunist countries and other polities undergoing systemic transformation, few notions have been more widely and reflexively embraced than the claim that "strong executive power" aids political and economic advancement. In most postcommunist countries where power is concentrated in the executive, electorates and constitution-makers have preferred presidential systems to parliamentary ones, and executive power has been vested in a president rather than a prime minister. Mighty presidents have been

hailed as saviors from statelessness, dictatorship, national dependence, and economic crisis.

Yet few generalizations are based on flimsier evidence. Indeed, superexecutivism—understood here as overweening, largely uncontrolled executive power—
has resulted in all manner of pathologies in the postcommunist world. In Russia,
superpresidentialism has impaired the legitimacy of the post-Soviet regime and of
democracy, arrested the development of sociopolitical organizations, enfeebled
state agencies and undermined state capacity, and diminished the accountability
of officialdom to the citizenry. In no respect is Russia exceptional; superpresidentialism has exerted similar effects in other postcommunist polities as well.

By *superpresidentialism* I mean specifically a form of regime that may be considered a democracy (or a partial democracy), insofar as regular elections are
held for power holders and the latter normally observe basic associational and
communicative rights.[2] Thus, superpresidentialism may be contrasted with dictatorship such as that found in Azerbaijan since 1993; Belarus and Kazakhstan
since roughly mid-decade; and Serbia, Tajikistan, Turkmenistan, and Uzbekistan
since the late 1980s and early 1990s. It may also be contrasted with moderate
presidentialism and semipresidentialism such as that found in Georgia since
mid-decade, as well as in Lithuania, Moldova, Mongolia, Poland, and Romania;
and with parliamentary regimes such as those in Bulgaria, the Czech Republic,
Estonia, Hungary, Latvia, Macedonia, Slovakia, and Slovenia. In contrast with
these other forms, superpresidentialism includes the following features: a sprawl-
ing apparatus of executive power that dwarfs other state agencies in terms of its
size and the resources it consumes; a president who enjoys the power to legislate
by decree; a president who controls most of the powers of the purse; a legislature
that cannot repeal presidential decrees and that enjoys little authority and/or
scant resources for exercising oversight of the executive branch; provisions that
render impeachment of the president virtually impossible; and a court system
that is controlled wholly or mainly by the chief executive and that cannot in practice serve as a significant check on presidential prerogatives or abuse of power.

In the postcommunist region since the end of the 1990s, superpresidentialism
is found in Russia, Kyrgyzstan, and Armenia. Ukraine is an ambiguous case; its
regime includes several but not all of the components listed above. In some respects it exemplifies superpresidentialism; in others, moderate presidentialism.
Several countries have constitutions that are semipresidential or even parliamentary in form, but also presidents who took advantage of national crises and constitutional ambiguities in a manner that enabled them to establish essentially superpresidential regimes. Croatia under Franjo Tudjman and Albania under Sali
Berisha serve as the region's exemplars of this phenomenon. Superpresidentialism, or at least most of its features, is also found in some polities outside the postcommunist region, including the Philippines, Korea, Argentina, Brazil, and
Peru—although one might argue that the last of these by 1997 or 1998 would be
better classified with authoritarian regimes such as those in Kazakhstan and
Azerbaijan.[3]

The Paradox of Superpresidentialism

Superpresidentialism in Russia has been paradoxical in several respects. First, and most generally, it has influenced politics in a manner diametrically opposed to that prophesied by its apologists. It was, and often still is, touted as the institutional guarantor of political stability and constancy. In practice, as will be discussed below, it has ensured volatility in multiple realms of political life. Second, it was created and supported during the late Soviet and early post-Soviet periods by anticommunist revolutionaries who regarded it as a weapon of democratization and reform, but in practice it has stymied both. The origins of the overweening presidency in Russia are found in the democratic movement's push to undermine communist power by withdrawing Russia from the USSR and in its concurrent attempt to create a powerful post for the politician who would lead the struggle to end communist domination. The spring 1991 referendum in Soviet Russia, in which a majority voted to found a presidency of the republic elected directly by the people, was essentially a vote against the communist regime and for an open polity. Virtually all voters knew that Boris Yeltsin, the de facto leader of the anti-Soviet movement, enjoyed unrivaled personal authority in Russia and would certainly capture the new office. One may even posit that voters created the office specifically for Yeltsin.[4]

The paradoxical career of superpresidentialism continued after the June 1991 election that brought Yeltsin to the new office. At the time, the Soviet Union remained in existence, though it was in the midst of its death throes. Yeltsin's moral and personal authority as the new president of the RSFSR far outstripped his legal authority, which was murky. Following the collapse of the Soviet system after the abortive putsch in August 1991, Yeltsin's personal authority grew from formidable to immense. As difficult as it might be to imagine from the vantage of the post-Yeltsin period, Yeltsin emerged from the putsch with the status of a demigod. He enjoyed charismatic authority in the exacting, Weberian sense of the term, meaning that he was widely regarded in his own society as a doer of extraordinary deeds, a holder of distinctive powers, and a liberator from a widely despised, time-worn way of life.[5]

Yeltsin therefore began his post-Soviet presidential career with towering stature but undefined formal powers. The Soviet-era constitution was still in effect—a patchwork document of outdated provisions and fictions (such as that which declared the Supreme Soviet to be the organ of highest authority) that had been modified by numerous Gorbachev-era amendments reflecting incipient liberalization and democratization. Despite the lack of constitutional clarity on the division of powers, Yeltsin used his overwhelming personal popularity and authority to gain temporary decree powers and the right to appoint his personal plenipotentiaries to provincial-level executive posts. From the outset of the post-Soviet period, therefore, the president enjoyed extraordinary power. As the relationship between Yeltsin and the Supreme Soviet grew more conflictual during late 1992 and early 1993, however, the future of the division of powers became uncertain, even as Yeltsin rapidly built large presidential and executive-ministerial apparatuses. Yeltsin's victory in the bloody showdown of October 1993 with his opponents in parliament, who were led by but not limited to communist and nationalist forces, buried the old Supreme Soviet and effectively ended the contest over presidential powers. Two months later, voters approved in referendum Yeltsin's proposed constitution, which codified the superpresidential system. As Stephen White rightly has noted, "After December 1993, it was the presidency that defined the character of the political system, as Yeltsin used his ascendancy after the dissolution of parliament to secure the adoption of a constitution that extended his already considerable powers."[6]

In all major realms of politics—in state-society relations, sociopolitical life, state-building, and the performance of state agencies—the overweening presidency has exerted pernicious effects. The following discussion outlines the multifarious and profoundly negative effects of the superpresidential system on Russian politics.

Tenuous Regime Legitimacy

The first arena in which superpresidentialism has undermined political development in Russia is that of state-society relations. Specifically, it has had a negative impact on the popular legitimacy of the post-Soviet regime. "Legitimacy" is a slippery concept. It must not be confused with mere "popularity," and it cannot be fully captured by public opinion polls; however, it does refer to a generally positive orientation among the populace toward the political regime. A regime is legitimate to the extent that the populace regards it as providing a satisfactory order and believes that no available alternative would be vastly superior.[7]

There is overwhelming evidence that the post-Soviet regime in Russia at the outset of the 2000s faces a serious crisis of legitimacy. Although various public opinion surveys conducted in postcommunist countries have turned up wildly disparate results on other subjects, there is considerable convergence among surveys showing that public trust in governmental institutions was exceptionally low and in decline during the 1990s. Even by the standards of postcommunist polities, in which trust in institutions is normally not high, Russia ranks very low.[8] The second indicator of a legitimacy crisis is found in the depth and universality of noncompliance with the law. Problems of public order are endemic to polities in transformation; but few major countries that have undergone regime change in recent decades have experienced the meltdown of public compliance with the law that has been manifested in post-Soviet Russia.[9] The third indicator of legitimacy crisis is the relative strength of parties that openly call for a change of regime. During the second half of the 1990s, the two largest parties in Russia in terms of membership and representation in the Duma (the lower house of parliament) were the Communist Party of the Russian Federation (CPRF) and the misnamed Liberal Democratic Party of Russia (LDPR). Some analysts have argued that these parties' willingness to play by established rules of electoral politics, which they indeed have done in parliamentary and presidential elections, indicates that they have embraced competitive, open politics and do not seek to overturn the regime.[10] The significance of the participation of such parties in electoral politics should not be dismissed lightly; but there are nevertheless good reasons to view such parties—as well as organizations such as the ultra-left Communists-Working Russia party, which came within one-half of a percentage point of clearing the 5 percent threshold needed for parliamentary representation in the December 1995 elections—as truly "antisystem" in their aspirations and intentions. Many leaders openly espouse a change of regime. Anatolii Lukianov, a CPRF leader and chairman of the powerful legislation committee in the Duma, calls for reestablishing "Soviet power," which he defines largely as the Soviet-era system of rule.[11] Indeed, it is difficult to read the literature produced and public statements made by such parties and their leaders without concluding that, like the Communist and Nazi parties in interwar Germany, these Russian parties are perfectly willing to play the game for the time being but nevertheless intend to push the polity toward much greater closure and authoritarianism if and when they gain the opportunity to effect such change.[12] The mere existence of such parties is not a sign of weak regime legitimacy; but their popularity and influence are.

Superpresidentialism has contributed to the legitimacy crisis in Russia by identifying the regime with a single individual in the popular imagination. Since so much power rests in the hands of a single person, it is unsurprising, especially in a fledgling democratic regime in a country with no history of open politics, that many citizens would come to associate the system with the person. Were Yeltsin the perfect politician, and were political, economic, and social circumstances in post-Soviet Russia rosy and auspicious, the consequences of such a public perception might not be grave for regime legitimacy. In fact, however, Yeltsin was not the perfect politician; and as in all other countries undergoing major transformation, in Russia much of the populace has faced onerous conditions. It was therefore important that Yeltsin, the leader of the democratic movement and the leading politician of the post-Soviet period, be able to share the blame for the hardships of transformation with other politicians, including the custodians of other offices. By concentrating so much power in his own hands, at least in formal terms, Yeltsin risked identifying the regime with his own government's policies, and his own government's policies with himself alone. In time, the crisis of his own popularity—which was inevitable—would become a crisis of regime legitimacy that might otherwise have been avoided. Citizens who opposed Yeltsin understandably may have perceived themselves as opponents also of the post-Soviet regime and perhaps even of the democracy that it supposedly embodied.

A comparison with other presidential systems enables us more fully to grasp the logic of this political phenomenon: In the United States, France, Poland, Mongolia, Lithuania, Moldova, and other polities that disperse power at the national level, politicians from different branches of government habitually blame one another for all of the country's woes—but they most often do so without actually targeting the political system itself. Most importantly, ordinary citizens in these countries also can pick their favorite target of blame without necessarily condemning the political system. As parliament and the president openly and unqualifiedly blamed one another in Poland for the country's high unemployment rate, so too did unemployed Polish workers at mid-decade—when unemployment reached 15 percent—have the opportunity to feel that their pain was inflicted by either the addle-headed, brutish, liberal-nationalist president, Lech Walesa, or the treacherous, uncaring, atheistic former communists who predominated in parliament. Neither option necessarily involved turning against the regime itself. As the 1990s drew to a close and unemployment and underemployment stubbornly remained stuck at distressingly high levels and violence for the first time poisoned what previously had been a highly peaceful transition, Mongolian herdsmen could blame either the conservative, intransigent, hidebound socialist president or the chaotic, out-of-touch, liberal, World Bank–loving parliament. The herdsmen could even blame the semipresidential system for encouraging political deadlock in 1998, as the president and parliament quarreled over who would fill the prime minister's post and the country was governed by an interim prime minister. But they would be, and have been, far less prone than have Russian agricultural workers to respond to frustration by throwing their support to political forces that stand for communism or extreme nationalism, indicting the regime as a whole by casting in their lot with forces that seek to overturn it.[13]

Ironically, the superpresidential system did not even work to benefit the president. Had institutions divided power rather than concentrating it in a single office, Yeltsin could have shared blame for the country's many economic and social woes and dislocations. By the late 1990s, blame for every problem was falling on the president's shoulders, even in matters that he could not really control. Coal miners, who stood staunchly behind Yeltsin at the time of the revolution in 1990–1991, placed Yeltsin's resignation at the heart of their demands during their strikes in summer 1998. Regional officials who previously had supported Yeltsin abandoned him in droves.[14] Yeltsin left office in complete disgrace, despised by the vast majority of Russians as the source of their many problems, rather than being admired as the revolutionary hero who had led Russia to independence and popular rule and who subsequently encountered difficulties along the road of postcommunist transformation. The dénouement of superpresidentialism in Russia was the destruction of the president's reputation as well as that of the post-Soviet regime.

Listless Societal Organization

One of the most salient characteristics of post-Soviet Russian politics has been the sluggish development of political parties and organizations of civil society. Membership in political parties in Russia remains among the lowest per capita in the postcommunist region. Most of the minuscule percentage who are members of political parties belong to the CPRF, the Russian successor to the CPSU; non-communist party development has been particularly torpid. Parties do play some role in structuring political competition in the Duma, but they do not enjoy a strong presence in society outside of the largest cities. Nor did trade unions, professional associations, and business associations establish a vital presence in Russia during the country's first post-Soviet decade. Social movement activity has been sporadic, severely limited in scope, and for the most part poorly organized.[15]

There are many possible explanations for the weakness of societal organization in Russia. Soviet repression of all nonstate forms of intermediation undoubtedly has left a legacy. Political parties and other autonomous organizations are generally less vigorous and robust in the postcommunist region than in other regions that have experienced an opening up of political access after a long spell of authoritarian rule. Even by postcommunist standards, however, Russian political society has developed particularly slowly.[16] Bulgaria and Mongolia, countries that started their postcommunist lives under conditions that did not favor the emergence of vigorous civil societies, have nonetheless outstripped Russia in the development and maturation of societal organizations. The Union of Democratic Forces (UDF) in Bulgaria and the National Democratic Party in Mongolia established themselves as strong, liberal, right-center parties with deep roots in society and a capacity for winning elections. Parties in Moldova and Romania, despite their mercurial character, are significantly better developed than are those in Russia. A well-differentiated and reasonably coherent party system evolved in Hungary during the 1990s. Slovakia, despite the presence of an autocratic prime minister during much of the decade, also developed political parties far more substantial than those in Russia. What is more, in each of these countries, social movement activity has been more vigorous than in Russia. The electoral victories of the UDF in Bulgaria in 1997, of President Emil Constantinescu in Romania in 1996, and of the National Democratic Party and its partner, the Social Democratic Party, in Mongolia in 1996 were preceded by mass mobilizations of ordinary citizens, human rights advocates, journalists, and nongovernmental organizations (NGOs) of many types. Social movements in these cases aimed to remove ineffective and corrupt parties from power, and in each country they scored victories. The youth-organized "Rock the Vote" campaign preceding Slovakia's fall 1998 elections enlisted young, first-time voters in a successful push to oust the government led by Prime Minister Vladimir Meciar. No social movements or parties of similar salience and power have emerged in Russia.[17]

Superpresidentialism is not the sole source of weakness in Russian political society, but it does exacerbate the problem. Superpresidentialism subdues the impetus for political and economic actors to invest in autonomous societal organizations. The strength of the stimulus to build parties depends in large part on the power of the legislature. Parliaments and parliamentary elections are where parties attract attention and resources, build their reputations, and find their voices. Parties normally control the nomination of candidates in elections to the legislature and organize competition within the legislature between elections. Parties do fulfill such functions in the Duma; but the weakness of this body compared to the executive branch provides ambitious politicians and societal actors with scant reason to seek their fortunes and advance their interests by constructing and contributing to political parties. Graft may seem a much more efficient way of pursuing one's goals than lobbying or working with this or that political party.

A superpresidential system tends to encourage the formation of small, closed, compact societal organizations that are adept at applying pressure on and currying favor with individuals in ministries and other executive-branch agencies. Indeed, the numbers of highly personalistic, well-endowed cliques representing business and financial interests mushroomed in Russia during the 1990s. These groups have defined the character and complexion of post-Soviet Russian political society much more than have political parties, interest groups (in the traditional meaning of this term), professional associations, trade unions, or social movement organizations. Other factors (e.g., the privatization process) also contributed to the emergence of this peculiar type of political society in Russia.[18] But this political society bears an elective affinity with superpresidentialism, and it is particularly likely to emerge under such a regime.

The stimulus to build political parties may have been stronger, even under the superpresidential system, had parties managed the nomination of candidates in presidential elections. Political parties in the United States and Chile are strong institutions not only because legislatures hold a great deal of power in the moderate presidential systems of both countries but also because parties in both countries play important roles in nominating presidential candidates. Hypothetically, one can even imagine how parties, if granted a de facto monopoly over nominating authority for election to the presidency, may evolve into reasonably strong organizations even in systems with relatively weak legislatures. One would expect such circumstances to foster the emergence of systems dominated by two broad-based parties, since presidential elections tend to push party systems toward consolidation.[19] Parties in two-party-dominant systems, no less than in multiple-party (or more highly fragmented) systems, may be and often are strong and vital institutions. Parties did not play leading roles, however, in Russia's first two presidential elections. Yeltsin's own view of parties was of considerable moment. From the outset of his struggle with other Soviet leaders in the mid-to-late 1980s through the ignominious end of his second presidential term in 2000, Yeltsin's stance toward parties was, at best, indifferent. He never consented to lead or join a party. Instead he preferred the haughty pose of the metapolitical popular tribune who represented "the nation" as a whole. Thus, the enervating effect of superpresidentialism on party development was exacerbated in the Russian case by the virtually nonpartisan character of presidential elections, which in turn resulted in part from the behavior and attitude of the president.

Whatever the presidents' or presidential candidates' specific views on parties, however, superpresidentialism itself clearly inhibits societal-organizational development. The postcommunist experience supplies a great deal of evidence. Lithuania, Mongolia, Poland, Georgia after 1995, Moldova, and Romania, each of which developed more vigorous political societies than did Russia during the first postcommunist decade, have moderate presidential or semipresidential systems, in which both parliament and president hold substantial power. In these countries, as well as in those with parliamentary systems (including the Czech Republic, Bulgaria, Hungary, Estonia, Latvia, Macedonia, and Slovenia), political society acquired a stronger organizational infrastructure than it did in Russia. Slovakia under the rule of Meciar (in 1994–1998) suffered from a form of superexecutivism that one might call prime-ministerial absolutism—a form that similarly concentrated power in the executive and that inflicted substantial damage on Slovak democracy. Still, since Slovakia's parliamentary system gave strong incentives to political and societal actors to build parties, political society in Slovakia was relatively spirited even under Meciar's rule. In contrast, the postcommunist countries with superpresidential systems—Armenia, Kyrgyzstan, and Ukraine, in addition to Russia—failed to develop strong party systems or other components of an effective and sturdy autonomous political society.[20]

Decrepit State Institutions

Superpresidentialism in Russia also has obstructed the growth of coherent state agencies and undermined state capacity. Evidence of weakness in the Russian state was plentiful at century's end; by most indicators, the state lacked any meaningful extractive capacity. Tax revenues in Russia as a percentage of GDP have been consistently very low. Despite several government campaigns to revamp the tax code and bolster the tax police, tax collection capacity declined in the second half of the 1990s, with the ratio of anticipated-to-actual revenues falling substantially. The agencies responsible for the maintenance of public order virtually disappeared from the business of law enforcement in many parts of Russia in the early 1990s and did not return. The agencies in charge of national defense also suffered decimation: The armed forces' preparedness, corporate moral, and institutional coherence plummeted to a point that would have made Argentina's armed forces in the early 1990s look hale and robust. What is more, central authority deteriorated vis-à-vis regional authority—and not through systematic and negotiated decentralization but by lack of means and will to maintain a federal order. Indeed, the very application of the notion of "federalism" to Russia, though widespread in the literature on Russia, is dubious. Russia is not a "federal" system in the same sense as are the United States, Germany, and Brazil; nor did it experience anything resembling the negotiated devolution that occurred during the Spanish transition in the 1970s and 1980s. Russia's "federalization" was far less orderly and well orchestrated even than the de facto federalism that has emerged in the past two decades in China, where central authorities have exercised considerable control over the pace and character of decentralization. In Russia, the center simply hemorrhaged power and capacity, and regional governments drew in as much as they could. This decentralization-by-default drastically undermined the coherence and strength of the Russian state.[21]

Superpresidentialism exerts its destructive effect on state agencies and state capacity mainly via the personalistic, anti-institutional impetus it imparts to politics. George Breslauer has aptly judged that Yeltsin's "approach to administrative organization of the presidential and executive branches was the antithesis of rationalization." The result, according to Breslauer, has been a chronic "instability of expectations" in state agencies.[22] In a similar vein, Zoltan Barany, in a discussion of the Russian military, has noted: "To the extent that there is civilian control, . . . it is an unregulated and personalistic arrangement. . . . The president established several institutions to aid him in controlling the armed forces. Some of these . . . were abolished as suddenly as they were called to life, highlighting Yeltsin's erratic leadership style and the specific political contingency by which their very creation was justified."[23]

Breslauer are Barany are right to assign a large part of the blame to Yeltsin, and in particular, to his mentality and leadership style.[24] Equally important to understanding the anti-institutional effects of Yeltsin's behavior is the character of the office that he held. Superpresidentialism creates and sustains anti-institutional personalism. The reason why Yeltsin's administration exerted profoundly deinstitutionalizing effects on Russia, and why the mighty and organizationally expansive administration of Franklin Delano Roosevelt did not do so in the United States, lies in the facts that the U.S. Congress and courts had formidable independent power prior to the Roosevelt presidency and retained that power during his incumbency, whereas Yeltsin faced no similarly well-established, competing branches of national government.

In what ways does undivided power, and particularly concentration of power in an overweening presidency, undermine institutional formation? The antiinstitutional thrust of superexecutivism is complex, but it is essentially found in the incentives that the ruler has or does not have to build institutions. If a single actor enjoys unquestioned mastery within a given realm, s/he has an interest in continually undermining the formation of foci of organization and influence that can challenge him/her. In his comparative study of state-building in the Third World, Joel Migdal discusses how rulers often encounter and indulge an anti-institutional urge in their efforts to transform society. Rulers even undermine institutions that they themselves created. Since institutions may serve as the seeds of rival power centers, rulers concerned with surviving in power and maximizing personal control—that is, all or almost all rulers—find themselves pursuing deinstitutionalization as soon as they have accomplished institutionalization. According to Migdal, "Bizarre as it may seem, state leaders with limited capacity to mobilize their public have themselves crippled the arms of the state, especially those organs that ultimately could have given the leaders not only mobilizational ability but also . . . enhanced security." Migdal sees the paradox as arising out of the nature of society. With special reference to Egypt under Gamal Abdul Nasser and several other postcolonial Third World cases, Migdal argues that the ruler's efforts at transformation run up against "the vast, but fragmented social control embedded in the nonstate organizations of society," which in turn "has dictated a particular, pathological set of relationships within the state organization itself, between the top state leadership and its agencies." Migdal therefore explicitly focuses on how society, with its multifarious and web-like structures of authority and control, shapes the state. In Migdal's view, the prior loci of societal power, including local influentials and strongmen, co-opt and gain control of the ruler's agents and agencies of transformation, forcing the ruler constantly to intervene to undermine his own agents and engage in counterinstitutional behavior in order to thwart the emergence of any challenge to him/her and to ensure his/her own survival in power.[25]

Migdal provides valuable insight into the deinstitutionalizing impulse. But he only illuminates the paradox and provides a glimpse at its possible sources. He does not fully unlock the logic of the deinstitutionalizing urge or show precisely under what conditions the opposite impulse might drive the ruler's behavior. There is no logical reason why "the vast but fragmented social control embedded in the nonstate organizations of society" must serve as the source of the ruler's suspicions that his agents will escape his dominion. Migdal focuses on Egypt and other countries where societies rich in long-standing clan or tribal ties, chiefdoms, strata of powerful and well-to-do peasants, and other sources of nonstate authority immediately encountered, meshed with, and at least partially co-opted state agents, thereby challenging rulers' transformational goals and supremacy. Even without the societal challenges that play a central role in Migdal's accounts and theory, one can easily imagine rulers fearing loss of control over their agents—especially if the latter are able to break out of exclusively vertical, dependent relations with a ruler and work within institutions that might escape the ruler's direct monitoring and command. In fact, Russia did not enter the post-Soviet period with, nor did it subsequently spawn, a dense, web-like society of the type that Migdal found in his postcolonial cases. The Soviet regime, and Stalinism in particular, leveled or greatly weakened classes, organizations of civil society, and groups based on ascriptive ties, including clans and tribal structures. Post-Soviet Russian society bears little resemblance to the societies Migdal investigated; yet its first president's anti-institutional habits of rule were, if anything, even more pronounced than Nasser's.[26] Like Nasser, Yeltsin feared institutions because they threatened to depersonalize power by empowering his agents and enabling them to elude his control.

How does the logic of politicians' attitudes toward institutions differ when power is dispersed? Politicians may still seek to avoid institutionalization. But under circumstances where power at the national level is dispersed among or between branches or camps, politicians are often guided by an urge to build institutions rather than undermine them. Indeed, the origin of most institutions is found in conflict between or among contenders for power. If one does not and cannot hope to achieve complete mastery over the polity, one's best strategy is often to outdo competitors in the construction of institutions that can serve as sources of support—even given the risk that such institutions may elude total control. The origins of most institutions, institutional development, and institutional innovation are found in *competition for the right to rule,* rather than in the process of ruling it-self. One may observe this phenomenon at work in multiple realms, though to this author's best knowledge, this logic has not heretofore been drawn out and applied explicitly to the problem of the separation of powers within constitutional systems in precisely the manner in which it is in this chapter.[27]

In the area of primitive state-building, Charles Tilly suggests that the impetus to construct institutions grows out of competition from rival states or proto-states, not from the practice of despotism within a single, unchallenged polity.[28] Dankwart Rustow's celebrated theory of the demise of authoritarian regimes is built on the notion that intense competition between evenly matched forces leading to dead-lock spurs the genesis of democratic institutions. According to Rustow, each party to the conflict comes to see that it cannot hope to impose its will and rule unilater-ally, and must engage in cooperation and institution-building in order both to compete with its antagonist and to create the conditions that insure that its antago-nist accepts its right to exist and to compete in perpetuity. Democratic institutions therefore emerge willy-nilly out of heated competition, not by design and bestowal from above.[29] Barbara Geddes argues that institutional reform in the civil service, in open, competitive polities, is most likely to emerge when political forces represent-ing rival interests (normally, political parties) are more or less evenly matched. As long as one party or coalition predominates in government, it will always face an ir-resistible temptation to use the civil service as its own patronage machine and therefore will not consent to reforms that promote institutionalization, profession-alization, or depoliticization of the bureaucracy.[30]

Interestingly, even Migdal's analysis points to the importance of competition and the dispersion of power for institution-building. Though Migdal does not draw out the logical implications of his own narrative, his story of the single case of successful postcolonial state-building, Israel, is replete with conflict, rivalry, and balancing among the creators of the new state. Indeed, the strife among the new state-builders and their organizations, the absence of a single overweening personage or organized force in the anticolonial movement, and the consequent necessity of resolving conflict by creating institutions stand out as the most salient differences between Israel and the cases of failed state-building. Migdal does not highlight these differences but instead stresses the skill of Israeli politi-cians and the structural characteristics of society.[31]

In sum, the concentration of power, particularly in a single individual or of-fice, exerts counterinstitutional effects. Institutions tend never to be born, to be subverted if they are created, or to rot from lack of reform even if they are not in-tentionally subverted. Conditions in which power is dispersed, in contrast, some-times stimulate institutional formation.

Unaccountable Officialdom

Not only has superpresidentialism debilitated Russian state agencies and under-mined the growth of state capacity; it has also bred highly unaccountable behavior among the custodians of state agencies. The accountability of officialdom is difficult to measure, but it may be observed in a number of realms. The extent to which officials' habits of governing demonstrate respect for and fear of the citizenry, and the extent to which major governmental decisions reflect the popular will, represent perhaps the two best indicators of official accountability.

Russian officials' habits of governing during the 1990s displayed no respect for or fear of the governed. Despite the presence of regular, open elections to the presidency, the legislature, and many local and provincial-level offices, officials habitually approached the governed with an attitude of haughtiness and detachment. Indeed, the Russian experience clearly demonstrates the inadequacy of electoral institutions alone to secure democracy with accountability. Like several major Latin American cases, the Russian case shows that the episodic political intervention of the citizenry via the ballot box is an insufficient condition—albeit a necessary one—for accountable government.[32]

The clearest sign of a government that scorns the citizenry is massive, all-pervasive corruption. This phenomenon is the emblem of unaccountable government, since people everywhere and always oppose the appropriation by officials of resources that otherwise could be invested in the provision of public services. High corruption always indicates low official accountability, though one can imagine the possibility of authoritarian polities where both corruption and accountability are low. Corruption is difficult to observe and measure. Some cross-national surveys that attempt to determine relative levels of corruption, however, provide aid in observation and measurement. Such surveys show corruption to be the very stuff of political life in Russia. In the most recent study conducted by Transparency International, Russia ranked 76th out of the 85 countries evaluated, meaning that in only nine countries was corruption more severe. Russia received the worst rating of the 12 postcommunist countries studied, ranking below Bulgaria, Ukraine, and Serbia. Corruption was also judged to be worse in Russia than in 14 of the 17 African countries included in the study. Among the 12 Asian countries assessed, only one—Indonesia—received a less favorable rating than Russia.[33]

The link between corruption and superpresidentialism is found in the executive's control over public expenditure and in the absence of meaningful external checks on executive-branch officials. Since the Russian regime invests most of the powers of the purse in the executive branch, the latter controls the disposal of most of the state's resources. Whenever parliamentary cooperation is desirable, the president's enormous discretionary powers enable him easily to buy the support of parliamentarians. Thus, Yeltsin was able to obtain support for his budgets even from a parliament whose majority was openly hostile toward him and his policies.[34] Corruption within the executive branch also rages unchecked due to the lack of oversight mechanisms. Since neither parliament nor the courts possess the means to investigate and monitor the executive, those who control the state's resources at the national level ultimately are accountable only to the president. Were he deeply committed to and able to control his subordinates, perhaps the president could circumscribe abuse of office for private gain. But Yeltsin's obvious incompetence in this matter allowed many officials, including top leaders such as former prime minister Viktor Chernomyrdin and former deputy prime minister Anatolii Chubais to convert state agencies into high-powered siphons through which they routed copious portions of the national wealth into their own personal bank accounts, portfolios, and real-estate empires in Switzerland, Cyprus, and the United States.

If the accountability deficit that Russian superpresidentialism aggravates is evident in officials' impudent use of office for private enrichment, it is also obvious in several major governmental misdeeds that probably never would have been perpetrated had there been a more equitable division of powers among the branches of government. The most flagrant and catastrophic of these blunders was the invasion of Chechnya in 1994. The attack was plotted by Yeltsin and a handful of officials in charge of the agencies of coercion, without consultation with the legislature or public debate. From the day it began, the war enjoyed virtually no support in parliament or in the broader public. Opponents of the war included not only Yeltsin's traditional communist detractors but also virtually all major liberal politicians and organizations. If the parliament had held more authority in the matter, the war might never have been initiated in late 1994. And if members of the Duma and of the general public had been able to assert their wishes even after the war had been launched, Russian forces would have been withdrawn quickly from Chechnya, saving 40,000 civilian lives and sparing the army serious losses of fighting capacity, prestige, and morale.

Conclusions on the Pathologies
of Superexecutive Power

Superpresidentialism has thwarted progress in every major sphere of political life in Russia. It has undermined the legitimacy of the post-Soviet regime and even perhaps of democracy itself; stunted the growth of nonstate political organizations; checked the development of an efficacious state; and deterred the emergence of accountable government. The devastating influence of superexecutive authority is compounded by the mutually reinforcing effects that its various pathologies exert on each other. For example, the lack of accountability and the unresponsiveness of officialdom further diminish incentives for citizens to organize and join autonomous political organizations, including political parties and interest groups, since such participation is unlikely in any way to affect policy. The reverse relationship also obtains: Without strong parties and other intermediary organizations that continually pressure, constrain, and monitor the political class, the citizenry cannot hold officialdom accountable, save during its episodic participation in elections. This vicious circle is also evident in the relationship between the weakness of intermediary societal organizations and the debility of state agencies. Decrepit and underinstitutionalized state structures reduce incentives for citizens to become involved in the parties, groups, and movements that seek to influence those state agencies. In the absence of a strong state, civil society has nothing to push up against. An underdeveloped civil society, in turn, cannot provide the human and organizational capital and pressure from below needed to energize and indurate state institutions.[35]

It may be argued, with some merit, that not all of the maladies here ascribed to superpresidentialism are due to the institution itself and that some should be attributed to the officeholder. Educated in the old *nomenklatura* and its ways of politics, sidelined by health problems for much of his tenure, and limited in his intellectual capacities, Yeltsin cannot be considered a particularly energetic, imaginative, or capable president. But the institutional arrangements that define the constitutional system—in particular, the extent to which power is separated and dispersed—have been far more important than the personal attributes and inclinations of the chief executive. All of the problems discussed here with regard to Russia also have afflicted the other countries in the postcommunist region with superpresidential constitutions during the first post-Soviet decade. Armenia, Kyrgyzstan, and Ukraine developed a remarkably similar syndrome of pathologies, including crises of regime legitimacy, low and declining stocks of energy in political society, waning state capacities, and increasingly out-of-touch officials. It is difficult to attribute these phenomena to the leaders themselves without reference to the superpresidential system. None of the individuals who occupied the presidency in these countries were widely considered to be particularly dull, venal, arrogant, or incompetent figures at the outset of their tenure in power. Yeltsin, for all his limitations, was the iron-willed and politically adept leader of a great revolution, the first politician in Russia's thousand-year history who made it to the top by virtue of his support from the people as a whole rather than by birth, control of coercive power, corridor-wisdom, flattery, or chicanery. Armenia's first president, Levon Ter-Petrossian, like Yeltsin, was a courageous and beloved spokesman for both democracy and national independence. Kyrgyzstan's first and current president, Askar Akaev, a highly accomplished, charming, and intelligent academician, was similarly regarded as the father of his country's democracy and independence. Ukraine's two presidents, Leonid Kravchuk and Leonid Kuchma, lacked the overwhelming personal appeal of Yeltsin, Ter-Petrossian, and Akaev, but each nevertheless at one time enjoyed great stature and popular appeal. All of these leaders, moreover, were respected in the West; each was, at least at one time, seen widely in the international community as a guarantor of democratization, stability, and reform.

Only in retrospect did these postcommunist leaders seem, to citizens in their own countries as well as to observers from abroad, to have been haughty, misguided, autocratic, or detached from their people. Their offices were in large part to blame for their personal transitions from states of grace to disgrace (or in the best case, severely tarnished grace). In fact, the expansiveness of the powers of their office magnified the pernicious effects of the leaders' mistakes. Importantly, it also abetted the growth of a megalomania that may be less likely to emerge in leaders whose offices are adorned with less pomp and splendor, and who are constitutionally obligated to share fundamental powers with other agencies that are entirely beyond their control. Few of those who knew him at the time of regime change in Kyrgyzstan or abroad then could have imagined the courtly and urbane Akaev adorning public buildings with banners emblazoned with his own visage, or presiding over a society in which university students, in the best Soviet tradition, were obligated repeatedly to cite and laud his writings and speeches in their papers and dissertations, regardless of the scholarly appropriateness of doing so. And yet, by mid-decade, Kyrgyzstan had fallen into such a state.

The importance of the character of the office emerges even more clearly in a broader comparative perspective. Several postcommunist countries adopted arrangements that include a presidency whose powers are substantial but also circumscribed by powerful legislatures. Poland, Romania, and Lithuania provide the clearest examples. In none of these three countries did any of the pathologies discussed above appear in nearly as severe a form as in the Russian case, or for that matter, in the Armenian, Kyrgyz, and Ukrainian cases. One is hard pressed to attribute the differences to leaders rather than institutions. To say that the former presidents of Poland, Romania, and Lithuania (respectively, Lech Walesa, Ion Iliescu, and Algirdas Brazauskas) somehow constituted a more distinguished and far-sighted group than did Yeltsin, Ter-Petrossian, Akaev, Kravchuk, and Kuchma would require formidable powers of imagination, or strictly post hoc thinking that fails to account for *why* the former set of leaders, even after electoral defeat (in the cases of Walesa and Iliescu), left office with both their good names and their countries' political systems intact. It is difficult to argue that either Walesa or Iliescu was any more interested in depersonalizing power and building strong state institutions for their own sake or in fostering the development of a vigorous civil society, including opposition movements and parties, than were Yeltsin and Akaev. But the Polish and Romanian presidents operated in semipresidential systems that continually pruned their autocratic ambitions, exposed their most expansive conceptions of themselves as delusions, and contained the effects of their mistakes. The regime also forced the presidents to hone their skills at politics and governance, since they really had to compete with their adversaries, and not only during election campaigns. They lacked the options of bypassing, ignoring, and quashing their foes.

Although the generalizations offered here with regard to the postcommunist world might not hold true outside it, it might well prove fruitful to investigate how or whether the pathologies examined here manifest themselves in polities in other regions. The four disorders identified in the Russian case might indeed be more endemic in Brazil, Peru, Korea, and the Philippines, with their overweening presidents, than in Chile, Uruguay, or Taiwan, with their more balanced systems. A great deal of further research would be required to establish a firm basis for evaluation.

If this chapter is correct in its argument that superexecutivism engenders pathologies in the political system, then neither a redistribution of power within the executive branch nor the election of a new president will remedy Russia's political underdevelopment. During Prime Minister Yevgenii Primakov's tenure from fall 1998 to spring 1999, some observers argued that a great deal of power had drifted from the president to the prime minister and that the time of Russian superpresidentialism was past.[36] But the combination of a stronger prime minister and a weaker president in Russia proved a transient configuration arising from the president's incapacitation, and it could hardly have mitigated the effects of superexecutivism. The regime does not operate in a manner in which the president and the prime minister exert mutual checks over one another, as was demonstrated by Yeltsin's successive purges of prime ministers during his last two years in office. The president appoints the prime minister, and the latter serves at the president's pleasure. Russia's problem is superexecutivism—a bloated, muscle-bound executive that is neither balanced nor monitored by the legislature or the courts. No temporary or even lasting reallocation of power within the executive branch could remedy the deleterious effects diagnosed here. Russia needs a regime that disperses power at the center—either moderate presidentialism or semipresidentialism—and a more autonomous and authoritative judiciary. Nor will a new helmsman repair the ship. The new president may prove more vigorous and effective than Yeltsin, but the institution that promoted political underdevelopment in the beginning will remain in place and continue to consign Russia to political backwardness.

Notes

1. Charles de Secondat, Baron de Montesquieu, *The Spirit of the Laws* (Cambridge, U.K., 1995), 157 [first published 1748].

2. On Russian superpresidentialism, see, among other works, Eugene Huskey, "The State-Legal Administration and the Politics of Redundancy," *Post-Soviet Affairs* 11, no. 2 (1995): 115–143; Timothy J. Colton, "Superpresidentialism and Russia's Backward State," *Post-Soviet Affairs* 11, no. 2 (1995): 144–148; Timothy J. Colton, "Boris Yeltsin, Russia's All-Thumbs Democrat," in Timothy J. Colton and Robert C. Tucker, eds., *Patterns in Post-Soviet Leadership* (Boulder, 1995), 49–74; Robert Sharlet, "The Politics of Constitutional Amendment in Russia," *Post-Soviet Affairs* 13, no. 3 (1997): 197–227; Philip G. Roeder, "Varieties of Post-Soviet Authoritarian Regimes," *Post-Soviet Affairs* 10, no. 1 (1994): 61–101.

3. Scott Mainwaring and Matthew Soberg Shugart, eds., *Presidentialism and Democracy in Latin America* (Cambridge, U.K., 1997); Juan J. Linz and Arturo Valenzuela, eds., *The Failure of Presidential Democracy* (Baltimore, 1994); Gabriella R. Montinola, "Parties and Accountability in the Philippines," *Journal of Democracy* 10, no. 1 (January 1999): 126–140; Steven Levitsky, "Fujimori and Post-Party Politics in Peru," *Journal of Democracy* 10, no. 3 (July 1999): 78–92.

4. See Michael Urban, *The Rebirth of Politics in Russia* (Cambridge, U.K., 1997), 240–244.

5. Max Weber, *The Theory of Social and Economic Organization* (New York, 1947), 64, 328, 358–363. On Yeltsin's extraordinary role and authority in the early post-putsch period, see "Nad vsei Rossiei bezoblachnoe nebo," *Rossiia*, October 16–22, 1991; "Boris Yel'tsin: 100 dnei posle pobedy," *Rossiia*, October 23–29, 1991.

32 M. Steven Fish

6. Stephen White, "Russia: Presidential Leadership under Yeltsin," in Ray Taras, ed., *Postcommunist Presidents* (Cambridge, U.K., 1997), 38.

7. See Weber, *The Theory of Social and Economic Organization,* 124–132, 324–329.

8. Richard Rose and Doh Chull Shin, "Democratization Backwards: The Problem of Third Wave Democracies" (unpublished ms., 1999); USIA [United States Information Agency], Office of Research and Media Reaction, *Opinion Analysis,* March 15, 1999; Richard Rose, "Postcommunism and the Problem of Trust," in Larry Diamond and Marc F. Plattner, eds., *The Global Resurgence of Democracy,* 2d ed. (Baltimore, 1996), 251–263.

9. See the works of Louise I. Shelley, including "Post-Soviet Organized Crime," *Demokratizatsiya* 2, no. 3 (Summer 1994): 341–358; Stephen Holmes, "What Russia Teaches Us Now," *American Prospect* 33 (July-August 1997): 30–39; M. Steven Fish, "The Roots of and Remedies for Russia's Racket Economy," in Stephen S. Cohen, Andrew Schwartz, and John Zysman, eds., *The Tunnel at the End of the Light: Privatization, Business Networks, and Economic Transformation in Russia* (Berkeley, 1998), 86–137.

10. See Michael McFaul, "Lessons from Russia's Protracted Transition from Communist Rule," *Political Science Quarterly* 114, no. 1 (Spring 1999): 103–130.

11. Author's interview with Anatolii Lukianov, Moscow, December 19, 1995.

12. On antisystem parties and their participation in electoral politics, see Giovanni Sartori, *Parties and Party Systems: A Framework for Analysis* (Cambridge, U.K., 1976). For unequivocal evidence of the noncommitment of both communist and nationalist parties in Russia to the existing political regime, see, for example, G. A. Ziuganov, *Za gorizontom* (Orel, 1995); Sergei Kurginian, *Rossiia: Vlast' i oppozitsiia* (Moscow, 1994); Veljko Vujacic, "Gennadiy Zyuganov and the 'Third Road,'" *Post-Soviet Affairs* 12, no. 2 (1996): 118–154; or peruse any issue of the newspapers *Sovetskaia Rossiia* or *Zavtra,* both of which are controlled by and speak for communist and nationalist organizations.

13. On Poland, see Andrew A. Michta, "Democratic Consolidation in Poland after 1989," in Karen Dawisha and Bruce Parrott, eds., *The Consolidation of Democracy in East-Central Europe* (Cambridge, U.K., 1997), 66–108. On Mongolia, see M. Steven Fish, "Mongolia: Democracy without Prerequisites," *Journal of Democracy* 9, no. 3 (July 1998): 127–141.

14. "Rossiiskie regiony vkliuchaiutsia v bor'bu za otstavku Yel'tsina," *Nezavisimaia gazeta,* July 1, 1998; "Soglasie budet nedolgim," *Izvestiia,* March 16, 1999.

15. Michael McFaul, *Russia's 1996 Presidential Election: The End of Polarized Politics* (Stanford, 1997), 83–88; M. Steven Fish, "The Predicament of Russian Liberalism: Evidence from the December 1995 Parliamentary Elections," *Europe-Asia Studies* 49, no. 2 (1997): 191–220; M. Steven Fish, *Democracy from Scratch: Opposition and Regime in the New Russian Revolution* (Princeton, 1995), 210–230; Marc Morjé Howard, "Demobilized Societies: Understanding the Weakness of Civil Society in Post-Communist Europe," (Ph.D. dissertation, University of California, Berkeley, 1999).

16. By *political society* I mean both political parties and the organizations normally subsumed under the rubric of civil society. I distinguish between state and societal organizations, with the latter being defined in terms of their autonomy from the state. In contrast with other authors, however, I do not draw a hard line between political society (which some analysts define as political parties alone) and civil society (meaning nonparty forms of societal organization). See M. Steven Fish, "Russia's Fourth Transition," in Larry Diamond and Marc F. Plattner, eds., *The Global Resurgence of Democracy,* 2d ed. (Baltimore, 1996), 274, note 1.

17. M. Steven Fish, "Postcommunist Subversion: Social Science and Democratization in East Europe and Eurasia," *Slavic Review* 58, no. 4 (Winter 1999); M. Steven Fish, "Moving Backwards: The Dynamics of Democratic Erosion and Reversal in the Postcommunist World," Working Paper no. 2.67, Center for German and European Studies and the Center for Slavic and East European Studies, University of California, Berkeley, 1998.

18. Fish, "The Roots of and Remedies for Russia's Racket Economy," 88–91.

19. Giovanni Sartori, *Comparative Constitutional Engineering* (New York, 1994); Arend Lijphart, "Presidentialism and Majoritarian Democracy," in Linz and Valenzuela, eds., 91–105; Matthew Soberg Shugart and John M. Carey, *Presidents and Assemblies: Constitutional Design and Electoral Dynamics* (Cambridge, U.K., 1992).

20. Fish, "Moving Backwards"; M. Steven Fish, "The End of Meciarism," *East European Constitutional Review* 8, no. 1-2 (Winter-Spring 1999): 47–55; Ilya Prizel, "Ukraine between Proto-democracy and 'Soft' Authoritarianism," in Karen Dawisha and Bruce Parrott, eds., *Democratic Change and Authoritarian Reactions in Russia, Ukraine, Belarus, and Moldova* (Cambridge, U.K., 1997), 330–369; Elizabeth Fuller, "The Fall from Democratic Grace," *Transition*, November 15, 1996; Eugene Huskey, "Kyrgyzstan: The Fate of Political Liberalization," in Karen Dawisha and Bruce Parrott, eds., *Conflict, Cleavage, and Change in Central Asia and the Caucasus* (Cambridge, U.K., 1997), 242–276; Kathleen Collins, "Clans, Parties, and Politics: The Failure of Political Parties in 'Democratic' Kyrgyzstan" (unpublished ms., 1999). I am focusing here exclusively on countries that may be considered democracies or partial democracies and am excluding from analysis the autocracies with personalistic dictators who take the name "president," which are Azerbaijan, Belarus, Kazakhstan, Serbia, Tajikistan, Turkmenistan, and Uzbekistan.

21. Fish, "The Roots of and Remedies for Russia's Racket Economy"; Kathryn Stoner-Weiss, "The Russian Central State in Crisis: Center and Periphery in the Post-Soviet Era" (unpublished ms., 1999); Zoltan Barany, "Corrupt Generals, Hungry Soldiers: The Armed Forces in Russian Politics" (unpublished ms., 1999); Charles H. Fairbanks, Jr., "The Feudalization of the State," *Journal of Democracy* 10, no. 2 (April 1999): 47–53; Gabriella R. Montinola, Yingyi Qian, and Barry R. Weingast, "Federalism, Chinese Style: The Political Basis of Economic Success in China," *World Politics* 48, no. 1 (October 1995): 50–81; Anatol Lieven, *Chechnya: Tombstone of Russian Power* (New Haven, 1998); "Novoe obostrenie politicheskogo krizisa v Moskve," *Nezavisimaia gazeta*, March 18, 1999.

22. George W. Breslauer, "Evaluating Yeltsin as Leader" (unpublished ms., 1999).

23. Barany, "Corrupt Generals, Hungry Soldiers."

24. Breslauer, "Evaluating Yeltsin as Leader"; Barany, "Corrupt Generals, Hungry Soldiers."

25. Joel S. Migdal, *Strong Societies and Weak States: State-Society Relations and State Capabilities in the Third World* (Princeton, 1988), 172–173, 181–237. Quoted passages appear on 207.

26. For explication, compare the depiction of Russian society found in Fish, *Democracy from Scratch* (esp. 21–24, 52–64, 210–218) with that offered by Migdal of the cases on which he builds his theory. For another telling portrait of societies and state-society relations that resembles Migdal's, see Naomi Chazan, "Africa's Democratic Challenge," *World Policy Journal*, Spring 1992: 279–308.

27. The main advantage of dispersing power, explicated originally and most forcefully by Montesquieu and James Madison, is normally seen in the creation of barriers to tyranny rather than in the promotion of institutional development. See Montesquieu, *The*

Spirit of the Laws, 156–166, 325–327; Alexander Hamilton, James Madison, and John Jay, *The Federalist Papers* (New York, 1961), 308–313, 320–323.

28. Charles Tilly, *Capital, Coercion, and European States,* A.D. *990–1990* (Oxford, 1990).

29. Dankwart Rustow, "Transitions to Democracy: Toward a Dynamic Model," *Comparative Politics* 2, no. 3 (April 1970): 337–363.

30. Barbara Geddes, *Politician's Dilemma: Building State Capacity in Latin America* (Berkeley, 1994).

31. Migdal, *Strong Societies and Weak States,* 151–173.

32. Among other works, see Guillermo O'Donnell, "Delegative Democracy," *Journal of Democracy* 5, no. 1 (January 1994): 55–69; idem, "Horizontal Accountability in New Democracies," *Journal of Democracy* 9, no. 3 (July 1998): 112–126; and Terry Lynn Karl, "Dilemmas of Democratization in Latin America," *Comparative Politics* 23, no. 1 (October 1990): 1–22.

33. "The Transparency International 1998 Corruption Perceptions Index," at www.transparency.de/documents/cpi/index.html (April 1999).

34. Robert G. Moser, "Constitutional Design and Democratization: Executive-Legislative Relations in Russia, 1991–1998" (unpublished ms., 1999).

35. Jonah D. Levy, *Tocqueville's Revenge: State, Society, and Economy in Contemporary France* (Cambridge, Mass., 1999), 12–15, 293–318; Fish, *Democracy from Scratch,* 73–75, 122–125.

36. See "Lovushki: O paradoksakh rossiiskoi politicheskoi zhizni razmyshliaet politolog Liliia Shevtsova," *Trud,* March 18, 1999.

3

Personalism Versus Proceduralism

Boris Yeltsin and the Institutional Fragility of the Russian System

George W. Breslauer

University of California, Berkeley

Russia's fundamental problem is that it doesn't have any credible fiscal rules or any fiscal administration.

—**Michel Camdessus, Managing Director,**
International Monetary Fund (*San Francisco Chronicle*, July 18, 1998)

I do not claim to be able to discuss the philosophy behind economic reform.
—**Boris Yeltsin,** *Zapiski prezidenta* (Moscow, 1994, 235)[1]

The collapse of the Russian financial system in August and September 1998, the threat of rising social protest, and the increased tendency toward fiscal separatism among regional elites highlighted a key gap in the country's political and economic development during the 1990s. Russia has indeed broken with the communist system and replaced it with formal organizations that bear a family resemblance to the structures of a capitalist economy and liberal democracy. But these formal organizations are largely shells that do not necessarily contain the processes necessary for the democratic regulation of political, social, and economic exchange. Under Russia's current system of crony capitalism and illiberal democracy, organizational processes are driven by personalistic considerations that override both efficiency calculations and procedural propriety. Although it is not necessarily incompatible with economic growth and political stability, this system is relatively feeble, fragile, and susceptible to collapse when shaken by external shocks. In this regard, Russia's system is similar to that in a number of Asian countries that underwent economic collapse in 1997 and 1998, after decades of impressive growth rates. Russia experienced a similar collapse in 1998, but without a preceding period of growth or wealth-creation. In contrast, Russia's GDP had declined markedly throughout the 1990s.

It is now obvious that the infrastructure of Russian public administration operates with little of the procedural impersonality required for the cohesion of a market economy and representative democracy. Russia lacks regulatory institutions that can ensure tax collection, protection of property rights, enforcement of contracts, and procedural propriety in the financial sector. It lacks police, legal, and judicial institutions that can ensure physical security for the populace and rule of law in the adjudication of social conflicts. And it lacks a system of nationwide or sectoral political parties that channel societal demands into the political arena and that link regional politicians to those at the center through a political-organizational relationship of mutual dependence. On this much there is consensus in the theoretical literature: The proper functioning of a market economy, rule of law, and representative democracy requires such institutions. The legitimacy, effectiveness, and ultimately, stability of an advanced industrial society hinge on the qualities of such structures.[2] Russia is therefore institutionally fragile. Before we can ask how to overcome this condition, we must ask how it came to be.

Lessons of the Crisis

A debate has begun in the West over the lessons to be learned from the current crisis. Some observers argue that a collapse was all but inevitable, regardless of what Yeltsin had done during his years as Russia's president. There are three explanations that run along these lines, though they are not mutually exclusive. One is cultural, and argues that Russian culture had never developed orientations compatible with impersonal markets, rule of law, or representative democracy. A second is institutional, claiming that the administrative fragmentation, tacit privatization, and widespread criminalization of the Soviet state during the late Gorbachev era—or in some versions of the argument, present under Brezhnev—constituted a legacy that the Yeltsin regime could not possibly overcome in so short a period of time. A third argument for inevitability is circumstantial: that Gorbachev had made a mess of the Soviet economy, the Soviet Union, and Soviet foreign economic relations by 1991. The result was a rupturing of economic relationships, which could not be surmounted by the Yeltsin regime. When we combine these explanations, treating them as mutually reinforcing components of the legacy bequeathed to Yeltsin, the image of futility and inevitability becomes that much more credible.

An alternative approach to the question of historical causality treats the current situation as a product of contingent policy choices made by Boris Yeltsin and his governments from 1991 to 1998, either under foreign pressure or autonomously. Without denying that the above-mentioned constraints were real, this argument claims that the constraints did not predetermine the outcome; that is, opportunities were missed to relieve these constraints and to alter the trajectory of Russian development.

Thus, according to this argument, a corrupt, weak state might have been difficult to avoid, given the initial conditions; but the scope and depth of political corruption and criminalization, and the "virtual economy" of 1998,[3] were products of specific policy choices made in 1992–1995: the approach to macroeconomic stabilization; the privatization programs of 1992 and 1994; and the "loans for shares" program of 1995. The fragility of democratic institutions might have been a product of the "dual power" built into the constitution that was in force in 1991, exacerbated by the disorientation and political conflict engendered by Russia's loss of its empire and global role. But the political meltdown of 1998 was a product of choices about party-building and state-building made in fall 1991 and choices about constitutional design made in 1993 and 1994. Limited adherence to "rule of law," and spotty protection of the population from physical insecurity, might have been inherent in the aftermath of any state's collapse, but the minuscule progress in building legal and judicial institutions, and the extent of police withdrawal from law enforcement, were products of decisions made in 1992 and of a continuous lack of priority given to legal-institutional development. Persistent defiance of central authority by the government of Chechnya might have been the bane of any Kremlin leader. But the costs and consequences of the war against Chechen secession were products of policy choices made by the Yeltsin leadership in 1994 and 1995. The Russian state might have been institutionally underdeveloped in any case, given the time it takes to build effective institutions; but the extent of its underdevelopment and fragility was a product of neglect and of policies that undermined institutional goals.

We thus have two sets of arguments: one based on the notion that culture, structure, and circumstance were determinant, and the other based on the notion that leadership—in this case, bad leadership—was determinant. It is not easy to choose between the two, for we are in the realm of counterfactual speculation. Had Yeltsin done things differently in each of these policy realms, we would have been better positioned to assess the resilience of cultural, institutional, and circumstantial constraints on change. But in many realms of policy, Yeltsin's initiatives either acquiesced in or exacerbated the situation he inherited. Hence, we cannot say with confidence how much would have been different had Yeltsin acted differently.

What we can do is document Yeltsin's personalistic and patriarchal leadership style and show how that style reinforced inherited constraints, and in many respects, created new ones. His style emphasized personalistic considerations and political rationality at the expense of procedural development and systemic legitimacy, thereby contributing to the institutional fragility that plagues Russia to-day. He may not have been fully aware of this dynamic and may have been gen-uinely befuddled by the consequences of his actions, but that is a separate issue.[4] The purpose of this chapter is to document Yeltsin's personalistic style and its im-pact on institution-building in post-Soviet Russia. The sources for this study are memoirs and speeches by Yeltsin, book-length memoirs by officials who worked for him, interviews with a number of the latter individuals, and secondary litera-ture on the Russian policy process.

Perhaps the Russian bureaucracy defies reform and smothers all efforts at ra-tionalization. Unfortunately, Yeltsin never really tested this proposition. If Yeltsin's successors wish to build a stable, market democracy that is integrated into the multilateral institutions of the rich democracies, they will have to break with the mentality that informed Yeltsin's choices, and develop strategies for institution-building that make up for time lost and damage done. Moreover, they will have to do so in a context in which many constraints on change have arisen that did not exist in 1992.[5] If they do eventually launch such a program, we will be better positioned to assess the ongoing resilience of cultural, institutional, and circumstantial obstacles to change.

Yeltsin's Personalistic Leadership Style

Yeltsin is notorious for having concentrated enormous formal power in his hands as Russian president. This was consistent with his lifelong urge to be in charge. Such a self-image can be traced to the early stages of his life and career. As he wrote in his autobiography, "For more than thirty years now, I've been a boss. . . . Not a bureaucrat, not an official, not a director, but a boss. I can't stand the word—there's something about it that smacks of the chain gang. But what can you do? Perhaps being first was always a part of my nature."[6] An ear-lier autobiography records many stories of the leadership role he played among his friends and of his penchant for assuming the preponderance of risk—as, for example, when he insisted on being the one among his friends to disarm a grenade, and lost two fingers in the process.[7] People who knew him early in his career, in Sverdlovsk, report that he was an assertive, demanding, and harsh boss.[8] Those who knew him when he was first secretary of the Moscow party organization aver that he was a "true party despot."[9] He viewed himself at the time as a turnaround artist who needed to be unconstrained in restructuring his domain.[10]

The urge to rule with as few institutional constraints as possible followed Yeltsin into the Russian presidency. Of course, he rarely had the luxury of doing so. As a member of the Interregional Group of Deputies within the Congress of People's Deputies in 1989, he was schooled by Andrei Sakharov and members of the democratic caucus, in the procedural ways of a democratic society. As chair-man of the RSFSR Supreme Soviet from 1990 to 1991, he had to bargain hard to build minimal winning coalitions for his initiatives. As the popularly elected president of Russia, from June 1991 until August 1991, he bargained and compromised with Gorbachev over the terms of the Union Treaty. And for two years after his election as president of independent Russia (in January 1992), he locked horns with the Supreme Soviet and its chairman Ruslan Khasbulatov over matters of power, policy, and the terms of a new constitution.

These constraints tested Yeltsin's commitment to democratic procedures and institutions. It would be unfair to claim that he behaved like an uncompromising autocrat in these contexts. To be sure, he was an able and hard bargainer, and his emotions at times got the best of him. But he also made frequent efforts to strike deals with his opponents and to push for legislation based on compromise.

Yet, at key points, his patience ran out and his personalistic urge came to the fore. After the August 1991 coup, he banned the newspapers that had supported the coup editorially—until his advisers convinced him that this was incompatible with a commitment to democracy. In fall 1991, instead of using his enormous political authority and resources to help build democratic political parties, he declared his intention to stand "above parties"—a commitment he reiterated in advance of the December 1993 and December 1995 parliamentary elections, much to the dismay of democratic activists. From fall 1991 to 1993, he demanded and secured the right to rule by decree when the parliament refused to endorse his initiatives. In summer 1993, he decided to dissolve parliament—a right he did not yet possess—having concluded that fruitful compromise was impossible. In his second autobiography, he admits his disillusion with parliamentary democracy, and its unsuitability for Russia.[11]

Although Yeltsin's personality inclined him to seek personal control, it is important to bear in mind that personalism is not necessarily the same as despotism—though all despots are by definition personalistic. Personalism is a form of rule in which the leader is not held accountable—formally, regularly, and frequently—to institutions that can substantially constrain his discretion. But personalistic rulers can be generous, proper, and temperate; they are not necessarily tyrannical, capricious, or corrupt. Yeltsin's self-image was that of a patriarch: a strict but benevolent father-figure.

Yeltsin as Patriarch

Within his inner circle, Yeltsin demanded total loyalty to himself and his commands. He exercised maximal discretion over his subordinates' lives both public and (at times) private. There was nothing impersonal about these relationships, nothing based on procedural propriety or official prerogatives other than his own. The staff and officials of the presidential administration and executive branch were his retainers, not his lieutenants—his political "family," not his cabinet. He conceived of himself as a paterfamilias rather than as the chief executive of a corpus of professionals.[12] As former press secretary Vyacheslav Kostikov has noted in his memoirs, Yeltsin considered himself "something like the father of an extended family" *(semeistvo).* He enjoyed flaunting his patriarchal authority, and liked it when he had the opportunity to demand that somebody apologize for a bureaucratic bungle: "Ask papa for forgiveness."[13]

Memoirs by his associates and those by Yeltsin himself are laced with examples of the language of patriarchy and filial intimacy. Kostikov affirms that Yeltsin harbored a great deal of sentimentality, almost love, for Yegor Gaidar, and says that Gaidar was Yeltsin's "alter ego" *(vtorym ya)*.[14] Yeltsin is reported to have referred to Anatolii Chubais and Boris Nemtsov as "like sons to me."[15] Yeltsin's ghost-writer and eventual chief-of-staff, Valentin Yumashev, appears in a photograph with Yeltsin in one memoir, with a caption that reads: "For the President, V. Yumashev is almost like a son. It is not for nothing that his patronymic is Borisovich."[16] Erstwhile media director Oleg Poptsov has noted Yeltsin's "infatuation" with his young advisers in early 1992,[17] a word also used by an "outsider" student of Yeltsin's leadership.[18] Kostikov's memoir is entitled *Love-Affair with a President*.[19]

During the 1980s, Yeltsin's relationship with his bodyguard Aleksandr Korzhakov was so intimate that the two exchanged blood from their fingers on two occasions to affirm their eternal loyalty to each other as "blood brothers" (Yeltsin was in his mid-50s at the time).[20] Korzhakov has referred to a vacation he and Yeltsin took in 1986 as a "honeymoon."[21] Yeltsin was the designated "wedding patriarch" at the marriage of Korzhakov's daughter.[22] Streletskii writes of the psychology of those responsible for guarding party and governmental officials under Yeltsin: "Bit by bit they are turned into 'members of the families' of those they are guarding."[23] Tellingly, after Yeltsin rebuked Korzhakov in May 1996 for getting involved in politics, the latter proclaimed to Yeltsin's daughter Tatiana, "It would be an understatement to say that I no longer love Boris Nikolaevich." Tatiana reportedly flew into a rage at this statement.[24] Yeltsin's patriarchal self-conception also encompassed members of the military leadership. Colonel Viktor Baranets, one-time press secretary in the Russian Ministry of Defense, reports that Defense Minister Grachev "loved" Yeltsin and that the two men once declared their "eternal friendship and love" for each other. When he awarded Grachev a special presidential gold medal in a public ceremony, Yeltsin declared that it was his "personal gift."[25]

In this context, the key to political longevity and influence was to capture the attention and the ear of the patriarch. But this had to be done with all proper deference. Indeed, when seven members of Yeltsin's staff wrote a joint letter to their boss in 1994, urging him not to repeat his embarrassing, apparently drunken, performance in Berlin, Boris Nikolaevich was livid. His reaction was that of a patriarch rather than an executive: He demanded that each of them admit their "guilt" and express "repentance."[26]

Within this familial context, Yeltsin felt free to be an abusive parent. Like Napoleon, he would dress down military commanders in front of their subordinates, as he did Defense Minister Igor Rodionov and Chief of the General Staff Viktor Samsonov just before firing them.[27] Nor were the military the only victims. Other members of Yeltsin's cabinet were subjected to open, verbal abuse: Foreign Minister Kozyrev, Interior Minister Yerin, and Nationalities Minister

Yegorov are specifically mentioned in memoirs as having received such treatment,[28] and Kostikov hints that Prime Minister Chernomyrdin was also publicly scolded by Yeltsin.[29] On occasion, particularly when he had been drinking, Yeltsin was also physically abusive. He "played the spoons" on the heads of ranking assistants, and when the others in the room responded with laughter, augmented the speed and force of the spoon-pounding, as well as the number of heads being pounded.[30] Another time, traveling on a boat down the Yenisei River, the president lost patience with interruptions from his press secretary and ordered his bodyguards to toss the man overboard. When his bodyguards hesitated on the assumption that he was kidding, he reiterated that he was serious, and he saw that the hapless press secretary went over the side.[31]

Yeltsin's abuse of his most dependent and servile subordinates did not cease at the boundaries of the Russian executive offices. Others have written about how he played the spoons on the head of the president of Kyrgyzstan, Askar Akaev.[32] Unless this was mutual, good-natured play (not clear from the memoir account), it is a stunning indicator of the extent to which Yeltsin considered portions of the CIS to be members of his household.

Although Yeltsin frequently abused his subordinates and dependents, he could also be a generous benefactor to his political family. He enjoyed bestowing gifts (usually expensive watches) on members of his staff.[33] Such gestures reached beyond the inner circle, as Yeltsin received innumerable requests for special favors—tax exemptions, in particular—from representatives of regional and sectoral interests. Reportedly, he found it difficult to say "no" in the face of opportunities to assist friends, maddening his budget-conscious finance minister in the process.[34] This tendency extended also to "friends" outside the Russian Federation. Gaidar reported in his memoirs his fear that Yeltsin, if left alone with the leaders of Belarus during economic policy negotiations, would concede more than Russia could afford.[35] An interviewee confirmed that such fears were well-founded, but not because of Yeltsin's (very real) ignorance of economics or his ideological commitment to CIS integration; rather, what drove Yeltsin in such conversations was paternalism and a sense of communalism. As this interviewee put it, Yeltsin's expressed sentiment was: "We're a family here. Let's dispense with formalities! Why should we wrangle? Here, I'll give you this!" This attitude extended beyond Russian-Belarusian relations, according to this insider, helping to explain Russia's flexibility in relations with Ukraine and Kazakhstan (the latter, regarding Caspian Sea oil). The same interviewee averred that in CIS relations, Yeltsin "could be generous to a fault."

Yeltsin thought of himself as "director of all of Russia,"[36] whose election as president had validated his right to interpret the will of the people. Because of his overwhelming victories in confrontations with the old system and in free elections, he didn't believe he had to account for or explain himself to anyone.[37] But he also thought of himself as a "people's tsar,"[38] benevolent and caring, though strict when necessary. When he offered reassurances to the populace that their pain would shortly ease, he was performing the role of a Russian priest, lifting the spirits of his flock.[39] On a tour of Russia in 1992, he brought along hundreds of millions of rubles for "gifts to the working people." He knew that this violated the prevailing economic policy, "but he considered it possible for himself to make tsarist gestures."[40]

The Evolution of Yeltsin's Style

Yeltsin entertained a personalistic self-conception throughout his political career; he always wanted to be "in charge." But his operating style evolved over time, with patriarchalism becoming a dominant orientation only after 1993. Memoirs by his close aides of the late 1980s rarely mention the traits emphasized here, stressing instead his charismatic personalism.[41] Several memoirs by people who worked with Yeltsin both before and after 1993 distinguish between the early President Yeltsin and the late President Yeltsin, with the midpoint being sometime in 1993. Before then, Yeltsin was a populist who was confident of his ability to mobilize the masses against his political adversaries. He also enjoyed enormous charismatic authority within his entourage, and rational-legal authority that derived from his public election to the Russian presidency in June 1991. In addition, within his inner circle, while demanding the deference due a patriarch, he was also accessible, consultative, and receptive to a range of policy advice. By late 1993, however, Yeltsin had lost confidence in his ability to rally the masses, a conclusion reinforced mightily by the results of the December 1993 parliamentary elections.[42] His memoirs published in 1994 end with the prosaic promise to give the Russian people "stability and consistency in politics and the economy" and with the declaration that "the only definite guarantor of calm is the president himself," both of which are features of a patriarchal orientation.[43] The system-builder had evolved into an authoritarian system-manager. Thereafter, we are told, Yeltsin's presidential administration took on still more of the attributes of a "court" and increasingly lost the attributes of a cabinet.

Gaidar, in fact, wrote that around this time Yeltsin began to present himself as a benevolent tsar surrounded by a huge court.[44] Increasingly over time, Kostikov reports, Yeltsin referred to himself in the third person.[45] According to Korzhakov, Yeltsin began to be heavily preoccupied with his personal security.[46] He also narrowed the circle of those to whom he would turn for advice, and allowed the security personnel in his entourage to have a major influence on policy.[47] As Kostikov lamented, "We ['democrats'–G.B.] were pained that in relations with Boris Nikolaevich, a steady disappearance of democratism, accessibility, and relations of trust was occurring."[48] One former associate explains this trend as a joint product of the physical pain and exhaustion Yeltsin experienced at this time and the emotional anguish of having "lost" the December 1993 parliamentary elections after having expended so much energy to prevail over the Supreme Soviet in 1993. He had been expending so much "negative energy" for so many years that by 1994 the members of his entourage felt they could bring him bad news only when it was packaged with three times as much good news.[49] Whatever the exact cause of the change, it was unmistakable. It led Gaidar to remark to Kostikov in January 1994 that "we must return Yeltsin to Yeltsin,"[50] which meant that they must find a way to curb Yeltsin's authoritarian impulse, reinforce his democratic strain, and prevent him from relying excessively on alcohol as an escape. Yeltsin had evolved from a "people's tsar"[51] to an embattled, increasingly reclusive autocrat. His personalism, constant throughout his years as president, had metamorphosed from populist and consultative to patriarchal and exclusionary.

Personalism Versus Institution-Building

The Benefits of Personalism

Some theorists believe that transitions to market democracies require strong executive leadership in order to break through the constraints on change. Others argue that a parliamentary system is a precondition for consolidating a market-democratic breakthrough. Given this lack of theoretical consensus, Yeltsin's personalism need not be treated as a self-evident obstacle to progress. Indeed, given his concern to overturn the formal structures of communist power and to replace them with the formal organizations of a capitalist economy and a liberal democracy, integrated into Western organizations, within the territorial boundaries of the Russian Federation of December 1991, and resistant to both communist restoration and fascist reaction, one could argue that in the near term Yeltsin's personalistic approach to leadership went far toward those ends. He forced through changes that created the framework for such a system. In these respects, Yeltsin was indeed an institution-builder.

Yeltsin and his staff designed and won ratification of the Russian Constitution of 1993, which, however flawed, finally provided a consistent constitutional framework for the nascent Russian state. The parliamentary and presidential elections of 1993, 1995, and 1996 took place as scheduled, and although they were procedurally flawed in several respects, their outcomes were probably legitimate. Yeltsin resisted the temptation to postpone or cancel the gubernatorial elections of 1996–1998, even though they threatened to diminish his political leverage over regional elites. He also resisted the temptation to postpone the presidential election of 1996, despite the fact that in January 1996 his public approval rating had fallen to 7 percent and some of his advisers were recommending postponement.

Similarly, Yeltsin resisted the temptation to roll back the civil rights won by Russians under Gorbachev: freedoms to criticize, organize, worship, and travel. Books, newspapers, and television shows regularly roasted or ridiculed the president. They sharply criticized many of his policies—at times, to the president's dismay and shock. These institutions survived despite Yeltsin's presumed distaste for such personal attacks.

With respect to transformation of the economic system, Yeltsin, in the name of creating a class of property holders who would fight to prevent communist restoration, sponsored a program of privatization that allowed the transfer of state property into private hands at a rate and on a scale that exceeded anything seen before in world history. Thus, Yeltsin was the "founder" of Russia's oligopolistic and plutocratic but nonetheless capitalistic economy.

In his policies toward Russia's regions, Yeltsin sponsored a series of bilateral treaties and agreements between Moscow and individual regions and republics that flexibly defined the respective obligations of the center and the periphery. The Constitution of 1993 tried to rein in centrifugal forces by prescribing a strong role for Moscow. But that same document left many areas to joint jurisdiction and failed to specify the mechanisms for resolving ambiguities and conflicts. Such ambiguities were consistent with Yeltsin's urge for personal flexibility in striking deals with the heads of different "subjects of the Federation," and consistent with the prevailing realities: the disparate resource bases of the regions, the varying levels of resolve of their leaders, the lack of consensus among regional governors and republican presidents about constitutional principles, and the center's frequent incapacity to enforce its writ. Only in the case of Chechnya did Yeltsin resort to military force.

In the realm of nation-building, Yeltsin consistently fought against those who would define the Russian Federation as an exclusionary, ethnically Russian entity. Instead, he sponsored and loudly argued for a civic and tolerant definition of citizenship in Russia, and his definition of policy on these matters prevailed.[52]

At the international level, Yeltsin was one of the architects of the Commonwealth of Independent States, established to foster peaceful relations among the successor states to the Soviet Union. Although he rhetorically defended the rights of Russian-speakers resident in the successor states, he also insisted that such issues be resolved peacefully. And when the governments of other CIS states resisted Russian pressures for "dual citizenship," Yeltsin backed off on the issue.[53]

In relations with the "far abroad," Yeltsin encouraged and monitored the negotiation of a NATO-Russia Charter as a way of making NATO expansion palatable to the Russian political elite. He also successfully negotiated the expansion of the G-7 into the G-8.

On the basis of this record, if one values the fundamentals that Yeltsin put in place—assuming these institutions survive the current turmoil—one could arrive at a positive evaluation of Yeltsin's contribution to Russia's recent political-economic development and international integration. In fact, this is the basis for positive evaluations that are already on record.[54] These emphasize Yeltsin's role as founder of a new order and as guarantor of that order against communist restoration, fascist ascendancy, and secession from the Russian Federation. Indeed, these were precisely the roles that Yeltsin conceived for himself in the "struggle for Russia."

Macrostructural Vulnerabilities

And yet, one could argue that Yeltsin's urge to found and guarantee a new order of things as quickly as possible, and to do so through personalistic leadership, planted the seeds of crisis that have been growing for several years and have finally begun to flower. In the political realm, Yeltsin's primary macroinstitutional accomplishment—the Constitution of 1993—established a framework that is so overcentralized and in certain respects so rigid that it inhibits the system's adaptation to a changing environment. The new constitution established a presidential system under which the powers of the president are enormous, including vast powers of decree, and those of the parliament and the Constitutional Court are very limited. It is almost impossible constitutionally to impeach the president, and equally difficult to amend the constitution itself. The constitution was designed to ensure that the president would be (by far) the highest authority in the land, largely unaccountable to institutions and primarily answerable only to the people, via subsequent presidential elections.

Such discretion provides the president with strong incentives to ignore or infantilize the other branches of government. The constitution makes it easy for the president to dissolve parliament, but nearly impossible for parliament to impeach the president. The courts, like parliament, are greatly underfinanced, whereas the presidency and the executive branch are hugely bloated with redundant personnel. Given the resources available to the president, his capacity to bribe or intimidate members of parliament by far exceeds their capacity to threaten him. The overwhelming power of the presidency vis-à-vis other central institutions ensures that the general direction of policy is likely to reflect the president's preferences. But this also means that policy will depend largely on the wisdom and foresight of the president, that policy elaboration will not be the product of a parliamentary consensus-building process, and that an infantilized parliament will likely engage in obstruction in those realms of policy within which it has some discretion.

Yeltsin's "superpresidentialist"[55] constitution also eliminated the office of vice president so that no future VP could turn against the president the way Yeltsin's vice president, Aleksandr Rutskoy, had in 1992 and 1993. The lack of a vice presidency in a system in which the president has such extraordinary powers means that any sign of presidential ill-health—or the anticipation of such—sets off a chain of political maneuvering and demagogic rhetoric in anticipation of a new election. The legal ambiguity about the definition of "incapacitation" becomes magnified. Efforts to alter the constitution to establish a vice presidency, or even to mandate that the prime minister serve out the former president's term before a new election, are impeded by the impossibility of amendment. Moreover, the constitution provides an incentive for those most hopeful of winning the next election to oppose its amendment. Why reduce the powers of an office that you have reason to believe you can capture?[56]

In the economic realm, Yeltsin's privatization program amounted to the greatest case of insider trading in history. It was consistent with Yeltsin's urge to build an economic elite as quickly as possible—an elite that would support him politically and serve as a powerful bulwark against communist restoration. But the extraordinary concentration of wealth and conspicuous consumption that this program allowed, along with the illicit, often criminal, means by which that wealth was acquired and the crony capitalism that resulted, has nurtured a widespread sense of social injustice that could explode into rage or public protest at any time. The mass impoverishment resulting from the chosen strategy of macroeconomic stabilization (i.e., liberal monetarism) gives a powerful economic motivation for protest to new members of the economic underclass. Even if ideological and organizational obstacles to the mobilization of mass protest prove insurmountable,[57] socioeconomic pressures could eventually lead to the victory in presidential and parliamentary elections of a populist-authoritarian alternative.

Similarly, Yeltsin's decision to wage war in Chechnya to defend the territorial integrity of the Russian Federation proved disastrous for all concerned. The human toll—among Chechens, Russian civilians in Chechnya, and soldiers of Russia's armed forces—was enormous. We probably will never know whether the war deterred other regional executives from contemplating secession. But certainly the costs of the war further undermine the legitimacy, stability, and effectiveness of the Russian government, however popular the decision in 1999 to once again invade Chechnya.

Above all, Yeltsin's determination to stand "above political parties" as "director of all of Russia" has inhibited the development of political parties that provide the organizational buttress for stable, representative democracy. In fall 1991, and again in fall 1993 and 1995, Yeltsin was presented opportunities to sponsor reformist presidential parties that might have helped build muscular, nationwide political organizations. These could have expanded the mobilizational capacity of antirestorationist forces and strengthened the organizational bond between politicians in the center and those on the periphery. The Russian president certainly controlled sufficient material resources to invest in such a venture. Instead, Yeltsin opted for an ad hoc, personalistic approach to leadership, accepting no obligations to any particular organization and remaining free to shift support bases as his intuition dictated. Although this approach was consistent with his self-image as a leader and his conception of the kind of leadership Russia needed to found and guarantee a new order of things, it left the political system demonstrably underdeveloped and fragile.

Yeltsin's Mentality: Microinstitutional Blind Spots

Yeltsin's self-image as a leader influenced his political strategies for accumulating and wielding power. However, to understand his policy priorities and to appreciate why he neglected microorganizational development, we must also explore his values, perspectives, and beliefs.

Yeltsin believed that the Russian bureaucracy was a quagmire that could serve little useful purpose. He wrote in his memoirs that both the Russian bureaucracy and the Russian people required a "strong hand" to extract them from their inertia and their nihilistic behavioral patterns. Unified, strong command was more important than rule of law. In Yeltsin's words: "everyone knows that we Russians do not like to obey all sorts of rules, laws, instructions, and directives. . . . Rules cut us like a knife."[58] "Somebody had to be the boss," he wrote in his second book of memoirs. "Russia's main paradox was that . . . there had not been any real powerful leader in the Republic of Russia." At present, people "are almost incapable of doing anything themselves." Two or three presidencies will have to go by, he asserted, before this situation would change.[59] Gorbachev's problem, according to Yeltsin, was that he did not understand this: "Was he organically capable of playing the role of a severe, uncompromising master?" Gorbachev should have known better, Yeltsin wrote, for he had plenty of evidence: Whenever Gorbachev got tough with the obstreperous Congress of People's Deputies, it acceded to his demands. But when he was weak, it attacked him.[60]

These beliefs attracted Yeltsin to a breakthrough strategy for building a new order in Russia. A plan that was subsequently dubbed "shock therapy" sounded to him like the approach he was looking for. It promised quick results at the macroeconomic level, with none of the procrastination he found so maddening in Gorbachev's policies.[61] It was consistent with campaignism, commandism, and "struggle," which had been common features of the Stalinist and post-Stalinist administrative cultures in which he had grown up. As former parliamentarian Valentin Fyodorov has noted, this approach also filled the cognitive vacuum left by evaporating confidence in the previous ideology, and appealed to Yeltsin's neo-Soviet mentality in that it was simple and clear-cut in its principles and required resolve and political decisiveness in implementation.[62]

The so-called shock therapy approach was reductionist in that it focused on the individual citizen, promising to cure Russians of the lethargy into which they had fallen. As much as the strategy was a macroeconomic prescription for economic stabilization, it was also based on an implicit theory of behavioral and cultural change. If people—regardless of their cultural backgrounds—were put into situations in which survival depended on their exercising entrepreneurial initiative, they would finally overcome their lethargy and seek out opportunities. As Yeltsin put it, in retrospect, "Sometimes it takes a sharp break or rupture to make a person move forward or even survive at all"[63]—an observation based on personal experience, for he had put himself through just such a wrenching cognitive and value transformation during 1988, after being purged from the Soviet leadership.[64] Presumably, sustained behavioral change ultimately would bring attitudes into conformity with behavior, transforming lethargy and envy into initiative and achievement. Judging from Yeltsin's statements about economic reform,[65] neither the success of behavioral and cultural transformation nor that of macroeconomic stabilization and liberalization hinged on microinstitution-building, which could come later, developing naturally in the course of things. To Yeltsin, this was perhaps a positive feature of the strategy, for it circumvented or decommissioned the bureaucracy rather than seeking to reform or restructure it.

To Yeltsin, cultural transformation would also be a product of generational change. Those who would not or could not adapt to the stringent new requirements would be replaced by the new generations reaching their twenties and thirties in the 1990s. He saw himself as the leader of a revolution that would bring those new generations into positions of authority in the polity, economy, and society. For the most part, he assumed the older generation of citizens incapable of adjusting to capitalism, having been ruined by the old system. But Yeltsin's candor revealed his own Leninist-Stalinist "campaign" mentality. For example, Yeltsin wrote that as head of the Moscow City Committee, he strove to replace compromised workers in Moscow shops with "young, 'uninfected' [*nezarazhennaya*] staff."[66] When discussing economic reform in his second book of memoirs, he praised tough, independent, ambitious young people, who possessed "an entirely new psychology."[67] Russia's backwardness could not be overcome until generational change had taken place: "We must finally admit that Russia comprehends democracy poorly—not merely for global, historical reasons but for rather prosaic ones: the new generation cannot break its way into power. The Socialist mode of thinking has left its imprint on all of us . . . . The new generation must come to the forefront as quickly as possible."[68]

This emphasis on demographic change may have been perspicacious, but it also reinforced Yeltsin's inattention to microinstitutional development. For if energy, enthusiasm, "democratic" orientations, and a work ethic were decisive, then organizational rules and administrative efficiency were less important. To a considerable extent, Yeltsin believed that "cadres decide everything"—an idea consistent with one strand of Soviet political culture. There were no fortresses that "uninfected" young people could not storm, once they were given an electoral voice, hired in large enough numbers, liberated from the command economy, and given a fungible currency to fuel economic ambition and exchange.

A most telling indicator of Yeltsin's blind spot was his treatment of microinstitution-building in his second book of memoirs, which was written in 1994. Notably, this volume says very little about processes of institution-building required to consolidate the new order, even though it was written at a time when the pinch of organizational deficiencies was starting to become obvious. And when he did occasionally mention the problem, it was either: (1) in a passing, ritualistic reference to a highly generalized need (e.g., for "rule of law"); (2) focused on organizational forms, not internal organizational processes (e.g., we now have a stock market); (3) reflective of a fatalism or beffudlement about efforts to transform the Russian bureaucracy (e.g., what can you do!); or (4) an effort to blame others for current deficiencies (e.g., it was parliament's fault).[69] For the most part, however, the problem of institution-building was ignored in favor of lengthy discussions of cadres policy. In a similar vein, when corruption was mentioned, it was treated as a cultural or individual failing and not as a social problem that could be solved through changes in institutional incentives.

Personalism Versus Rationalization
of the Russian Bureaucracy

Yeltsin's self-image and beliefs undermined administrative efficiency throughout his years in office. His organization of the presidency and his manipulation of the executive branch did much to strengthen his grip on the formal reins of power and perhaps to make possible the achievement of his general goals. But they simultaneously strengthened the corrupt bureaucracy's capacity to avoid rationalization and therefore undermined the sustainability of Yeltsin's achievements. In all public administration there is an inherent tension between the requirements of political control and those of administrative efficiency. What distinguishes administrative leaders is how they deal with this tension, and whether their solutions strike a balance that is consistent with the realization and consolidation of their general policy goals. Leaders like Charles de Gaulle, Franklin Delano Roosevelt, and Kemal Ataturk understood this. In Yeltsin's case, the sacrifice of administrative rationality to the requisites of political control and personalistic leadership was such as to threaten the sustainability of his program. I will not try to determine whether Yeltsin's shortcoming in this regard was due to a preference for short-term power maximization, distaste for the detailed, programmatic thinking needed to tackle the reform of public administration, or fatalism about the unreformability of Russia's bureaucracy. What is clear is that bureaucratic fragmentation, corruption, and unaccountability got worse as a result of the approach to administrative control that Yeltsin employed.

Take, for example, his approach to the organization of advice within the presidency and the articulation of interests within the government. On both scores, Yeltsin's preferred approach was individualized, antiprocedural, and anti-institutional. Within his personal staff and advisory corps, Yeltsin resisted the crystallization of even informal constraints on his power over the "children." He did not conceive of the political organization of his staff as a rational distribution of formal powers *(polnomochiya)*. Instead he wanted to maintain fluidity and redundancy of jurisdictions in order to maximize his capacity to play his subordinates off against each other and to maximize their sense of dependence on him for protection against the others. According to a former, high-level staff member,[70] Yeltsin wished to get advice from staff members on an individual, not a collective basis. He did not want his staff to get together, work out a common viewpoint on an issue, and present it to him as a collective judgment. Nor did he care to meet with them as a group. Instead, he wanted each of them to come to him individually with their ideas. When they defied this preference, he retaliated.

Personalism also informed Yeltsin's approach to interest articulation and aggregation. As noted earlier, he was highly responsive to particularistic pleading for tax exemptions, licensing, and the like. He also preferred to deal with governors, military commanders, and ministers on an ad hoc, individual basis rather than through their organizations. Although there may have been a political rationality to some of these preferences, the effect was anti-institutional in that they undermined the development of organized collectivities on which modern public administration is based. As Eugene Huskey has aptly observed, it was "a style of rule associated more with traditional monarchs than modern chief executives."[71]

Yeltsin's cadres policy also was antiprocedural. Even after securing ratification of his superpresidentialist constitution of December 1993, he violated its terms with impunity by using his decree authority to fill ministerial posts that he had no legal prerogative to fill. In other realms of policy, too, Yeltsin's liberal emission of decrees frequently exceeded his constitutional authority.[72]

Yeltsin's approach to administrative organization of the presidential and executive branches was the antithesis of rationalization; indeed, it was reminiscent of Khrushchev's approach of the early 1960s: constant reorganization, high turnover of personnel, and the regular creation of new units with jurisdictions that duplicated those of existing units.[73] The Presidential Administration evolved into a huge bureaucracy, larger in size than the CPSU's Central Committee apparatus and with at least as many departments. But there has been woefully little rationalization of jurisdictions within the apparatus and between the apparatus and the ministries. Officials of the apparatus were left with neither the assurance of stability nor the information they needed to perform their jobs.

In theory, one could view the blurring of jurisdictions and the inhibition of stable expectations as a textbook-rational way to organize a presidential administration. Organization theorists have long known that formal organization charts are a poor guide to how organizations actually run—or ought to run. U.S. president Franklin Delano Roosevelt found it useful to establish redundant jurisdictions to ensure that he received a variety of viewpoints and had access to multiple sources of information on the same situation.

This was not how Yeltsin's presidential administration and executive branch were run. Instability of expectations had less to do with the sequencing of tasks than with the continued existence of the agency and the maintenance of perquisites and privileges that accompany employment in the Presidential Administration. Here the blurring of jurisdictions has not been a functional means of ensuring diverse viewpoints so much as a proliferation of redundancies that leave units unclear as to who actually is responsible for task fulfillment. The exponential increase in the size of the administration did not foster a healthy coverage of all issues so much as a duplication of the governmental-ministerial structure within the presidential branch, a duplication of jurisdictions between the two branches, and a proliferation of decisional arenas to which bureaucrats and others could turn to subvert the implementation of presidential decrees or parliamentary legislation. The frequent creation and abolition of agencies left officials little time for programmatic thinking and focused their attention largely on personal political survival.

More generally, Yeltsin preferred to manipulate diversity in ways that played factions off against each other and thereby maintained or enhanced his leverage as the "ultimate arbiter." Yeltsin included within the Presidential Administration representatives of all political orientations save intransigent communists and radical nationalists. This is certainly a rational strategy for maintaining power. It can also be a rational strategy for eliciting a diversity of inputs: Both FDR and French president François Mitterrand, ably employed such a strategy. But they did so in a relatively strong institutional context and in a way that left most incumbents feeling reasonably secure in their jobs. If, instead, the ultimate arbiter frequently shifts back and forth between preferred factions and forces the losers to pay with their jobs, the result is more likely to be sycophancy, individualized efforts to curry the favor of the patriarch, or collective efforts to destroy the credibility and favor of competing factions. Yeltsin's modus operandi has been to fire leading officials and their deputies with great frequency, and sometimes to balance one arbitrary dismissal with another dismissal of an equivalent figure in the opposing faction.[74]

One result of such a strategy is that ideological or professional factions crystallize within the Presidential Administration for mutual protection against the unpredictable commander. Factions will spend a great deal of time attempting to compromise each other in the eyes of the ultimate arbiter. Another result of the general atmosphere of profound uncertainty and insecurity is widespread and deep-seated corruption within the Presidential Administration and the executive branch. Uncertain as to what actions are likely to fulfill the tasks assigned to them; equally uncertain as to how long they will keep their jobs regardless of their performance; finding themselves in a privileged position that affords many opportunities for using public office for private material gain; and knowing that they might not be able to gather such resources—or avoid criminal prosecution—outside of government, officials generally find it too tempting to resist feathering their nests while the opportunity is there. In sum, rather than engendering a healthy, low level of competition and uncertainty, Yeltsin's approach to microadministration of the presidential and executive branches succeeded in protecting his personal power against challenge but failed to create the institutional support needed for rational decisionmaking.[75]

This leadership style not only undermined rationalization of the administrative apparatus; it also subjected Yeltsin to decisional overload that often paralyzed policymaking. Yeltsin was a victim of his own success in destroying the communist system, in that he ruled as president without the benefit of an established apparatus of officials to organize the flow of information to him and the implementation of his requests. Even a healthy leader would initially have been burdened by this deficiency. But Yeltsin was not a healthy man; he suffered from a weak heart, a painful back injury incurred in Spain in 1990, and a regimen of medications that exacerbated his seemingly manic-depressive mood swings. Over time, his press secretary reports, the burden of decisional overload took a further toll, leading Yeltsin to avoid documents, appointments, and increasingly, decisions.[76] Nonetheless, Yeltsin resisted the obvious conclusion—that he should delegate more decisionmaking authority to others—perhaps fearing a dilution of his authority or the crystallization of threats to his power.[77] Indeed, even when he did not fear losing control, Yeltsin's patriarchal self-image predisposed him to take credit for all distributions of benefits. In a telling example of this "big man" mentality, Yeltsin told a U.S. subcabinet agency director, whom he met at a reception during a summit meeting, not to bother dealing with his ministerial counterpart in Moscow but instead to come directly to him.[78]

Perhaps decisional overload, combined with Yeltsin's expressed fatalism about reforming the Russian bureaucracy, explains the blind eye he usually turned to allegations of corruption within his administration. This is a curious feature of his presidency. Few observers see Yeltsin as a man who held his office largely for personal material gain. In Sverdlovsk, he was not noticeably corrupt. And when he was first secretary of the Moscow Party Committee, from 1985 to 1987, he was famous for his anticorruption campaigns. Yet, despite regular speeches as president about the need to root out corruption, memoirists report a tendency in Yeltsin to avoid following up on reports of corruption in his administration.[79] Resignation, fatigue, and a lack of ideas about how to accomplish his goals—in Moscow he had been frustrated in his efforts and befuddled at the seemingly unending scope of corruption[80]—may have combined to deter him from tackling corruption.[81]

If such was the case, it would be symptomatic of still another characteristic of Yeltsin's that hobbled his capacity to consolidate the policy accomplishments of his presidency. He simply did not understand the contradictions between his leadership style and the requirements of administrative rationality. Put differently, he did not understand that his initiatives usually made the situation worse on that front. Vague decrees that either circumvented parliament or violated the constitution had the dual effect of leaving interpretation up to the bureaucrats and of undermining the credibility of parliament as a force for oversight or discipline of the bureaucracy. The result was that the bureaucrats had the intellectual and political space to ignore or reinterpret decrees to their benefit.[82]

Indeed, it would not be too harsh to say that Yeltsin was not a programmatic thinker. He understood the general direction in which he was determined to push the country. And he understood the general directions he was determined to avoid taking. But when it came to elaborating complex programs that would move the country forward toward the preferred end-state, Yeltsin fell short. He admitted as much regarding economic reform in his second book of memoirs, published in Russian in 1994; but he excised the admission from the English translation that was published abroad.[83] Other Russian memoirists (among them one of Yeltsin's foreign policy advisers) have asserted that Yeltsin lacked a political strategy or philosophy of transformation;[84] some have cited his frequent bouts of depression or his native ambivalence as the causes of his squandering of political opportunities.[85] Whatever the sources of Yeltsin's policy choices, the implications for policy were clear: programmatic incoherence. Similarly, Yeltsin's conscious strategy of balancing and playing off factions against each other helped him to maintain his political autonomy as the ultimate arbiter and allowed him to maintain a broad and shifting centrist political base. But it also left his programs hostage to political considerations, which usually resulted in a counterproductive alternation of policy directions rather than a consistent program based on an appreciation of the interdependence among policy realms. Yeltsin seems not to have understood a key requirement of successful transformational leadership: finding a workable balance between macro- and microinstitution-building; between the achievement of near-term ends and longer-term consolidation of gains; and between political rationality and programmatic coherence.

Conclusion

Culture, institutions, and inherited circumstances are three causal factors that fatalistic observers have pointed to as determinants of the malaise in post-Soviet Russia. Rather than pin the blame on Yeltsin and his policy choices (or on international institutions and foreign governments that pressured him to adopt some of these policies), these analysts argue that the inheritance bequeathed to Russia in 1992 would have led to an unhappy outcome, regardless of the best efforts of those in power from 1992 to 1998. From this perspective, failures on the microorganizational front should have been expected.

The evidence discussed in this chapter cannot disprove this counterfactual claim. But it does point to policies embraced in 1992–1998 that exacerbated the negative features of the inheritance and created a still more fragile structure of public administration. Moreover, it highlights the leadership style of Boris Yeltsin: personalism, short-term political rationality, and macroinstitution-building geared toward preventing a communist restoration—all to the detriment of microinstitution-building.

Are Yeltsin's perspectives and personality unique to him? Or do they reflect a broader Russian "type" of leader and leadership that was a product of the situation? Certainly, the kind of personalistic leadership that Yeltsin stood for can be found in many member-states of the Commonwealth of Independent States. This suggests that situations of institutional fragmentation, such as followed the collapse of communism and the USSR, may favor the rise of personalistic leaders. Moreover, vacuums of political power tend to favor those who would seize and abuse that power. But institutional fragmentation was common to almost all postcommunist countries, whereas only some of them succumbed to personalistic leadership and failed to build a solid institutional foundation. Perhaps Yeltsin should be conceived of as a type of leader, significantly a product of his upbringing in Soviet culture and structures, who abhorred institutionalized checks on his leadership ability and was inclined to exploit and abuse the opportunity to aggrandize power. Once he made that choice, and once he enforced it in fall 1993, his own fears of the alienation engendered by his actions would lead him continuously to reinforce his power and to keep imagined opponents off balance. From this perspective, personalism was perhaps good for Yeltsin (as per the goal of staying in office), but bad for Russia.

But how bad was it for Russia? Could the benefits achieved under personalism have been attained without personalistic leadership? Would a weaker executive have been able to avoid gridlock or restoration? How do we weigh the positive results of Yeltsin's policies against the downside? This is not the place to answer that question. But events in Russia in 1998 and 1999 suggest that the system Yeltsin constructed was like a skeleton without ligaments: prone to collapse when it loses its artificial supports or when it meets countervailing force. The organizational system indeed collapsed, and society did not rush to fill the vacuum, either for good or for evil. The country has remained relatively stable (i.e., stagnant) since then. We shall see whether that situation lasts.

Notes

An earlier draft of this chapter was presented at the conference "Russia on the Eve of the 21st Century," in Berkeley, California, May 14–15, 1999. Part of the chapter was published as George W. Breslauer, "Boris Yel'tsin as Patriarch," *Post-Soviet Affairs* (April–June 1999): 186–200. I would like to thank Robin Brooks, Leonid Kil, Matthew Bencke, and Ilya Vinkovetsky for valuable research assistance; the Carnegie Corporation of New York for financial support; and participants at the May 1999 conference for their comments.

1. This statement was omitted from the English-language edition, Boris Yeltsin, *The Struggle for Russia* (New York, 1994); see p. 145.

2. See Douglass C. North, *Institutions, Institutional Change, and Economic Performance* (New York, 1990); Richard Hofstadter, *The Idea of a Party System* (Berkeley, 1970); William Riker, *Federalism: Origin, Operation, Significance* (Boston, 1964); for a trenchant demonstration that even F. Hayek understood the need for institution-building to buttress a market economy, see Jacques Sapir, "Russia's Crash of August 1998: Diagnosis and Prescription," *Post-Soviet Affairs* (January-March 1999); for a similar argument, coupled with a stimulating analysis of the clash between proceduralism and *sobornost'* (organic unity) in post-Soviet Russia, see Nikolai Biryukov and Victor Sergeyev, *Russian Politics in Transition* (Aldershot, U.K., 1997). Note also a leading, congratulatory study of Russian privatization in the 1990s that ends on an ominous note about the dangers deriving from Russia's underdeveloped regulatory system (Joseph R. Blasi, Maya Kroumova, and Douglas Kruse, *Kremlin Capitalism: Privatizing the Russian Economy* [Ithaca, N.Y., 1997], 179–181); and a study of Russia's 1996 presidential elections that ends with a chapter warning about the likely negative consequences of the lack of intermediate institutions linking state and society (Michael McFaul, *Russia's Presidential Election of 1996* [Stanford, 1997], chapter 7). There is plenty of controversy in the literature on the role of the state in economic development, but I have never seen a refutation of the minimalist claim I have advanced here.

3. Clifford G. Gaddy and Barry W. Ickes, "Russia's Virtual Economy," *Foreign Affairs* (September-October 1998): 53–67.

4. Yeltsin regularly gave speeches and issued decrees on the need for rule of law, a strong judiciary, reliable tax collection, and the rooting out of corruption, but little progress, or negative progress, was made in these realms under his guidance.

5. See Dmitri Glinski and Peter Reddaway, "What Went Wrong in Russia?: The Ravages of 'Market Bolshevism'," *Journal of Democracy* (April 1999).

6. Boris Yeltsin, *The Struggle for Russia* (New York, 1994), 179.

7. Boris Yeltsin, *Against the Grain* (New York, 1990), 29.

8. Pilar Bonet, "Lord of the Manor: Boris Yeltsin in Sverdlovsk *Oblast'*," Kennan Institute Occasional Paper, no. 260 (Washington, D.C., 1995), 1; Pilar Bonet, "Nevozmozhnaya Rossiya: Boris Yel'tsin, provintsial v Kremlye," translated from the Spanish by G. Luk'yanova, *Ural* (Yekaterinburg), no. 4 (April 1994): 24, 141; and Yeltsin's self-depiction: "A provincial first secretary was a god, a czar—master of his province" (Yeltsin, *Against the Grain*, 70).

9. Aleksandr Korzhakov, *Boris Yel'tsin: Ot rassveta do zakata* (Moscow, 1997), 49, 51; see also Lev Sukhanov, *Tri goda s Yel'tsinym* (Riga, 1992), 20.

10. Yeltsin, *Against the Grain,* 108–119.

11. Yeltsin, The *Struggle,* 238.

12. For fuller documentation and discussion of Yeltsin's patriarchal style, see George W. Breslauer, "Boris Yeltsin as Patriarch," *Post-Soviet Affairs* (April-June 1999).

13. Vyacheslav Kostikov, *Roman s prezidentom: Zapiski press-sekretaria* (Moscow, 1997), 8, 25.

14. Ibid., 157, 278.

15. *Financial Times*, September 16, 1997.

16. Valerii Streletskii, *Mrakobesiye* (Moscow, 1998), last page, unnumbered. Note also the following observation by a Russian journalist: "Presidential policy has long been a family business, in which Yumashev is admitted with the rights of a relative" (Aleksandr Gamov, in *Komsomol'skaya pravda*, July 8, 1998). What Gamov missed is that in Yeltsin's political family, relatives did not have "rights."

17. Oleg D. Poptsov, *Khronika vremyon tsarya Borisa* (Berlin, 1995), 269.

18. Fyodor Burlatsky, interview, Moscow, June 1998.

19. See Kostikov, *Roman*. During an interview with me in Moscow in June 1998, an erstwhile presidential aide explained that in the early 1990s, Yeltsin "loved" his young advisers and they "loved" him in return.

20. Korzhakov, *Boris Yel'tsin*, 223.

21. Ibid., 63.

22. Ibid., 243.

23. Streletskii, *Mrakobesiye*, 24.

24. Korzhakov, *Boris Yel'tsin*, 358.

25. Viktor N. Baranets, *Yel'tsin i yego generaly* (Moscow, 1998), 230, 170, 248–249. This highly detailed memoir is written in a way that suggests a real effort to be objective, although it also draws blunt conclusions.

26. Ibid., 220–223; Kostikov, *Roman*, 328–331.

27. Baranets, *Yel'tsin i yego generaly*, 77, 122.

28. Yegor Gaidar, *Dni porazheniy i pobed* (Moscow, 1996), 107–108, 333–334; Korzhakov, *Boris Yel'tsin*, 52–53.

29. Kostikov, *Roman*, 347.

30. Korzhakov, *Boris Yel'tsin*, 81–82.

31. Ibid., 253–254.

32. Ibid., 82. This anecdote was corroborated by other presidential associates (none of them admirers of Korzhakov) whom I interviewed in Moscow in June 1998.

33. Korzhakov, *Boris Yel'tsin*, 54. As Korzhakov notes, the notion that *shef darit* (the chief or patron gives a gift) was supported by Yeltsin's practices during his Sverdlovsk days as well.

34. Kostikov, *Roman*, 216–217; Eugene Huskey, *Presidential Power in Russia* (Armonk, N.Y., 1999); Anatol Lieven, *Chechnya: Tombstone of Russian Power* (New Haven, 1997), 171; Victor M. Sergeyev, *The Wild East: Crime and Lawlessness in Post-Communist Russia* (Armonk, N.Y., 1998), 117–118. Huskey reported that Finance Minister Lifshits had lamented that Yeltsin did not understand the economy "and tries to help everyone . . . , but some people need to be imprisoned rather than helped," and that Economic Minister Yasin had complained that Yeltsin had "his favorite directors who can open any doors" (*Presidential Power*, 57, 137).

35. Gaidar, *Dni porazheniy i pobed*, 183–184.

36. Kostikov, *Roman*, 306–307; see also Poptsov, *Khronika vremyon tsarya Borisa*, 283.

37. Kostikov, *Roman*, 304.

38. Fyodor Burlatsky, *Glotok svobody,* vol. 2 (Moscow, 1997), 315.

39. Kostikov, *Roman,* 21–22.

40. Ibid., 42–43; Huskey *(Presidential Power)* argued that Yeltsin conceived of the presidency as "the country's primary institutional patron" and of the president as standing above all branches of government and sending "emissaries" to them. The evidence displayed in the present article supports Huskey's characterizations.

41. Sukhanov, *Tri goda*; Viktor Yaroshenko, *Ya otvechu za vsyo* (Moscow, 1997).

42. Kostikov, *Roman,* 151–152; Gaidar, *Dni porazheniy i pobed,* 223–231, 313–314; Korzhakov, *Boris Yel'tsin,* 330.

43. Yeltsin, *The Struggle,* 292. In Kenneth Jowitt's words: "As a mode of leadership, patriarchalism has historically had several distinguishing features, including a stress on orderly rather than charismatic (i.e., highly random and arbitrary) management, direct concern with the economic welfare of the social unit involved, personalized attention to solidarity issues, and emphasis on authoritarian and disciplinary behavior" ("An Organizational Approach to the Study of Political Culture in Marxist-Leninist Systems," *American Political Science Review* [September 1974]: 1190). Yeltsin's rhetorical stress on stability, however, was accompanied by an arbitrary, not orderly, approach to stern, patriarchal leadership.

44. Gaidar, *Dni porazheniy i pobed,* 295.

45. Kostikov, *Roman,* 308.

46. Korzhakov, *Boris Yel'tsin,* 133.

47. Gaidar, *Dni porazheniy i pobed,* 300.

48. Kostikov, *Roman,* 322.

49. Confidential interview, Moscow, June 1998; see also Korzhakov, *Boris Yel'tsin,* 251.

50. Kostikov, *Roman,* 296.

51. Burlatsky, *Glotok svobody,* 315.

52. For the evidence, see George W. Breslauer and Catherine Dale, "Boris Yeltsin and the Invention of a Russian Nation-State," *Post-Soviet Affairs* (October-December 1997): 303–332.

53. For the evidence on this score, see Igor Zevelev, "Russia and the Russian Diasporas," *Post-Soviet Affairs* (July-September 1996): 265–284.

54. Dmitry Mikheyev, *Russia Transformed* (Indianapolis, Ind., 1996), chapters 5–7; Leon Aron, in *Sunday Times* (London), September 6, 1998: "Yeltsin has finally become a victim of his own blunders and of the crushing burden of the Soviet economic, political, and social legacy. But the creator and guardian of the most tolerant and most open regime in Russian history will be missed very soon, and very sorely, if he is replaced by the kooks and troglodytes from whom, until two weeks ago, his broad back had shielded Russia and the world."

55. Stephen Holmes, "Superpresidentialism and Its Problems," *East European Constitutional Review,* vol. 2-3, no. 4-1 (Fall 1993-Winter 1994): 123–126.

56. For more on these constitutional vulnerabilities, see George W. Breslauer, "Political Succession and the Nature of Political Competition in Russia," *Problems of Post-Communism* (September-October 1997).

57. Stephen E. Hanson and Jeffrey S. Kopstein, "The Weimar/Russia Comparison," *Post-Soviet Affairs* (July-September 1997): 252–283.

58. Yeltsin, *The Struggle,* 139–140; see also 148: "Unfortunately, the law-enforcement agencies are adapting very slowly and poorly to this new crime phenomenon. That's the typical Russian style."

59. Ibid., 6, 18–19, 7.

60. Ibid., 17, 109.

61. As he put it in introducing the reform (*Sovetskaya Rossiya*, October 29, 1991): "The time has come to act decisively, firmly, without hesitation. . . . The period of movement with small steps is over . . . . A big reformist breakthrough is necessary." As translated and quoted in Anders Aslund, *How Russia Became a Market Economy* (Washington, D.C., 1995), 64.

62. Valentin Fyodorov, *Yel'tsin* (Moscow, 1995), 27–28, 55; see also Gaidar, *Dni porazheniy i pobed*, 105.

63. Yeltsin, *The Struggle*, 149.

64. Yeltsin, *Against the Grain*, 203–210; 216–239. Observation of this parallel between societal shock therapy and his own personal reappraisal appears also in Mikheyev, *Russia Transformed*, 89.

65. See Yeltsin, *The Struggle*, passim; also his speech introducing the reform strategy, as published in *Sovetskaya Rossiya* (October 29, 1991).

66. Yeltsin, *Against the Grain*, 118 (the Russian original is in Boris Yel'tsin, *Ispoved' na zadannuiu temu* [Sverdlovsk, 1990], 112). In both the Russian and the English versions, Yeltsin was sufficiently self-conscious about the connotations to put the word "uninfected" inside quotation marks.

67. Yeltsin, *The Struggle*, 146.

68. Ibid., 290–291. For other references in Yeltsin's memoirs to the crucial role of the younger generation, see *Against the Grain*, 183, 234, 253; and *The Struggle*, 126–127, 151–152, 291. Yeltsin also invoked this perspective to explain his firing of the cabinet in March 1998 and its replacement with a new team of young reformers, led by 36-year-old Sergei Kirienko. See Yeltsin's interview in *Komsomol'skaya pravda* (April 1, 1998). When this renewal of the "breakthrough" strategy led instead to the crash of the ruble in August 1998, Yeltsin tried to go back to an emphasis on social stability and political experience, firing Kirienko and nominating Viktor Chernomyrdin. This squares with the pattern of discussion in *The Struggle* (126–127, 155, 168, 169, 200–201, 222–223), where young cadres are praised for their contributions to transformative goals, while "experienced" cadres are praised, and recruited, for their contributions to consolidative goals: efficiency and the maintenance of social stability.

69. See *The Struggle*, viii–ix (not in the Russian edition), 7, 19, 127, 129, 141, 148, 158, 169, 175, 226–227. For a seminal analysis of the antiprocedural thinking that has dominated among the post-Soviet, Russian elite, see Biryukov and Sergeyev, *Russian Politics in Transition*.

70. Interview, Moscow, June 1998. Published confirmation of this characterization can be found in Korzhakov, *Boris Yel'tsin*, 221.

71. Huskey, *Presidential Power*, 50.

72. Martha Merritt, "If Checks Won't Balance: Parliamentary Review of Ministerial Appointments," in Graeme Gill, ed., *Elites and Leadership in Russian Politics* (London, 1998), 18–19; Biryukov and Sergeyev, *Russian Politics in Transition*, 260–269.

73. Huskey refers to the last of these tendencies as "the politics of redundancy"; see Eugene Huskey, "The State-Legal Administration and the Politics of Redundancy," *Post-Soviet Affairs* (April-June 1995): 115–143.

74. According to Kostikov (*Roman*, 210), when Yeltsin formally fired his vice president, Aleksandr Rutskoy, he also fired cabinet member Vladimir Shumeiko. The latter had done nothing wrong, but Yeltsin told Kostikov that Shumeiko had to be "sacrificed" in order to "balance off" the firing of Rutskoy.

75. Baranets (*Yel'tsin i ego generaly*, 50) argues that the bloated and impenetrable mechanism of Russian political decisionmaking allowed Yeltsin to exercise ultimate control over his bureaucracy, including military officialdom. Every minor decision had to be processed by a multitude of organizations and administrative departments and only then submitted to the president for final approval. When Yeltsin was incapacitated, the situation became even worse. Many of the most pressing problems of strategic or tactical importance never got solved and kept accumulating. See also Lieven (*Chechnya*, 294–299) for a case study of the impact of this leadership style on military reform in Russia.

76. In the words of Kostikov (*Roman*, 306–307): "Coming into his office, I often found him seated behind an empty table in deep, morose thought. He missed his earlier role of 'Director of all of Russia.' And it seemed that [he] was losing his head in the face of the scale of the deeds he enumerated for himself in his Constitution." Kostikov also reported that during his entire period as president of Russia, Yeltsin was in physical pain from a variety of ailments, including severe back and leg pain (Ibid., 196)—an observation supported by Korzhakov (*Boris Yel'tsin*, 202).

77. Korzhakov (*Boris Yel'tsin*, 310) reports that in fall 1993 Prime Minister Chernomyrdin began trying to persuade Yeltsin to grant him more responsibilities and duties in order to lighten the presidential workload. Yeltsin, according to Korzhakov, was deeply suspicious and feared that Chernomyrdin might be seeking more formal power or be planning to run against him in 1996.

78. Personal communication, not for attribution.

79. Streletskii, *Mrakobesiye*, 155–156; Kostikov, *Roman*, 216.

80. He admitted as much in public speeches at the time, and later summarized his dilemma in Yeltsin, *Against the Grain*, 115–119.

81. In an unpublished book manuscript, Jerry Hough has suggested another possible reason, grounded in political rationality: that by implicating a wide range of officials and politicians in corruption, Yeltsin enhanced the political elite's dependence on his staying in office to protect them from prosecution.

82. This point is made and documented in Sergeyev, *The Wild East*, 84ff; and in Biryukov and Sergeyev, *Russian Politics in Transition*, 260–269.

83. See the quotation from Yeltsin that heads this chapter.

84. Poptsov, *Khronika vremyon*, 431; Kostikov, *Roman*, 300–301, 323–324; and Aslund, *How Russia Became a Market Economy*, 91.

85. Gaidar, *Dni porazheniy i pobed*, 106–107, 310–314; Kostikov, *Roman*, 141–142, 168–169, 174; Korzhakov, *Boris Yel'tsin*, 315.

4

Russia's Second Constitutional Court

Politics, Law, and Stability

Robert Sharlet

Union College

A s Russia enters the twenty-first century, one of its main objectives continues to be the creation of a stable society ruled by law. Ancillary to this endeavor is the ongoing task of institution-building, which is an essential part of the larger, longer-term process of democratic state-building; in essence, the building or restructuring of core legal institutions into a viable legal system. These include such familiar institutions of law as the courts, the prosecutor's offices, the bar, and the law codes and statutes. A rule-of-law society also requires other supportive institutions, such as police, a prison system, and law schools. Absent these components of an integral legal process, it would be difficult to contemplate the construction of a state's regulative and adjudicative networks, not to mention its extractive and administrative capacities, which also are defined by law.

In this chapter, I focus on the Russian Constitutional Court (RCC)—one of the newer additions to Russia's spectrum of legal institutions, and one that has grown in stature and importance within the political system. This has especially been the case of the second Constitutional Court, which was first convened in 1995 and has gradually accrued to itself the values and attributes that eluded its ill-fated predecessor, the first Constitutional Court (which functioned from 1991 to 1993). These values include the accrual of moral prestige and political capital, along with the attributes of institutional stability and jurisprudential predictability. Subtly but steadily, the second Court has gained respect and even some deference from the power centers of the Russian polity, the executive and legislative branches. This promising phenomenon, with its positive potential for Russia's political development, bears watching.

Prologue and Questions

The new Russian Constitution of 1993 is a political document framed in the language of law. As such, it represents a "power map" or outline of the configuration and distribution of political power in the state, in society, and in state-society relations. Because a democratic constitution is essentially a metapolitical framework for the day-to-day operation of the polity, it necessarily requires explication, translation, and interpretation if it is to provide effective parameters for institutional and individual behavior in a given society. In a civil law system, constitutional explication is supplied by legal scholars who produce learned commentaries; in a common law system, this work falls to judges, who make case law. In both systems, constitutions are translated into the laws needed for the governance of a society. Finally, the function of interpreting the constitution in matters of dispute or uncertainty falls to the high courts—in the United States, to the Supreme Court; in Europe (including Russia), to special tribunals called constitutional courts.

Thus, the Russian Constitution charges the Constitutional Court with the task of closely reading, studying, analyzing, and authoritatively interpreting the fundamental law in cases of disputes between qualified parties as well as in instances of ambiguity or uncertainty in the constitutional text. The Court's purpose has been to resolve disputes within the constitutional framework and to help ensure the smooth and peaceful operation of the political system by clarifying and occasionally even emending a particular constitutional article. The demands on the RCC have been especially heavy since its inception in 1991, as Russia has made its way through a rather difficult transition from political authoritarianism and economic centralism toward a democratic polity and a market economy. Whereas the first RCC struggled with a much-amended, patchwork constitution, the second Court's task has been complicated by the fact that the new constitution contains a number of gaps, omissions, and ambiguities.

If a constitution distills a society's political choices about power, then the institution created to interpret the document has a political character. As a scholar of the U.S. Supreme Court has bluntly stated: "The [U.S.] Constitution is a political document; it serves political ends; its interpretations are political acts."[1] A French scholar, taking into consideration European experience with judicial review, has argued that constitutional courts have a "hybrid, semi-judicial, semi-political nature." He added that these courts certainly perform familiar judicial functions; but since, in addition, "they operate as mediators, implementing a system of checks and balances . . . they are also highly political bodies."[2]

One of the RCC justices has gone even further, characterizing the Court as "both quasi-judicial body and quasi-legislative body" in the sense that it functions as both a negative and positive legislator in striking down unconstitutional rules and creating new legal norms.[3] It was in this spirit that a Russian constitutional law text described the RCC: "The Constitutional Court is a legal institution. Since it operates in a system of intersecting legal and political relations, applying its decisions on the basis of the Constitution which has politico-legal content and meaning, the Constitutional Court therefore also functions as a politico-legal institution."[4] A leading Russian Constitutional Court justice concurred, calling the Court "a synthesis of a governmental agency, a juridical institution, and a [social] science research institute."[5]

The short history of the RCC can be recited briefly. The first post-Soviet, Russian republic operated under the heavily revised 1978 Constitution of the Russian Republic, which provided for parliamentary supremacy as well as a strong presidency. Due to political and personal differences among the principal actors, legislative-executive relations were extremely conflictual, causing serious political instability and eventually degenerating into a zero-sum political game. Throughout the life of the first post-Soviet republic, the first Constitutional Court sought to mediate disputes and conflicts between the branches of power, but it eventually was caught in the political crossfire. Having prevailed over parliament by military force in October 1993, President Boris Yeltsin suspended the RCC, declaring that because of its politicization and tilt toward the legislature, the Court had contributed to the instability and collapse of the republic.

From the ashes of October emerged the new Constitution (that of the second Russian republic), which was followed in mid-1994 by a significantly revised Constitutional Court statute. The complement of justices from the first RCC was grandfathered into the second Court, but newly created seats had to be filled. After many months of debate over judicial nominations and appointments, in March 1995, the new justices were seated and the second RCC got under way, ending a hiatus of nearly a year and a half. During its five years of existence, the second Court has quietly pursued its legal tasks, while maintaining a considerably lower profile politically than did its predecessor.

For various reasons, the second Russian republic has been marked by relative political stability—or to paraphrase Ted Gurr, the persistence of political institutions, to which I would add the existence of mechanisms affording the possibility of orderly social change over time.[6] To what extent has the second Constitutional Court contributed to this outcome? Has the Court become a responsible part of the third branch, playing its role in the system of checks and balances slowly emerging under the Constitution's separation of powers doctrine? Or, as its critics say, has the second RCC become "the fifth wheel of the carriage of Russian autocracy"?[7]

To answer these questions, let us compare the first and second Courts for the purpose of highlighting changes in the current Court's judicial structure, functions, and roles (as well as incumbents), and its resulting jurisprudence since 1995. At the heart of this investigation is a critical inquiry as to how well the second Constitutional Court has handled the potentially fractious mix of politics and law in Russia's continuing, tumultuous transition.

Comparative Constitutional Justice

To determine to what extent the second Constitutional Court has contributed to or detracted from the political stability of the second Russian republic, I briefly compare the experiences of the first and second Courts in terms of (1) the constitutions under which they operated, and their respective conceptions of constitutional control; (2) the statutes that guided their work; (3) the judicial and extrajudicial behavior of the justices—especially the respective chief justices; (4) the ensuing patterns of jurisprudence of the two Courts, emphasizing the effect of the second Court's decisions on the goal of advancing the rule of law in Russia; and (5) how well the Zorkin Court and the Tumanov-Baglai Court have handled the relationship of law and politics in their work.

The Constitutional Frameworks

The first Constitutional Court labored under the much-revised 1978 Constitution, which had been amended over 300 times in the final years before the USSR expired in 1991. As previously mentioned, a main feature of this document was its endowment of the senior body of the two-tier parliament with the power to amend the Constitution legislatively by a two-thirds majority. It was in fact through parliamentary amendment that the first RCC was given constitutional life. Its enabling statute, the law on the Court, was passed in 1991, and was subsequently amended a year later to permit verification of the constitutionality of political parties' charters in connection with the impending Communist party case.[8] Given parliament's leverage over the Court's constitutional and statutory status and the ease of amending either document, it was no surprise that the first RCC adopted a pro-legislative tilt in its decisions from the outset.

In contrast, the second RCC has worked under the 1993 Constitution—a document not without problems but nonetheless a model of clarity and coherence in comparison with its predecessor. This constitution is oriented to favor the presidency, and it was designed to be very difficult to amend. The statute establishing the second Court, a federal constitutional law requiring supermajorities in the bicameral parliament, was enacted in 1994, the first year of the second republic. Thus, the second Court has little fear that its constitutional authority or its statutory powers will be altered without an exceptional consensus. However, the Court has had reason to be concerned that the chief executive may use his control over the brethren's ample fringe benefits, as Yeltsin did during the first republic, to express his pleasure or displeasure with a particular ruling or decisional trend.

The most significant change from the 1978 to the 1993 Constitution was that the RCC could no longer take up cases on its own initiative. Many observers felt that the so-called auto-initiative provided by the 1978 Constitution had led the first Court deep into the troubled waters of Russian transitional politics, where it eventually foundered. Under the 1993 Constitution, the second Court may carry out judicial review only in cases that come to it from petitioners granted judicial standing.[9] In lieu of the lost initiative power, the second Court has been constitutionally endowed with a new interpretive function.[10] On petition from the president, the government, either house of parliament, or the legislative bodies of the federation subjects, the Court may provide authoritative interpretations of the

Constitution when a particular section of text gives rise to ambiguity or uncertainty of meaning.

Western observers have agreed that the Court's new function of issuing binding interpretations is "political"[11] and potentially formidable.[12] As Sarah Reynolds, a major student of the Court, has observed, "The interpretive role of the Court is likely to be a very powerful one and of very great importance in the development of a state that is functional, stable, just, and democratic."[13] Professor Vladimir Tumanov, the first chief justice of the second Court, expressed satisfaction that the new interpretive authority would allow the Court to move away from the literalism of Soviet judicial tradition and toward a style of interpretation more open and more conducive to translating constitutional clauses into reasonable, pragmatic legal rules for everyday matters of governance.

When asked whether the Court might exceed its new mandate to interpret the Constitution and instead create new constitutional norms, Chief Justice Tumanov acknowledged that norm creation, usually on fairly narrow questions, would be inevitable in the interpretive process. This would be especially the case when the interpretive function was employed "in filling gaps in the constitutional text"—a procedure that Tumanov dubbed "supplementary interpretation."[14] Subsequently, Justice Nikolai Vitruk confirmed Tumanov's position, adding that the new constitutional norms created would be primarily "procedural."[15]

Another associate justice, Boris Ebzeev, explicitly pointed out that the Court's decisions in interpreting constitutional clauses "essentially become part of the Constitution." He also called attention to an aside by Tumanov during his response quoted earlier—to wit, that because the Constitution is a rigid document difficult to formally amend, the new interpretive function provided essential flexibility. Justice Ebzeev emphasized this point, arguing that the Court's interpretations lead to the "'silent transformation' of the Constitution, i.e., changing it without amending the constitutional text."[16]

Before moving on, it should be noted that because petitions for binding interpretations may only arise from the political branches of the Russian system, the Court's new power represented not only an opportunity but also a challenge to be used judiciously. Mindful of this, the justices developed internal criteria for vetting requests for constitutional interpretation—in effect, constraints designed "to prevent [the Court from] being drawn into political conflicts."[17]

Lastly, the transition from the 1978 to the 1993 Constitution entailed fundamental changes in the RCC's status in the system of constitutional control as well as changes in the nature of the process of judicial review in Russia. After the collapse of the first republic and the suspension of the first Court, the future of the RCC in the Russian political system was uncertain. The Court's reputation had been tarnished by events, and its institutional prestige was at a low ebb. President Yeltsin's handpicked draftsmen, who were rushing a pro-presidential draft constitution to completion in fall 1993, were considering absorbing the RCC into the Supreme Court, as the latter's special bench for constitutional questions. As then Acting Chief Justice Vitruk reported, this proposal was vigorously resisted by himself and his brethren, who subsequently successfully argued and lobbied for the retention of the Constitutional Court as an autonomous body and for its inclusion in the draft constitution.

However, the legacy of the first Court had certain consequences for its successor. The president's constitutional draftsmen demoted the RCC from its status as the supreme judicial body of constitutional control[18] to that of coequal partner with the Supreme Court and the Higher Commercial Court.[19] This change was more than semantic and symbolic. In the first republic, Russia had borrowed Europe's centralized model for judicial review of the constitutionality of legislation. This was the exclusive domain of the first RCC. However, for the purpose of reducing the Court's preeminence and power in the political system, and presumably to lighten its immense caseload as well, the new Constitution left open a door for the other high courts to encroach upon the RCC's previously singular prerogative. This was accomplished through the demotion described above, combined with the introduction of the principle of the direct applicability of constitutional norms consistent with democratic constitutional practice.[20]

As a result, the Russian Supreme Court openly challenged the RCC's erstwhile hegemony in constitutional judicial review. The second Constitutional Court did not remain passive, but instead insisted on its primacy in the constitutional verification process, in the tradition of European constitutional tribunals. A lively exchange of dicta between the two high courts ensued, with justices from both courts entering the lists in the learned law journals. The Supreme Court fired the first shot with a decree or "guiding instruction" in late 1995, which directed the lower courts, under the guise of the direct application of the Constitution, to carry out judicial review with the option but not the requirement of subsequently referring the case to the RCC.[21]

Replies from the RCC included a rebuttal from retired Chief Justice Tumanov, who insisted that referral from the ordinary courts should be "obligatory," not optional.[22] The current chief justice, Marat Baglai, responded sharply, saying that "there is no basis to talk about the Supreme Court 'duplicating' or 'preempting' the powers of the Constitutional Court."[23] The nearly full bench of the RCC, in turn, issued a strong rebuttal to its brother courts in the *Judicial Review* case, in which the Legislative Assembly of the Karelian Republic had petitioned the RCC to interpret the interrelationship between itself and the other high courts, the Supreme Court and Higher Commercial Court, as defined in Chapter 7 (on the "Judicial Branch") of the Constitution. In the majority opinion (with two dissenting), announced in June 1998, the second Court strongly asserted its "exclusive authority to examine the constitutionality of normative acts enumerated in Article 125.2.a & b of the Russian Constitution."[24]

Just a year earlier, Peter Maggs, a highly respected specialist in Russian civil law and judicial practice, had observed "broad possibilities for the exercise of constitutional jurisdiction by the commercial courts" in addition to the longer-term trend underway since 1993 in the courts of ordinary jurisdiction.[25] In a magisterial study of the Supreme Court's jurisprudence, another American scholar noted that in the second republic, Russia had moved away from the centralized model of judicial review "to a system marked by elements of diffusion and redundancy," and concluded that "the Constitution now speaks through two ultimate judicial voices in Russia, with the benefits and disadvantages that such a dual system might be expected to provide."[26] Although the second Court's 1998 ruling, in theory, constituted a binding interpretation on the subject, it remained to be seen whether it could successfully stem the emergent trends toward concurrent judicial review. For instance, just several months after this ruling, the Supreme Court issued a decision directly challenging the RCC—a challenge that met with sharp criticism from the State Duma's permanent representative to the Constitutional Court, who declared it "procedurally untenable."[27] Still, the question must be asked: Will the RCC ruling on the books in this instance become the law in action?

Statutory Guidance

The Constitutional Court statutes of 1991 and 1994, reflecting the respective constitutions empowering the institution, operationalized the necessary broad strokes of the constitutions' clauses into the myriad organizational details necessary for institution-building. Even before the end of the first republic, the justices of the first RCC, including even the highly activist chief justice, Professor Valerii Zorkin, agreed that the Court's 1991 statute needed revision based on their collective experience on the bench. Although events outran the possibility of statutory revision, the gist of the Court's operational problems was later summed up by Acting Chief Justice Vitruk when he said, "The Constitutional Court is not the fire brigade"—a phrase his successor Chief Justice Tumanov of the second Court was later fond of repeating.[28]

Since the justices themselves, together with representatives of the president and parliament, drafted the bill, which following committee work, floor debate, and amendment in the State Duma became the 1994 Federal Constitutional Law on the Constitutional Court, it is not surprising that the spirit of Vitruk's criticism found its way into the revised law. In fact, the RCC's jurisdiction was both trimmed and augmented; access to the Court was narrowed; and changes in the institution's internal structure and operations were written into the new statute. For instance, the Court's jurisdiction over political parties was eliminated, and disputes over jurisdiction and competence among institutional political actors within the separation and division of powers were added to the second Court's mandate. Also, the Court's jurisdiction over judicial practice was dropped from the 1994 law. This erstwhile part of the first Court's jurisdiction had greatly added to case overload during the first republic, as described by Alexander Blankenagel, a prominent German law professor and consultant to the RCC:

> The Constitutional Court presented itself as the master of all courts: division of labour or function-specific cooperation with the other court system was unacceptable: no confidence in the other courts and their capacities to master the task of in-

terpretation of ordinary law, let alone the application and interpretation of the Constitution. So nearly every question, of ordinary law down to the lowest administrative ordinance, of constitutional law up to the basic principles of justice was appropriated: this was the fight of the lonely loner against the illegalisms and unconstitutionalisms everywhere, and the possible deputy sheriffs being just as bad, could not be relied on. The Constitutional Court tried to be a judicial everything: the general collapse saved it from being submerged by the appropriated everything.[29]

Thus relieved of responsibility for the constitutional supervision of judicial practice, the second Court was authorized to receive specific case referrals on constitutional issues from judges in the ordinary and commercial courts. Over five years later, however, there have in fact been very few such referrals, perhaps reflecting the trends discussed in the previous section whereby the other courts tend to be gradually poaching on the second Court's judicial review turf.

The rules on standing, or the question of who has access to the second Court, were made more restrictive. For example, in the first republic any parliamentary deputy who failed to realize his political objectives in the legislative chamber had the option of turning to the first RCC—thus, to paraphrase one Court justice, turning the Court into a third house of parliament. Under the new rules for the second Court, no fewer than 20 percent of the complement of either chamber of parliament must endorse either a petition for relief or an interpretation. This effectively means that a petition requires a minimum of 90 deputies of the Duma (the lower house), or 35 senators from the Federation Council (the upper house).

The 1994 law has also redesigned the Court's internal structure, from the first Court's single chamber to a plenum of the full bench and two divisions of roughly equal size. Certain cases are heard only before the full plenum—for example, petitions for constitutional interpretation—whereas other cases are assigned by the chief justice to one or the other division, allowing the second Court to hear two cases simultaneously. This structure generally follows that of the German Constitutional Court, which being widely considered the most successful European constitutional court, had the greatest influence on the RCC in both of its incarnations. However, the Russian Court did deviate from the German model in certain respects.[30]

The new statute also implemented changes in Court size and in the criteria for judicial selection. The 1993 Constitution enlarged the second Court from 15 justices to 19. In fact, the first Court had only 13 members, the last two seats never having been filled during the nearly two-year life of the Court. Thus, the 1994 law provided for six seats to be filled before the second Court could sit, elect its officers, and begin hearing cases. Selection criteria were also tightened, while judicial tenure was shortened. Under the 1991 law on the Court, anyone 35 years or older was eligible for appointment and could enjoy life tenure until the mandatory retirement age of 65. The 1994 law raised the age minimum to 40; required that a judicial candidate have 15 years of legal experience; and limited tenure to one twelve-year term or age 70, whichever occurs first.

At its first sitting, in early 1995, the composition of the second Court was something of an anomaly—the original 13 justices served under the "life tenure" rule of the 1991 law, whereas the new appointees were limited to a fixed term but could serve five years longer under the 1994 statute. As the Court was still under a cloud from the events of the first republic, the president and parliament apparently sought older and wiser or at least more experienced jurists for the new Court, and intended to keep it on a shorter leash.

In the first republic, justices of the first RCC were chosen by the Congress of Russian People's Deputies upon nomination by political parties, parliamentary factions, and other institutions. In the second republic, the 1994 law provided for judicial nomination by the president on the basis of recommendations from a judicial qualifications commission, and for final appointment by simple majority vote of the Federation Council. The enlargement of the second Court, ostensibly to accommodate the German two-chamber division (although the German Court has only 16 members), was probably actually intended to allow President Yeltsin to "pack" the Court with friendly justices, since a majority of the original 13 members had been opposed to him even before his suspension of the first Court.

Yeltsin's court packing plan, however, was thwarted by the senators of the upper house, who during fall 1994 refused to support four of the president's most liberal nominees, three of whom were resubmitted and rejected twice by the Federation Council.[31] Thus, it took nearly seven months to fill the six vacancies on the second Court—a task that by law was to be accomplished within 30 days of the signing of the new statute (an unrealistic time period, by U.S. standards). The 1994 Court statute had been signed into law in July 1994, and the nineteenth justice, Marat Baglai, was not appointed until February 1995.

A final noteworthy change from the 1991 to the 1994 RCC statute concerned the powers of the chief justice within the Court. Under the first Court law, the chief justice could hold the leadership position until mandatory retirement from the Court or voluntary resignation from the post. In the meantime, the chief had wide discretionary authority over the hiring and firing of the professional staff that made up the Court's Secretariat. The 1994 law made the chief justice more accountable to the brethren. Staff can be hired and fired only on the advice and consent of the plenum; the chief justice is elected for a three-year term, with a two-term limit; and the chief justice can be removed from the post by his or her fellow justices.

Acting Chief Justice Vitruk's verdict on the first RCC law was most apt. Noting that the legislative draftsmen borrowed extensively and eclectically from foreign models, he concluded that the 1991 statute overbuilt the first Court, "which could not bear the weight of its own construction."[32] The drafters of the 1994 statute sought to avoid past mistakes, most notably the descent into the cauldron of partisan politics—apropos of which the coauthors of the first Western casebook on Russian law shrewdly observed that although a constitutional court cannot avoid some exposure to politics due to policy considerations, and "because constitutional adjudication is always value-laden, procedural rules may prevent unnecessary politicization" of the constitutional process. In the case of Russia, they pointed to the stripping away of the Court's previous right to initiate its own cases as one particularly important procedural safeguard incorporated into the second RCC.[33]

Judicial and Extrajudicial Behavior

Conventional wisdom holds that the suspension of the first RCC was largely due to Chief Justice Zorkin's proclivity for extrajudicial behavior, which had drawn him and the Court deep into the turbulent politics of the day. There is indeed much truth to this view, but it neglects the design flaws and dysfunctional features built into Russia's first attempt at constitutional adjudication, which also contributed to the Court's political collisions and final end. As I have written elsewhere, Zorkin was as much a "judicial politician" as a jurist, but that alone did not doom the first RCC. Structural and functional problems embedded in the institutional design of the first Court must also be weighed in the balance.[34]

As we shall see in this section, extrajudicial behavior did not cease with Zorkin's pressured resignation from the chief justiceship in October 1993. As already noted, Vitruk, the acting chief justice during the long interregnum between the first and second Courts, was himself occasionally guilty of extrajudicial pronouncements that crossed the line between law and politics. The difference was that Vitruk was on the side of the angels: To wit, he was saying the right things, or at least what the power brokers wanted to hear as they contemplated the fate of the Constitutional Court in Russian politics. To his credit, Acting Chief Justice Vitruk's extrajudicial commentary played a major role in saving the Court and affording it a second opportunity to help steer a safe course for Russia to the future.

Part of the problem was that many Russian judicial players could not easily discern the line between appropriate judicial conduct and inappropriate extrajudicial remarks, given their earlier socialization into the highly politicized Soviet legal process and their success in advancing up the hierarchy. An Austrian specialist on the RCC caught the essence of the problem exceptionally well: "Russian Constitutional Court justices are products of the Communist nomenklatura system. They would not have reached their positions without the political loyalty and adaptability required by that system."[35]

An added difficulty in staffing the RCC in both the first and the second republics has been that most of the appointees were legal academics with long careers in academe and no judicial experience or understanding of judicial temperament and behavior. Of the original 13 justices, only one had any practical legal experience—in his case, as a prosecutor. Was it any wonder that one of their number dubbed their early decisions "academic reports"? The six new appointees of the second republic brought to the second Court its first and for a time its only professional judge. Later, after the mandatory retirement of Chief Justice Tumanov at age 70 and the death of Justice Ernst Ametistov in 1998, the Court acquired two more justices with prior judicial experience.

The argument here is not that the constitutional bench primarily requires experienced judges. The Court is after all both a legal and political institution; hence, justices with political experience and a broader legal theoretical bent are also needed. The point remains that 17 of 19 justices on the Tumanov Court, and subsequently 15 of 19 on the Baglai Court, were talented jurists but had little or no practical experience of the law before their appointments.

Let us turn to the subject of how the chief justices of the second RCC acquitted themselves judicially and extrajudicially. Leaving aside Zorkin, whose performance is well known, we will focus for a moment on the successive chiefs of the second Court—Tumanov (1995–1997) and Baglai (1997–present). Although elected chief justice by a modest majority of his peers (11–8), Tumanov may have been the ideal navigator to steer the new second Court through the early part of its institutional journey. At age 68 when appointed to the Court, Tumanov was destined to retire in two years and therefore nicely fit the role of short-term, interim chief. A prominent legal academic expert in "bourgeois" legal philosophy, with only brief service as a legislator prior to his elevation to the Court, Tumanov brought neither judicial experience nor managerial skills to the bench.[36]

What he did bring, however, was much needed by a divided Court facing a skeptical political elite. Tumanov was a worldly, politically sophisticated chief justice with good diplomatic skills, who well understood that the resuscitated RCC would have to re-earn the trust and confidence of the power brokers to ensure its longer-term survival and institutional growth. The theme of his brief tenure was to avoid inciting "the presidential administration against a still weak court"[37]— not a brave posture but probably a politically realistic one for 1995 and 1996, the latter of which was a presidential election year. If Tumanov's administration of the Court had a mantra, it would have been the "golden mean," his favorite approach to any problem facing the Court during his incumbency.[38] A critic, scornful of his timid judicial navigation, later derided Tumanov as he left office for his "golden halfheartedness."[39]

Professor Marat Baglai, Tumanov's successor as chief justice, could not have been more different. A businesslike labor law academic with some administrative experience, Baglai was described as "the least politicized justice who suits everyone."[40] He was the RCC's third chief justice, elected in early 1997 to serve a three-year term. In his inaugural remarks to the press, Chief Justice Baglai equated the second Constitutional Court with a "sturdy ship" that would stay the course to "promote the stabilization of the constitutional system, and most importantly, to protect the rights of our citizens."[41] In spite of this restrained rhetoric, the new chief justice struck out on a far more challenging course than his predecessor.

Extrajudicially as well, the two chief justices behaved quite differently. Tumanov made no effort to be publicly discreet about sensitive cases in which the president had a vital political stake. On the contrary, he used his regular press conferences to signal the presidential administration on his pro-Yeltsin tilt and to explain how he expected to lead the Court in particular cases. He first did this in spring 1995, concerning the politically charged Chechen case, and then again several months later at a press appearance where he candidly aired his pro-administration views on a pending petition related to the parliamentary elections later that year. In both instances Tumanov violated the 1994 Court law, which forbids justices to discuss publicly cases that are either before the Court or may be headed to the Court.

Baglai has been more circumspect in public appearances. In a radio interview in late 1998, as he was discussing the Court's work on individual rights cases, he referred to a public issue still of concern to many: the question of whether rooms in a communal apartment could be privatized. Then he quickly added: "This case is currently being considered by us. That's why at the moment I cannot tell you anything on this issue."[42] Compared to two liberal justices who openly spoke out against the Communist party presidential candidate in 1996 while ostensibly addressing a constitutional law issue, the chief justice has been very careful in his other extrajudicial interventions as well, addressing the specific issue at hand in a careful and factual manner.

All of Baglai's public statements have been firmly grounded in the Constitution. Sometimes his remarks supported the president's position on an issue; on other occasions, he spoke critically of the administration in his defense of the Constitution. For instance, on several occasions during the late 1990s, Baglai publicly argued against various proposals to amend the Constitution, a principled position on which he happened to be in concurrence with the president. On another issue, he occupied the middle ground, welcoming the prospect of a Russian-Belarusian union but also pointing out the constitutional obstacles and implications that would need to be considered. On the other side of the political ledger, during the temporary governmental crisis in spring 1998 over Yeltsin's repeated nominations of Sergei Kirienko as prime minister, Baglai ended public speculation on a possible dissolution of the Duma should it reject the candidate a third time, stating that dissolution would not be just an option but a constitutional imperative for the president.

On that same occasion, he also firmly rejected a presidential adviser's suggestion that should dissolution occur, Yeltsin could issue a decree changing the federal law on parliamentary elections prior to the constitutionally mandated elections to the successor Duma. The chief justice denied that the president had any right to unilaterally change a law under the Constitution, saying, "A presidential decree abrogating a law is impossible in our country."[43] Conversely, in early summer 1998, as the government was trying unsuccessfully to push a package of anticrisis legislation through the lower house, Chief Justice Baglai publicly reaffirmed that both the constitution and an earlier RCC decision supported the president's authority to issue temporary decrees in the absence of prevailing legislation.

Although the idea of a U.S. chief justice speaking extrajudicially on a wide range of public issues would be abhorrent to our more settled legal culture, it is

TABLE 4.1　Classification of Cases Decided by the Russian
Constitutional Courts, 1992–1998

Type of Case	Zorkin Court	Tumanov-Baglai Court
Separation of powers	42%	10%
Individual rights	30%	60%
Federalism	28%	30%

SOURCE: Author's compilation.

possible that in the very different Russian political context Chief Justice Baglai's periodic sallies into the public arena in defense of the Constitution might have had the positive effect of encouraging constructive constitutional dialogue between the elites and among the attentive public.

Patterns of Constitutional Jurisprudence

Russian constitutional jurisprudence can be divided into three types of cases: constitutional or separation-of-powers cases; federalism or center-periphery cases; and the wide spectrum of individual rights cases. Using this typology, Table 4.1 shows a comparison of the types of cases decided by the first and second Constitutional Courts. The first set of percentages shown was provided by a senior official of the RCC Secretariat,[44] and the second set are estimates made by Chief Justice Baglai in mid-1998.[45]

The first category—separation-of-powers cases—is of greatest interest for our examination of the relationship between the RCC and political stability or instability in Russia. As can be seen above, the Zorkin Court was primarily engaged in what one American judicial observer presciently called "too much heavy lifting"; that is, in cases involving the president, the parliament, and legislative-executive relations, which would eventually lead to its breakdown.[46] In its initial case, in the first month of Russia's post-Soviet period, the Zorkin Court took on the president on the issue of internal security. In that case, given that Chief Justice Zorkin had to privately persuade Yeltsin to accept the Court's ruling that his executive decree merging two internal security agencies was unconstitutional, Zorkin should have known what lay ahead as Russia began its transition from authoritarianism and introduced the concept of judicial review.

Instead, Zorkin continued to lead the new Court headlong into political conflicts involving the other branches of the government. The constitutional process was not prestigious enough, nor was the cloak of law thick enough, to fully muffle these rancorous conflicts and reduce them to quiet legal problems. Each encounter with the power structures left the Court more frayed, with its initial stock of goodwill further diminished among the elite. Although the purpose of a constitutional court as first conceived by Austrian legal theorist Hans Kelsen was primarily to act as a check on the legislature, ensuring that its output was compatible with the constitution, the Zorkin Court in its first 15 months acted mainly as a check on the executive branch within the separation-of-powers doctrine. Only in its last six months in 1993 did the Court, by then openly accused of antipresidential bias, hastily turn its jurisprudential spotlight fully on parliament in an attempt to redress the imbalance in the public perception of its work. By then, however, the deeply divided first republic was hurtling toward its end, and it was too late for the Zorkin Court to attempt to regain the legal high ground and the political center.

The lessons of the rise and fall of the first RCC were not lost on Chief Justice Tumanov as he assumed leadership of the politically rehabilitated and legally reconstructed (second) Court in early 1995. The above data, which reflect the full two years of Tumanov's tenure but only the first year of Baglai's term of office, nonetheless make evident the second RCC's relative avoidance of collisions with other centers of power in the government. During its first year of operation, the Tumanov Court largely addressed narrow issues of technical jurisprudence in cases involving legislative procedure and the formalities of the constitutional amendment process, along with a number of individual rights petitions and a few federalism cases.

The one great exception was the Chechen case of summer 1995, which arose out of the Russian Federation government's military campaign to rein in its rebellious Chechen Republic. Tumanov assiduously tried to avoid this political hot potato, and failing to do so, telegraphed via the press his pro-presidential position even before the opening hearing. The Chechen case, in which parliament challenged the constitutionality of Yeltsin's war decrees, could not have come at a worse time for the second Court, which was then only in its fourth month of existence. The deliberations were further complicated by the nearly concurrent onset of peace negotiations between the Chechen forces and the Russian government, just across town.

Not to belabor what is well known, Tumanov and the Court majority succumbed to political expediency, confirming as constitutional President Yeltsin's use of military force in Chechnya. In one of a number of dissents in this case, Justice Zorkin lamented that the Court had "become a hostage of political emotion"—a conclusion confirmed by Chief Justice Tumanov's extrajudicial acknowledgment that "legal argument was sometimes adjusted to political goals."[47] A grateful Yeltsin soon after issued a presidential decree showering the justices and their families with a wide range of fringe benefits and other amenities, including cars, vacations, and shopping vouchers.[48]

The second and final year of Tumanov's tenure as chief justice was relatively quiet on the separation-of-powers front, with only an occasional pro-executive decision, such as the Procedural Irregularities Case of 1996. In this case, an authoritative interpretation of Article 107—the "Federal Laws and the President" clause—was sought by the two houses of parliament over the president's refusal to either sign or veto certain passed bills within the time period allotted by the Constitution. Yeltsin's refusal was based on his objections to mail balloting in the Federation Council and to proxy voting in the lower chamber. He filed a counter-petition to that effect, which the Court majority endorsed, finding that the president could return bills unsigned and without veto (thereby avoiding the possibility of being overridden) in instances when procedural irregularities had occurred in legislative roll calls.[49]

A similar quiescence continued during most of 1997, year one of Baglai's term as chief justice. Late that year, however, the Baglai Court began to find its voice. In a series of cases, the Court bucked presidential policies or preferences, or at the very least made decisions inconvenient for executive authority. In a case decided in December 1997, the Court ruled that the government could not demand that enterprises privilege tax payments before paying wages.[50] During spring 1998, the Court issued two decisions in quick succession, ordering the president to sign the duly passed Trophy Art law on World War II booty, and confirming the constitutionality of the five-percent cutoff in the law on parliamentary elections governing the allocation of party seats in the Duma.[51] Following these decisions, during a June meeting, Yeltsin reportedly admonished Chief Justice Baglai for the recent trend in Court-presidential relations.

The presidential warning apparently had little effect on the imperturbable chief justice, as the second RCC continued through 1998 and into 1999 to issue decisions that, at a minimum, demonstrated its growing authority and independence of the other branches of government. Some of these cases involved taking on the government for unconstitutionally cutting the budget line for support of the judiciary; ending political and legal speculation that Yeltsin might, if he wished, be able to run in the presidential election of 2000, in effect for a third term; and declaring the further imposition of death penalties unconstitutional unless defendants were afforded their constitutional right to choose jury trials. The latter decision, announced in early 1999, no doubt rubbed parliamentary proponents of capital punishment the wrong way and discomfited various executive branch law enforcement constituencies that opposed further expansion of the jury trial beyond the original nine provinces where it had been instituted.

In mid-1999, the Court revisited the issue of the so-called World War II trophy art captured from Nazi Germany—this time, on the basis of a presidential petition arguing that the 1998 law barring the return of any of the art works was unconstitutional. Declining to find the statute invalid, the Court did declare certain parts of it unconstitutional in a legally well-crafted and politically astute compromise ruling, which afterward was praised by both sides in the controversy, the Kremlin and parliament.[52]

By the fifth anniversary of the second Russian Constitutional Court, at the dawn of the twenty-first century, one could conclude that the second Court had overcome the legacy of its predecessor and had gained a surer institutional footing.

Politics, Law, and Constitutional
Justice in Russia

Even for the great John Marshall of early American legal history, there was peril in the "shadowy borderland between law and politics," and finding safe passage through that uncharted territory was the major challenge of his chief justice-ship.[53] Chief Justice Zorkin, who was not equipped either by temperament or by circumstance to navigate the perils of Russian politics and law, failed this challenge. Although it was technically extraconstitutional, Yeltsin's decree of October 7, 1993, suspending the first Constitutional Court, represented a just political verdict on the chief justice's extrajudicial activities, calling him to account for transforming the Court "from a body of constitutional justice into an instrument of political struggle."[54] In quest of stability, Zorkin and his Court in the final analysis unintentionally became a source of increasing instability and ungovernability.

Zorkin's successors fared better. Chief Justice Tumanov, who sought to avoid Zorkin's mistakes, erred in the opposite direction, bending more than necessary to the political winds. Still, he must be given credit for guiding the new second RCC safely for two years. This period permitted institutional convalescence and recovery, and afforded the Court the opportunity to slowly rebuild its reputation as a juridical institution. The subsequent chief justice, Marat Baglai, who held a more hard-edged view of the distinction between law and politics, nonetheless has steered the Court safely as well, although on a much more adventurous course. In his textbook on Russian constitutional law, the chief justice assured his readers that the second Court has been alert to the dangers posed by the intrusion of politics into the work of constitutional adjudication.[55]

In a 1998 media interview, Baglai perhaps best captured the paradox of the RCC's place in the Russian landscape, insisting that the Court was "outside politics," while conceding with a touch of frustration that political matters still managed to penetrate the institution, under "the general cloak of the law."[56] In the final analysis, though, it was Vladimir Tumanov, echoing Alexis de Tocqueville's observations on nineteenth-century America,[57] who made the wisest observation about the relationship of politics, law, and constitutional justice in contemporary Russia: "When they say that the Court should not examine political issues, this is nonsense. The Constitutional Court is doomed to address political issues. . . . The Americans have learned to view every political issue as a legal problem. That's the trick."[58]

In sum, the Tumanov Court may have been the "fifth wheel of the carriage of Russian autocracy," but the Baglai Court earned the institution a reputation as a fair and evenhanded tribunal of constitutional justice. Today the Court is increasingly recognized as the keystone of the third branch. Under Chief Justice Baglai's effective leadership, the Russian Constitutional Court has made significant contributions to the relative political stability of the second republic, translating possibly contentious political disputes into manageable judicial issues and providing a forum for negotiating change through constitutional adjudication.[59]

Notes

1. Paul Brest, "Constitutional Interpretation," in Leonard W. Levy et al., eds., *Judicial Power and the Constitution* (New York, 1990), 163.

2. Yves Meny, *Government and Politics in Western Europe*, 2d ed., rev. Andrew Knapp and trans. Janet Lloyd (Oxford, U.K., 1993), 343.

3. Justice Gadis Gadzhiev, "Influence of the Constitutional Court of the Russian Federation on the Legislative Process," in Mentor Group, *The Russian Forum for Legal and Economic Affairs* (Boston, 1999), 49.

4. V. A. Kriazhkov and L. B. Lazarev, *Konstitutsionnaia iustitsiia v Rossiiskoi Federatsii* (Moscow, 1998), 61.

5. "Acting Constitutional Court Head Interviewed," *Rossiiskie vesti*, September 28, 1994, Foreign Broadcast Information Service, *Daily Report: Central Eurasia* [hereafter, FBIS-SOV], September 30, 1994: 22, interview with Nikolai Vitruk.

6. See Jan-Erik Lane and Svante Ersson, *Politics and Society in Western Europe*, 4th ed. (London, 1999), 296.

7. Quoted in Herman Schwartz, *The Struggle for Constitutional Justice in Post-Communist Europe*, ms. ch. 5 (Chicago, forthcoming) [hereafter cited as Schwartz, ch. 5].

8. See Robert Sharlet, "The Russian Constitutional Court: The First Term," *Post-Soviet Affairs* 9, no. 1 (January–March 1993): 19–20.

9. Constitution of the Russian Federation [of 1993] (Moscow, 1994), Arts. 125.2, 125.4, and 125.5 [hereafter cited as Constitution].

10. Constitution, Art. 125.5.

11. Herbert Hausmaninger, [transcript of conference presentation on the second Russian Constitutional Court] *American University Journal of International Law and Policy* 12, no. 1 (1997): 101.

12. Jane Henderson, "The Russian Constitutional Court," *Russia & the Successor States Briefing Service* 3, no. 6 (December 1995): 23.

13. Sarah J. Reynolds, editor's introduction to "The Russian Constitutional Court Revisited," *Statutes & Decisions* 31, no. 4 (July-August 1995): 6.

14. V. A. Tumanov, "Konstitutsionnyi sud Rossiiskoi Federatsii: Interv'iu Predsedatelia Konstitutsionnogo Suda Rossiiskoi Federatsii Prof., Doktora iurid. nauk V. A. Tumanova zhurnalu 'Gosudarstvo i pravo,'" *Gosudarstvo i pravo*, no. 9 (1995): 6–7.

15. Justice Nikolai Vitruk's remarks in "Kruglyi stol zhurnala 'Gosudarstvo i pravo': Sovremennoe sostoianie Rossiiskogo zakonodatel'stva i ego sistematizatsiia," *Gosudarstvo i pravo*, no. 2 (1999): 27.

16. B. S. Ebzeev, "Tolkovanie Konstitutsii Konstitutsionnym Sudom Rossiiskoi Federatsii: Teoreticheskie i prakticheskie problemy," *Gosudarstvo i pravo*, no. 5 (1998): 9, 12.

17. Gadzhiev, "Influence of the Constitutional Court of the Russian Federation on the Legislative Process," 50.

18. Konstitutsii Rossiiskoi Federatsii [of 1978 as amended through spring 1993], *Obozrevatel': Spetsial'nyi vypusk*, vol. 2, no. 17–18 (1993), Art. 165.

19. Constitution, ch. 7.

20. Constitution, Art. 15.1.

21. "Decree on Courts' Application of [the] Constitution in Administering Justice of 31 October 1995," *Rossiiskaia gazeta,* December 28, 1995, in *FBIS-SOV* (January 25, 1996): 17–22, esp. pt. 3.

22. "Sovershenstvovanie pravosudiia v Rossii: Interv'iu glavnogo redaktora zhurnala s V. A. Tumanovym," *Gosudarstvo i pravo,* no. 12 (1998): 17.

23. Predsedatel' Konstitutsionnogo Suda Rossiiskoi Federatsii, Chlen-Korrespondent Rossiiskoi Akademii nauk M. B. Baglai otvechaet na voprosy zhurnala 'Gosudarstvo i pravo,'" *Gosudarstvo i pravo,* no. 2 (1998): 6.

24. "Delo o tolkovanii otdel'nykh polozhenii statei 125, 126 i 127 Konstitutsii Rossiiskoi Federatsii," *Vestnik Konstitutsionnyi Sud Rossiiskoi Federatsii* [hereafter *VKS*], no. 5 (1998): 58.

25. Peter B. Maggs, "The Russian Courts and the Russian Constitution," *Indiana International & Comparative Law Review* 8, no. 1 (1997): 114.

26. Peter Krug, "Departure from the Centralized Model: The Russian Supreme Court and Constitutional Control of Legislation," *Virginia Journal of International Law* 37, no. 3 (1997): 786.

27. Valerii Lazarev, "Role of the Constitutional Court of the Russian Federation in the Enhancement of Democratic Principles in Russian Legislation," in Mentor Group, *The Russian Forum for Legal and Economic Affairs,* 19.

28. "Acting Constitutional Court Head Interviewed," *FBIS-SOV* (September 30, 1994): 23.

29. Alexander Blankenagel, "Coming of Age of the Russian Constitutional Court" (1995), 72–73. This is the first part of a book-length manuscript in preparation on the Constitutional Court from its inception to the present.

30. Donald P. Kommers, *The Constitutional Jurisprudence of the Federal Republic of Germany,* 2d ed., rev. and expanded (Durham, N.C., 1997), ch. 1.

31. Henderson, "The Russian Constitutional Court," 25.

32. Nikolai Vitruk, "Constitutional Justice in Russia: Results and Prospects," in Mentor Group, *The Troika for Russian Constitutional Affairs: Securing the Foundation of the Russian Constitution* (Boston, 1994), 38.

33. Gennady M. Danilenko and William Burnham, *Law and Legal System of the Russian Federation* (New York, 1999), 70.

34. Robert Sharlet, "Chief Justice as Judicial Politician," *East European Constitutional Review* [hereafter cited as *EECR*] 2, no. 2 (Spring 1993): 32–37.

35. Herbert Hausmaninger, "Towards a 'New' Russian Constitutional Court," *Cornell International Law Journal* 28 (1995): 382.

36. V. A. Tumanov, *Contemporary Bourgeois Legal Thought: A Marxist Evaluation of the Basic Concepts* (Moscow, 1974).

37. Schwartz, ch. 5.

38. "Vladimir Tumanov Reports Before Recess," *Segodnia,* July 25, 1996, trans. in *Current Digest of the Post-Soviet Press,* 48, no. 30 (1997): 11.

39. Quoted in Schwartz, ch. 5.

40. Ibid.

41. "Marat Baglai Is New Chairman of Constitutional Court," *Nezavisimaia gazeta,* February 21, 1997, trans. in *Current Digest of the Post-Soviet Press* 49, no. 8 (1997): 12.

42. "Constitutional Court Chairman [Marat Baglai] Interviewed," *Radio Ekho Moskvy,* October 21, 1998, trans. in *World News Connection* [hereafter cited as *WNC*], available at wnchlp@apollo.fedworld.gov (October 22, 1998).

43. "Russia," *EECR* 7, no. 2 (Spring 1998): 27.

44. Sergei Bobotov, "Constitutional Justice: A Comparative Analysis," in Mentor Group, *The Troika for Russian Constitutional Affairs*, 23.

45. "Constitutional Court in No Hurry on Trophy Art, Electoral Laws," Interfax, June 2, 1998, *RFE/RL Newsline* 2, no. 105, part 1 (June 3, 1998). This report is based on a public announcement by Chief Justice Baglai.

46. Sharlet, "The Russian Constitutional Court," 5.

47. Quoted respectively in Schwartz, ch. 5; and in William E. Pomeranz, "Judicial Review and the Russian Constitutional Court: The Chechen Case," *Review of Central and East European Law* 23, no. 1 (1997): 48.

48. Hausmaninger, *American Univ. J. of Int'l L. and Policy* 12, no. 1 (1997): 105.

49. See "Delo o tolkovanii otdel'nykh polozhenii stat'i 107 Konstitutsii Rossiiskoi Federatsii," *VKS*, no. 3 (1996): 5–14.

50. See "Delo o proverke konstitutsionnosti punkta 2 stat'i 855 Grazhdanskogo kodeksa Rossiiskoi Federatsii i chasti shestoi stat'i 15 Zakona Rossiiskoi Federatsii 'Ob osnovakh nalogovoi sistemy v Rossiiskoi Federatsii,'" *VKS*, no. 1 (1998): 23–31.

51. See "Delo o razreshenii spora ob obiazannosti Prezidenta Rossiiskoi Federatsii podpisat' priniatyi Federal'nyi zakon 'O kul'turnykh tsennostiakh, peremeshchennykh v Soiuz SSR v rezul'tate Vtoroi Mirovoi voiny i nakhodiashchikhsia na territorii Rossiiskoi Federatsii,'" *VKS*, no. 4 (1998): 11–20; and "Delo o proverke konstitutsionnosti riada polozhenii Federal'nogo zakona 'Ob osnovnykh garantiiakh izbiratel'nykh prav i prava na uchastie v referendume grazhdan Rossiiskoi Federatsii,'" *VKS*, no. 5 (1998): 28–41.

52. See statements by the minister of culture and by Gennadii Zyuganov, leader of the Communist faction in the Duma, in, respectively, "Russian Restitution Decision Does Not Exclude Germany," and "Zyuganov Sees Restitution Decision as 'Reasonable,'" ITAR-TASS (in English), July 20, 1999.

53. Charles F. Hobson, *The Great Chief Justice: John Marshall and the Rule of Law* (Lawrence, Kans., 1996), 151.

54. Quoted in Vitruk, "Constitutional Justice in Russia," 45.

55. See M. B. Baglai, *Konstitutsionnoe pravo Rossiiskoi Federatsii* (Moscow, 1998), 635.

56. "Constitutional Court Chairman Interviewed," *WNC* (October 22, 1998).

57. Quoted in Gavin Drewry, "Political Institutions: Legal Perspectives," in Robert E. Goodin and Hans-Dieter Klingemann, eds., *A New Handbook of Political Science* (Oxford, U.K., 1996), 199.

58. Quoted in Robert Ahdieh, report on the second Russian Constitutional Court for the Rule of Law Consortium, Washington, D.C. (September 1995), 15.

59. The quality of court leadership has been no less a factor in the progress of Russian constitutional justice than in the development of the U.S. Supreme Court. At crucial historical moments in American history, the Court has been associated with such notable chief justices as John Marshall, Roger B. Taney, and Earl Warren.

5

Institutional Decline in the Russian Military

Exit, Voice, and Corruption

Kimberly Marten Zisk

Barnard College, Columbia University

W hy was the Russian military so passive and acquiescent at the close of the twentieth century, in the face of terrible institutional decline? During the Gorbachev and Yeltsin years there were repeated warnings by outside analysts as well as members of the officer corps that quality of life had deteriorated so badly in the military that things might get to the boiling point, and the military might enter politics in some extraconstitutional fashion. Yet despite the failed putsch effort launched against Gorbachev in 1991 by a few members of the military and security forces, and despite Yeltsin's success at calling in the troops on his side in his violent confrontation with the legislature in 1993, the Russian military did not turn out to be a very powerful or independent actor in Russian domestic politics. A close reading of what the Russian officer corps said about itself in the late 1990s shows that the military recognized that it had become a rather marginal social actor.

Military officers as individuals lacked broad societal authority and respect, even if the military as an abstract institution continued to hold a privileged place of relative trust in the increasingly cynical Russian mind-set.[1] The military also lacked the resources, discipline, and morale that would be required for officers to play a significant role in domestic politics. The troops were increasingly uneducated, unfit, and unruly. Garrisons and bases often had no assured access to daily needs such as food, fuel, housing, and a living wage for personnel; and both the troops and the officer corps were plagued by corruption, internal violence, and suicide. While President Yeltsin may have threatened to call in the troops again in the late 1990s (as he hinted he would do in July 1998) against political opponents or agitators,[2] it is questionable whether many units would have responded if he had actually tried, and likely that the response would have been half-hearted and partial at best.[3] The army was disintegrating.

Defense Minister Igor Sergeev made real strides in beginning much-needed military reforms during these years. If the reforms are ever fully implemented, they have the potential to turn the bedraggled remnants of the Soviet military into a tighter, more professional, and more appropriate armed force for the smaller Russian state. But military downsizing and reorganizing require a lot of money, which the Russian military did not have in the Yeltsin era; nor was there any obvious means for the military to get the money it needed, given Russia's endemic fiscal and monetary crises. As a result, Sergeev's reform measures were only partially implemented. The partial reforms caused a great deal of personal suffering, anguish, and opposition in the officer corps, leaving the armed forces in even worse shape in terms of discipline and morale than they were before. (This may be the real explanation behind Sergeev's April 1999 claim that downsizing of the forces was being stopped because of NATO intervention in Yugoslavia.)[4]

When Russian military operations against rebel forces in the breakaway republic of Chechnya resumed in fall 1999, just before Yeltsin left office, many observers saw this as an attempt to placate frustrated Russian officers. What started out as air strikes against reputed terrorist strongholds quickly grew into an all-out ground invasion designed to redress the failures of the 1994–1996 Chechen war. The influence of hard-liners within the General Staff seemed to be on the ascendancy, as Russian military leaders aimed to rebuild the reputation of their fighting machine by using more effective tactics against the rebels this time around.[5] Yet an easy victory in Chechnya was far from assured; long-standing resource and morale problems continued to hamper Russian military effectiveness on the ground.[6] The institutional weaknesses plaguing the Russian officer corps could not be easily solved. Nonetheless, there was still no credible evidence of any concerted effort by the Russian military to intervene in politics (at least not beyond the military policy advocacy role that every military institution in any country plays), even in the uncertain months of the post-Yeltsin transition.

The relative passivity of the Russian officer corps in the face of massive institutional decline may seem odd, but it is understandable once the incentives facing individual military officers are clarified. Although the military as a whole was unhappy, there was neither the means nor the motive for many individual officers to take concerted political action in reaction to their unhappiness. The state had no money to be redistributed to the military. Leading or even backing an authoritarian coup would not enable the military to solve its institutional problems. Given endemic bureaucratic corruption, massive capital flight, pervasive tax evasion, and continuing international investment ambivalence toward Russia, even an authoritarian regime appeared unlikely to be able to produce the funds that would put the military back on its feet. Furthermore, following the debacles in Afghanistan and in the earlier round of fighting in Chechnya, and given extensive public knowledge of the brutal and often deadly hazing of new recruits *(de-dovshchina)*,[7] even an authoritarian regime would be unlikely to make the Russian military a respectable career choice for ambitious young people in the near future.[8] Over 80 percent of Russian young men by the late 1990s hoped to evade the draft, and according to official Ministry of Defense figures (which may be understated by a factor of two), 40,000 troops deserted between 1994 and the first half of 1998.[9] As we shall see below, few young people chose to make a career in the officer corps, either.

Political economist Albert O. Hirschman noted in 1970 that members of institutions in decline have two basic choices when they become dissatisfied: They can exercise voice, or express their discontent through political means; or they can exit, deserting the institution for greener pastures.[10] Those who remain loyal to an institution are likely to try to voice their unhappiness first, in an effort to repair the damage and rebuild their home; but if there is no institutional response, exit becomes the most attractive option. It is not surprising that when years of complaints failed to garner an improvement in officers' living conditions—which in fact deteriorated as time went on—many officers with talent and resources solved their personal financial and social problems by leaving the service as soon as they could and going into business or other civilian employment. Around half of the officers surveyed in 1997 indicated that they planned to leave the military as soon as their current tours were up,[11] and these plans do not seem to have been altered by the August 1998 crisis in the civilian economy.[12]

Some officers were unable to exit, however, probably because they lacked either the skills or the willingness to accept risk and to adapt easily to competition in the market economy.[13] Hirschman argues that the inability to exit can empower those with no alternatives, since their clamoring voices and increasingly raucous protests tend to become more and more intolerable to those in authority over time.[14] Yet the Russian authorities in the Yeltsin era overcame this situation by offering a third alternative to exit and voice. Unable to produce the resources necessary for institutional rejuvenation, they instead implicitly encouraged disaffected officers to use institutional decline for their personal gain. Those who were unable to exit adapted by moonlighting, with the blessings of the defense ministry, as private security guards or in other positions in commercial structures. This secondary employment further damaged military cohesion and discipline, since officers in effect had two masters, and lines of hierarchical authority were no longer clear or determinant. The situation was made worse by the fact that much of this private economic activity occurred at the direct expense of the military. Stealing from military coffers became common, most often either through direct theft of weapons and equipment or by cooking the books on procurement orders for food and other supplies.

This alternative—corruption of the declining institution—is one that Hirschman did not foresee.[15] Corruption, of course, further harmed discipline and cohesion, and thus morale, making any unified collective action on the part of officers in the future even more difficult to contemplate. Private economic interests split the officer corps along multiple, crosscutting lines, giving many an incentive to support the status quo. The status quo, after all, made both legitimate private business operations and unchecked theft from the state possible. This further fragmentation of the officer corps prevented any unified political response of outrage.

Repeated warnings by some military officers and their supporters of a nationwide military "social explosion" or military-backed coup thus appeared to be paper tigers designed to extort more money out of the state. This does not mean that voice ceased to operate as a strategy. As time went on, its forum merely shifted, responding to the fragmentation of economic interests within the officer corps. In desperation, officers and troops serving in individual garrisons began to resort to local protests, often with the support of mayors and provincial governors. The military began to reflect the fragmentation of the Russian state and society as a whole; troops and officers increasingly joined the miners, the defense industry workers, and the teachers and scientists who had already been involved in such local protests for years.

I would argue that this scenario does not make civil war or violent political separatism more likely, since even locally concentrated officers do not form cohesive organizational groupings. However, any such argument must address claims from within the Russian officer corps that this fragmentation represents a return to a dangerous historical pattern of revolution.

In 1997, Lt. Col. (in reserves) Anatolii Panov asserted that the military environment corresponded to that of the revolutionary period from 1905 to 1907, when local mutinies and rioting became common as soldiers started to agitate against the tsar.[16] At first blush Panov's analogy sounds forced and inaccurate, since the mutinies of that earlier era were carried out by conscripts against their commanding officers, whom they saw as elitist representatives of a repressive and alien state.[17] Conscripts viewed these officers as members of a social class to which they could never aspire, and resented the fact that society was passing them by and becoming increasingly Westernized. The soldiers, mostly peasants conscripted for long tours of duty, stopped obeying orders, and often took out their frustrations on local civilians, in uncontrollable riots and pogroms.

Similar class concerns and conscript anger at officers were not the primary causes of army unrest in the late 1990s. In fact, as the military officer's profession became less and less attractive from both a social and an economic standpoint, the Russian officer corps was increasingly drawn from the same relatively uneducated and economically immobile stratum of society that produced the unfortunate conscripts.[18] Most importantly, the protests that occurred across the Russian military in these years (including a refusal to obey orders, the technical definition of mutiny) were led by officers.[19]

Although the social class distinctions at the twentieth century's opening are not analogous to the situation at its end, the underlying factors of poverty and alienation from the state that fueled the earlier protests were in fact present in the latter. The second time around, the poverty and alienation were shared by the troops and officers; and in fact, the troops may actually have had better future prospects than the officers. Desertion became an almost socially acceptable choice in Russia, given the prevalence of *dedovshchina* as an explanation for it. The youngest male members of Russian society (those who were subject to the draft) had the best chance of finding jobs in the civilian market—certainly, a better chance than those who chose the military profession because they had no viable alternative. Revolutionary local protests and riots may indeed reemerge from Russian garrisons, but they are likely to be led by officers rather than against them. In the concluding section of this chapter I speculate about what this may mean for Russian society in the future.

Officers' Views of Military Hardships

The basic outlines of the terrible situation of the Russian military in the 1990s are well known and need not be repeated here in detail. Suffice it to say that plenty of reasons existed for officers to have been tempted by revolutionary promises of a stronger military institution in the future. Neither officers nor troops were paid on time; many officers and their wives and children lived in abysmal conditions because adequate housing was unavailable; smooth demobilization of those officers who were made redundant by military reform plans was hampered because little severance pay or relocation assistance were available for them, despite laws on the books and promises by the state to the contrary; food supplies for the troops were found to be contaminated or otherwise inadequate; the amount of time given to combat training was very low because adequate fuel was lacking to fly planes or send ships on exercises; *dedovshchina,* the brutal hazing of new recruits by more senior troops, was rampant[20] and often led to murder or suicide; corruption of the officer corps was prevalent, ranging from illegal sales of weapons and supplies to the commandeering of troops for private slave labor on dachas or in officer-owned businesses; death rates of both servicemen and officers from accidents, murder, and suicide soared; and as a result of all of these things, draft-dodging was at epidemic levels and the officer corps hemorrhaged its youngest and most talented officers. All of these facts have been well reported both in the West[21] and in many Russian national newspapers, especially *Moskovskii Komsomolets* and *Nezavisimaia gazeta (NG).* They were also the basis of strident complaints made by the late retired Gen. Lev Rokhlin, who used his Duma seat and his Movement in Defense of the Army as a platform to call for President Yeltsin's impeachment.

Rather than concentrating on what outsiders and those with avowedly political goals have said about the military, I decided to see what Russian military officers said about themselves when they were writing in military newspapers and journals—in other words, when they were communicating with a Russian military audience rather than lobbying civilian politicians. What I discovered is that there is no real variation in what military officers said to different audiences. Although there were some exceptional cases (which appeared primarily in the defense ministry's official newspaper, *Krasnaia zvezda*) in which officers pretended that military reform was proceeding smoothly and that their problems were well on their way to being solved, the vast majority of articles reveal that officers agreed that the situation in the military was poor, and told each other about their problems frequently.

For example, in the monthly ground forces journal *Armeiskii sbornik*, the commander of the Moscow Military District, Col. Gen. Leontii Kuznetsov, wrote:

> The insufficient strength level of District troops in personnel, weapons, military equipment, and supplies; [the] low intensity of combat training; [the] uneven nature of financing; and the decline in prestige of military service are having a negative effect on the overall status of troop combat readiness and on keeping the battle management system in a working condition, and they also considerably hamper fulfillment of operational, mobilization, and combat training plans and [resolution of] social problems. Since all this . . . negatively affects the combat effectiveness of troops as a whole, a search for nontraditional and nonstandard ways and means of keeping it at the requisite level has become the main content of practical activity of the command element.[22]

Kuznetsov went on to say that "the reduction in force, problems of social and legal protection of personnel, and the decline in prestige of military service are having a serious effect on servicemen's moods and behavior."[23]

In the same issue of the journal, Lt. Gen. Aleksandr Voronin summarized virtually without comment a NATO report on the status of the Russian armed forces, noting:

> They are shocked by the miserable situation of officers and enlisted men. . . . Living and everyday conditions of Russian servicemen and their families are described here as dreadful. It is no accident that many officers and enlisted men end their lives each year . . . by suicide . . . . The genuine surprise of the NATO military and parliamentarians is evoked by the fact that flight operations have become a rarity at many air bases . . . [and] that Russian Navy surface ships put to sea only in exceptional instances. In addition, the West believes that the RF Armed Forces are demoralized. Once powerful, they have turned into a "fig leaf."[24]

Military officers were even willing to admit the extensiveness of corruption in the officers corps. Stories about illegal activity were legion in the military press, and are perhaps further indications that group solidarity had broken down. *Nezavisimoe voennoe obozrenie* (*NVO*), an occasional military and defense industry supplement to the daily *NG*, reported that a military court in the Pacific Fleet had sentenced a submarine commander and other high-ranking officers to prison for grand theft of fuel, and stated that similar cases were pending against

seven other admirals and generals. The article noted that in several different instances "it has been necessary to remove the commanders of some units and their
deputies from their posts and call them to account for covering up [such]
crimes."[25] During the summer of 1998, Russia's chief military prosecutor, Gen.
Yurii Diomin, was reported to be very angry because the Duma granted wholesale amnesty to all generals and admirals who were under investigation for
crimes of corruption but who had received medals for combat action; thirteen of
his cases were prematurely closed by this action[26]—perhaps indicating that state
authorities truly did see corruption as a means of limiting the exercise of voice by
disaffected officers. Even *Krasnaia zvezda,* which tended to be more circumspect
about the problems of the military, noted that the Group of Russian Forces in the
Caucasus (serving as peacekeepers in Abkhazia) had special problems with corruption, especially because commanding officers were stealing the wages the state
sent to the "dead souls" (i.e., fake employees) on their payrolls.[27]

Blaming State and Society

Despite their willingness to voice openly their lack of combat preparedness and
the fact of military corruption, there was nonetheless a tendency for military officers not to take responsibility for these problems and instead to blame them on
the crisis of the wider Russian society and especially on a lack of adequate funding. For example, an *NVO* article told the (most likely apocryphal) story of an
anonymous lieutenant colonel (given the name Bezbrezhnii), a decorated hero
who specialized in mine and bomb clearing, who was convicted of selling on the
black market the mines and bombs he had cleared, and who was sent to prison as
a result (he apparently did not report the existence of all the cleared materiel to
the authorities). Although the article presumably was intended as a warning to
those who might copy his strategy, it concluded with what sounds like a complaint against the state, justifying this officer's actions:

> After all, it is in fact unbearable to live for a long time in debt. And the government is
> in no hurry to settle accounts with us. One puts a bullet through his head while on
> duty, another dies quietly by hanging himself in the shower, a third steps through the
> window of an upper-story apartment. . . . And then here, in the Bezbrezhnii affair—
> "sitting on money." Buyers are common and the money isn't bad.[28]

In a similar vein, Lt. Gen. Vladimir Fedorovich Kulakov, head of the Main Directorate of Educational Work in the military, candidly admitted that *dedovshchina* was an "ulcer that eats away at Army discipline and undermines military foundations," and said that "the problem of people's deaths continues to be
one of the most acute problems of Army reality." He spoke of how eradicating
this ulcer was one of the main tasks of educational and psychological work in the
military. Yet he then proceeded to blame society for the army's ills: "Its origins lie
in schools . . . . It has penetrated many walks of life of our society. In the military

medium the old-timer always protected the young soldier or sailor. *Dedovshchina* was carried into the Army from outside. It is very difficult to fight this phenomenon . . . because its roots are in society."[29]

His assessment was clearly oversimplistic. It is true that violence has long been endemic in many sectors of Russian society and that *dedovshchina* has been difficult to control, especially since the Russian military lacked a cohort of professional, experienced, noncommissioned officers who could supervise the barracks in off-duty hours (Russia did not even begin to develop a military police service until 1994).[30] But violence inside the barracks was certainly exacerbated and even encouraged by the violence that officers routinely committed against service personnel under their command[31]—something that the officer corps could have controlled if it had chosen to set a good example for the troops.

There was in fact within the officer corps a tendency to blame most of the military's problems on a lack of funding and attention from the state. As two colonels who are faculty members in the Department of Military Finance and Economics at the State Financial Academy wrote, "Given the discrepancy between the volume of finances allocated and that required, military organizational development is turning into a process of destroying the state's military structure."[32] Destruction of the armed forces was occurring, say these officers, but occurring because of outside forces, not because of problems that the military could solve on its own.

Personnel Questions

Senior officers were particularly concerned about a growing deficit of junior officers. The Russian armed forces had been top-heavy for many years, and one of the centerpieces of Sergeev's reforms was an effort to reduce the size of the command staff, sending mid-level and senior officers into early retirement.[33] Ironically, however, the military simultaneously needed scores of new lieutenants each year to take over the command of platoons and companies and fill basic training posts. According to military sociologist Maj. Dmitrii Pozhidaev, over 80 percent of officers who left the army at this time were doing so "ahead of schedule" (i.e., before they were required to retire), and 35 percent of those leaving were under age 30.[34] Russian motorized infantry and armor divisions were reportedly left with 25 percent of their lieutenant positions vacant, and began sending senior enlisted soldiers and reservist troops through ten-month crash training courses to ensure an adequate command staff at lower levels.[35]

Many senior officers blamed this situation, not surprisingly, on funding problems. As an article in *Krasnaia zvezda* lamented:

> Unfortunately, the current situation of the Russian Armed Forces is not attractive for our young compatriots. The officer cadre has decreased significantly; problems with financing, lack of housing, insufficient supply of the latest types of weapons and equipment—all this, of course, does not bode well for the authority of the gun-

slingers. It is not surprising that a difficult situation has arisen in the ground forces today, especially at the level of the platoon, company, and battalion.[36]

Yet on this issue, at least, not all senior officers evaded responsibility for the situation. A major part of the problem, according to Col. Gen. Ilia Panin, who headed the defense ministry's Main Directorate of Cadres and Military Education, was that Russia's officer training programs left their graduates with only a narrow set of specialized skills that lacked utility in the market economy.[37] This meant that few young people sought career advancement by joining the military, since they could not transfer the experience they gained there into promotions in the civilian job market. Panin suggested that military education be reformed to give its recipients the same kind of basic higher education they would receive at civilian universities. In other words, when profitable exit seems possible at some future point, entry becomes more attractive than if the organization appears to be a dead end.

Panin also noted that senior officers did not sufficiently mentor their junior colleagues:

> When . . . there is indifference or even rudeness on the part of commanders and offi-
> cers in charge, aggravated by . . . everyday disorder, young officers submit a request
> for discharge from military service . . . . One has to fight for every lieutenant, not
> leave him without a commander's attention in his period of development as well as
> during his entire subsequent officer career.[38]

This view was seconded by Vice Adm. V. Yarygin of the navy's personnel and military education department. Noting that there was "no money, no living accommodations . . . only problems" for young officers, he added: "As we see it, young officers do not want to serve because their superiors do not pay enough attention to their needs and problems. Moral stimuli are lacking, you see."[39]

Yet even here it was possible for officers to lay the blame at the feet of the Russian state. Undoubtedly a large part of the reason why moral stimuli were lacking among the senior officers was that these officers were miserable about their own career prospects and focusing on their own survival at a time of difficulty. Their own futures became uncertain under the reform plans that Defense Minister Sergeev initiated. In the words of Rear Admiral Diakonov of the Northern Fleet, "With what thoughts will a young officer serve if he has before his eyes the example of a senior comrade who devoted his best years to service in remote Polar garrisons and who found himself, after release into the reserve, without work and without the opportunity to move into housing?"[40]

Goals of Military Reform

The primary goal of military reform was to save money and rationalize the country's defenses, using a drastically smaller but better prepared and equipped active military. A large reserve officer corps was intended to back up the smaller, active forces, to be called up as necessary during wartime.[41] Officer and troop levels were to be cut severely, with hopes of reaching the target size of a 1.2-million-person military in 1999. (Outside estimates indicate that the real size of the Russian military had not been much larger than this when reforms began; but the prereform unit structure was designed for a capacity of 1.7 million people, and many of these positions were vacant, leaving units seriously understaffed.) Simultaneously, the various command hierarchies were to be combined, leaving a much smaller number of organizational units, staffed at much higher levels of readiness. Nuclear deterrence became the primary focus of defense activity, replacing the traditional Soviet predilection for covering all contingencies, including large-scale conventional war. Conventional force planning would be centered on preparedness to contain smaller, local conflicts on Russia's borders and in the interior.[42] Officers began speaking of maintaining parity with the West at a nuclear level only, recognizing that Russia lacked the money to match NATO conventional force levels.[43]

Many long-standing separate force structures were eliminated or merged, and huge numbers of officers (at the level of 40 to 45 percent in many of the services) were discharged into early retirement. The old divisions between the various armed services were eliminated, with the goal of eventually retaining only three groups: most likely, the ground forces, air force, and navy, although there was also talk of leaving the strategic rocket forces a separate unit and combining the navy and air force into a single service.[44] The military space force and the rocket-space defense force were successfully merged into the strategic rocket forces, which Sergeev saw as a transitional service that would be reorganized by 2005.[45] Similarly, in February 1998, the air force was merged with the air defense force, and 40 to 45 percent of those services were scheduled to be laid off by June 1998, including 24 generals.[46] This involved the elimination of several entire regiments and brigades.[47] The Baltic and Pacific Fleets integrated pieces of the ground forces into their command structures, eliminating a layer of senior army officers and many units.[48] Personnel levels in both the navy and ground forces in the Kaliningrad and Leningrad military districts were scheduled to shrink by 40 percent by the year 2000.[49] In addition, more than 40 military higher education schools were consolidated or shut down.[50]

Officers' Views of the Reform Process

Although it was widely recognized within the officer corps that layoffs and restructuring were absolute economic necessities, the way the reforms were implemented provoked a great deal of hostility and anger. The basic problem was that hundreds and even thousands of officers in particular localities were suddenly laid off without being given any housing, significant severance pay, or useful job retraining or other relocation assistance. When we recall that a huge number of officers left voluntarily to take jobs in the civilian sector, it is a good guess that a fairly large percentage of the officers who were *involuntarily* laid off as a result of restructuring were those lacking the resources and skills to easily find employment elsewhere. Because whole units were often decommissioned, the burden of social welfare for those with no alternatives fell on the shoulders of particular cities and provinces.

From the time of the first debacle in Chechnya (when talk of the need for radical structural reform in the military began) through mid-1997, high-level opposition within the presidential Security Council and in the defense ministry repeatedly derailed any attempt at significant reform.[51] But by the end of 1997, Sergeev, as the latest in a line of rapidly changing defense ministers, had gained enough authority to begin implementing his reform program. This apparently was made possible both because President Yeltsin finally made military reform a high priority within his administration, and because officers' back wages were (at least temporarily) paid off that fall.[52] Throughout 1998, real reorganization and downsizing occurred.

Three trends are apparent when we look at officers' responses to this process. First, strong interservice rivalry emerged in the military as each branch argued that its role was uniquely vital for the future of Russian security. Thus, airborne troops commander Col. Gen. Georgii Shpak wrote of the "growing role of airborne and airmobile troops" in the doctrines of the United States and its NATO allies, complaining that "a comparative analysis. . . shows that the proportion of airborne troops in the overall [Russian Federation] armed forces structure is low and there is a tendency toward its further decrease." He argued that instead "the airborne troops must become a most important component of the armed forces and the foundation of immediate reaction forces."[53] Simultaneously, Maj. Gen. of Aviation (retired) Valentin Rog argued that strike and reconnaissance aircraft had made the most decisive contribution to warfare since the 1940s, and that precision air strikes continued to play "the deciding role" in what he termed "peacekeeping" operations (such as the NATO strike during the operation Croatian Storm). He argued that the only way to ensure air force effectiveness was to maintain a centralized command structure emphasizing the importance of aviation, since "elevation of the air force role in warfare is not someone's subjective wish, but an objective historical process."[54] Meanwhile, Rear Adm. (retired) Georgii Kostev made a case for the cost-effectiveness of submarine-launched nuclear weapons as compared to those of the land-based strategic rocket forces, and complained about the priority that land-based ICBMs nonetheless received under Sergeev's leadership. He noted the growing strength of the Turkish navy and the U.S. Seventh Fleet in the Mediterranean just off Russia's borders, and complained: "The [Russian Federation] Ministry of Defense tries to close its eyes to such realities and is concerned more with preserving capabilities for deploying fronts of the Great Patriotic War model, based on military districts . . . .The impression forms that the Ministry of Defense is paying no attention to all of this."[55]

Of course, these highly varied claims were mutually incompatible. The military budget had been drastically curtailed, and not every service branch could receive the highest priority in funding. Although these arguments are completely understandable and perhaps even predictable given the radical restructuring of the forces that was under way, this interservice rivalry further eroded the possibility of any unified military action against the reform plan. Each branch, and in many cases each unit within a division, was competing against the others for survival, which made cooperation unlikely.

The second trend, which followed directly from this rivalry, is that senior officers began to criticize and undercut the defense ministry, blaming it for the tenor of reforms. This is particularly significant when we are making predictions about future political action by the military, because the ministry remained under the leadership of uniformed officers. Other officers, not civilians, were being blamed for the hardships of the reform process, destroying any possibility of a unified military uprising against the center. In fact, the move toward a large-scale ground war in the second Chechen conflict was widely seen as the victory of one military faction over another—namely, against the defense ministry leadership, which preferred to cut conventional forces in order to concentrate on nuclear deterrence.

Those whose units had been eliminated or merged into other command structures spoke out against the reforms, complaining that the choices made by the defense ministry left lethal gaps in state security. One common argument was that as command staff levels were cut in potential theaters of domestic military operations, it would be increasingly difficult to control troops in crisis situations.[56] A similar complaint, with slightly different reasoning, was made by Lt. Gen. Mukhamed Batyrov, who had commanded ground troops in Kamchatka until he was told to transfer his units to the command of the Pacific Fleet as part of the reorganization plan. He suggested that in the event of an invasion from the east, it would be his troops who would repel an aggressor, not the navy, and that it was therefore a mistake to relieve him of his command. In what may be an extreme example of an order being countermanded, Batyrov said in February 1998 that the commander of the Far East Military District, Col. Gen. Viktor Chechevatov, had given him "a verbal directive to stop transferring equipment and other property to Pacific Fleet forces." Later press reports indicated that Chechevatov had succeeded in convincing the Ministry of Defense to halt the transfer of troops.[57] In this case, a complaint led to a technical mutiny (a refusal to obey orders) that impeded the progress of reform.

The fact that officers' complaints have been public and have sometimes involved mutiny indicates how much the cohesion one normally associates with a professional military command has broken down in Russia. Pavel Felgengauer, a civilian reporter who often has seemed to speak on behalf of high-ranking military officers, claimed that "the morale of Russia's military is nearing the breaking point"; that "military reform is the main cause of the growing discontent"; and that "many [commanders] even say they would have preferred a civilian politician as defense minister to Sergeev," since his focus on nuclear deterrence to the detriment of a balanced force structure was "absurd" and left him "not fit to command Russia's military."[58]

The worst problem, in the eyes of many officers, was that an insufficient amount of money was allocated to cover the demobilization process, leaving officers who were transferred to the reserves without pay and housing.[59] The air force went so far as to set up an emergency telephone hot line for those displaced by the merger with the air defense forces, and Commander in Chief Anatolii Kornukov started holding bimonthly receptions both in his office and at bases to "deal with individuals' problems."[60]

One resulting development that obviously disturbed the Yeltsin administration greatly was the growing activism of the Movement to Support the Army, which was staffed largely by retired military officers and appeared to attract many current officers, even though the latter were legally barred from joining any political organization. (This explains the prevalence of rumors that Rokhlin's murder in July 1998 was politically motivated, despite the confession by his wife Tatiana and her resulting prosecution for murder.) Particularly unnerving was the statement made immediately following Rokhlin's death, by Viktor Iliukhin, Rokhlin's successor as chair of the Duma Security Council and head of the Movement, calling on officers "not to fulfill orders, not to disarm, and not to leave military settlements if those demobilized are not provided with housing and compensation."[61] Rokhlin himself never publicly suggested that officers should mutiny;[62] but his Movement is reported to have distributed flyers in May 1998 on the territory of the Volgograd 8th Guards Corps (which Rokhlin at one time commanded), urging officers to disobey orders in conjunction with a national demonstration that Rokhlin planned.[63] In response to Iliukhin's statement, the Main Military Prosecutor's Office in Russia issued a counterstatement warning that acts of military disobedience were punishable under the Criminal Code by up to five years in prison, and urging its representatives in the field to "resolutely cut short" any mutiny they observed.[64] (Iliukhin, as a Duma deputy, was immune from prosecution, even if his statement had been considered an incitement to mutiny.)

These facts indicated a growing level of political activism among Russian military officers. However, the sort of rebellion they encouraged was limited to passive disobedience. The Movement did not call for officers to take action, to march on the defense ministry, impede the functioning of federal offices, or to turn their arms against their superiors. Instead it told officers to ignore orders to alter the status quo. In effect, it asked officers to use their voice to protect the third alternative to exit—namely, the use of an underfunded and overstretched status quo for individual self-interest.

The third trend flowing from this situation is that local protests against reorganizations and lay-offs at particular bases and garrisons became more frequent over time and were often supported by local governmental authorities. Such protests seem to have begun in 1997;[65] they were reportedly widespread by spring 1998,[66] and intensified further over the following summer. By July 1998, a group of naval officers in St. Petersburg who were ordered to move their families off decommissioned ships where they had been living (in the absence of sufficient military housing) went on a hunger strike and refused to leave the ships.[67] Officers' wives at the Uzhur Strategic Missile Forces base in Krasnoyarsk blocked a road to prevent their husbands from going on duty, and rallied for two hours, demanding their husbands' back pay.[68] An army major in Nizhnii Novgorod commandeered a tank from his garrison and ended up leading a large rally, also demanding payment of back military wages.[69]

Krasnoyarsk governor Aleksandr Lebed cited the rally of the officers' wives in an infamous open letter to Prime Minister Sergei Kirienko, in which he demanded that back wages be paid and suggested that otherwise he might take over jurisdiction of the strategic missile base, including its launch authority.[70] (This appears to have been a jest rather than a real threat, since launch authority could not physically be transferred to the local level.) Lebed also demanded that two local military schools scheduled to be closed under the reform not be shut down, and criticized the merger of air defense and air forces on the Chinese border as detrimental to Russian security interests.

Lebed's letter is unusually strident, but his attempt to interfere in the military reform process was not an unusual step for a regional leader to take. Similar calls for particular installations to be kept open, or for authority over them to be transferred to the gubernatorial level, were reportedly made by the governors of Murmansk, Karelia, Khabarovsk, Primorsk, Kamchatka, Chukotka, Kaliningrad, Khakassia, and Stavropol.[71] This should not be surprising, given that provincial governors and other local officials were increasingly contributing to the expenses of local garrisons from their own funds, often on the explicit request of the defense ministry.[72] For example, reserve officer training programs in the Moscow Military District were funded by the Moscow oblast and raion administrations;[73] and several other city or regional governments "adopted" Russian navy ships, acting as their patrons.[74] In part this undoubtedly aided the political ambitions of regional officials looking for good publicity. In part it also reflected the increasing share of the social welfare burden that was shifted to regional budgets, making pay for decommissioned officers an important local concern.

Implications for the Future

The usually sober-minded editorial staff of the *Economist* magazine opined in 1998 that a military coup was becoming a real possibility in Russia.[75] Yet what the analysis presented above suggests is that although military officers may indeed become more and more directly involved in politics, they are unlikely to do so in any kind of cohesive fashion. The economic interests of Russian military officers are in competition against each other. Political action by the military is likely to be fragmented along both service and geographical lines, and is more likely to affect particular localities than to destabilize the Russian state as a whole. It is also likely to be of limited aims, because so many officers benefit at an individual economic level from institutional breakdown.

Will this trend lead to revolutionary local protests, or perhaps local warlordism? There is some evidence that as municipal and provincial governments have "sponsored" particular ships and even land-based garrisons, these sponsored bases have taken on a cohesive local character. For example, Rear Adm. Diakonov stated in late 1998 that because the Moscow oblast sponsored the *Adm. Kuznetsov* aircraft carrier, 200 residents of Moscow oblast have now been assigned to that ship, and that Murmansk's sponsorship of the *Adm. Nakhimov* nuclear cruiser has caused 80 Murmansk residents to be assigned there. Diakonov claimed that "up to 20 percent of the conscripts arrive in the fleet based upon targeted recruitment, knowing beforehand that they are going to 'their' ship, where they are awaited and where they will . . . meet their compatriots."[76] According to another report, Vladimir oblast ran a contest in which the prize-winning conscripts were assigned to a particular border troop detachment and a particular unit in Moscow oblast, and similar contests were being held in Elista, Tomsk, and many other cities.[77]

However, these reports do not suggest that bases sponsored by local governments are located on local soil. If anything, the fact that one oblast sponsored a base located in another oblast suggests regional *integration* through the use of regional military resources, rather than disintegration. Even if a significant minority of troops and officers on a particular ship or at a particular base share a home region, it does not follow that the entire garrison will exhibit loyalty to a regional governor over national authorities if push comes to shove and the governor tries to secede from Russia. The situation bears watching; but there is as yet no reason to believe that regional loyalty and solidarity on the part of local bases will supersede competing economic interests among undisciplined officers—especially since radical political change might threaten the opportunities for corruption and theft that so many officers now exploit.

There is speculation that the Yeltsin administration planned the military reform process deliberately to ensure that competition over scarce resources would keep the military divided and controlled. Perhaps, the speculation goes, Yeltsin knew that the drastic reform that was needed would provoke outrage, and he preferred to have complaints expressed at an individual or local level, rather than facing a unified military backlash that could lead to a coup attempt. This speculation is fueled by the growth of resources granted to other, non–defense ministry security services under Yeltsin, especially the interior ministry troops and newly independent border guards, who might presumably be convinced to defend the state from an attempted defense ministry coup. In fact, as the pace of military reforms accelerated, defense ministry representatives supported the notion of more cross-ministry cooperation with interior ministry and border guard troops, including joint peacekeeping exercises in the Caucasus.[78] Valid military logic lay behind this position; one of the problems the Russian forces encountered in the first Chechen conflict was a lack of coordination across troops from the various ministries, and by the time of the second Chechen conflict it appeared that the defense ministry had more successfully integrated control over this mixture of units. But it is probably no accident that the military statements favoring this integration tended to talk about the importance of keeping command of these joint operations based in the existing military districts (i.e., under the control of defense ministry officers).[79] Joint training under military command might also lead to the development of joint interests, or at least to the defense ministry's knowledge about what was going on inside the other power ministries.

Given that the military reform plans were drawn up by senior military officers, it is unlikely that the intention was to cause the forces to split away from each other, since this outcome undercuts military effectiveness as least as much as it does political cohesion. What is more likely is that the defense ministry was doing the best that it could at a time of constrained resources and rampant corruption, and that military policy confronted the same reality of Russian regionalism and gubernatorial activism that Russian budgetary, tax, and privatization policies had also encountered.

A Revolutionary Model?

If these trends continue, then the situation in the Russian military in the future might indeed come to resemble partially that of 1905–1907, with individual garrisons becoming uncontrollable from time to time, as they are demoralized and politicized by those with revolutionary agendas. Some officers will undoubtedly come to support the notion of a radically different government, especially if the post-Yeltsin regime does not appear able to solve the military's resource problems. Yet it is unlikely that every officer in a particular garrison would be willing to risk life and limb for the political ambitions of any regional leader, given the crosscutting regional and economic loyalties that are prevalent in the Russian military today.

At the moment, it is virtually unthinkable that the Russian officer corps as a whole would support a revolution along the lines of the Bolshevik takeover in 1917. There is simply no issue on the horizon that can cut across the varying interests of officers to unify them behind a particular radical program—especially since the option of exit, as Hirschman predicted, carries off many of the best and brightest who might otherwise lead a cohesive push for change.[80] In the absence of a revolution today, many disaffected officers can either line their own pockets by stealing from the state, or quit and try their hands at legitimate business. The possibility of exit or corruption limits the likelihood of antiestablishment violence. Furthermore, the Russian officer corps today lacks the sense of corporate cohesion that has provoked military coups in Latin America and southern Europe in the past. Perceived military interests today are being threatened by other military officers (namely, those sitting in the defense ministry in Moscow); and what threatens one service arm tends to benefit another. All military officers are not suffering equally.

The significant effects of this breakdown of military cohesion may be negative for society as a whole, as those trained in the use of weapons choose to fend for themselves in an anarchic environment. Military breakdown may contribute to an increase in crime and other forms of antisocial behavior. Serious political repercussions, nonetheless, are much more likely to be international than domestic. Continuing financial desperation already encourages individual officers to sell Russian weapons illegally on foreign as well as domestic markets. And if local mutinies end up affecting the behavior of Russian peacekeeping troops stationed in Georgia, Tajikistan, or Moldova, for example, troops may take unauthorized actions that go against the interests of the Russian state.

A partial example of this may have been seen in June 1999, when Russian troops assigned to the Stabilization Force (SFOR) peacekeeping operation in Bosnia suddenly marched into war-torn Kosovo ahead of the KFOR peacekeeping schedule agreed to by the United Nations, to the surprise of NATO officials and apparently of the Russian Foreign Ministry. Although the exact chain of events in this case remains murky, credible reports indicate that the action may have been spearheaded by a faction led by Gen. Viktor Zavarzin, for personal— and ultimately careerist—reasons.[81] Zavarzin had served as the Russian military representative at NATO headquarters, but had been recalled and apparently punished by his superiors after he failed to discover or predict the exact starting time of NATO air strikes against Serbia during the Kosovo crisis. Zavarzin is reported to have wanted revenge on NATO as well as to restore his reputation at home. He suddenly appeared in Bosnia at the Russian SFOR base and communicated by radio to Moscow with Gen. Anatolii Kvashnin, chief of the General Staff. In turn, Kvashnin apparently presented the troop transfer plan to President Yeltsin for signature only half an hour before the operation began. So although the action taken thus appears to have been "authorized," it did not follow the path one would normally associate with major military undertakings that have strong diplomatic repercussions. The plan may in fact have been put into effect the same day it was hatched by a few generals.[82] It succeeded in boosting Zavarzin's career, since he received a medal for this action; but it certainly was not well conceived from an operational point of view, since within a week the Russian troops occupying the Pristina airport were reduced to begging for water from the British KFOR forces surrounding them.[83] The hypothesis that this action was inaugurated by a faction of generals rather than by cohesive state policy is strengthened by the fact that within days Russian defense minister Marshal Sergeev signed an agreement with U.S. defense secretary William Cohen that put Russian forces in Kosovo basically where NATO had intended them to be all along, in small units under a unified, NATO-led command. In other words, the Russian military as a whole made no attempt to subvert the generally cooperative approach that Russian diplomats decided to take toward the Kosovo situation, even though a group of generals was able to commandeer the reins of policy temporarily. In fact, the Russian military leadership has gone out of its way to support the Russian KFOR troops who are cooperating with NATO, reportedly paying them salaries ten times the level of troops not facing immediate combat,[84] at a level equal to those fighting in Chechnya, so that they feel on an equal footing with their NATO counterparts.

Effective and cohesive political action at the national level is unlikely to emerge from the Russian military anytime soon, given the circumstances described here. For this situation to change, loyalty to the institution and to its core values has to reemerge among the officer corps, replacing both exit and corruption as attractive options. If down the road the officer corps can once again articulate a clear and convincing purpose for its existence that is reflected in its size and structure, then a common sense of patriotism and duty will lead Russian society to regain its traditional respect for the officer corps, and will allow the officer corps again to respect itself. At that point, control of corruption and encouragement of professionalism will follow naturally from the desire of the institution to reform itself in order to preserve its image and its own well-being. Simultaneously, the military will once again become a real force in Russian society.

The one note of caution that must be sounded in conclusion is that internal reform of the Russian military organization in the future need not be in a direction that solidifies democratic civilian control. There are multiple, credible reports that the extremist nationalist political movement led by Aleksandr Barkashov, Russian National Unity (RNE, in its Russian acronym), which is widely seen to be a violent, neo-Nazi organization, has been directing its youth cadres into military, police, and internal ministry careers in an effort to gain influence in those institutions. The Russian military leadership apparently welcomes and even encourages these efforts, since the young men who go through RNE paramilitary training are much more disciplined and physically fit than the average draftee or officer recruit.[85]

If the RNE recruits of today become the leading officers of the Russian military in a generation, and if their numbers and continuing connection with the RNE are sufficient for them to retain the values indoctrinated in them as teenagers, military corruption and disorder will become a thing of the past. Cohesion and organizational loyalty will reappear. Yet liberal democratic political institutions may fall victim to this rebirth of the Russian military institution. It is at this point that a military-backed authoritarian coup would become a real possibility, if the fledgling democratic Russian state remained in the kind of disarray seen at the end of the Yeltsin era. Loyalty would trump exit and corruption; and the Russian military might then assert a unified voice, demanding order and promising its delivery should the state be unable to oblige.

Notes

1. The Russian Center for Public Opinion Research (VTsIOM) reported that the level of "complete trust" in the armed forces fell from 39 percent in 1993 to 27 percent in 1997, even though the military remained the second most trusted institution in society (after the Russian Orthodox church) when compared against the political leadership and the other power structures. A majority of respondents believed that the draft should be abolished. Polls done by other organizations indicated that respondents in Moscow and St. Petersburg saw the army beset by poor standards of professionalism (including bullying of re-

cruits) and "insufficient intellectual potential of the leadership." See Natalia Shchenkova, "One Million Two Hundred Thousand to Join the Ranks: The Rest . . . ," *Rossiiskie vesti,* July 30, 1997, as reported in *FBIS-UMA* 97–212; and "About the Wish of the Youth to Serve in the Russian Armed Forces," East European Press Service, *Defense and Security,* May 25, 1998, as reported in the Internet Securities International on-line press database.

2. See David McHugh, "Yeltsin Courts Generals, Hints at Plot," *Moscow Times,* July 11, 1998, and "Yeltsin Says Authorities Can Foil Coup Plan," *Radio Free Europe/Radio Liberty (RFE/RL) Newsline* 2, no. 131, pt. 1 (July 13, 1998).

3. A 1996 study sponsored by the Lawrence Livermore National Laboratory and led by Deborah Yarsike Ball indicated that over half of the officers surveyed in a variety of Russian regions would be prepared to ignore orders to become involved in domestic political disputes or unrest. See Ball, "How Reliable Are Russia's Officers?" *Jane's Intelligence Review,* May 1996: 204–207.

4. "Russia Rethinking Military Downsizing," *RFE/RL Newsline* 3, no. 68 (Apr. 8, 1999).

5. See David Hoffman, "War Gives New Clout to Russian Military," *Washington Post,* Dec. 5, 1999; Eva Busza, "Chechnya: The Military's Golden Opportunity to Emerge as an Important Political Player in Russia," Program on New Approaches to Russian Security (PONARS) Policy Memo no. 98 (Cambridge, Mass.: Harvard University, Davis Center for Russian Studies, Dec. 1999); and Mark Kramer, "Civil-Military Relations in Russia and the Chechnya Conflict," PONARS Policy Memo no. 99, Dec. 1999.

6. In addition to the above sources, see Michael J. Orr, "Some Provisional Notes on Current Russian Operations in Dagestan and Chechnya," available on line at www.ppc.pims.org/csrc/russ_chech1.htm (Dec. 1999); and Michael R. Gordon, "The Grunts of Grozny," *New York Times Magazine,* Feb. 27, 2000.

7. Within the first month after the Ministry of Defense set up a hot line for *dedovshchina* complaints, it received 2,000 calls. See David Filipov, "Thousands Flee Russia's Brutal Military," *Boston Globe,* June 14, 1998.

8. According to one source, "military sociologists" claimed: "Prejudiced coverage of the Armed Forces problems in the media . . . plays a negative role . . . . Within the last seven years not a single movie was produced which showed the Armed Forces in a positive light. All of this contributes to the formation of an unattractive image of the Armed Forces in the public conscience and the generation of the wrong notions about the military service among the people" ("About the Wish of Youth").

9. Filipov, "Thousands Flee."

10. Albert O. Hirschman, *Exit, Voice, and Loyalty: Responses to Decline in Firms, Organizations, and States* (Cambridge: Harvard University Press, 1970).

11. All officers who were on active duty in 1993 signed a five-year contract that was to expire in 1998. A 1997 poll indicated that 50 percent of those officers intended to leave the service when their contracts expired. See Stuart D. Goldman, "Russian Conventional Armed Forces: On the Verge of Collapse?" Congressional Research Service Report no. 97–820 F (Washington, D.C.: Library of Congress, Sept. 4, 1997), p. 23. According to a mid–1998 *Izvestiia* poll, 55 percent of officers surveyed planned to stay in the military—which of course means that 45 percent did not. See "Only One-Fifth of Soldiers Live on Their Pay," *RFE/RL Newsline* 2, no. 132, pt. 1 (July 14, 1998).

12. Vladimir Mukhin, "Ground Troops Reduction Completed: Their Strength Level Decreased Tenfold in Nine Years," *Nezavisimoe voennoe obozrenie (NVO)* [an occasional supplement to *Nezavisimaia gazeta (NG)*], no. 9 (Mar. 12–18, 1999), as reported in Foreign

Broadcast Information Service *Daily Report (FBIS)-SOV* 1999–0322. His observation is based on interviews at the ground troops main directorate.

13. For an application of this argument to the situation of Russian defense industrial workers and managers, see Kimberly Marten Zisk, *Weapons, Culture, and Self-Interest: Soviet Defense Managers in the New Russia* (New York: Columbia University Press, 1998).

14. Hirschman, *Exit, Voice, and Loyalty*, pp. 65–66.

15. Hirschman (*Exit, Voice, and Loyalty*, p. 33) argues that "the voice option is the only way in which dissatisfied customers or members can react whenever the exit option is unavailable." Corruption could, however, be included in his category of "internal exit" (p. 113), where members who do not leave an organization physically nonetheless drop out of its established norms of functioning.

16. Anatolii Mostovoi, interview of Anatolii Panov, "Revival of Officers' Assemblies," *NVO*, no. 29 (Aug. 9–15, 1997), as reported in *FBIS-UMA* 97–225.

17. John Bushnell, *Mutiny Amid Repression: Russian Soldiers in the Revolution of 1905–1906* (Bloomington: Indiana University Press, 1985).

18. Anatol Lieven, *Chechnya: Tombstone of Russian Power* (New Haven: Yale University Press, 1998), p. 273.

19. These include the multiple instances where commanding officers refused to lead their troops into Chechnya (see Goldman, "Russian Conventional Armed Forces," pp. 27–28), as well as other, more recent protests that have been reported across the country and are discussed later in this chapter.

20. According to a military sociologist, between 50 and 70 percent of recruits surveyed reported "the presence of nonregulation relationships in units and subunits," which is how the Russian Defense Ministry officially refers to *dedovshchina*. Maj. Dmitrii Pozhidaev, "The State and Revolution: Modern Problems of Society and the Army Through a Sociologist's Eyes," *Armeiskii sbornik* no. 9 (Sept. 1997): 16–19, as reported in *FBIS-SOV* 97–350.

21. For excellent recent examples, see Goldman, "Russian Conventional Armed Forces," and Lieven, *Chechnya*.

22. Col. Gen. Leontii Vasil'evich Kuznetsov, "Armed Forces: Problems, Solutions," *Armeiskii sbornik* no. 3 (Mar. 1998): 4–9, as reported in *FBIS-SOV* 98–146.

23. Ibid.

24. Lt. Gen. Aleksandr Voronin, "The Russian Armed Forces Through Western Eyes," *Armeiskii sbornik* no. 3 (Mar. 1998): 13–15, as reported in *FBIS-SOV* 98–142.

25. Vladimir Georgiev, "Army Crime Threatens Russia's Security," *NVO* no. 10 (Mar. 13–19, 1998), as reported in *FBIS-UMA* 98–078.

26. V. Yermolin, "Amnestied Commanders Go On Running the Show," *Russkii telegraf,* July 31, 1998, as reported in the *Defense and Security* compilation (available through the ISI Emerging Markets on-line press service), Aug. 2, 1998.

27. Maj. Vladimir Mokhov and Maj. Vitalii Denisov, "Zagranichny: Shlagbaum" [Border Guards: A Barrier], *Krasnaia zvezda,* June 17, 1998.

28. Valerii Drobot, "Ofitser za reshetkoi" [Officer Behind Bars], *NVO* (electronic version available through ISI Emerging Markets on-line press service in Russian), June 26, 1998.

29. Aleksandr Shaburkin, interview of Lt. Gen. Vladimir Fedorovich Kulakov, "At First Hand: Ideological Niche of Military Service," *NVO*, Oct. 3–9, 1997, as reported in *FBIS-SOV* 97–307.

30. Ibid.

31. Lieven, *Chechnya*, p. 292.

32. Col. Aleksandr Mikhailovich Batkovskii and Lt. Col. Igor Nikolaevich Kuznetsov, "Shortage of Finances Fraught with Disintegration of Army," *NVO*, Feb. 12, 1998, as reported in *FBIS-UMA* 98–056.

33. Pavel Felgenhauer [Pavel Felgengauer], "Kremlin's Rank Obsession," *St. Petersburg (Russia) Times*, Dec. 1–7, 1997; Anatolii Bukharin, interview of Col. Gen. Vladimir Nikolaevich Yakovlev, Commander in Chief of the Strategic Rocket Forces, "Armed Forces: Problems, Solutions," *Armeiskii sbornik* no. 2 (Feb. 1998): 4–9, as reported in *FBIS-SOV* 98–167; "Ground Forces Reorganization Continues," *NVO*, Mar. 17, 1998, as reported in *FBIS-SOV* 98–076; and A. Bondar, interview of Adm. Kuroedov, "No Problems, Only Tasks," *Na strazhe Zapoliaria* [the newspaper of the Russian Northern Fleet], July 1, 1998, as reported in the *Defense and Security* compilation (available through the ISI Emerging Markets on-line press service), July 1, 1998.

34. Pozhidaev, "The State and Revolution."

35. S. Ishchenko, "Officers Are Baked Like Pancakes," *Vo slavu rodiny* [the Belarusian Defense Ministry Newspaper] no. 93 (1998), as reported in the *Defense and Security* (Russia) compilation (available through the ISI Emerging Markets on-line press service), July 1, 1998.

36. Vladimir Matiash and Feliks Semianovskii, "Polkovodtsy XXI veka" [Commanders of the 21st Century], *Krasnaia zvezda*, June 9, 1998.

37. Col. Gen. Il'ia Grigor'evich Panin, "Pulse of Military Reform," *Armeiskii sbornik* no. 2 (Feb. 1998): 10–15, as reported in *FBIS-SOV* 98–167.

38. Ibid.

39. S. Daskal, interview of Vice Adm. V. Yarygin, "Funds Are Being Saved, Combat Readiness Is Increasing," *Strazh Baltiki* [the newspaper of the Baltic Fleet], July 7, 1998, as reported in the *Defense and Security* compilation (available through the ISI Emerging Markets on-line press service), July 29, 1998.

40. P. Lysenko, interview of Rear Adm. Aleksandr Gennadievich Diakonov, "Training and Education: Always the Leading Edge," *Morskoi sbornik* 12 (Dec. 1998): 50–53, as reported in *FBIS-UMA* 99–032.

41. Vladimir Matiash, interview of Col. Gen. Yurii Dmitrievich Bukreev, "Voiska meniaiut oblik" [The Troops Are Changing Their Look], *Krasnaia zvezda*, June 18, 1998.

42. Igor D. Sergeev, "Voennaia doktrina i reformirovanie Vooruzhennykh Sil Rossiiskoi Federatsii" [Military Doctrine and the Reform of the Armed Forces of the Russian Federation], *Krasnaia zvezda*, June 17, 1998; Maj. Gen. Anatolii Fillipovich Klimenko and Col. Aleksandr Arkadievich Koltiukov, "The Basic Document on Military Organizational Development," *NVO* no. 6 (Feb. 13–19, 1998), as reported in *FBIS-SOV* 98–107.

43. Rear Adm. O. Shkiriatov and A. Zolotov, "Some Approaches to Reforming Russia's Armed Forces," *Morskoi sbornik* no. 4 (1997): 18–21, as reported in *FBIS-SOV* 97–203; Vladimir Mikhailovich Zakharov, doctor of military sciences, "Defense on All Azimuths," *NVO* no. 38 (Oct. 10–16, 1997), as reported in *FBIS-SOV* 97–328; Col. Gen. Vladimir Yakovlev, cited in "Korotko" [Briefly], *NVO*, June 26, 1998 (available through the ISI Emerging Markets on-line press service, in Russian).

44. Goldman, "Russian Conventional Armed Forces," p. 41.

45. Sergeev, "Voennaia doktrina."

46. "Commander Discusses Merger of Air Force and Air Defense Troops," *RFE/RL Newsline* 2, no. 28, pt. 1 (Feb. 11, 1998).

47. Vladimir Mukhin, "Reform Process Took in the Bulk of Troops," *NVO* no. 19 (May 22–28, 1998), as reported in *FBIS-SOV* 98–190.

48. Ibid.

49. Sergeev, "Voennaia doktrina."

50. "Army Plans More Cuts Among Officers, Military Schools Face Closure," Interfax, Mar. 7, 1998, as reported in *BBC Summary of World Broadcasts* SU/D3170/S1.

51. Lieven, *Chechnya,* pp. 294–299.

52. Goldman, "Russian Conventional Armed Forces," pp. 40–43.

53. Col. Gen. Georgii Ivanovich Shpak, "Armed Forces: Problems, Solutions," *Armeiskii sbornik* no. 8 (Aug. 1997): 6–9, as reported in *FBIS-SOV* 97–307.

54. Maj. Gen. of Aviation (ret.) Valentin Rog, "Armed Forces: Problems, Solutions," *Armeiskii sbornik* no. 11 (Nov. 1997): 4–9, as reported in *FBIS-SOV* 98–042.

55. Rear Adm. (ret.) Georgii Georgievich Kostev and Sergei Ivanovich Patyrev, "The Navy in the Millstones of Reform," *NVO* no. 37 (Oct. 3–9, 1997), as reported in *FBIS-SOV* 97–307.

56. Andrei Korbut, "Four Military Districts Will Be Eliminated," *NVO,* June 8, 1998, as reported in *FBIS-UMA* 98–159.

57. Igor Frolov, "Ferment Intensifies in the Russian Army," *NVO,* Mar. 3, 1998, as reported in *FBIS-UMA* 98–062.

58. Pavel Felgengauer, "Defense Dossier: Army Morale at a New Low," *Moscow Times,* Mar. 12, 1998.

59. For example, see V. Izosimov, interview of Maj. Gen. Yurii Usynin, commander of the Saratov Missile Engineering School, "Missile Engineering School in Saratov marks 80th Birthday," *Saratov,* June 26, 1998, as reported in the *Defense and Security* compilation (available through the ISI Emerging Markets on-line press service), July 8, 1998.

60. Oleg Litvinov, "Air Force Commander in Chief's Hot Line," *NVO,* June 24, 1998, as reported in *FBIS-UMA* 98–175.

61. "Defense Ministry Accuses Iliukhin," *RFE/RL Newsline* 2, no. 140 (July 23, 1998).

62. "Military Prosecutor's Office Deal Retaliating Strike," *Russkii telegraf,* July 24, 1998, as reported in the *Defense and Security* compilation (available through the ISI Emerging Markets on-line press service), July 27, 1998.

63. Ivan Kurilla, "Rokhlin Looks for Support on Volgograd Military Bases," *Russian Regional Report,* Internet Edition, May 7, 1998.

64. "Military Prosecutor's Office Deal Retaliating Strike," and "Supporters of Opposition Army Movement May Face Criminal Prosecution," Radio Rossiia, July 23, 1998, as reported in the *Defense and Security* compilation (available through the ISI Emerging Markets on-line press service), July 23, 1998.

65. Goldman ("Russian Conventional Armed Forces," p. 32) reports that an airborne brigade in Stavropol refused to go on exercises until they received their back pay.

66. Frolov, "Ferment Intensifies in the Russian Army."

67. NTV, "Servicemen Protest as Cuts in Russia's Baltic Fleet Leave Them Homeless," July 8, 1998, as reported by *BBC Worldwide Monitoring* (available through the ISI Emerging Markets on-line press service), July 16, 1998.

68. "Officers' Wives Are on Strike," *Izvestiia,* July 25, 1998, as reported in the *Defense and Security* compilation (available through the ISI Emerging Markets on-line press service), July 29, 1998.

69. "Facing Tanks, Defense Ministry Is Scared," *Tribuna,* July 25, 1998, as reported in the *Defense and Security* compilation (available through the ISI Emerging Markets on-line press service), July 29, 1998.

70. Vladimir Georgiev, "Lebed's Nuclear Ultimatum," *Nezavisimaia gazeta,* July 28, 1998, as reported in *Russian Press Digest,* on-line version.

Kimberly Marten Zisk

71. Igor Frolov, "Temperature of Russian Army Approaches Boiling Point," *Komsomol'skaia pravda*, Mar. 3, 1998, as reported in *FBIS-UMA* 98–062.

72. Goldman, "Russian Conventional Armed Forces," p. 32.

73. Kuznetsov, "Armed Forces: Problems, Solutions."

74. "'Piotr Veliki' Secretly Hopes for Presidential Patronage," *Kommersant-Daily*, July 28, 1998, as reported in the *Defense and Security* compilation (available through the ISI Emerging Markets on-line press service), July 31, 1998.

75. "Russia's Crisis: Could It Lead to Fascism?" *Economist*, July 11, 1998, p. 20.

76. Lysenko interview of Diakonov, "Training and Education."

77. Vladimir Mukhin, "Rank and File: Ministry of Defense Satisfied with Results of Draft–98," *NVO* no. 3 (Jan. 29–Feb. 4, 1999), as reported in *FBIS-SOV* 1999–0215.

78. "Russia's 58th Army Begins Military Exercises in North Caucasus," and "Russia: Joint Command Exercise Under Way in North Caucasus," both ITAR-TASS, July 27, 1998.

79. Col. Gen. Leonid Zolotov, head of the Frunze Military Academy, "Vzaimodeistvie silovykh struktur" [Cooperation of the Force Structures], *Krasnaia zvezda*, June 16, 1998.

80. Albert O. Hirschman, "Exit and Voice: An Expanding Sphere of Influence," in idem, *Rival Views of Market Society and Other Recent Essays* (Cambridge: Harvard University Press, 1992), p. 90.

81. See Phil Reeves, "NATO in Kosovo: The Five-Minute Hero," *Independent* (London), June 20, 1999.

82. See Viktor Baranets, "Serbs Kissed the Dust-Covered Armor of Our BTRs," *Komsomol'skaia pravda*, June 15, 1999.

83. Andrew Jack, "Russian Elite Forces Pushed into Peacekeeping Role," *Financial Times*, June 18, 1999.

84. See "Russian Troops in Dagestan Get Top Dollar," Agence France-Presse, Aug. 17, 1999, as reported in the ClariNet on-line news service, which cites the Russian Defense Ministry as saying that KFOR troops are being paid $1,070 per month while troops serving in non-combat situations at home are earning $100 per month.

85. For examples, see Pavel Guskov, Mayak Radio Network broadcast in Russian, Oct. 29, 1996, as reported in *FBIS-SOV* 96–204; Aleksandr Golubev, "Brothers in Arms: MVD Professionals Train Barkashovites," *Obshchaia gazeta*, May 15–21, 1997, as reported in *FBIS-SOV* 97–107; and Dmitry Babich, "The National Socialists," *Moscow Times*, Apr. 24, 1999.

PART II

Economy

6

Stability and Disorder

An Evolutionary Analysis of Russia's Virtual Economy

Clifford G. Gaddy

The Brookings Institution

Barry W. Ickes

Pennsylvania State University

The much-heralded "transition to the market" in Russia is now widely recognized to be a far more complex and open-ended process than many at first expected. Boris Yeltsin's last state-of-the-federation speech to the Duma reflected this realization: "We are stuck halfway between a planned, command economy and a normal, market one. And now we have an ugly model—a crossbreed of the two systems." Yeltsin's mixing of metaphors—the spatial with the biological—reflected the fundamental confusion in logic that has plagued economic policy-making in post-Soviet Russia. A hybrid—the biological mixture of two genotypes—is not a halfway point. If it were, the current dilemma would be simpler to resolve.

This chapter offers an analysis of the evolution of Russia's current economic system, which due to its unusual (some would say unique) characteristics has been referred to here as the "virtual economy." We pay particular attention to the interaction between economic reform policies and the adaptive behavior of enterprise directors, which has blunted the efficacy of attempted reforms. In concluding, we explore the dire implications of the virtual economy for Russia's internal stability and development as well as for its international security.

The critical question for Russia's future development is whether the current situation represents a transitory detour or a fundamental crisis of transition. The future success of the Russian experiment depends on a successful economic transition. If the current crisis is merely a temporary detour, its implications for Russia's fundamental stability are not too severe. We argue in this chapter, however, that Russia's economic development has evolved into a new system—*a virtual economy* (Gaddy and Ickes 1998, 1999, and forthcoming; Ericson 1999)—that is stable in the near term but is not conducive to sustainable economic development.

In order to explore the potential future development of the Russian economy, one must first analyze how the economy got stuck. That is the primary question posed by the Russian experience for the economics of transition. Some argue that the virtual economy is just a continuation of the Soviet economy. This is not quite right; although there are important legacies from the Soviet period, it is important to understand how agents have *adapted* their behavior.

The virtual economy is the result of behavioral adaptation in the wake of incomplete shock therapy. The debate between proponents of shock therapy and of a gradualist approach centered around details but shared a common technical view of the reform problem.[1] That is, the argument between the two factions was about the pace of reform and not its nature. We assert that this technical focus led to an incomplete understanding of enterprise behavior, resulting in policies too narrowly focused on economic instruments.[2] The narrow approach induced enterprises to adapt their behavior in ways that crystallized into the virtual economy.

In analyzing this process, we have used an evolutionary construct that exposes the behavioral adaptation at the very core of the virtual economy. Because it is equally important to understand the larger context in which the system developed and which will shape its future, we also examine the current economic system in the context of the fundamental policy imperatives facing post-Soviet Russia. This examination reveals that at the most basic level, the virtual economy was a result of Russia's inability to satisfy its multiple imperatives simultaneously.

The Soviet Roots of the Virtual Economy

The roots of the virtual economy lie in the largely unreformed industrial sector inherited from the Soviet period. At the heart of the phenomenon are the large number of enterprises that still produce goods but destroy value.[3] An enterprise destroys value when the value of inputs it purchases from other enterprises exceeds the value of the output that it produces.[4]

To understand the phenomenon of value destruction, one must understand Soviet pricing practices. Raw material inputs were underpriced in the Soviet economy.[5] Their prices were based on the operating costs of extraction, ignoring rent (that is, disregarding the opportunity cost of using the resources now rather than in the future). No doubt this practice harmonized with the short-term goal of increasing production; scarcity pricing might have induced more conservation, which would have militated against production increases. This bias in raw material prices fed into the system of industrial prices. Heavy consumers of energy were, in effect, subsidized. So too were heavy users of capital, thanks to the absence of interest charges. In short, the costs of production were calculated on the basis of an incomplete enumeration of costs.

In addition, the system was biased toward certain users. Many commodities bore two different prices—one for use by heavy industry, and the other for light industry. This bias would feed into the calculation of the costs of production of these goods in such a way that goods produced by high-priority sectors would appear to have lower costs of production than those produced by low-priority sectors. The distortions created by such pricing practices masked the true productivity of economic sectors, leading economic policymakers during the post-Soviet transition to make decisions based on faulty assumptions.[6]

Because the pricing system disguised the relative efficiency of various activities, the true viability of these activities would become apparent only after economic liberalization. Once prices began to reflect costs, many sectors that earlier had appeared to be creating value turned out to be destroying it.[7] The extent to which the Soviet economy produced the wrong things in the wrong way could only be gauged after liberalization. This effect was magnified by the simultaneous adjustment to world market prices.[8] Many industrial enterprises could not recover their costs, once prices moved to market-clearing levels. The raising of prices on goods produced only led to unsold output. Price liberalization revealed the extent to which value added in the Soviet economy was in fact created in the energy and raw materials sector; but it had the effect of making price reform appear to be the destroyer of the manufacturing sector. Russians' recognition of the nonviability of value-destroying enterprises thus has been hampered by the popular argument that failed policies of reform are to blame.[9] Policy has suffered as a result. Much of the change that has occurred in the sectoral distribution of output since the end of planning is due more to price liberalization than to substantial changes in the structure of the economy.[10] The Russian economy remains a hyperindustrialized system composed of enterprises that would not be viable in a market economy, supported by transfers from energy and raw materials sectors.

There is one other key difference between the Soviet economy and the current Russian economy that should be discussed here: Under Soviet conditions, the transfer of value from energy and raw materials to industry was merely an accounting convenience with no effects on how the economy operated. Industry appeared more productive than it actually was; but this distortion was immaterial to the operation of the system. In the Russian economy, on the other hand, the transfer of resources from energy and raw materials to industry must be *induced*. The transfer of value is no mere accounting convenience but reflects a redistribution of income. To maintain this transfer of value, the owners of assets that are contributing value must be induced to continue to contribute that value.[11] To the extent that the payment necessary to induce the value transfer leaves the system (for example, in the form of capital flight), the Russian economy has less total value with which to support government, compared with the Soviet economy.

The Nature of Reforms

The central idea behind Russian and other marketizing economic reforms is to influence enterprise behavior via budget constraints—that is, to force enterprises to increase revenues or cut costs in order to satisfy the constraints of their budgets.[12] A profit-maximizing firm will respond to budget constraints in appropriate ways, either by reducing costs or by increasing revenues.

Budget Constraints

An enterprise can relax the pressure exerted by its budget constraints in several ways. First, it can increase efficiency, raising the amount of output that it obtains from the same given inputs. Secondly, it can reduce the amount of inputs purchased, although this approach may also reduce future output and revenue, if the inputs are key to production. Third, the enterprise may increase sales through better marketing, obtaining a better price for output. Fourth, the enterprise can temporarily forego investment. If the capital stock depreciates, however, this has long-term consequences for production.[13] Fifth, the enterprise can borrow, if credit is available and the enterprise is sufficiently attractive to investors. However, any borrowed sums must be repaid in the future, with interest.

Conversely, when subsidies are reduced or taxes increased to enterprises, their budget constraints harden. In Soviet times, subsidies were a necessary feature of a regime that required production of goods independent of cost considerations.[14] In the post-Soviet transition, most direct subsidies have been reduced, although many indirect subsidies remain in place, with tax offsets and other special deals being a key feature of the environment. It is crucial at present that direct and indirect subsidies be eliminated and taxes be collected, forcing enterprises to meet budget constraints through market methods.

Market Distance.   Reform via the budget constraint is based on the assumption that an enterprise's survival depends on its profits. The tightening of the budget constraint impinges on profits, forcing enterprises to increase their efficiency. Of course, this approach also weakens all enterprises at impact, before adjustment. But the idea is that the strongest will survive and grow even stronger.[15]

The underlying notion on which this approach is based is the *monotonicity* of reform. This means that the effects of the shock on an enterprise depend on the degree of the enterprise's inefficiency. We can think of enterprises in terms of the distance they must traverse to produce a marketable product.[16] Let $d_i \in (0, \bar{D})$ be the distance of enterprise i. An enterprise that produces a product it can sell in world markets has $d_i = 0$, while a completely inefficient enterprise has $d_i = D$. Transition starts with some initial distribution of enterprise distance.[17] The greater is d, the less viable the enterprise. Suppose that $\underline{d}$ is the cutoff point for viability: that is, all enterprises with $d_i = \underline{d}$ are not financially viable.

Now consider the effect, for example, of an increase in tax collection. This tightens the budget constraint for all enterprises, essentially increasing d_i for all i. Those enterprises that were closest to the break-even point, $\underline{d}$, are pushed beyond it. The pressure to restructure is greatest for the enterprises closest to this point, but all feel the pressure. The more inefficient the enterprise, the greater the shock. The most inefficient may be wiped out by the shock, but healthier enterprises will grow stronger as a result of the intervention.

This unidimensional view of restructuring—that reform means reducing d_i—lies at the heart of much reform advice.

Relational Capital.   Now suppose that the organism has another survival tool: relational capital. Enterprises vary in their inherited stock of relational capital. Some enterprises (directors) have very good relations with local and/or federal officials and with other enterprises. The stock of these relationships determines the types of transactions that can be supported (barter versus cash, prepayment, and the like). Relational capital is goodwill that can be translated into informal economic activity.[18]

Let r_i be the stock of relational capital of enterprise i. The actions that an enterprise takes can affect its stock of r_i. Just as investment augments the physical capital stock, enterprises can also invest in and build up relational capital. For example, the enterprise can perform services for local government. This action may enhance the enterprise's relationships with local officials, and thus increase its capacity to conduct informal activities in the future. It is important to recognize that the augmentation of relational capital is costly.

The key point is that relational capital can aid enterprise survival. Enterprises that have high d may survive by exploiting relational capital, r_i.

R-D Space

A consideration of relational capital shows that the conditions that initially characterize enterprises in transition are two-dimensional. Enterprises can thus be located in r-d space as in Figure 6.1.

It is clear that the greater is d_i, the greater is the minimal level of relations necessary for survival. Although relations can allow an enterprise to compensate for greater distance, some enterprises have such poor initial combinations of r and d that they are unviable. Not only are these enterprises situated far from the market, but the quality of their relations with officials and other enterprises is poor. Clearly, the minimum level of relations needed to survive increases with distance. So we can imagine a boundary (*VC* in Figure 6.1) with a positive slope separating the region of viable enterprises from those that are not viable.[19] How steep *VC* is depends on the institutional setting.[20] In a fully transparent economy, relations may compensate little for great distance. If officials are more corrupt, then relations may be much more important.

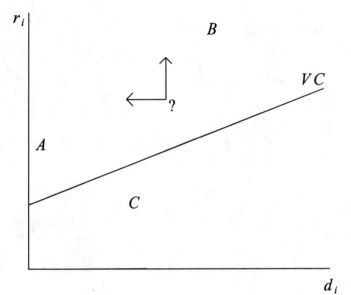

FIGURE 6.1   R-D Space

Source: Clifford Gaddy and Barry W. Ickes, "To Restructure or Not to Restructure: Informal Activities and Enterprise Behavior in Transition," working paper, William Davidson Instititure, May 1998.

In this two-dimensional environment, the effects of market-type reforms need not be monotonic. That is, a tightening of the budget constraint does not necessarily put the greatest pressure on those enterprises that are most inefficient (that have the highest d). Those that invested in r are relatively better off. If investment resources are limited, then the relevant issue for an enterprise is the relative return to investing in distance reduction and relational capital.[21] Our analysis shows that these relative returns depend on the nature of reforms and on the choices made by individual enterprises.

Privatization of Relational Capital

One of the most important but least examined results of economic reform in Russia has been the privatization of relational capital. In Soviet times, personal relations, connections, and influence *(blat)*[22] were important to the system's functioning. The primary benefit to the enterprise director lay in increased ability to fulfill the economic plan. In the highly distorted regime of central planning, supply failures were a feature of daily life. Relations with local party officials and with other enterprise directors were often crucial to obtaining scarce inputs. In the late Soviet period and even more so during economic reform, the autonomy of the director increased as the force of the plan weakened. One consequence of this was that directors obtained the capability to appropriate the returns from the relationships they had developed.

For directors to be able to appropriate returns, enterprises had to continue to function: Much relational capital was enterprise-specific and existed in the form of relationships with directors of other enterprises, often those in related lines of activity. Directors could not cash in this relational capital but could derive benefits from it as long as their enterprises continued to operate.

To appropriate rents, the successful enterprise director utilized relationships to obtain inputs and find customers. If the enterprise produced marketable products, personal relationships would be of lesser importance, and workers would be less content to see a portion of the income of the enterprise diverted by directors; but for an unviable enterprise, the alternative to a director's appropriations was enterprise closure. Faced with this tradeoff, workers were comparatively willing to accept the personal enrichment of directors who had shown themselves capable of keeping their operations going.

The privatization of relational capital helps explain why directors have fought so hard to keep enterprises open that have few prospects in the market economy. The frequent success of their efforts is explainable by the symbiotic relationship between workers and directors: Workers need the directors to keep unviable enterprises afloat and keep their jobs; and directors need the unviable enterprises and their workers in order to exploit relational capital.

Mutation and Resistance:
An Evolutionary Analysis

Enterprises' and directors' exploitation of relational capital to survive in a more hostile environment can be thought of as a mutation. This view fundamentally contradicts that of the reformers who designed the Russian privatization, who viewed Soviet-type enterprises as typical of all enterprises encumbered by political controls. The notion was that without government control, and with hard budget constraints, enterprises in Russia would behave like "normal" enterprises.[23] That is, once political controls were lifted, they would maximize shareholder value, like any firm in the West.

This conventional view ignores the fact that the post-Soviet enterprise had available to it survival strategies unavailable to the "normal" enterprise. The enterprise in the virtual economy produces goods that can be used for barter or for tax offsets but that cannot be sold on the market. It can also procure inputs at a lower cost because relations allow it to pay in nonmonetary forms. However, the cost of pursuing such strategies is lack of transparency, which makes it impossible to attract external funds for restructuring. Hence, the enterprise in the virtual economy finds it prohibitive to reduce distance, and the market-oriented enterprise cannot engage in the survival strategies available to the virtual enterprise.[24]

Partially implemented policies of economic shock therapy produced a sudden change in the environment facing enterprises, but the effects of the reform were not monotonic, as had been intended. Enterprises that chose transparency found themselves at a competitive disadvantage to those that invested in, or had initially high, relational capital. Enterprises that had invested in this alternative means of survival were less affected by the reform. These enterprises proved immune to the very shock therapy that had been designed to force them either to change or to shut down.

The overall economic effects of this development may extend far beyond the initial group of mutant enterprises. Enterprises tend to imitate behavior that they see as successful. If some enterprises in the virtual economy survive without undertaking costly restructuring, then other enterprises may choose to follow this behavior. The system may rapidly tip.

We do not argue that Russia's economic reforms were ill-conceived,[25] although we do believe that they were excessively focused on the budget constraint. The greatest shortcoming of the reform process lay in the partial implementation of policy decisions. For the most part, reforms that would have shut down loss-making enterprises were shunned because their consequences were deemed intolerable.[26] Clearly, the effective hardening of budget constraints was an implicit assumption necessary to the therapy of tight money and liberalization. The fact that hard-budget constraints were avoided through investment in relational capital means that reforms were not fully implemented.

Incomplete Therapy

Incomplete shock therapy failed to wipe out loss-making enterprises. A new mutant strain emerged with the survival strategies available in the virtual economy. The mutation and survival of unviable enterprises made it harder for new, viable enterprises to compete. The greater the number of mutant enterprises exploiting virtual strategies, the greater the relative disadvantage for market-type enterprises, because mutant enterprises operate under rules that market-type enterprises cannot use.

This problem can perhaps be better understood by analogy to that of multiple-drug-resistant (MDR) tuberculosis (TB). MDR strains of TB are never found in the wild. Genetic resistance to particular drugs occurs naturally but is diluted by the overwhelming prevalence of drug-susceptible organisms. In the natural environment, there is no evolutionary advantage to genetic resistance to antimicrobials of synthetic origin. The introduction of synthetic antimicrobials provides the selective pressure for resistant organisms to become predominant. In other words, human intervention creates the selective pressure in favor of MDR. The primary mechanism by which this happens is an *incomplete* regimen of treatment (or poor adherence to a proper regimen). The incomplete regimen wipes out the drug-susceptible organisms, leaving the field open to drug-resistant varieties.

A straightforward analogy can be drawn to enterprise behavior. In a competitive environment, there is no selective advantage to investing in relational capital; reducing market distance is the key to viability. Incomplete therapy in Russia, however, did not create such an environment. Relational capital continued to result in a positive payoff, in terms of enterprise fitness and survival. For enterprises that possessed sufficient relational capital, the opportunity to survive via virtual strategies became a viable option. Hence, the burden of therapy was on the enterprises that did not have, or chose not to invest in, relational capital. Incomplete therapy imposed a *relative* burden on enterprises that chose to act in a "normal" manner. It provided selective pressure that favored the mutant enterprise. This is similar to the outcome for a TB patient who does not take the full complement of anti-TB drugs or follow a multiple-drug regimen.[27]

Behavioral Adaptation

In the biological world, evolution relies solely on relative fitness. The proportion of mutants is limited by the frequency of mutation. In social evolution, however, change can occur not just through replication but through adaptation.[28] Enterprises can *imitate* behavior observed to be successful. If some enterprises are able to survive without undertaking costly restructuring, then other enterprises may choose to follow this behavior. Hence, once virtual economy strategies appear to be working, the system may rapidly tip.

The speed at which this process unfolds depends on the pattern of interaction among enterprises. Conservatively, one could model the adaptive (imitative) process with the asumption that enterprises were equally likely to interact with any type of enterprise. Payoffs are determined solely on the basis of population frequencies for the economy as a whole. One could argue, however, that enterprises may be more likely to interact with like-minded enterprises. For instance, enterprises in the production sector tend to interact with the same enterprises that they dealt with under central planning. This could lead to further bifurcation. If agents tend to interact with like-minded agents, this may reinforce behavior.[29] This suggests that the presence of nonrandom interactions could strengthen the virtual economy trap.

Policy Ineffectiveness

All of the shocks that have occurred since the start of transition have had greater relative impact on enterprises working according to the rules of the market economy. Attempts to increase the intensity of reform have focused on hardening the budget constraint without any actions to reduce the payoff from relational investments. Such policy measures illustrate the principle that in the virtual economy populated by mutant enterprises, conventional policy prescriptions will not work as expected. Below we consider two examples.

Transparency. The first illustrative example of a policy that has unintended consequences is that of increasing enterprise *transparency*. An essential element of market reform is that enterprises make their financial activities more transparent. The implicit bargain of market reform was that greater transparency would be rewarded by greater access to credit. Financial markets require transparency, as do foreign investors. Of course, transparency also makes problems more apparent. But if the only way to obtain external financing is to take the plunge to greater transparency, then enterprises will choose this costly option.

The problem with choosing transparency is twofold. First, transparency precludes the use of strategies that rely on relational capital. Second, transparency is essentially irreversible. If there were no *r*, then those enterprises with greater *d* would be disadvantaged. The move to greater transparency would have the greatest benefits for enterprises that are closest to the market. Hence, the fitness of the most efficient enterprises would be enhanced relative to loss-making enterprises. The problem is that when relational capital is an available survival strategy, enterprises that choose transparency may find themselves at a relative disadvantage.

This argument has important implications for discussions of the role of corporate governance. Inadequate corporate governance is a severe problem in Russia, one that inhibits investment, especially foreign investment.[30] The conventional view is that weak corporate governance is a key barrier to external finance for Russian enterprises. This is an important argument, but it is critical to keep in mind that the opposite is also true: The low probability of attracting external finance inhibits the development of good corporate governance. There are two parts to this argument: First, enterprises that have very high *d* see very little return upon improving corporate governance. Even with very transparent relations they are unlikely to attract external financing, because the expected return is so low. Second, enterprises that may have higher expected returns face the twin problems of high interest rates and increased tax incidence. The fiscal problems of the Russian government increase the cost of external finance. In addition, an enterprise that chooses to reduce *d* faces increased relative tax incidence from entering the monetized part of the economy, which also reduces the expected return. Hence, enterprises led by directors who fully understand the connection between good corporate governance and external finance may *choose* not to implement the former because the benefits are insufficient.

The relative disadvantage faced by enterprises that choose transparency is due to the extremely high cost of external finance. Even apart from problems of corporate governance (which are in any case less severe in transparent enterprises), the fiscal policy of the Russian government has crowded out much investment. Transparent enterprises have not received the intended benefits of transparency, but they have paid the costs of refraining from the use of relational capital. Enterprises that choose transparency are now more vulnerable than they were before. This is especially true when there is a tax crackdown. High tax rates that result from fiscal weakness and campaigns to increase tax collections mean that the greatest pressure falls on enterprises with the most transparent accounts.

Tight Money.   A second example of a policy that is rendered ineffective by the virtual economy is that of tight money. An essential element of shock therapy is a tight monetary policy aimed at stabilizing the price level. Indeed, most critics of so-called shock therapy have pointed to tight monetary policies as one of the prime causes of reduced industrial output. Certainly, tight money is an essential element of the tightening of budget constraints. If credit is lax, there is less pressure on enterprises to restructure.

Tighter credit is a perfect example of a policy that is supposed to hurt all enterprises and to have the greatest impact on the least efficient. The policy of tight money is premised on the assumption that reform is monotonic. If survival via investment in relational capital is feasible, then this assumption is invalid. Enterprises that invest in relational capital may insulate themselves against credit shocks. Tight money then has greater relative impact on those enterprises that have invested in reducing distance. The "fitness" of the latter enterprises relative to those that invested in relational capital is reduced by tight monetary policy. This induces imitation, and virtual behavior spreads.

Enterprises in Russia were able to use relational capital to insulate themselves from the stringency of the budget constraint. The ability to pay for inputs, and to pay taxes in kind rather than in cash, provides them with an advantage compared to those that must use cash. Barter typically costs the paying enterprise less than an equivalent *nominal* amount of cash. If it were not so, then the enterprise would sell the output for money, and pay with the proceeds.[31] Hence, once barter became more common, even enterprises that could afford monetary payment chose barter.

To place this observation in the context of our evolutionary analysis: The transition process was perturbed by the tightening of credit during 1995 and the ruble corridor, which induced a mutation in enterprise behavior. In particular, monetary tightening evoked the use of barter. Lack of liquidity may have induced enterprises to engage in nonmonetary behavior. Once this mutation occurred, the stability of virtual behavior implies that barter would persist even if the initial conditions that shocked the system were no longer present.

This account fits with recent empirical studies of barter. It has been argued by Commander and Mumssen (forthcoming), for example, that barter became widespread in Russia in response to the monetary tightening of 1994 to 1995. Yet, as demonstrated in Guriev and Ickes (1999), barter does not seem related to the financial position of the enterprise. The latter study also shows that there is a lock-in effect of barter: Once enterprises resort to barter, it becomes cheaper for them to continue to do so.

The key point is that the importance of relational capital and of networks of relationships among enterprises preceded the imposition of tight monetary policy. When that policy was implemented, its intended effects were countered by enterprises' resort to virtual strategies. Tight monetary policy penalized the wrong enterprises. It reinforced barter—a phenomenon that clearly preceded the tightening of credit—and provided a relative advantage to those whose relational capital was sufficient to support barter. This leaves the interesting counterfactual: If tight money had been imposed earlier—*before* the mutation—would it have been more effective because virtual behavior had not yet consolidated?

Implications for the Future

What are the implications of our analysis for the future evolution of the Russian economy? Is the virtual economy a stable institutional setting? Or is it a temporary resting point that will soon become a historical curiosity?

The argument in favor of the historical curiosity position rests on the notion that the virtual economy cannot sustain itself over the long run. Several facts give credence to this argument. First, the linchpin of the virtual economy—the manufacturing sector—is made up of old capital and old labor. One expects that over time these factors will wear out. Because capital replacement in loss-making enterprises is nearly nonexistent, this sector's role in the economy as a whole gradually will shrink.

A second approach considers the question from the standpoint of *infusion of value*. We know that the operation of the virtual economy depends on the continued infusion of value—most importantly from Gazprom, but also from the new private sector and external sources. One could argue that in principle there are no serious limits to further infusions of value. As long as actors are willing to support the system, this peculiar development will persist. The capacity of the system to tap value is not unlimited, however. Firstly, the gas and oil sector—the most important source of value in the economy—has suffered from inadequate investment. Analysts suggest that this deficit will severely hamper production in the future. In a sense, the current operation of these sectors overstates true value production.[32] Inadequate investment means that current levels of value creation cannot be maintained indefinitely. Secondly, foreign investors have been less willing to invest in the Russian economy since the August 1998 crisis and the ensuing default on short-term government debt (GKOs). It is not clear how long the aftereffects of this shock will linger, but the optimistic scenarios that led to foreign investment have been shattered. Moreover, international financial institutions appear more reluctant to increase aid levels above what is needed to keep Russia more or less current on its debt repayment (we say "more or less," because the debt is continually being rescheduled).

The third source of value is Russia's domestic private sector. However, the capacity of this sector to provide value to offset losses incurred elsewhere is limited. The continued operation of the virtual economy places a heavy tax on new activity.

Whatever the levels of infusion of new value, the virtual economy still redistributes that value in an inefficient manner, and much value is lost in the process. First, value is destroyed in production by an uncompetitive manufacturing sector. Second, value is leaked from the system. Some leakage is necessary, to keep value-adders in the system (the "good leakage")—for example, payoffs to Gazprom so that they will continue to subsidize loss-makers; but much is unnecessary and is actually a form of looting. Third, barter—the characteristic form of exchange in the virtual economy—by its very nature involves substantial transaction costs.

In sum, the potential sources of value infusion are waning, and value continues to be lost inside the system as well as to the outside. Russian policymakers will continue to attempt to solve these problems. Slowing the loss of value on the one hand and increasing the value infusion on the other might enable the virtual economy to sustain itself indefinitely; but let us assume that the present trend of gradual decline in value prevails. The question then arises: What happens as the system runs out of value?

The Primitivization of Production: Shrinkage

Understanding how the economy adapts to a reduction in the total amount of value to be circulated is key for assessing the evolution of the economy. The optimistic scenario has enterprises choosing to restructure in order to survive. With resources no longer being infused into the system from Gazprom and other sources, enterprises must survive on their own—hence, restructure. This presupposes, however, that the investment decisions—or rather, the lack thereof—of the past eight years can easily be undone. It presumes that the distance that must be traversed to reach the market has *not* increased during the period of postponed restructuring. This assumption is, of course, unwarranted.

What happens to enterprises when the value pump ceases to flow? One possibility is bankruptcy. Enterprises may simply cease production. This is rather unlikely, however, in the case of Russia. Rather than cease production, Russian enterprises on the verge of bankruptcy may transform themselves by limiting their activities, a process we call *shrinkage*. This transformation generally involves a radical reorientation and in some cases a complete alteration of production lines. This is not the primary characteristic, however. Rather, the key characteristic of the shrinking enterprise is increasing withdrawal from the market—in both its conventional (monetized) and its virtual (demonetized) variants.[33]

An enterprise that has seen the value of its relational capital dissipate will cease production of nonmarketable, value-destroying goods (ones that consume more in the value of their inputs than they produce). At the same time, given that the enterprise's distance to the market has increased during transition, the opportunity to shift to producing marketable products is practically nonexistent. With a sufficient infusion of external finance, presumably any enterprise can be restructured sufficiently to produce marketable goods. But enterprises that have migrated toward the southeast corner of *r-d* space are the least likely to be able to attract any external funds, let alone sufficient ones. The alternative for the enterprise is to survive by radically insulating itself from market forces. It will employ its capital stock to produce goods that use little or no purchased inputs, and it will increasingly focus on the survival of its workers. This means more small-scale, primitive production and less specialization.

Ironically, this enterprise is, in a purely technical sense, more efficient than it was before. Before, the plant was attempting to produce, on as large a scale as it could, a good that destroyed value. The more it produced, the less it contributed to the economy. Now, because the plant uses few or none of the valuable inputs that it previously did, its activity is less socially harmful. Indeed, the enterprise may even be adding value. But it is doing so on a drastically reduced scale of production.[34]

This transformation of the enterprise via shrinkage is rational, and it is efficient. Less value is destroyed in the new activity. However, there is another side to this development that is less propitious for the country's economy. Shrinkage may also involve a write-off of human capital—a waste to society, and a permanent loss to the economy.

Stability and Disorder

Ironically, Russia's virtual economy conserves old structures and relationships, yet is destructive to society. The virtual economy is a system that operates to prevent changes that need to take place for economic performance to improve. It postpones the day of reckoning for enterprises and institutions that should have left the scene at the onset of transition.

Implications of the Virtual Economy's Stability

The implications for Russia's economy if it continues along this track are dire. We can see this by examining four issues that are of key importance to Russia's economic survival: (1) economic growth; (2) development of the private sector; (3) the national integrity of the economy; and (4) the ability of the public sector to fulfill its tasks and obligations.

Economic Growth.   In the virtual economy, official growth figures mean little. Virtual (that is, illusory) prices result in illusory GDP. The economy may appear to grow, but it actually contracts. For the short term and middle term, this system is likely to remain stable. But the stability comes at a huge hidden cost, since the virtual economy undermines the future competitiveness of the economy by discouraging the modernization of physical and human capital. Indeed, the virtual economy acts as a barrier to restructuring.[35] Thus, the economy continues to grind down. The further it goes, the less competitive it is.

The Private Sector.   The fate of the true private sector—the value-adders outside the virtual economy, including foreign joint ventures—is a vital issue for

Russia's future. The virtual economy bears a curious relationship to the private sector: It will not eliminate it, since it needs a private sector in order to survive. It needs cash as well as the social safety valve that the private sector provides. Yet dominance by the virtual economy is incompatible with a genuinely independent, prosperous private sector. Consequently, small businesses will exist, but they will be prevented from supplying public sector customers. They will not be allowed to develop as subcontractors to larger enterprises. More seriously, as value-adders producing for the market (that is, selling for cash), they will be subject to a heavy tax burden. The virtual economy will therefore squeeze the private sector to get the cash it needs (taxes); and it will constrain the private sector to protect the market it needs.

National Integrity. The virtual economy tends to fragment the national economy into smaller, self-contained, local economies. This trend is evident in Russia, where local government budgets are already more "virtualized"—demonetized—than even the federal budget. Local governments protect the local markets for the benefit of their local, virtual economies. In the post-August crisis, regional and local governments intensified the tendency toward localism by introducing measures to hoard goods locally and ban exports, especially of food, even to other regions of Russia.

The Public Sector. The public sector will be smaller and more demonetized, and as stated above, more localized. The federal governmental budget is key. Look at the recent record: In 1997, Russia's federal government collected less than 60 percent of its taxes in monetary form. Its cash tax revenues came to barely U.S.$23 billion at 1997 exchange rates. Even if we add to that its other sources of monetary revenues—privatization sales, customs duties—the government was able to raise no more than about U.S.$40 billion (not counting funds borrowed at home and abroad). With its highly publicized tax collection campaign at the beginning of 1998, the government was slightly more successful in raising cash; but as the virtual economy model predicted, the extra cash to the budget came at the expense of the rest of the economy, helping to precipitate the financial collapse of August 17.

Since the default, tax collection in real terms has been below 1997 levels. Moreover, the devaluation of the ruble against the dollar has put the Russian government in a much worse situation as regards foreign debt repayment, greatly increasing its debt burden. As a result, the government has fewer resources at its disposal and continues to fall far short of providing the basic public services for which it is responsible.

The failure to adequately fund government agencies at all levels has meant that these agencies are becoming the bureaucratic analogues of self-subsistence farms. Government employees use government assets and government time to earn enough to keep themselves alive, to grow food, or to perform other tasks necessary to survival. Little or nothing is left for serving the public. In the case of some civil servants, whose jobs serve no useful purpose, this trend may be acceptable. For many others, it is damaging, both for their own health and well-being and for the citizens they are supposed to serve. And for some critical categories—the military is the best example—it may be disastrous.

Time Is the Enemy

The virtual economy has been consolidated since about 1994. It might be argued, however, that the entrenched adaptation of enterprises to the virtual economy does not mean that they cannot eventually restructure. Improvements in the economic environment could alter the relative payoffs of market and virtual strategies, leading to real economic restructuring. Such an improvement in the economic environment could occur, for example, if the tax system is improved, or if the ruble depreciates in real terms.

The notion has merit, but it ignores the fact that delayed restructuring has important consequences. Foremost among these is that the distance that enterprises must traverse increases with time. The initial d_i with which enterprises begin the transition is relative to the world standard. If the world standard is advancing, then an enterprise that simply maintains its current level of efficiency will see its distance *increase*. Hence, the payoff to that enterprise from investing to reduce distance will decline over time. Delayed restructuring increases the margin that must be overcome for an enterprise to become competitive.[36] This raises the relative payoff for engaging in virtual strategies. Hence, stagnation may make the virtual economy more stable.

We can outline four reasons for this bleak conclusion that time is not on the side of Russian economic reform:

1. First and foremost, the critical implication of the adaptation of behavior is that the system to be reformed is not the same as it was in 1991 and 1992. The Russian economic system has evolved and adapted as a form of institutionalized protection from and resistance to market reform. Over time, increasingly larger parts of the economy have been drawn into these institutions. The resistance to reform is thus more robust than ever. As a result, any program of radical and comprehensive economic reform today has almost no popular appeal. The prospects are years of pain and dislocation, with few if any compensating benefits to the population except in the rather distant future. (This popular view contrasts with that typical between 1991 and 1992, when the new reforms granted a great deal of personal freedom to individuals, both political and economic.)

2. The consolidation of the virtual economy has had an adverse effect on the younger generation. Contrary to hopes, young people, in order to survive and succeed in this system, develop behavior more appropriate to the virtual economy than to a market economy. Although some in the new generation appeared to have broken out of the rut, they were still a

minority. Most have not. The younger generation is not an automatic guarantor of change.

3. Even if there were a willingness in enterprises to change and adapt and become competitive in the market, this has become a greater technical challenge than it was six or seven years ago. Things were bad enough then. Even by official Soviet standards, a huge proportion of equipment in Russian industry was physically obsolete when reform began in 1992. The Russian economy needed massive modernization. It has not had it. As a result, a physical plant that was generally old and uncompetitive to begin with is now seven years older and even less competitive. Less drastic but still important has been the loss of human capital. The people who worked in those uncompetitive industries who felt that they had a chance in the new market economy left and tried their chances there. The people who remained behind tend to be the least productive.

4. Finally, there is a steadily worsening macroeconomic barrier to successful modernization of the Russian economy: the country's permanent debt trap. Russia continues to build its debt up, not down. This is true not only of the financial debt but also of society's cumulative, unpaid, nonpecuniary costs—especially damage to the environment and the undermining of public health. These are costs that must someday, somehow be paid.

Compared to six or seven years ago, the process of real economic reform—defined as reasonably complete marketization, monetization, and modernization—in Russia today would be (1) more unattractive to begin with; (2) more difficult and more costly to complete successfully; (3) more painful for the population to endure; and (4) more burdened by accumulated, unpaid debts, in the broadest sense. The virtual economy is a trap.

Escaping the Virtual Economy Trap

If the virtual economy represents an adaptation of behavior to what would otherwise be an unsustainable environment, as we have argued, then the answer of how to escape this trap can come only from an examination of this broader environment.[37] We suggest that this environment was created by the impossible linkage of three goals or imperatives of post-Soviet Russian policy.

The Impossible Trinity[38]

The overriding imperative for any state is national survival. The definition of national survival and the cost of meeting this imperative depend on the external environment in which the country is located as well as on the dominant vision of the nation shared by the leadership. It is critical nonetheless to recognize that national survival is an imperative; it is impermissible to allow other policies, no matter how desirable in themselves, to seriously threaten the very existence of the nation. National survival, guaranteed first and foremost by national defense, is naturally a policy imperative for Russia.

Post-Soviet Russia's goal of shedding its totalitarian past added two additional policy imperatives: development of democracy and a modern, transparent market economy. Under the specific circumstances in which Russia found itself after the demise of the Soviet Union, the three elements of this trinity were fundamentally irreconcilable.[39]

Russia entered the transition with security needs inherited from the Soviet era, albeit with an economy only about 60 percent of the size of the Soviet Union's. These needs were compounded by the breakup of the Union, which created new external borders that Russia alone would have to defend. Even without any short-term economic problems, the objective security imperative would have pressed heavily on the smaller economy; but national economic collapse further reduced Russia's capacity to meet its security needs.[40] In order to sustain an adequate defense capability, Russia would have had to spend more on defense than the people of the newly democratic country would have supported, given general economic conditions. Hence, Russia could not fulfill all three imperatives in the trinity. One of the elements—security, democracy, or market economy—had to be sacrificed.[41]

Given that the Russian leadership had committed itself to the new imperatives of democracy and market economy, the only way out was to redefine the security imperative. The end of the Cold War was taken by many to mean that Russia's security needs would be much reduced. With a less hostile security environment, Russia could satisfy the security imperative, implement democracy, and take on economic reform. Hence, the initial attempt to solve the dilemma of the impossible trinity was affected by maintaining a pretense with respect to the first imperative, national security. In the first few years, government leaders in the West as well as in Russia pretended that Russia had less of a security dilemma than it actually did and that its defense capability was stronger than it really was. The idea that "the Cold War is over" led to Russian expectations that the West would ensure a better international environment for a newly cooperative, marketized and democratized Russia. This was the essence of Kozyrev's foreign policy: lessening international tensions in order to foster reforms. At the same time, everyone pretended that Russia's strength was much greater than it was.

NATO's eastward expansion and continued exclusion of Russia ended the pretense of a peaceful environment; and the first Chechen war ended the pretense of Russian strength. It was evident that the only way to meet the security imperative was to devote more resources to defense. But if security is the ultimate imperative and pretense about it is no longer possible, then Russia's leaders must choose between abandoning democracy and abandoning the market economy. In the event, the pretense was shifted to the economy. Russia ended up with a nontransparent, pretend market economy. This virtual economy allowed for greater government spending on defense than was politically (democratically) feasible, thanks to the nontransparent mechanisms of offsets, barter, and other nonmonetary transfers.

This version of events has a provocative implication. To the extent that Russia was able to make serious moves toward the market in the early years of transition, it was in part because pretense was concentrated on the security imperative. Once the possibility of continued pretense vis-à-vis the security imperative was eliminated, Russia had to shift the pretense to either democracy or the market economy. The price of preserving real freedom was a halt to serious efforts to create a true market economy.

The Way Out

Russia's fundamental dilemma is the discrepancy between its security needs and its economic capacity. If that discrepancy is not eliminated but merely covered up, Russia is likely to proceed in a much less benign direction than is now the case. With security imperatives pressing ever more heavily on a steadily decreasing economic capacity, the options available to Russian leaders will not be attractive. Given that the security imperative must be met, a resort might be made to heavier dependence on nuclear weapons, which would reduce the costs of meeting security needs. However, as the example of nuclear weapons makes clear, cheaper tools and methods for maintaining national security are often more dangerous.

An alternative reaction to an ever-shrinking resource base might be to end the pretense with regard to the economy. As the economy shrinks, it will be ever more difficult for the Russian state to extract resources through pretense and through the voluntary contributions of value-producers induced to contribute so that they can continue to benefit from good leakage. At that point, the security imperative will come into conflict with the goals of a market economy and democracy. It is hard to see how a return to a centrally planned economy could be accomplished without the abandonment of democracy.

Two things are required to avert that scenario: (1) Russia's security needs have to be lowered; and (2) its economic wealth must be increased. And these two goals must be accomplished in that order: Russians will never be able to abandon the pretense of the virtual economy in favor of a true, transparent market economy until they can be certain that their national survival is not at risk.

Notes

We are grateful to the other contributing authors to this volume for their comments on early drafts of this chapter. The chapter also benefited greatly from our extensive discussions with Bruce Blair, Richard Ericson, Vijay Krishna, and John Steinbrunner.

1. See, for example, the work of Dewatripont and Roland (1995) and Stiglitz (1999).

2. Political reasons were at least as important. But the misunderstanding of enterprise behavior altered the compromises that reformers were willing to make. A crucial role also

was played by the international security environment, as discussed below, in the section subheaded "The Impossible Trinity."

3. It is important to note that activities can temporarily appear to be value-destroying because of a decline in demand—for example, during a strong recession. Our concern here, however, is with activities that have been value-destroying in the longer term. For a fuller analysis of value destruction, see Gaddy and Ickes (forthcoming).

4. To assess whether value is being created or destroyed, one must consider the crucial factor of market prices: The same configuration of activities can produce value at one set of prices and destroy it at others. The Soviet economic system, under which prices were set by central government planning offices, separated domestic prices from the world market. Given Soviet prices, which placed a high premium on defense output, economic activity produced value. Only in comparison with outside opportunities for using the same resources does the phenomenon of value destruction come into play.

5. See Ericson (1997) for a discussion of calculation of national income in the Soviet economy, and of the implications of pricing rules on the measurement of sectoral income.

6. See Ericson (1997) for an analysis of the implications of arbitrary pricing for the apparent and actual production of value added in the Soviet economy. Ericson (1988) was the first study to formalize the dual nature of the Soviet economy in terms of priority (military) and nonpriority sectors.

7. It is perhaps more accurate to say that the end-users in the Soviet regime—the Communist party—placed a high value on the output of the defense sector, and that with the end of the regime, the value of defense production shrank dramatically.

8. This point was emphasized in Bosworth and Ofer (1995).

9. This confusion of nonviability with failed reform is exacerbated by the reform-induced recession common even among successfully marketizing economies.

10. This fact becomes apparent when sectoral output for the Soviet period is measured at world prices. Consider, for example, the contribution to industrial output from electrical energy, fuel, and forestry and timber products. In 1991, at Soviet prices, these sectors contributed 17.1 percent of total output. At world prices, however, these sectors amounted to 51.6 percent of total output! See OECD, *Russian Economic Survey* (1995), chapter 1.

11. This process of inducing the owners of assets to contribute value relates to the notion of "good leakage," discussed in Gaddy and Ickes ("To Restructure..."1998).

12. A related aspect of marketizing reforms has been the bargain between reformers and enterprises: Become transparent, and the cost of borrowing will be reduced. Because credit is more likely to flow to enterprises that have more transparent books, and because firms in countries undergoing economic transition suffer from credit constraints, there should be great incentive to clean up the books so as to attract credit. Of course, this holds true only if credit is actually available, as discussed below.

13. This is clearly a popular strategy employed by many Russian enterprises.

14. The soft-budget constraint of a Soviet-type enterprise (Kornai 1992) involved *ex post* subsidies. During marketization, soft-budget constraints often have been transformed into tax arrears and arrears to other enterprises.

15. The image suggested is that of vaccination, during which minute amounts of a virus are introduced into the bloodstream in order to trigger the immune system's production of antibodies. The rationale for hardening budget constraints was that the organism, if appropriately stressed, could be induced to restructure its behavior in order to increase its long-run viability.

16. The notion of market distance is discussed at length in Gaddy and Ickes (1998).

17. Let μ_i be i's share of GDP (or employment); then $\Omega = \int_i (d_i \, \mu_i) \, d_i$ is a measure of the average distance of the economy from the market—the initial gap that must be overcome in transition. Under the initial conditions in Russia, [Oomega] was larger than in other marketizing economies.

18. It is important to note that relational capital contributes to production. Hence, investing in relations is *not* the same as rent-seeking.

19. Note that the position of the *VC* line will depend on how open the economy is. Enterprises that would be unviable (for given *d*) in an open economy may be viable if the economy is autarkic.

20. As *d* increases, we may further suppose that the minimum *r* necessary for survival increases at an increasing rate.

21. Enterprise decisionmaking to reduce distance and invest in relations is analyzed in Gaddy and Ickes (1998).

22. See Ledeneva (1998).

23. This was articulated clearly by several key architects of Russian privatization. See, for example, Boycko, Shleifer, and Vishny (1996, 65): "In our view, controlling managers is not nearly as important as controlling politicians, since managers' interests are generally much closer to economic efficiency than those of the politicians."

24. In practice, the boundary is rarely so sharp. *See Gaddy and Ickes ("To Restructure . . . ," 1998)* for a discussion of *Igor's* rules for successful enterprise management in Russia.

25. That argument has been made quite often recently, most notably in Stiglitz (1999).

26. This argument is developed further in Gaddy and Ickes (forthcoming), using the concept of impermissibility.

27. In fighting TB it is crucial to follow a multiple-drug regimen, because the virus mutates so dramatically that a unitary drug regimen is ineffective.

28. This difference has been explored in various contexts by Boyd (1997) and Young (1998).

29. Young (1998) has shown that if agents interact in sufficiently small, close-knit groups, then the length of the period within which the evolutionary process can be expected to approach its asymptotic distribution is independent of the number of agents or of the initial state.

30. See Blasi, Kroumova, and Kruse (1997, 176–181) for a discussion of the effects of corporate governance problems on the attraction of investment. This issue also was recently taken up by Stiglitz (1999).

31. This may not be a valid generalization in all cases, as invisible costs may be associated with the use of cash. For example, cash payments may attract the attention of criminals, who will assume that cash is regularly kept on the premises occupied by enterprises remitting or receiving payment in cash. Likewise, barter may carry certain tax advantages. In addition, an enterprise that signals that it has cash on hand may find it harder to delay wage payments to workers. For further discussion, see Gaddy and Ickes (1998).

32. For an analysis of Gazprom, for example, see the report by Deutsche Bank, "Gazprom: Show Me the Money," September 29, 1999.

33. For a further analysis of the concept of shrinkage, see Gaddy and Ickes (forthcoming, chapter 7).

34. Gaddy and Ickes (forthcoming, chapter 7) provide a concrete example of such an enterprise: Kvarts, a former television manufacturer in Omsk, which now produces potatoes.

35. See Ericson and Ickes (forthcoming) for an analysis of the virtual economy trap. In that model, even enterprises that have positive expected returns from restructuring choose not to follow through with it, because the costs of leaving the virtual economy outweigh the benefits.

36. It is as if the *VC* line in Figure 6.1 is shifting upward over time.

37. Just as in natural history, changes in the macro environment (such as climatic changes) altered the course of evolution (led to the extinction of dinosaurs).

38. See Gaddy and Ickes (forthcoming, chapter 9) for a more extensive discussion and analysis.

39. This expression was first used by Robert Mundell to describe an economic policy that was aimed at simultaneously achieving a fixed exchange rate, an independent monetary policy, and a regime of capital mobility.

40. We assume that this is an unprecedented event, and another aspect of Russia's unfortunate situation of losing the peace rather than the war.

41. This analysis underscores how different Russia's situation was in comparison to that of Poland or even China—neither of which had Russia's security needs. Poland, in fact, had its security needs lessened due to the dismantling of the Warsaw Pact and NATO expansion. China does not have the problem of insecure borders that plagues Russia. Russia is unique in its mismatch between economic capacity and national security demands. An excessive defense burden helped destroy the Soviet economy. The new Russia, economically weaker than its predecessor, could not possibly sustain an even greater defense burden than that borne by the USSR.

References

Blasi, Joseph R., Maya Kroumova, and Douglas Kruse. *Kremlin Capitalism: Privatizing the Russian Economy.* Ithaca, N.Y., 1997.

Bosworth, B., and G. Ofer. *Reforming Planned Economies in an Integrating World Economy.* Washington, D.C., 1995.

Boycko, Maxim, Andrei Shleifer, and Robert Vishny. *Privatizing Russia.* Cambridge, Mass., 1996.

Boyd, R. "Population Structure, Equilibrium Selection and the Evolution of Norms." To be published in proceedings volume for conference on *Economics and Evolution* held at the International School for Economic Research, University of Siena. Ugo Pagano, ed ., Cambridge University Press, U.K., June 1997.

Commander, Simon, and Christian Mumssen. "Understanding Barter in Russia." In Paul Seabright, ed., *The Vanishing Rouble.* Cambridge, U.K., forthcoming.

Dewatripont, M., and G. Roland. "The Design of Reform Packages under Uncertainty," *American Economic Review,* 85(5), December 1995.

Ericson, R. E. "Priority, Duality, and Penetration in the Soviet Command Economy." *RAND Note N–2643-NA.* Santa Monica, Calif., 1988.

_____. "The Structural Barrier to Transition: A Note on Input-Output Tables of Centrally Planned Economies." Columbia University Discussion Paper no. 9596–31, revised. New York, March 1997.

_____. "Comment on an Accounting Model of Russia's Virtual Economy," *Post-Soviet Geography and Economics,* 40(2), March 1999: 103–109.

Ericson, R. E., and Barry W. Ickes. "An Equilibrium Model of the Virtual Economy," *Review of Economic Design,* vol. 6, forthcoming.

Gaddy, Clifford, and Barry W. Ickes. "To Restructure or Not to Restructure: Informal Activities and Enterprise Behavior in Transition." Working paper, William Davidson Institute, Ann Arbor, Mich., May 1998.

_____. "Russia's Virtual Economy," *Foreign Affairs,* 77(5) September-October, 1998.

_____. "A Simple Four-Sector Model of Russia's Virtual Economy," *Post-Soviet Geography and Economics,* 40(2), March 1999: 79–97.

_____. *Russia's Virtual Economy.* Washington, D.C., forthcoming.

Guriev, Sergei, and Barry W. Ickes. "Barter in Russia." In Paul Seabright, ed., *The Vanishing Rouble.* Cambridge, U.K., forthcoming.

Kornai, Janos. *The Socialist Economy.* Princeton, 1992.

Ledeneva, Alena V. *Russia's Economy of Favours.* Cambridge, U.K., 1998.

Organization for Economic Cooperation and Development (OECD). *Russian Economic Survey.* Paris, 1995.

Stiglitz, Joseph E. "Whither Reform: Ten Years of the Transition." In *Annual Bank Conference on Development Economics.* Washington, D.C., 1999.

Young, Peyton. "Diffusion in Social Networks." Johns Hopkins University working paper. Baltimore, Md., 1998.

7

Russia in the Information Age

Emma Kiselyova
Manuel Castells
University of California, Berkeley

Postcommunist Russia is managing four simultaneous transitions: from totalitarianism to democracy; from a command economy to a market economy; from "democratic centralism" to democratic federalism; and from the industrial era to the information age. In this chapter we have focused on the fourth dimension of the Russian transition, which in our view constitutes a fundamental component of Russia's evolution in the twenty-first century.[1] The ability of the new Russia to perform better than its Soviet predecessor under the new technological paradigm will condition the wealth, power, and social development of Russia in the twenty-first century, which in turn will shape the country's relationship to the world at large.

Information Technology Industries in Russia:
Crisis and Restructuring

For a major industrial producer like Soviet Russia, the most direct path of transition to the information age would have been the upgrading of its information technology industries and the development of domestic industrial producers of semiconductors, computers, telecommunications equipment, and consumer electronics. But the electronics industry in Russia lagged far behind the technological level of the electronics industry in the United States, Europe, or East Asia in the 1980s, and in the first half of the 1990s it collapsed. However, between 1995 and 2000, incipient signs of recovery appeared in particular segments of information technology markets. Interestingly, although the industrial crisis primarily affected the defense-oriented industries, the recent rebirth of a Russian electronics industry has been driven by demand from business firms and affluent consumers.

The root of the problem is the backwardness of the Soviet Union's information technology industries. A study of microelectronics factories in Zelenograd (a city near Moscow, at the heart of the Soviet equivalent to California's Silicon Valley) conducted by Castells from 1991 to 1993 revealed a lack of sophistication in products and processes, despite the high quality of scientists and engineers.[2] This retardation in development extended to the low end of the electronics industry, consumer electronics, where products could not match international standards. In 1991, the final year of the Soviet Union's existence, Russia exported some 80,200 television sets with a total value of U.S.$5.6 million, and imported 460,000 sets with a total value of U.S.$300 million. The same year, Russia exported only 800 videocassette recorders (VCRs), and imported 416,000 VCRs.[3]

The reasons for the lag in Soviet development of information technologies lay deep in the structure of the Soviet system. They include the complete domination of the industry by military requirements; the subsequent isolation of the Soviet industry from technological supplies and exchanges with the rest of the world; and the constraints on diffusion of technological knowledge and information in civilian industry and in society. As a result of this technological backwardness, when Russian military markets began to shrink in the 1990s, technological obsolescence prevented Russian microelectronics and computer firms from competing with foreign companies, both abroad and in the domestic market. The total value of chip production in Russia declined from a relatively low U.S.$1.5 billion in 1989 to an incredible $385 million in 1995. The most advanced segments of the industry were devastated: Out of 140 microelectronics manufacturers existing in 1990, 130 had closed down by 1995. For the remaining 10 firms, manufacturing costs increased by 4,000 percent. These companies and several remaining telecommunications equipment producers were barely surviving in the mid-1990s as subcontractors for low-technology Asian companies, producing toys and digital watches.

When in 1996 Castells interviewed a second time the engineers of the leading microelectronics company that he had studied in Zelenograd in 1992, they reported that 50 percent of their factory was producing shampoo for the Russian market. One of the most technologically advanced companies still in the microelectronics business in Zelenograd, Mikron, became a joint venture with Hua Ko Electronics, a Hong Kong firm that bought 50 percent of Mikron's shares for U.S.$18 million. Indeed, the most profitable business in Zelenograd became the sale of assets and shares to foreign investors. But there were few takers. In 1997, the Russian government, realizing the strategic importance of salvaging the microelectronics industry, announced priority credit lines for Russian microelectronics companies engaging in partnerships with foreign firms that were willing and able to transfer advanced production technology. Three Zelenograd semiconductor firms were targeted for development. Two of them, Mikron and Angstrem, claimed annual sales increases from 1994 to 1997; but the largest part of their production consisted of 4- by 6-inch wafers at the lower end of productivity and quality. Angstrem, which was studied by Castells in 1992 and 1993, had been the star of Soviet microelectronics. It was slated to begin production of 8-inch wafers and 0.5-micron chips; but lack of funding and the impossibility of accessing new technology blocked these plans. In 1997, Angstrem finally built the 55,000-square-foot "clean room" that its managers had dreamed of in 1993. They had the room at last, but no equipment, since the price for an up-to-date manufacturing line had gone up to about U.S.$300 million. Having spent $120 million on this expansion—most of it government funding—Angstrem was still seeking an additional $200 million from potential foreign partners. Angstrem also had ambitions of building an even more advanced facility, capable of achieving a line width of 0.35 micron, at a cost of $800 million in additional equipment—an obviously unreachable dream.

In another effort to revive Zelenograd, the government provided a credit guaranty for $42.5 million to Elma, a semiconductor materials firm in Zelenograd, to create a facility capable of producing an 8-inch wafer. However, both the technology and the capital had to come from foreign firms. With no Western partners in sight for such an ambitious project, these plans had to be shelved. Zelenograd's firms were condemned to technological obsolescence in an extraordinarily competitive, global market.[4] Looking for a revival of the strategically crucial microelectronics industry, the Russian government in June 1997 designated Zelenograd as a special economic zone, dedicated to high-tech investment. The zone offered foreign firms a customs-free warehouse for goods to be reexported, and a substantial tax reduction. Yet there were no significant takers. Intel in 1997 sold $370 million worth of products in Russia, where its sales had been increasing annually by 50 percent. Yet it preferred to serve the Russian market from other locations rather than risk investment in local production facilities.[5]

The reluctance of foreign companies to invest in Zelenograd, or in Russia for that matter, is best explained by the following example, which has become symbolic of the fate of foreign investment in Russian electronics: the rise and fall of an IBM PC factory in Zelenograd. In 1993, IBM linked up with Kvant, a former military electronics enterprise, to produce 40,000 PCs per month for the Russian market. Under an agreement with the Russian government, IBM-Kvant would be exempted from taxes on imported components. This exemption was essential precisely because there was no reliable supplier of components in Russia. IBM-Kvant was a commercial success. According to business sources, in 1995, Russians bought close to 1 million PCs, 40 percent of which were supplied by IBM. IBM-Kvant employed 1,000 workers, and the value of its output was estimated at around $960 million per year. In 1994, the Russian parliament had approved a law eliminating the tax exemption on imported components (for a value of about 8.5 percent of the cost of the finished product). This law put IBM at a competitive disadvantage with the Russian trading companies that were importing finished PCs, mainly from China and Southeast Asia, that continued to be tax exempt. This was precisely the intent of the law's drafters in the Duma, who were swayed by a powerful lobby of import/export companies. On February 27, 1996,

IBM stopped assembling PCs in Zelenograd. Most of the workers were idled, and the plant was converted into a repair and maintenance shop for IBM PCs imported into Russia. For all practical purposes, PC production stopped. As for Kvant, it diversified its activity in order to survive. In 1997, for instance, one particular division of the company was working in the following areas: chip design for a Western firm; development of a parallel computer system for a domestic customer; prototyping image processing units; and conducting market research.

Lacking technology, equipment, supplies, and know-how, Russian microelectronics industries often became low-level subsidiaries of low-level Asian producers, or in the best cases, subcontractors of specific tasks for Western firms. The exception was a small number of firms that continued to work for the Russian defense ministry, using imported components and foreign technology (either licensed or copied through reverse engineering). The defense ministry was rightly worried about Russian technological dependence on Western suppliers. However, its emphasis on keeping defense electronic firms in operation and in isolation from the international market has reproduced the mistake of the Soviet era, undermining these firms' competitive capacity and locking them into obsolete technologies. Malcolm Hill, evaluating the interaction between electronics firms and the Russian military, concluded that "in some instances, the influence of the military sector has increased rather than diminished in the electronics industry, as attempts to diversify away from defense production have met with a number of difficulties related to market competitiveness for civilian products."[6] Because this relative isolation makes many Russian microelectronics products unfit for advanced electronic warfare, the Russian military ends up seeking an increasing proportion of its supplies on the international market, thus reducing market share for the Russian suppliers after locking them into a backward, homegrown technology for security reasons.

The crisis in microelectronics was echoed in the advanced computers industry. After reviewing the evidence on the state of high-performance computing in Russia in 1997, P. Wolcott and M. N. Dorojevets concluded, "As the waves of reform have washed over Russia, established Soviet industries, like high-performance computing, have been nearly swept away."[7]

The demise of civilian industries of microelectronics, advanced computers, and telecommunications manufacturing industries has had far-reaching consequences for Russia. First, it has left the new Russian economy entirely dependent on imports for its advanced technological infrastructure. For example, imports of electronic components had grown from nothing in 1990 to about 40 percent of the total Russian components market in 1997 (Analog Devices was making major inroads in supplying Russian companies, by agreement with the Russian distributor Argussoft).[8] Second, it has eliminated the possibility of industrial know-how that could make possible the existence of Russian firms as part of an electronic producers network. The dependence of Russia, still a nuclear superpower, on foreign supplies and know-how in advanced electronics and communications technology has limited its defense capabilities to existing nuclear weapons, preventing Russia from again becoming a credible, autonomous power in conventional warfare.

However, there are promising signs that all is not yet lost: Although Russia's military- and industry-oriented production has been devastated during the transition period, its PC and software industry is flourishing, driven by demand from business people and professionals.[9] According to the International Data Corporation (IDC), PC purchases in Russia in 1996 exceeded the previous year's level by 20 percent, and in 1997, by an additional 33 percent; and in 1997, 1.4 million personal computers were sold in Russia, valued at a total of U.S.$1.9 billion. Before the economic crisis of August 1998, purchases of PCs were growing at an annual rate of about 10 percent. The majority of buyers were first-time users engaged in private industry or in the professions, and government agencies. It was projected that in 2000 Russia would become the fourth-largest PC market in Europe.

Most significantly, local PC makers account for 71 percent of the Russian market, and most of these firms are new: There were about 1,500 PC makers in Russia in 1998. Although foreign firms, led by Hewlett Packard and Compaq, also maintain a strong presence in the Russian marketplace, local brands are much more competitive because of their considerably lower prices and despite their relatively deficient customer service. It should be noted that Russian PC makers, like their counterparts in western Europe, are primarily assemblers of low-cost electronic components produced in Asia. In August 1998, when the Russian economy crashed, PC sales plummeted, and they still had not recovered in March 1999. Nonetheless, a report prepared by International Data Corporation in September 1998 identified considerable growth potential in Russian computer markets, evidenced by the previous sustained level of demand.

Simultaneously with the growth of the PC industry, a number of small software companies have sprung up in Russia. The scientific and technical potential of universities, research institutions, and state enterprises has found its way into this new industry. Entrepreneurs sometimes pursue unorthodox paths, appropriating available software and reconfiguring it to suit customers' needs. Indeed, software piracy is pervasive in Russia. During his visit to Russia in 1997, Bill Gates urged the Russian government to curb the growing market for pirated software, which was cutting into Microsoft's sales in Russia—an indirect tribute to the skills of Russian programmers. In August 1999, the Ministry of the Interior estimated that 85 percent of software programs on the Russian market had been pirated, with total sales of about U.S.$15 million—indicating a fivefold increase in just two years.[10]

However, some of the best software talent is leaving Russia for better opportunities abroad. Many programmers have migrated to the United States to work (a few of them on a green card but most on temporary visas), attracted by headhunters such as Alternative Technology Resources, which supplies companies in the United States with programmers on two-year work contracts. Other companies, such as Sun Microsystems, are setting up offshore development centers in third countries, staffed by engineers from Russia and elsewhere, working on new products for the company via on-line, joint engineering.[11] In a word, Russians are indeed entering the information age— not in continuity with the obsolete, military-oriented electronics industry of the Soviet era but with their bare brains, fueling both local consumption and global production.

The Security Implications of Russia's Technological Lag in Electronics

In the twenty-first century, defense capabilities are largely dependent on electronic technologies. The current Russian electronics industry seems incapable of providing the equipment needed to modernize the Russian military.

Russia does have access to microelectronics and computer equipment on the international market, but it also faces major obstacles in importing such equipment. The United States—the only potential supplier of cutting-edge information technology, other than Japan—has imposed export controls on technologies with potential for military use. The problems encountered by Convex and IBM in attempting to export high-performance computers to Russia in 1995 and 1996 are instructive. Although Russia claimed that it was purchasing the computers in compliance with the Comprehensive Test Ban treaty—that is, for "civilian uses," including safety control in Russia's nuclear laboratories—the U.S. government determined that there was a danger of possible military use, and revoked the export licenses. Russia nonetheless managed to obtain a number of powerful, high-performance computers that it could not produce domestically.[12]

But although Russia can in some cases evade export controls, it still faces an expensive, difficult, and protracted struggle to access technology by this route, always remaining a step (or several steps) behind the U.S. military. The fundamental obstacles to technological modernization remain the dismantlement of the Soviet scientific establishment and the lack of fiscal resources either to update military procurements or to invest in defense-oriented R&D, due to the ongoing national economic crisis. According to Sharon Leiter, a Rand Corporation expert on Russian defense science, the number of scientists in Russia declined by one-third from 1990 to 1993, and 70 percent of Russian mathematical researchers left the country. The defense science budget suffered a substantial decline, reaching the same low level as the civilian science budget: In 1997, both were officially set at about U.S.$3 billion (actual spending may have been even lower). In Leiter's assessment: "This loss is having a negative impact on basic theoretical, applied, and defense science. Until the federal government acts decisively to put into place the appropriate mechanisms for promoting development of the innovative R&D sector, the continuing shrinkage of the Russian science and technology base will accelerate."[13] The Russian military will be increasingly dependent on foreign technology. A full-fledged modernization of the armed forces seems financially out of reach for Russia in the near term. According to a special report published in 1998 by the journal *Vlast'*, defense investment in technology, advanced military equipment, and R&D decreased by a factor of 14 from 1990 to 1995. To redress the technological obsolescence of the Russian armed forces as of 1998 would take an overall investment in the vicinity of U.S.$30 billion, a sum that is simply not available to the Russian government.[14]

One of the international security implications of this technological lag in the Russian military is a dramatic weakening of the fighting capability of Russia's conventional forces. This could be an ominous development for the world's security. NATO's attack on Yugoslavia in 1999 prompted considerable fear and hostility in Russia, both in the citizenry and in the political leadership: most Russians felt threatened. A Cold War wind started to blow again, with the Russian military feeling that its weakness could lead to further humiliation and even to a possible attack on Russia. Minister of Defense Igor Sergeev, on April 26, 1999, declared that the government was planning to use all available resources to extend the life span of Soviet military equipment, including the nuclear arsenal, and to upgrade it as much as possible. On April 29, Yeltsin signed a series of decrees instructing the armed forces to step up the readiness of both tactical and strategic nuclear weapons. Evidently this renewed emphasis on nuclear deterrence was due to the perception among the Russian leadership that the country would be at a technological disadvantage in fighting a limited, conventional war, and to the fact that Russia feels threatened and vulnerable after the war in Yugoslavia. In this military logic, the distance between a possible conventional armed confrontation involving Russia and a possible nuclear exchange has dramatically decreased, precisely because Russia must resort to an old and devastating technology (nuclear weaponry) to compensate for its handicap in new, information technology–based armament.

At an academic meeting in May 1999, our assumption that NATO's bombings would incite Russia's military to shift from outdated conventional armament to a defense based on nuclear weapons was met with strong criticism from experts on Russia. Nevertheless, in late June 1999, Russia carried out a military exercise including simulated nuclear strikes. According to the script, Russia had come under attack by a Western "force" using nonnuclear weapons. At first Russia also tried to limit its attack to conventional forces; but when these defenses proved ineffective, the nuclear arsenal was brought into action. In the words of Defense Minister Sergeev, "The exercise tested one of the provisions of Russia's military doctrine concerning a possible use of nuclear weapons when all other measures are exhausted."[15]

Russian Telecommunications:
Information Superhighway or Private Driveways?

Telecommunications and information systems are the backbone of the computer networks that constitute the infrastructure of the information age. Studies by Diane Doucette, by Robert Campbell, and by Rafal Rohozinski have provided conclusive evidence of the retardation of Soviet and post-Soviet Russian telecommunications, as a result of Soviet policies.[16] Official international statistics for 1994 put the number of telephone lines per thousand persons in Russia at 162, in contrast to 602 for the United States and 371 for Spain. According to Russian official statistics, in 1996, only 48.7 percent of urban households and 19.7 percent of rural households had access to a private telephone. In addition, there was considerable regional disparity in the access to telephone service: 76.9 percent of urban households in northwestern Russia had access to a telephone, as compared with 64.5 percent in central Russia, 42.1 percent in western Siberia, and 32.2 percent in eastern Siberia.

In 1991, independent Russia inherited the fragmented telecommunications structure of the Soviet Union. That year, only 55 percent of telephones were connected to the Public Telephone Network. The rest belonged to a variety of "branch systems" dependent on government ministries and industrial enterprises or specific to the special, military-related telecommunications network. This fragmentation continued and even intensified during the postcommunist era, as many banks, financial institutions, trading groups, corporate services, and business conglomerates created their own satellite-based links. As the various systems were privatized in a disorderly fashion, the results have been lack of coordination, uneven quality of service, and absence of an integrated telecommunications grid providing a basis for universal access. Lack of investment, along with the resultant delay in technological upgrading of the private infrastructure, also contributed to an increasing gap between public service and private networks, and between residential telephony and business-related telephony. In 1996, more than 9 million customers were awaiting installation. An Economist Intelligence Unit report estimated in 1997 that to meet the demand for new lines as well as to replace obsolete ones, 2 million lines would have to be installed every year until 2005. According to the Russian Ministry of Communications, the gradual upgrading of the nation's telecommunications infrastructure to meet international standards, including the installation of a digital telecommunications network— scheduled to take place between 1995 and 2005—would cost about U.S.$40 billion.[17] Although foreign investment in Russian telecommunications doubled in the 1990s, it did not reach even $500 million in 1995, and it was substantially reduced after the 1998 economic crisis. And foreign investment is crucial, as evidenced by the fact that imported digital systems were in use by 90 percent of new telephone exchanges in Russia in 1998.[18]

In addition to the Ministry of Communications, several semiprivate companies created during privatization currently participate in the telecommunications market. Rostelekom has primary control over long-distance telephony and international communication, despite its deteriorating service and high prices. Svyazinvest, the large national holding company for Russian local carriers, controls local communications in most areas. In July 1997 (over the objections of the Duma and of the Federal Service for Export Controls), it was partially privatized: 25 percent of its stock was sold, for U.S.$1.875 billion, to Mustcom, a consortium including Oneximbank, Deutsche Morgan, and George Soros's Quantum Fund. On the whole, foreign investment in Russian telecommunications is hindered by a complex regulatory environment, which makes returns highly unpredictable. Many markets are monopolized by Russia's largest telecommunications companies.[19]

One area is wide open to foreign investment and technology: wireless, cellular, and satellite-based telecommunications. Russian authorities began to issue GSM licenses in 1996, and by the end of 1996 they had licensed 40 regions for GSM.[20] Foreign companies seemed interested in entering the cellular telephony market in Russia. The dominant player in this field is Cellular Vision of Russia, a joint venture of the American company Cellular Vision, Svyazinvest, and the Russian government. Fujitsu is installing wireless digital microwave facilities in the Western Urals, and Rostelekom/Global Star is launching a joint venture company (Globaltel) to provide satellite services by 2002. In contrast with the lagging traditional telecommunications infrastructure, the cellular market in Russia was growing at an accelerated pace by the end of the 1990s, in spite of the high price of a cellular phone (in 1997, the equivalent of U.S.$2,500). It was estimated that the number of cellular phones in service would approach 1 million in the early years of the new century, up from 6,000 in 1992. Although only a small fraction of the population uses cellular communications, these users may represent the dynamic, entrepreneurial core of the new market economy. However, the problem is that there is as yet no nationwide, integrated cellular network. Given the distances between nodes in Russia's vast territory, the variety of codes, and the fragmentation of markets licensed to various companies, the technical and business problems of integration are staggering.[21] Therefore, the development of cellular telephony is in fact increasing the social and territorial fragmentation of the telecommunications infrastructure.

Satellite-based telecommunications may be the most important development in Russian communications, as it has facilitated the growth of specialized networks that cater to the strategically important functions in business and government. Russia began actively to seek foreign participation in satellite telecommunications as early as 1990, when the Institute of Automated Systems—the leader in the design of packet switched networks in the former Soviet Union—and the American company San Francisco/Moscow Teleport established the first joint American-Soviet venture, SOVAM Teleport, to provide international telecommunication services using computer networks.[22] By 1997, several semiprivate companies were using satellite communications and digital technology to link Russia and its regions internationally, particularly focusing on communications for financial transactions.[23] On November 22, 1998, Russia's first commercial satellite, a Bonum-1, modeled on the Hughes HS-376HP, was launched from Cape Canaveral. With a 50-channel capacity, the satellite is being used for direct television broadcast service and for data transmission. Financing came from Russian financial institutions, Chase Manhattan Corporation, and the U.S. Export-Import Bank.[24] The Russian oligopolistic media sector, controlled by various financial groups, has also entered the telecommunications field to ensure autonomous broadcasting capability.[25]

Connectivity in Russia is geographically specific, with the greatest access traditionally having been provided in the northwestern and central regions. For example, a local fiber-optic network was developed in Moscow as early as 1994. Using mostly Russian equipment, the Prospective Technologies Agency planned eventually to provide the whole Moscow area with a broadband communications network.[26] Satellite communications are targeted on Moscow, St. Petersburg, and the major regional nodes. Access to international connections is often provided via private, satellite-based channels.

Connectivity is also functionally specific: Banks and financial institutions have focused on their global connectivity since the early 1990s. Needing access to global networks of information and financial exchange, and unable to wait for an improvement in Russian telecommunications infrastructure, Russia's financial institutions set up their own systems, focusing first on improving their internal networking capabilities. One early, critical investment was in wide area networking technology designed for both internal and external communications. The high cost of this technology caused small banks and local banks gradually to fall by the wayside and prompted the consolidation of larger banks, because only large financial corporations had the necessary resources to invest in advanced communication technology.[27] The World Bank and the European Bank for Reconstruction and Development participated in this selective development of telecommunications and information systems with an information technology scheme established in 1996 under the Financial Institutions Development Program that was intended to improve information technology and training for 40 Russian banks and to promote electronic links between them and their Western partners.[28] The U.S. government adopted a similar strategy, supporting the linkage of new American business centers in major regional nodes of Russia to global financial networks.[29]

In sum, the weak development of telecommunications and information systems in Russia goes hand in hand with the development of specialized, satellite-based connections linking regional nodes with Moscow, and Moscow with the world. Together, these two trends have produced a newly networked economic geography that reflects the uneven development of the information society.

The Development and Structure of the Russian Net[30]

The origins of the Russian Net illustrate the meaningful, contradictory relationship between the Soviet system and the information society. State-sponsored attempts to build computer networks in the 1980s (e.g., Akademset and IASnet) failed, largely due to lack of interest on the part of potential users, scientists, and managers, many of whom feared the networks would facilitate a tightening of bureaucratic control over their activities. A number of scientists and engineers used research facilities to start independent networks of their own design. Out of these grassroots efforts the current Russian Net eventually emerged.[31]

RELCOM/DEMOS[32] was the earliest of these computer networks, and today it is among the largest. It was created in Moscow in 1990, through a collaboration between researchers from the Kurchatov Institute of Atomic Energy and the DEMOS Lab of Moscow State University, where a group of physicists were developing a Russian version of UNIX. By the end of 1991, RELCOM/DEMOS had over 20,000 users in more than 120 cities. RELCOM (not the Internet) had become synonymous with the Russian Net for the Russian media and remained so until 1996. It has always been a very decentralized network, with different companies and institutions exchanging E-mail with Moscow's RELCOM node, each node and end user paying on a per byte basis for information sent and received. RELCOM has been a quasi-commercial network since its beginning. In 1992, RELCOM and DEMOS split, and SP-DEMOS became purely commercial. AO-RELCOM became the first Russian hybrid ISP, being operated by the Kurchatov Institute but at the same time a publicly traded company. So, as Rohozinski has observed, AO-RELCOM was somewhat protected from the vagaries of the market during its developmental stage.

Alongside the various commercial networks established in Russia in the 1990s were a number of educational and scientific networks aimed at linking domestic universities and research institutions and providing a channel for their communication with foreign academic institutions. One of these networks was the Freenet. Founded by the Zelinsky Institute of Organic Chemistry in 1991, the Freenet links universities and research institutes, serving about 350 academic institutions. Other research-oriented networks include REDLINE, created in 1994 by the Ministry of Education and the trade union of workers in education and science, and funded by the U.S. Agency for International Development and the Eurasia Foundation; RELARN, created in 1993 under an agreement between the Ministry of Defense and the Russian Academy of Sciences, the Kurchatov Institute, and a number of other leading research institutes; RIPN, founded in 1992 by the Committee on Higher Education and the Kurchatov Institute; RUNNet, started in 1994 under the program "Universities of Russia"; and UNICOR (University Networks of Knowledge), set up in 1992 by the State Committee on Higher Education.[33] In the late 1990s, the Russian Net has become a highly developed and diversified structure.

The national infrastructure of computer networks based on TCP/IP protocols (IP networks) includes backbone channels for traffic exchange within the country as well as channels for connection with foreign Internet networks. The picture is diverse, and lines between categories are sometimes indistinct. For instance, regional providers may operate their own high-capacity international channels, or academic networks might use their capacity to provide commercial Internet services.

National networks include the following major commercial networks: Eunet/RELCOM, Glasnet, Global One Russia, Internet/Russia (formerly DEMOS), Portal, Rolnet JS RTC, Rostelecom, Sovam Teleport, and Teleport-TP. The main academic and research networks are RBNet, Freenet, MSUNet,

RELARN-IP, RSSI, RUHER/Radio-MSU, and RUNNet. Among these networks we should also mention the projects developed by the Open Society Institute (Soros Foundation).

There is also an alternative network, FIDONET. Rohozinski conducted an in-depth field study of the origins and diffusion of this special network, which was developed in the 1980s by a young American anarchist to serve as a global, non-commercial and noninstitutional computer network running parallel to the Internet. According to Rohozinski's field research, in 1996, Global FIDONET included 33,000 nodes in six zones. The Russian segment (FIDONET-7) in May 1998 included 4,469 linked nodes in 90 separate oblast-level networks, with up to 100,000 users. Rohozinski stated that the presence of FIDONET in Russia is considerable and growing.[34] However, our own on-line interviews in Novosibirsk (one of FIDONET's original nodes) do not confirm the current importance of this alternative network, which according to these reliable informants is primarily used by the very young and does not really concern most of the Internet population.

Internet Traffic Exchange Within Russia: IX Nodes

Cooperation among the major national and regional ISPs in organizing the rational exchange of IP traffic within the country was extremely important for Russia. Until 1996, all connections between the different Russian networks were realized via the global Internet. In other words, the user with access to one network could reach a server from another Russian network (even located in the same city!) only by surfing the global Net, using up the precious, limited capacity of external backbone channels. The resultant bottleneck was eased by the creation of IX (Internet exchange) nodes where different ISPs could allocate their backbone routers to allow peering with no inter-network channels and thus without additional costs. In 1999 there were two IP-traffic exchange nodes in the country: M9-IX in Moscow, and B-IX in St. Petersburg. The exchange is regulated by bilateral agreements and does not provide for multilateral connections. Only seven commercial and academic ISPs participated in the first Moscow exchange agreement, but more than 20 other companies had joined by early 1998.

Connection to the Global Internet

The capacity of Russian international telecommunications channels has grown quite rapidly—from about two Mbps in 1995 to 15 Mbps in 1996, and to 70 Mbps by early 1998.

In 1997, several companies operating on the national level began to establish their own international channels. The quality of IP service improved, and the channels were working at full capacity because of new subscribers. New channels added in 1997 included a connection to the MCI network (through Rostelecom)

**TABLE 7.1　International Connectivity of Russian Networks, 1998
(by ISP and Capacity)**

Moscow

Glasnet: BBNplanet (U.S.), 1 Mbps, MCI (U.S.), 2 Mbps
Global-One: 3 channels to U.S. and Europe, total 8 Mbps
Demos: MCI (U.S.), 6 Mbps
Comstar: Concert/Btnet (Great Britain), 2 Mbps
Macomnet: Teleglobe (Canada), 2 Mbps
Relcom: EUnet/ (Netherlands), 4 Mbps; EUnet (Finland), 2 Mbps; MCI (U.S.), 4 Mbps
Rosnet: BBNplanet (U.S.), 2 Mbps; MCI (U.S.), 2 Mbps
PTT-Teleport Moscow: MCI (U.S.), 2 Mbps; UUNET (U.S.), 2 Mbps
Sovam Teleport: 3 channels to U.S. and Europe, total 6 Mbps
Teleport TP: NyserNet (U.S.), 2 Mbps
Elvis-Telecom: Teleglobe (Canada), 2 Mbps
FREEnet: DTAG (Germany), 256 Kbps
MSUnet: MCI (U.S.), 512 Kbps
ORC/RAS net: DFN (Germany), 2 Mbps
Radio-MSU: DFN (Germany), to Hamburg, total about 2 Mbps
RSSI: NASA Internet (U.S.), 512 Kbps

St. Petersburg

RUNNet: NORDUnet (Finland), 2 Mbps; Teleglobe (Canada), 4 Mbps
WEBplus: Teleglobe (Canada), 2 Mbps
Metrocom: Teleglobe (Canada), 2 Mbit
NTO "Rusnet": Telecom Finland, 512 Kbps

SOURCE: Authors' compilation.

and to the network Teleglobe International, which was very active in the Russian telecommunications market in 1997. Table 7.1 shows the Russian networks' international channels as of late 1997 and early 1998.

One of the recent Internet communications technologies to reach Russia is DirectPC, developed by Hughes Network Systems. This Internet service system uses a regular channel (switched or leased) to request data from a client, and a satellite channel (up to 400 Kbps) to transmit requested data to another client PC by ISP.

In April 1998, the first Russian fast channel to the global Internet was put into operation by the Business Network, a powerful corporation uniting the resources of 6 Russian ISPs (including Rostelecom, RELCOM, and the Kurchatov Institute). By means of terrestrial fiber-optic cable with a bandwidth of 34 Mbps, this channel connects Moscow via St. Petersburg to Stockholm, and from there to the backbone of the UUNet, a leading international ISP. This project was aimed at correcting the bottleneck in Russian international electronic communications and thereby enhancing the developmental potential of the Russian networks.

Let us now examine some statistical estimates of the development of the Russian Net in the late 1990s. According to a 1998 report by the Russian Public Center for Information Technologies (ROCIT), by the end of 1998, there were in Russia between 150 and 200 national ISPs, and about 300 additional ISPs operating at the subnational level. Similar data for January 1999, collected and elaborated by Network Wizards, showed the Russian Net to be considerably smaller in absolute numbers than that in the United States, Taiwan, the Netherlands, and Finland. Even in per capita terms and in comparison with other, less developed countries, such as South Africa, the Russian Net came up short.[35] A special report published by *Ekonomika i zhizn'* (no. 73, April 1998: *Sibir'*) argues that although it lags behind in actual numbers, the Internet in Russia is growing at a pace similar to that in the United States. According to this source, the number of computers connected to the Net would have been at that date close to 200,000—twice as many as in winter 1997.

Another survey, conducted from October 5 to October 8, 1998, by Moscow University's Internet researcher, Alex Tutubalin, indicated that the financial crisis had not significantly slowed the growth of the Russian Net: The number of computers connected to the Internet in the *.su* domain had shrunk by about 40 percent since March 1998; but the total number of computers connected reached the figure of 238,887, including 16,1637 hosts with Intranet addresses.[36]

How pervasive is the use of computer networks in Russia? Debate rages around statistics on the demographics of the Russian Net. Yet an accurate statistical assessment is crucial to any assessment of Russia's integration into the Internet, which is the backbone of the global information age.

ROCIT has provided systematic, authoritative data in its annual report on the Russian Net for 1998. Based on its own surveys as well as on surveys by two of the leading polling firms in Russia, COMCON-2 and Gallup, ROCIT found that by the end of 1998 there were 180,000 Russian IP hosts in the *.ru* domain, and between 150 and 200 ISPs. About 250,000 users were paying for access to the Internet. Another 500,000 users had free access from their workplaces. About 600,000 users, including many in educational and research institutions, reported that they regularly used the Internet in their work.[37]

COMCON's survey, as reported by ROCIT, estimated a more widespread use of the Net. It reported 840,000 users in June 1998, of which 644,000 connected from their workplaces, and 268,000, from their homes. Net use had increased substantially, to a total of 1,081,000, in August 1998. Of this total, 852,000 had access from their workplaces, and 319,000, from their homes. Including all family members, it was estimated that there were about 600,000 home-based Internet users. Focusing on usage of the Net in higher education in Moscow, St. Petersburg, Yekaterinburg, and Omsk, the survey found that 40 percent of university staff and researchers and 30 percent of students had Internet access, but less than 50 percent of them used this access regularly.

A Gallup survey of Muscovites, conducted in September 1998, found 237,900 users visiting the Net daily, and 436,200 (or 6.2 percent of Moscow's adult population) visiting weekly. Usage on weekends was less frequent than on weekdays, emphasizing the predominantly work-related use of the Internet.

Combining and adjusting these data, the authors of ROCIT's 1998 report estimated a total of 1.5 million users, including E-mail users, and adding access from home, workplace, and educational institutions. Although these figures have been challenged by many Russian experts, they are relatively close to estimates provided by the international consulting firm IDC for June 15, 1999: The total number of Russia's Internet users was estimated to have increased from 384,000 in 1996 to 1.2 million in 1998—a threefold increase in less than three years.[38]

Tutubalin assessed the evolution of the Net between March 1998 and March 1999 by analyzing domains, web sites, and numbers of computers connected rather than end users. In this single year, domains increased by 97 percent; web servers increased by 86 percent in 11.5 months; and IP addresses increased by 40 percent in 10.5 months, indicating a trend toward smaller sites with fewer computers, linking up to the Net by themselves.[39] ROCIT's 1998 report shows an increasing commercialization of the Internet, as information services companies (80 percent of them self-financed) grew by 200 percent in 1998. Search engines such as Aport and Yandex, and Internet catalog providers such as AU and "1,000 Stars," experienced significant growth, with a total turnover of U.S.$6 million in commercial services. Internet advertising companies, such as Inter-Reklama and Russian Link Exchange, were also expanding their business. Private connection companies recorded a 1998 turnover of U.S.$5 million. Internet portals in Russia, as in the United States, seem to be the fastest-growing segment of the industry. Mergers are taking place, adding resources to the industry. The economic crisis of 1998 slowed the development of the Internet but did not affect the use of E-mail or the long-term prospects for Russian Internet growth. There is strong evidence that business firms and professionals are keeping their Internet use a priority.

Noncommercial Use of the Internet

Although Russia's regions lag considerably in the development of commercial Internet usage, they are benefitting from nonprofit foundations' and the government's efforts to set up a basic Internet infrastructure centered around universities, research centers, schools, and libraries. The most significant of these projects is one built around a contribution from the Open Society Institute using funds from the Soros Foundation. The Telecommunications/Internet Project is jointly funded and is being developed by the Russian federal government, local governments, and universities. It aims at establishing 33 university-based Internet centers around the country, with particular emphasis on the regions. By 1995, such centers had been founded in Moscow, Novosibirsk, and Yaroslavl. Their primary purpose has been to provide open access to Internet resources, thus encouraging the diffusion of information in areas such as culture, education, libraries, museums, health care, and human rights. The program also helped the development of Internet Training Centers. In 1998 there were 16 such centers operating in the country, from the Far East (Vladivostok) to the Northwest (Petrozavodsk).

One of the leading noncommercial Internet centers in the regions is the Novosibirsk Scientific Internet Center[40] located in Akademgorodok, the science town near Novosibirsk, in Siberia. This center was developed in the early 1990s, through the integration of several network-oriented programs initiated by university and academic institutions and by the city of Novosibirsk. It was one of the programs supported by the Open Society Institute in cooperation with the Russian Foundation for Basic Research, the Siberian Branch of the Russian Academy of Sciences, and the regional administration. The building of this Internet infrastructure allowed the Novosibirsk Center to participate in various international networking programs, such as the NICE project funded by the European Commission ACTS program, and the U.S.-initiated program MIRNet. Locally, several user organizations are connected via RRL links, and a metropolitan data communications network, based on frame relay technology, was being developed by the local PTT (post, telegraph, and telephone agency) in cooperation with the Novosibirsk Internet Center. The goal is to build a node along the emerging "Trans-Siberian Information Highway." Interestingly, the increasing communication capacity at this location led to a significant change in the direction of information flows. The initial ratio of in/out traffic, which was 1:5, changed to 1:3, meaning that external users were retrieving more informational resources from the system.

The Novosibirsk network has kept its noncommercial character while expanding its networking services to users such as health care organizations, regional museums, libraries, theaters, and art galleries. Libraries are now providing free access to a variety of users. Among the obstacles to the further development of their network the administrators of the Center cite the lack of a modern broadband infrastructure in Russia; the language problem, given the prevalence of English in Internet resources; and the need to provide tutorials at various levels, geared toward the staff members of institutions and toward users from the community.[41]

Overall, although education-based, noncommercial networks are aiding the diffusion of Internet technology among the Russian regions, a large gap remains between the level of Internet usage in the Russian regions and that in the largest metropolitan areas such as Moscow, due to regional inequality in educational and other resources.

The Russian Net has grown throughout the past decade to become a sizable phenomenon, spurred by a combination of the individual efforts of scientists, would-be commercial entrepreneurs, academic programs (seeking to link Russian higher education with the world), and self-educated Net users building virtual communities and information networks. However, its rate of growth lags behind that of the global Internet, and its diffusion, both in real numbers of hosts and users and in their proportion of the educated Russian population, seems disproportionately low. It is predominantly concentrated around Moscow, St. Petersburg, and other large urban areas, and is used primarily by young people and professionals. The lack of adequate telecommunications infrastructure outside Moscow, the limited diffusion of personal computers (in spite of its high growth rate), and the relatively high cost of connectivity (U.S.$20 dollars per month is a prohibitive rate for many Russian families) are the main factors slowing the diffusion of the Russian Net.

Internet and Business Management

This lag in the diffusion of Internet may prove costly for the productivity and competitiveness of the Russian economy, as well as for the quality of education and information processing. In 1998, Intel commissioned a study from COM-CON on the Russian market potential for information technologies.[42] Researchers surveyed managers of information systems in various sectors of the Russian economy, including finance, information technologies, and telecommunications. According to the conclusions of the survey, outdated computer equipment was found to hamper substantially management's performance and workers' productivity. Eighty percent of Russian managers of information technology complained about the considerable amount of time wasted because of low-performance computers. Eighty-eight percent of managers considered the Internet a very important working tool for increasing their company's competitiveness; yet they reported sporadic and inefficient use of the Internet in their firms. Eighty-five percent of managers claimed to have access to the Internet, but 84 percent thought they used it inefficiently. One-third of the managers stated that the slowness of Internet connection and information transmission was a major deterrent to more effective use. Although 82 percent of all respondents thought a web site an important company asset, only 50 percent reported the existence of a web site at their firms. In other words, although Russian information systems managers seem aware of the potential of the Net and are willing to use it, deficient telecommunications, lack of personnel training, and obsolete company structures appear to block the potential boost in productivity that the Net could bring.

The Internet Society

Because the social universe that revolves around the Russian Net is diverse and rapidly changing, little reliable information about it exists. Nonetheless, using the data that are available, we can ascertain the approximate dimensions of that universe as well as its basic demographic and geographic characteristics.

Who Are the Users?

As in other countries, users of the Net in Russia are mainly educated professionals: 55 percent are college graduates; and 50 percent are professionals, 15 percent,

managers, and 18 percent, students. One-third appear to be working in occupations directly related to information technology. A gender gap is apparent, with as
many as 85 percent of users being men (albeit, more recent, adjusted data indicate that a 70/30 split is closer to actuality).[43]

Another major demographic divide in the Russian Net universe pivots around
age: Only 15.2 percent of users are older than 45 years—an even smaller proportion than that of users between the ages of 16 and 19 (15.3 percent). This is a
powerful indicator of what appears to be the marginalization of Russia's older
population in the new information age, economically, culturally, and technologically.[44]

As for the geography of the Russian Net, residents of the main urban centers
predominate among users—particularly, Muscovites, who in 1997 accounted for
about 60 percent of Net users. However, it appears that this dominance had decreased to 50 percent of users by the end of 1998. Furthermore, Gallup Media estimated Muscovites' share at 30–45 percent in their survey of Internet users in
July 1999. Other sources have confirmed the dominance of the main urban centers.[45] Yet, the Russian web space is growing quickly. Almost all major cities, administrative oblasts, and okrugs have their own web sites. Many of these sites
seem to have been developed by self-trained local webmasters, as they are far
from perfect in design, text structure, interactivity, and navigability; they are often static and outdated. However, the process has at least begun: Sites exist. There
remains a substantial gap between the territorial diffusion of the web and the diffusion of Internet users in the population; although the web is expanding rapidly,
the number of users in nonmetropolitan areas is still very limited.

A major issue in the diffusion of Internet communication in Russia is language. Until 1996, the Web was, according to Specter, "under the absolute supremacy of the English language," which meant that Russia was being split into
two tiers: the cosmopolitan segment of the population, with easy access to a
plethora of informational resources; and the rest—a new "world of cultural and
intellectual ghettoes for people who cannot take advantage of what is out there in
English."[46] 1998 is considered a turning point in this trend, as Russian-language
content on the Net increased substantially that year. According to data from
Russian search engines Rambler, Aport, and Yandex, the number of Russian-
language documents grew during 1997 from 500,000 to 2,000,000, and the number of dedicated hosts, from 4,000 to 13,000.[47] A Russian-speaking user can now
surf an ocean of information—so much so, that there is already talk about an
"informational flood," the "danger of entropy," and necessity for more advanced
search engines and technologies.

As for the content, one can find everything on the Russian Net—both the good
and the bad—that is available on the global web. Is there something "purely Russian" in it? We think so, based on our direct observation of Russian web sites. Interaction on the Russian Net has a strong "communal" character like that of the
Russian "student collective"; everybody is welcome. Anecdote and joke sites are
the most popular, featuring distinctively Russian humor, and revealing a strong

trend toward the use of "humor therapy" as an indispensable part of Russians' survival kit. Most sites offer a warm and friendly environment, displaying spontaneous trust and the desire to help and to share. The style of expression used by some Internetters is playful, almost like that of kindergartners. Theirs is a very naïve culture, full of enthusiasm and frank and eager imitation of the foreign "elder brother" who got there first.

However, as was the experience of the "elder brother," in Russia the Net is losing its human face. "The Internet is approaching the end of the romantic period in its development," in the words of E. Genieva, president of the Open Society Institute in Moscow.[48] This newly discovered territory is being actively privatized and regulated, with its own set of rules of coexistence and property rights: Welcome to Net civilization, a world apart from anarchy.

As in other societies, in Russia the Internet faces serious problems: the uncomfortable coexistence of commercial and noncommercial networks; the lack of information security; infringements on intellectual property rights; and the tension between maintaining free access to information while protecting society from extremism (e.g., xenophobic propaganda), pornography, and incitement to violence, all of which are present on the Russian Net.

But there are also manifestations of creativity on the Net, which has been embraced with enthusiasm by the artistic and cultural intelligentsia. These groups are attracted by the promise of equal access and by the relative ease of using the Net as a tool and a medium. It facilitates the dynamic exchange of ideas and requires little monetary investment.

The Internet is being studied and experimented with in many quarters of the rich culture currently springing up in Russia. Intellectuals are reflecting on its "transcendental meaning" and implications for society, as they do with postmodernism, mass culture, democracy, communism, or fascism.[49] Current debates emphasize the end of the monopoly of the printing press and the death of distance and time. Global connectivity is expected to intensify the potential of intellectual life. Hypertext, literary games, and collaborative projects are not entirely new concepts (despite the new Russian word coined for the literature of the Internet, *neteratura*), but they blossomed afresh when they found a new medium for their existence, in the Internet.[50] The Internet opened a new space in the world of the arts, a space very different from the traditional, elitist, closed club with its rigid membership rules, strict hierarchy, and firm aesthetic criteria. The new world is open, democratic, very dynamic, and just waiting for conquerors. Still, there do not seem to be too many takers on the Russian Net. For instance, among information resources in 1998, web sites in the "culture and art" category accounted for 9.2 percent of total IR, but received only 7 percent of total hits.[51] This could mean that the supply of such sites exceeds the demand. On the other hand, foreign web sites (based abroad) are strongly present in cultural/literary IR on the Russian Net.[52] In demographic terms, Net art and *neteratura* sites are thinly populated islands of distinctive and elitist culture, clustered around Moscow and St. Petersburg, where most of the electronic magazines are published. Many of these magazines focus on the cultural life of these particular cities, merely projecting their longstanding rivalry as cultural capitals into the electronic age.[53]

One of the most important aspects of the Internet's contribution to social evolution as a whole is its *use in education.* The educational value of the Net is widely recognized in Russia. Cultural, legal, research, and academic institutions were the first to be connected to the Internet. In the early 1990s, a number of pilot projects were initiated by individual universities, supported by the program "Russian Universities," under the auspices of the Ministry of Education. This effort resulted in the founding of the RUNNet (Russian Universities Network) in 1994, and of the RBNet (Russian Backbone Network) in 1996. The Russian branch of the Open Society Institute (OSI) developed a high-speed backbone network in Moscow that connected the academic networks Freenet, Radio-MSU, and MSUNet with the computer networks of major research and educational centers located in southern Moscow. Regional telecommunications projects in Novosibirsk and Yaroslavl were also co-founded by the OSI. It is now possible to speak of an all-Russian infrastructure for computer telecommunications in science and higher education, well connected to the global Internet via Europe, North America, and Southeast Asia. With Russian-language resources being rapidly developed, the Internet is a growing resource for Russian education.

The problems of Internet use in education are under discussion in academic circles: One forum for the ongoing debate is the annual CIS conference on "New Information Technologies for Universities," held at Novosibirsk State University.[54] At the conference in March 1999, a wide array of questions were discussed: from the informatization of higher education to the use of computer technologies in the pedagogy of particular academic disciplines; the uses of computers in traditional classroom settings and at distant learning sites; and the teaching of information science in primary schools. Speakers reported their best case stories, shared their ideas on methodology, and complained about the lack of advanced software; there were as yet no electronic textbooks, manuals for students' independent study, and teaching programs for occupational retraining.

The need for a common informational-educational space prompted interuniversity cooperation in launching a remote electronic learning center: Several universities pooled their intellectual and informational resources to launch a higher educational consortium called the Open University of West Siberia. Founded in early 1998 by three universities, one year later the Open University had 14 member universities and colleges. These participating institutions appear to believe in the future of on-line education. However, some critics have argued that remote learning cannot fully substitute for face-to-face interaction because it downplays the role of the teacher as the main actor in the educational process. They fear that the quality of education will suffer and that control will be uncertain because of on-line circulation of exams and tests. At stake is the future of education as a social process including direct interaction between teachers and students. A new balance must again be struck between technology and social experience. Meanwhile, Russian universities are using the Internet even as they debate how better to use communication technologies while conserving pedagogic and academic values.

Nongovernmental organizations and grassroots movements, particularly human rights groups, are also avid users of the Net as a learning and teaching tool. Because they lack financial resources, such groups seek access to the Net in order to publicize their views, expose their critics, and build popular support. The often loose organizational structure of these groups is compensated for by on-line organization and communication, which makes tasks easier and multiplies the impact of their efforts. Because the Internet functions in real or chosen time, its use has facilitated the timely spread of information on which local and international NGOs rely for effective action. Western support groups also use Internet connections to link up with their Russian allies and keep their lines of information open to the world.

Do Russian Internet Users Have Distinctive Values?

There are no reliable sources of information on the values of the Internet population. But we can report on one interesting snapshot of the opinions and beliefs of a nonrepresentative sample of respondents to an on-line survey conducted by *Moscow News* from its web site, in 1998 and 1999. The respected weekly conducted a continuous (nonobtrusive) on-line poll of readers of its electronic version, asking one question each week.[55] An analysis of their archived responses to more than 40 questions provides an interesting profile of the average (though often unpredictable) Russian *netizen*.

Only 20.3 percent of respondents were able to make ends meet from one paycheck to the next, although 70.6 percent reported that their financial standing had improved during the previous ten years. Seventy percent of respondents did not fear the impact of new legislation on the provision of personal financial information for large purchases; 53.7 percent were willing to pay taxes on their total personal income, whereas 41.1 percent were not, and 4.8 percent were undecided. Only 25 percent liked the new national anthem of Russia, whereas 31.4 percent disliked it and 42.4 percent had "no emotions of any kind" toward it. Charity was the subject on which respondents were most conflicted: 57.5 percent were reportedly willing to offer aid to sick children (mainly monetary, but some also in the form of foodstuffs or caretaking); but in response to the question "Should beggars be given alms?," the respondents answered "yes," "no," and "I am not sure" in about equal proportions.

As for their political standing, 70.2 percent were against military action by Moscow to reestablish order in Chechnya; 52.7 percent approved of air strikes against Iraq; and 59.8 percent thought the Communist party should be banned. When asked in October 1998 whether Russia should provide Serbia with direct military assistance if NATO initiated a military operation in Kosovo, 44 percent said "yes."

When asked about the influence of A. Solzhenitsyn on their worldview, half acknowledged some influence. About 61 percent could recite at least one poem by Pushkin from memory. On the whole, they indicated a lack of trust in the mass media: About 43 percent would permit censorship of the *Moscow News* web site in order to prevent the circulation of extremist statements. Trust in the media was extremely low: Only about 8 percent trusted television broadcasts; 6 percent, radio; and 25 percent, newspapers. About 61 percent said they trusted no mass media outlet. Sixty-eight percent would vote in parliamentary elections "if elections were announced tomorrow." Their nation's economic and political outlook appeared dim: 52.7 percent thought Russia would not survive without IMF loans; 80 percent expected hyperinflation in the near future; 53.5 percent did not believe that the Primakov government could lead the country out of its current crisis; and about 55 percent were considering emigration as a way out of their personal problems in the Russian situation. Lastly, 80 percent declared that they would not stop using the Internet, even after the August 1998 crisis.

Since the first electronic edition of *Moscow News* was issued on line, 19.9 percent reported that they had purchased the newspaper's print edition for the first time, and 12.3 percent, that they had stopped buying it. But the most interesting finding is that 67.6 percent responded, "Where I live, you cannot buy it anyway." In this respect, the electronic medium seems a more reliable channel for communicating with the broad public than does print. More than two-thirds of respondents to this on-line poll were residents of nonurban areas.

Internet Penetration of Russian Society

It started as a phenomenon known only to computer literates and the professional, English-speaking elite; but today the Internet attracts a wider range of social and political groups. Its users now include many students and teachers, academics, office workers, managers, businessmen, and increasingly, bureaucrats and politicians. However, the Internet is still far from reaching the mainstream of Russian society. True, it has become fashionable in metropolitan areas to hang out in cyberspace. In April 1999, the Internet community in Moscow organized a live "Internet Party '99" ("With free vodka and strip-tease," "Everyone invited!"). Another, rather different manifestation of the virtual community's existence was a demonstration by young Internet users—mainly *fidoshniki* (subscribers to FIDONET)—in December 1997, against rising telephone rates in Moscow. The Internet cafes and bars cater to a highly diverse group of people, including intellectuals, kids, gays, and foreigners. Computer games simultaneously played by several players are a big attraction. Coupons for free use of the Internet are issued to patrons based on the amount of their regular (paid) usage.[56] Cyberspace is increasingly being studied and experienced by artistic and intellectual bohemians, and the fashionable *neteratura* circulates through the capitals of Russia.

However, the Internet is less developed in outlying regions. A study conducted by the Russian Academy of Sciences Institute of Social and Political Research concluded that Internet technology in Russia, outside of the largest cities, is rapidly becoming outmoded, leading to a situation similar to that in third world countries that are excluded from the global information community. Citizens of Russian regions are becoming "virtual homeless people," with no prospect of escaping their marginalization within the next years.[57]

This problem is more than the sum of negative economic, social, and technological trends. It is also a function of the lack of curiosity—of "stale air"—in remote areas of the country. There is little official effort to promote the diffusion of the Net—perhaps out of fear of uncontrolled flows of information. In the words of one speaker at a recent conference titled "Internet-Society-Individual": "There is no demand for it [Internet] in society. . . . Computer technologies are developing too fast. The computer elite does not realize that society has been exhausted by the pace of swift changes thrust upon it. Rapid change cannot be relentless. . . . It is necessary to get people interested, and to show them possible uses of new technologies."[58]

The mass media contribute to the Internet's unpopularity with the social mainstream. There are only a few periodicals that cover information technologies regularly (e.g., *Moscow Times, Novaya Sibir'*). But those who do write about the Internet focus on the dark side of the Net: computer piracy, viruses, thefts, disasters at the space stations, the health effects of radiation, madness as a result of Internet use, and information overload. These are the favorite computer-related topics for articles in the media. Basically, the Internet is depicted as an expensive way of obtaining news about crime and perversion. Why pay for it, when the radio is so much cheaper and more reliable?[59]

The specialized computer press is the honest servant of the computer business and represents the interests of producers but not of consumers. Aggressive competition between computer/software companies results in a steady flood of imperfect new versions of old products, with no adequate marketing information for users. No public reviews or comparisons of products are available, so users feel helpless. Some observers have noted that Russians take a quasi-mystical attitude toward computers: In the best religious tradition, users feel guilty when they cannot make a program work, and they never question its quality. The user interface is so unfriendly that a new type of interface is appearing: a human "mediator"—another user, who is more advanced in computing.[60] The growing amount of advertising is an obstacle as well: The commercialization of the Internet makes it less attractive to potential new users in the social mainstream.

Increasing Disarray Among Russia's Internet Pioneers

In 1999, the company DEMOS, the pioneer of the Russian Net, celebrated its tenth anniversary. The Net was ten years old; it was high time to take stock. Predictably, various collective reflections on the Internet appeared on-line in the first months of 1999. One in particular offers a unique perspective on the assessment of the Russian Net by those who created it.[61] Their main worry is that the concept of the Internet is gradually being reduced to that of various information technologies. In their view, the Internet is much more important than just another technology; it is a new culture of communication. As large, commercial Internet service providers take control of the networks, profits increasingly will come more from E-trade and advertising than from services (which will be practically free). In their view, three or four major companies will own the Internet in the United States. Similarly, the networks in Russia will be in the hands of between five and ten companies.[62] The managers of the Internet, rather than its users, will end up controlling it.

The Internet will be "McDonaldized": Everything will be standardized. The Internet will eliminate PCs and Windows; a personal web page on some site will replace the PC. The router will be the hardware. IP-telephony will die. The future is in 2 Mbps capacity provided for the user at every point of the globe. Financial firms and Internet companies are vying for control over the network, with electronic brokers enjoying a competitive edge.

The Internet also faces self-destruction due to increasing entropy. The more information resources expand, the more difficult it is to process information in a useful way. Search technologies are way behind the development of the Internet, inhibiting its informational potential.

If the Russian government does not provide financing for the further development of the Russian Net, there is a risk that foreign companies may gain control of it. Leading Russian programmers are already working for foreign firms. M. I. Davidov proposes that a giant joint-stock company be created to fund the Russian Net and to counter the national brain-drain. He argues in favor of a fund similar in size and substance to the United Energy Systems of Russia (the Chubais-led state oligopoly). This would be, in his widely respected view, the only certain way of avoiding the McDonaldization of the Russian Net.

The State and the Net

The Russian government realized the potential of Internet technology and accepted the idea of its development early on, as did local political leaders. Yurii Luzhkov, Moscow's mayor, was among the first to launch a web site during the 1996 presidential elections, using it to monitor the elections closely. In October 1997, Bill Gates "took Moscow by storm," opening the Russian market to his company's products.[63] Official government and Duma structures started to install computers and develop web sites. A breakthrough came in May 1998, when *netizen* Boris Yeltsin gave an on-line interview[64] in which he blessed the development of the Internet in Russia because "the future is in the information technologies." It is clear that the Kremlin sees the Internet as a matter of economic interest for Russia and as a political weapon that is best kept on its own side.

The concept of free and unmonitored exchange of information and ideas has interested everybody in Russia. Potential threats from the Internet to information security systems, as exemplified by the efforts of an active and growing group of Russian hackers, gained the attention of the Duma, which held several hearings on the topic (the first of them was titled "Threats and Challenges in the Sphere of Information Security"). In a different vein, George Soros's investment in the development of a Russian academic network was considered by Russian leaders an act of industrial espionage, potentially damaging to the interests of the Russian state; accordingly, it had to be controlled and counterbalanced by appropriate government actions.

The Duma started using the Internet to provide alternative information on its own activity, which Duma members felt was covered in a biased manner by the Russian media. Thus, the reaction of the political class was rather typical of politicians around the world: They were using the Internet, and attempting to control it, to further their own ends. In Spring 1999, the political parade of new web sites continued, with new actors entering the theater every day.[65] Politicians launched web sites not only to inform voters but to attract popular sympathy, with entire pages (or even separate sites) being devoted to their personal lives. Boris Nemtsov was the first to open two different sites: one political and another personal.[66] Web sites became an indispensable sign of being a modern political leader—so much so, that the president of Tatarstan, Mintimer Shaimiev, received his site as a birthday present from his staff.[67]

As for the control side of the equation, at the request of the Russian government the Russian Federal Security Service (FSB) has prepared regulations and technical requirements to facilitate field operative work in computer networks. An operation code-named SORM-2 (the Russian acronym for "System for Conduct of Investigation and Field Operations") has been planned, under which electronic devices are to be implanted in the web servers of each ISP, enabling the security services to intercept communications when necessary and as ordered by judicial authorities. The surveillance system was already in operation on traditional telephone lines. Recently, paging and cellular communication systems were included under the new surveillance procedures. Next in line is the Internet. Public reaction to early rumors about the FSB's regulation and control of telecommunications networks was very strong. Human-rights NGOs launched protest campaigns.[68] Foreign mass media also paid considerable attention to the matter. Some grassroots organizations in Russia have called for the development of a new electronic *samizdat* and have already established a Samizdat web site. In their view, the media are no longer free, having been conquered by corruption, business, and government. The Russian state is again suppressing autonomous expressions of dissent. Thus, the Internet is the new space of freedom, which must be defended and utilized as a new form of political organization, free speech, and unfettered communication.

Russian Internet providers are concerned not only about the potential violation of the constitutional rights of web users but also about their business. About

U.S.$100,000 will be required to install the SORM system in each network, at the expense of the ISPs, thus increasing their operating costs by as much as 10 to 15 percent. The SORM project is an acid test of the ability of the Internet, and of the society and business circles built around it, to resist renewed state security control over the development of informational resources. A last refuge from such intervention, similar to that developed in the United States, is tough-to-crack encryption technology that enables users to avoid undue interference. Since most Net users in Russia have little or no experience with encryption techniques, encryption technology is expected to become a booming business there in the near term.[69] Yet as in the United States, the Russian government is preparing legislative measures to make encryption illegal, with the exception of encryption procedures authorized by the government and used under controlled circumstances, where the government has access to the codes.

In August 1999, the Russian interior ministry opened a hot line on the Internet, inviting "malicious" hackers as well as computer security experts and all Internet users to discuss computer crime-related issues. One of the first texts published there was a press release on a new unit within the interior ministry: agency "R," established on August 14, 1999, to prevent high-technology crimes.[70] According to this document, the number of computer information crimes had increased fivefold in the previous two years, and 85 percent of all software products on the Russian market were pirated, with a turnover of about US$15 million. (By August 24, 1999, two criminal investigations had been initiated pursuant to information placed on the web site by users.)

Conclusion

There is an active debate on the Russian Net about the prospects of the information society. An insightful web site is the one established in 1997 by the Novosibirsk Institute of Economics, the Virtual Laboratory for Russian Economists and Sociologists, on the initiative of S. Parinov.[71] It is filled with technological optimism about the transformative potential of information and communication technologies. In the words of A. Shadrin, an economist at Moscow's Institute of Economic Problems of Transition: "The prospects of globalization of skilled labor, together with the development of on-line education, allow us to foresee a breakthrough in the dynamism of less developed countries. Advancements in computers and information technologies, and the decreasing cost of communications infrastructure, provide the conditions for the integration of developing countries in the global postindustrial space."[72]

However, these views contrast with Russia's current reality. On April 26, 1999, the World Bank issued a report on the state of poverty in the world. In the countries of the former Soviet Union and Eastern Europe, the bank calculated that there were 147 million people living below the poverty line of U.S.$4 a day. The equivalent figure for 1989 was 14 million. It is highly unlikely that the diffusion of information technologies, in the absence of broader trends of economic development and social reform, could reverse the structural crisis in Russian society. On the other hand, we should not underestimate the potential represented by a small but dynamic, entrepreneurial sector of Russian society. Nor should we ignore the critical role of information technology in ensuring the segmented connection of Russia to the global economy.

Indeed, if there is one recurrent theme in our analysis, it is dualization: dualization between a crumbling high-technology production system (most of it military-oriented), and a dynamic consumer market, albeit limited to a small segment of the economy; between a public telecommunications infrastructure still lagging behind the rest of Europe's in spite of recent modernization efforts, and specialized telecommunications links catering to business and global connections; between a small though fast-growing group of Internet users, and the population at large, which has remained aloof from technological change and is concentrating instead on survival; between the largest urban centers, the locale of most Internet users and information resources, and the rest of the country, served only by a narrow channel of electronic communications thanks to the courageous efforts of educational and research institutions; between the young and the old, as only about 15 percent of Internet users (the latter being a small minority of the general population) are older than 45 years; between men and women, although this is changing toward a more balanced gender distribution; between languages and cultural resources—between a highly educated, English-speaking, cosmopolitan stratum, and most Russians; more recently, between the commercial networks and the original, pioneer culture that gave rise to the Russian Net ten years earlier; and last but not least, between the growing use of cyberspace by the political class for their own advertising, and the attempt by the state to control citizens' free communication on the Internet.

These fundamental fault lines in the Russian information society exacerbate the social, economic, and political cleavages induced by a market economy that pushed 50 percent of the economy into barter; a polity that generated widespread distrust of the "democrats"; and a social policy that left about 40 percent of the population living below the poverty line. Furthermore, electronic communication enables dynamic segments of the Russian economy and society to connect with their counterparts around the globe, while evading the burden of poverty and backwardness borne by the rest of the country. This multidimensional dualism, expressed in cyberspace, splits Russia between the global and the local, with most valuables being global and most people being local.

Yet we have also observed the emergence of an ebullient, electronic civil society, out of communal sharing, entrepreneurialism, and intellectual curiosity. Although this dynamic group of *netizens* is small in size and influence, it is growing fast, and it is concentrated among the younger population—those who will create the new Russia. However, these words of hope may be grounded in little more than wishful thinking. The Internet-savvy, educated elite could use their capacity to link up with the world, in the midst of the harsh Russian reality, to find their own individual escape: first, in cyberspace, as they share in the networks of information, business, and dreams that populate the Internet galaxy; then, in many cases, by using this connection to physically leave Russia, building a new life in countries that more closely resemble the Internet tales. That they do not—that they find enough hope, material reasons, and spiritual companionship to stay and to spearhead Russia's entry into the new world—will largely determine the country's future in the information age.

Afterword: The Russian Internet in April 2000

The information technology revolution, with the Internet at its core, continues to expand throughout the world with unprecedented speed. Russia is no exception. Since the summer of 1999, when this chapter was written, important developments have taken place, generally along the lines suggested in our analysis. The one thing that did *not* happen was the Y2K disaster so feared by Western observers: No nuclear weapons security was jeopardized, no breakdown of infrastructure took place, and the "hotline" emergency communications links continued to operate. Given the widespread alarm about Russia's technical capabilities expressed in Western media during 1999, we must conclude either that Russia was not so unprepared or that the West overreacted in this matter.

Other matters were and remain more worrisome: In January 2000, a new Russian law was passed that expands the reach of the Internet surveillance project SORM-2. The power to monitor all Internet traffic in real time was extended from the FSB to include eight other agencies, among them tax inspectors, Kremlin security, border guards, and custom officers. To be sure, governmental monitoring of the Internet is not an exclusively Russian phenomenon, as evidenced by the U.S./U.K. surveillance operation Echelon, and by the U.S. F.B.I. Carnivore program. However, what is special in the Russian case is the degree of exposure that Internet users will have to potential abuse by corrupt or criminal elements with connections to the security agencies.

The Internet has become a battlefield not only of fierce virtual wars but also of real wars that incur a loss of human lives. In a striking example of today's geopolitical networking, the battles of the Chechen war were displayed on the World Wide Web—an effort not only involving Russians and Chechens but also Californians (one of the main Chechen web sites was based in that state).

Russian politics is now fully reflected in the Internet. During the March 2000 presidential campaign, because the Internet has been legally defined as a mass medium, "cyberviolations" of Russian laws on the dissemination of political propaganda during an electoral campaign were subject to monitoring and prosecution.

The Russian Net is expanding too quickly to permit the reliable tracking of its boundaries. New estimates of the number of its users in early 2000 ranged between 1.5 million and 6 million, and the number of web sites was estimated at between 18,000 and 25,000. The number of personal computers in Russia has increased to about 7 million, including 2 million home computers. The geography of the Internet is quickly changing as well: Siberians are now the most frequent users; will their region become "Cyberia"?

Last, but not least, in Russia as elsewhere in the world, the virtual world of the Internet reeks of real money, increasingly attracting investors both Russian and foreign. Leading figures in the Russian business world urge Russians to catch up with developed countries in their use of the Internet, seizing on it as a chance for developing Russia, in glowing language similar to Mikhail Lomonosov's classic prediction (that Siberia would become the source of Russian greatness). In early 2000, the first major Internet business projects came to light: Rambler, Top100, and iXBT. An important independent portal, *polit.ru*, went on sale. The contours of potential Internet giants started to emerge. The spheres of influence in Russian cyberspace are being redefined every day. The Russian state is struggling to catch up with private investors: The major financial institutions in Russia are preparing a large-scale strategic collaboration in Internet banking.

To maximize returns on their investments in Internet projects in Russia, companies must stimulate the growth of Net use among Russians. Therefore, it is likely that private business will lead the future growth of the Russian Internet, largely conditioning its structure and content. How firm the business sector's control of the Internet will be, with whom it will be shared, and how much of Russian cyberspace will be left to society in which to play, to exercise democracy, to practice communal life, to educate itself, and to communicate with the world, remains to be seen.

Notes

1. Our analysis is based on a variety of sources: firstly, on two studies by Castells on Russian information technology industries, conducted between 1990 and 1993, in Moscow, Zelenograd, and Novosibirsk. The first study focused on the development of Russian telecommunications, with an emphasis on microelectronics and telecommunications manufactures in Zelenograd. It was conducted in cooperation with Svetlana Natalushko, director of the advanced sociology program at the Institute of Youth in Moscow. The second study focused on the process of innovation in the Academy of Sciences' institutes of Akademgorodok (Novosibirsk) and their relationship to industrial enterprises and commercial applications. For summaries of these studies, see Manuel Castells and Emma Kiselyova, *The Collapse of Soviet Communism: The View from the Information Society* (Berkeley: University of California, International Area Studies, 1995). We have updated this information with our subsequent interviews and meetings with colleagues in Moscow and Novosibirsk, in 1995, 1996, 1997, 1998, and 1999. Second, we have used available information from both Russian and foreign sources on specific electronics businesses and industries referred to in the chapter. Third, we have relied on a few Western studies, which are cited in the endnotes. Our fourth and most important source has been the information on the Russian Net collected by Kiselyova in 1998 and 1999, via the Internet.

2. Castells and Kiselyova, *The Collapse of Soviet Communism.*

3. Malcolm Hill, "Russian Manufacturing in the Competitive Electronics Industry," *European Management Journal* 16, no. 4 (August 1998): 495–504.

4. Peter Clarke, "Investors Key to Russian Fabs," *Electronics Engineering Times,* no. 952 (May 5, 1997): 22; Hill, "Russian Manufacturing in the Competitive Electronics Industry."

5. *Electronic Business,* August 1998, available at www.eb-agm/registrd/issues/9808/0898bt.htm.

6. Hill, "Russian Manufacturing in the Competitive Electronics Industry," 50.

7. P. Wolcott and M. N. Dorojevets, "Making the Transition? High-Performance Computing in Russia," *Current Politics and Economics in Russia* 8, no. 2/3 (1997): 105–133. Quote on p. 127.

8. Mick Elliott, "Distributors Help Lift the Silicon Curtain," *Electronics Today* 23, no. 3 (March 1997): 19.

9. Michael D. White, "Russian PC Market Surges," *World Trade,* no. 8 (August 11, 1998): 24.

10. Data available at www.echonet.ru.

11. Gary H. Anthes, "The Russians are coming! The Russians are coming!" *Computerworld* 31, no. 41 (October 13, 1997): 87–89.

12. United States, General Accounting Office, "Export Controls: Sales of High-Performance Computers to Russia's Nuclear Weapons Laboratories," statement of Mr. Harold Johnson, Associate Director, International Relations and Trade Issues, National Security and International Affairs Division, April 15, 1997.

13. Paul Mann, "Russian Technology," *Aviation Week & Space Technology,* (May 26, 1997): 73.

14. *Vlast',* November 10, 1998: 91.

15. M. Gordon, "Maneuvers Show Russian Reliance On Nuclear Arms: Atomic Strike Simulated," *New York Times,* July 10, 1999.

16. Diane Doucette, "The Politics of Telecommunications in Russia," unpublished dissertation, University of California at Berkeley, Department of Political Science, 1995; Robert W. Campbell, *Soviet and Post-Soviet Telecommunications: An Industry under Reform* (Boulder: Westview, 1995); Rafal Rohozinski, "Mapping Russian Cyberspace: A Perspective on Democracy and the Net," paper delivered at the United Nations Research Institute for Social Development, Conference on Globalization and Inequality, Geneva, June 22, 1998.

17. Gordon Feller, "Further Financing Needed for Russian Telecoms," *Telecommunications* 30, no. 10 (October 1996): 20.

18. Global Business Networks, "Environmental Scan Report: Business in Russia" (Emeryville, Calif.: Global Business Networks, 1998).

19. "Telecommunications: Russia: A Legal Guide Supplement," *International Financial Law Review* (October 1997): 45–47.

20. *Telephony,* June 23, 1997: 34–35.

21. *Communications International* 38, no. 8 (August 1996): 12.

22. Vladimir Teremetsky, "Sovan Teleport: Telecommunications in Russia and Abroad," *IEEE Transactions on Professional Communication* 37, no. 2 (June 1994): 68–69.

23. Nicholas Mokhoff, "Russia's Communications Efforts Take to the Skies," *Electronic Engineering Times,* no. 948 (April 7, 1997): 106.

24. *Aviation Week & Space Technology* 149, no. 22 (November 30, 1998): 28.

25. For sources, see www.refrl.org/nca'special/rumedia1/rumedia2/rumedia3.

26. Timur Faroushkin, "Moscow Builds Fiber-Optic Networks," *Communication News* 31, no. 12 (December 1994): 22.

27. Karen Spinner, "Banking in the Wild, Wild East," *Bank Systems and Technology* 32, no. 4 (April 1996): 52–54; Gregory Dimitriev, "How Russia Got Frame Relay," *Communication News* 33, no. 7 (July 1996): 26.

28. *Euromoney,* no. 330 (October 1996): 91.

29. *Business America* 116, no. 7 (July 1995): 29–30.

30. Most of the sources we used in this study of the Internet are available at the web sites cited in the endnotes. Some of the information on ISPs has been obtained from the Russian Internet Yellow Pages: *Zheltye stranitsy Internet '98: Russkiye resursy,* eds. Y. Polyak and A. Sigalov (St. Petersburg: Piter Com, 1998).

31. Rohozinski, "Mapping Russian Cyberspace."

32. *RELCOM* stands for "Reliable Communication." *DEMOS* is the name of the Russian version of UNIX, developed by a team at Moscow State University.

33. Frank Ellis, *From Glasnost to the Internet: Russia's New Infosphere* (London: Macmillan, 1999).

34. Rohozinski, "Mapping Russian Cyberspace," p. 17.

35. ROCIT (Russian Public Center for Information Technologies), Annual Report, 1998 (Moscow).

36. See www.lexa.ru/ru-survey.

37. ROCIT, Annual Report, 1998.

38. See www.algo.ru/adaily/news.

39. See www.lexa.ru/ru-survey.

40. See www.nsc.ru.

41. Sergey Belov et al., "The Emerging Internet Landscape in Siberia," *Computer Networks and ISDN Systems* 30, no. 16–18 (1998): 1657–1662.

42. *Novaya Sibir',* March 22, 1998.

43. See www.rocit.ru/inform/page1.htm.

44. See www.comcon-2.com.

45. See www.gazeta.ru/daynews/31-08-1999.

46. Michael Specter, "World, Wide, Web: 3 English Words," *New York Times,* April 14, 1996: 1.

47. See www.algo.ru/colums/text/an/19980203.asp.

48. Reported (in Russian) at www.iol.spb.osi.ru.

49. Sergey Kornev, "Setevaya literatura i zaversheniye postmoderna," *Novoye literaturnoye obozreniye,* no. 4 (1998).

50. For a telling example of this literature, see "Virtual Ego," hypertext novel, posted at www.zhitinsky.spb.ru.

51. See www.rocit.ru/inform/page1.htm.

52. See www.mars.uthsca.edu/Russia; and www.members.tripod.com/chdyer/Russia.html.

53. See www.art.spb.ru; and www.fe.msk.ru/win/art.html.

54. *Novye informatsionnye tekhnologii v universitetskom obrazovanii* (Novosibirsk, 1999).

55. See www.mn.ru/index-mn.

56. V. Makeyev, "A Night on the Net," *Moscow News,* Dec. 18, 1997: 15.

57. E. Skorstova, in the Net conference posted (in Russian) at www.iol.spb.osi.ru.

58. N. Baranov, in ibid.

59. A few examples of such newspaper articles: "Off-Season Thoughts," *Moscow News,* no. 43, November 5–11, 1998; "Esli deneg doma net, potryasite Internet," *Komsomol'skaya*

pravda, December 18, 1998; "Internet Provocateurs," and "Helpful Tips for Prospective Assassins," *Moscow News,* December 3–9, 1998: 4.

60. Source posted on the Net at www.algo.ru/colums/text/an/19980203.asp.

61. See www.x7.dejanews.com/[st_m=gs]ge. . . NTEXT=.

62. ROCIT, Annual Report, 1998.

63. M. Lakhman, "Official Russia Embraces Internet," *New York Times,* February 21, 1998: 4.

64. See www.cityline.ru/VI/index.htm.

65. *Novaya Sibir',* March 20, 1999: 9.

66. See www.nemtsov.ru; and www.boris.nemtsov.ru.

67. *Moscow News,* no. 4, April 1999.

68. See the leading voice of protest at www.libertarium.ru; and S. Smirnov, at www.hro.org.

69. *Computerra* magazine, available at www.cterra.com/259/index.html.

70. See www.echonet.ru.

71. See www.ieie.nsc.ru/parinov.

72. See www.odn.ru.sth.

8

Organized Crime and Social Instability in Russia

The Alternative State, Deviant Bureaucracy, and Social Black Holes

Victor M. Sergeyev

*Moscow State Institute of
International Relations (MGIMO)*

The growth of deviant behavior in Russia since the late 1980s has important implications for the country's future. Before analyzing this behavior, however, we must first understand the concept of "criminality" as used in Russian public discourse. What is crime, in a society where laws and other legal acts change constantly? The interpretation of civil rights, of rules that guarantee freedom of information and that regulate the behavior of politicians and civil servants, especially those at the topmost level, remains unclear. The unpredictability of laws and regulations concerning business activities, export and import tariffs, taxes, and Central Bank regulations makes doing business in the country extremely difficult. Journalists do not hesitate to intrude into the private lives of politicians, and they openly use illegal means to uncover corruption. Politicians, in turn, refuse to step down from their offices despite public scandals, citing the presumption of innocence in their own defense. Government and Central Bank officials speculate in state bonds because there is no law against such behavior. The concept of criminal behavior is in constant flux in Russia today.

Crime in Russia is also unusual in that the main target of organized crime is not the private citizen (who is too poor) but the state. In most industrialized countries, the state is too strong to be a target of organized crime. But in Russia the state is extraordinarily weak in certain respects.[1] It is not weak in relation to individual citizens; on the contrary, in this respect it is quite strong. An ordinary citizen has little chance of winning any confrontation with the state, because the bureaucracy is powerful and the judicial system is subordinate to executive organs. Where the Russian state *is* weak is in relation to lobbyists and organized interests—a weakness due primarily to the fact that the legislative branch cannot control Russia's executive organs and the electorate exercises no control over the state. Despite the introduction of formal democracy, the state for the most part operates independently of public control. As a result, civil society has acquired a dual nature: It is formally sovereign but informally criminalized. Although it lacks the strength to force the state to enact laws it feels are appropriate, it has the capacity to ignore laws that the state enacts without its consent.[2]

Two factors have been instrumental in creating this state of affairs: the decay of the old state (the USSR), and the need to undertake radical economic reforms in the absence of a nationwide consensus about the nature of these reforms. The sudden disappearance of the USSR left what might be called a social "black hole" in Russia. Customary rules were flouted even as the system of state control was being dismantled. This was followed by an ill-fated attempt to introduce radical economic reforms, the implementation of which destroyed private savings and the well-developed Soviet social welfare system.[3] Most rank-and-file citizens found themselves in extreme economic distress, a condition that was aggravated by the complete lack of clues about how to survive the new hardships. Furthermore, the proclaimed "new order" and new rules of economic behavior were never implemented effectively. As a result, an enormous "gray zone" emerged between poorly implemented new laws and stable patterns of social behavior that had survived the Soviet collapse.[4]

Criminal activity in post-Soviet Russia benefited greatly from these circumstances. The collapse of the USSR and the legal confusion created by poorly designed and implemented reforms opened up unlimited opportunities for organizations, interests, and individuals powerful enough to profit from the new situation. From the start, the Russian public viewed much of what had been legitimized by the new order as criminal, especially the process of privatization. As illegal activity grew, this perception only deepened. At the same time, many customary aspects of social reality passed into history—first and foremost, the Soviet welfare state—taking with them the behavioral patterns on which social stability was based.

For these reasons, the phrase *criminal behavior* can best be understood in the Russian context as economic behavior that takes place in the black and gray sectors of the informal economy. It is not general criminality that currently endangers Russian social stability but rather specific types of deviant behavior made possible by the social confusion arising from the instability of rules and the uncertainty of expectations.

In this chapter I have used three particular phrases to characterize the consequences and dangers of this situation for Russia. *Deviant bureaucracy* refers to government institutions that use their power to privatize the state and make it serve their own interests. Different branches of government and different levels of state organizations have different and often conflicting interests, and there is thus a growing threat to the cohesion and unity of the state. Serious criminal allegations against politicians and high-ranking civil servants are common features of Russian public life. The government faces a barrage of criticism from regulatory agencies such as the Duma's Accounting Chamber and the prosecutor general's office. But in the present state of legal disorder, it is difficult to say exactly which actions go against the law and which do not. The gray zones between the traditional understanding of social order and the formal rules are just too broad.

Much of what takes place within these zones is carried out by groups that I refer to as the *alternative state*. The role of these institutions and organizations is to arrange and enforce contracts within the gray zone. Not all are, strictly speaking, illegal. Besides the mafia and various criminal groups, they include registered security agencies, legal firms, and various types of business organizations. Their principal feature is that although they are nongovernmental, they assume roles normally reserved for agents of the state. Here, too, we encounter a blending of formally criminal and formally innocent power patterns.

The final key concept is that of the *social black hole*. A permanent lack of funds renders the state unable to support and control the law-enforcement agencies in certain regions of the country. The most notorious case, of course, is Chechnya, which has lacked a law-enforcing regime since October 1991. To some extent, the vacuum was filled by the government of the Chechen Republic of Ichkeria. Nevertheless, before the renewed warfare in late 1999, power in many parts of Chechnya where official law enforcement was absent rested with the so-called "field commanders."

Unfortunately, similar conditions exist also in other parts of Russia where social order and social infrastructure have been destroyed. The best-known examples are certain areas of the Russian Far East. These are the predictable results of a society in which the welfare infrastructure is no longer operative; schools provide no teaching because teachers do not receive their salaries; heating cannot be paid for, and electric power is not even available; local transportation systems are cut off from the national network; and people cannot leave because they cannot afford travel tickets, to say nothing of new homes.

What social structures are likely to emerge in such situations? What are the likely political consequences if these black holes continue to grow? Answers to these questions are crucial for understanding the prospects for social stability in Russia.

The Shadow Economy and Organized Crime

Studying the shadow economy and organized crime is no easy task. First of all, one faces the problem of statistics. Official statistics often are vague and unreliable, representing only a small portion of reality. Russian criminal statistics, for example, show a decrease of criminal cases connected with bribes from the late 1980s to the mid-1990s—a result that dramatically contradicts the impressions of all impartial observers.

In the late 1980s, at the peak of perestroika, criminal communities and the shadow economy became central topics of public discussion. Earlier, the very existence of organized crime had been systematically denied by state officials. The sudden discovery of organized crime by liberal journalists during perestroika came as a shock to the public. The problem drew unprecedented public attention, and initial inquiries were made not by specialists in legal studies but by journalists.[5]

Growing openness about the extent of crime quickly turned the problem into an important political issue, which the two main opposing political forces at the time, communists and liberals, exploited to their benefit in accounting for the difficulties the country faced. Liberals viewed the growth of criminal communities as the legacy of communist rule, whereas communists saw it as the result of liberal reform.

By the mid-1990s, however, some serious studies of crime began to appear. Vadim Radaev, for example, classified types of economic activity based on the degree of their criminalization. He distinguished among the legal economy; the outlaw economy (activities in spheres free of legal regulations, such as the financial pyramid schemes of 1993 and 1994); the quasi-legal economy (activities in pursuit of goals that do not contradict the law but involve the use of illegal means); and the criminal economy (activities that directly contradict the intent if not the letter of the law).[6] V. Radlov, in contrast, used a typology based on the *means* employed by actors in the shadow economy and official attitudes toward the new sector. Steven Fish identified five factors that contributed to the formation of the Russian shadow economy: extraordinary natural resources, a privatization strategy that created a new oligarchy, the virtual withdrawal of the state from law enforcement, the market vacuum, and weak social organization. Out of twenty-eight countries considered in Fish's analysis, only in Russia were all five factors present.[7] Other examples of useful scholarship on this subject are works by R. Ryvkina,[8] D. Makarov,[9] and S. Glynkina.[10]

This literature provided a general picture of the shadow economy; but the picture lacked causal dynamics that could account for changes over time. An attempt to analyze the dynamics of the shadow economy and to assess its influence on social stability in Russia was undertaken by L. Kosals, who concluded that the shadow economy may have a dualistic effect.[11] While simultaneously promoting the growth of criminality, corruption, and inequality, the shadow economy also creates new jobs and stimulates the growth of civil society. Analyzing the balance between its negative and positive aspects, Kosals outlined two alternative scenarios for the future: a "radically liberal" outcome and a dictatorial one. His conclusions, however, were pessimistic in both cases: Both would lead to chaos.

I disagree with Kosals's conclusion because his analysis neglects the ongoing formation of new institutions and social practices that curb the trend toward chaos. For this reason, I propose a different approach—one that focuses on the inner dynamics of the state.[12]

Uncertainty, Trust, and Social Networks

We start with the idea of contract preservation. From the time of Hobbes, this notion has been central to political science. The state is traditionally seen as the main force that secures contracts and provides legal means to resolve disagreements about mutual obligations. What happens if contracts are made in realms of activity that society does not acknowledge as fully legitimate? For years, private business was illegal under Soviet law. Human minds and cultural attitudes are difficult to change even when laws have been altered. The contemporary economy is so complex and requires so much regulation that there is little or no chance for clearly defined business conditions to develop out of practically nothing in the course of several months or even years. Consequently, the entire economy has become a gray zone.

Social activities in the gray zone are not performed by organizations that are fully legitimate. Lack of legitimacy leads to the formation of communities that are not based on law but on customary mutual understandings among members. In this zone, the law-based state lacks any power to enforce contracts. An alternative power therefore emerges, a kind of invisible state that occupies the same territory as the visible one but operates according to its own laws.

Two questions are crucial for understanding how the alternative state functions. First, how are contracts executed without the help of the visible state's legal institutions? And second, how are contracts enforced? I have presented a detailed argument elsewhere that such a situation is identical to the well-known "cooperation dilemma" identified by political science.[13] The basic prerequisites for cooperative behavior in gray zones are a long experience of cohabitation, a long experience of collaboration, and a common origin and/or common language.

A culture of cooperation is not easily created in gray zones; but over the long term, cooperation in opposing or evading the visible state will form strong social networks, which gradually will develop into organizations with strong commitments. The permanent pressure exerted on such organizations by the visible state triggers psychological mechanisms of hierarchical behavior. Once created, such hierarchical organizations usually persist even under conditions where the original rationales for their activities have ceased to exist. The Italian mafia is a good example.[14]

The emergence of an alternative state presents another problem: When such an entity coexists with democratic political institutions, congruent or overlapping power patterns may undermine those institutions.[15] Social experiences within the democratic state and the alternative state are strikingly different. As democratic practices within state bodies compete with hierarchical practices in the social culture (which in their extreme form are manifested as crude domination over the weak), there is a growing risk that extreme forms of hierarchical behavior will permeate institutions of the visible state—especially law enforcement agencies and executive bureaucracy.

Alternative states over time tend to merge with visible ones. This process may be described as the privatization of state power. At its extreme, this process transforms the visible state into a mafia-type organization where patterns of behavior that agree with the formal laws are informally prohibited, and where actions that violate laws but agree with unwritten rules are viewed as an admission ticket to important positions within the bureaucratic hierarchy. Individuals who are unwilling to adapt present a danger to such a system, and they must therefore be eliminated by all means, including provocations and arbitrary accusations of incompetence.

The merger of the alternative and the visible states can, in equilibrium, yield a kind of congruence whereby the differences between their structures become insignificant and the average citizen cannot easily distinguish between them. The result is a deviant bureaucracy in which deviant behavior becomes a normal way of life—a social reality that is described elegantly in the short stories by Jorge Luis Borges. Individuals who seek justice from the visible state cannot be sure that their case will not eventually be adjudicated by participants in the alternative state. Such a possibility is far more terrifying in the Russian context than are Kafkaesque fantasies about the almighty bureaucratic machine run amok.

When the visible and the alternative states merge, the use of law for political purposes in pursuit of group interests becomes the rule rather than the exception. When a gray zone encompasses the entire society, everyone turns out to be formally guilty. However, it is impossible to punish everybody. Criteria for punishment are then taken from a different sphere, that of group interests. The state bureaucratic machine is used to legitimize the process of punishment in favor of private interests. No one can feel secure in such a society—and not because the bureaucratic machine is blind but because it is dominated by clearly understood interests.

Networks within such a state are usually unclear. Many persons involved in the activities of the alternative state may in fact not realize what kind of game they are playing. Consider, for example, a prosecutor initiating legal action against a person at the order of his superiors; he may well be ignorant of the particular interests he is protecting through what appears to be normal legal-institutional behavior.

Bureaucracy in the Gray Zone

Improper behavior on the part of the Russian bureaucracy has become a normal feature of its activities. Every day the Russian press provides new testimony about conflicts of interest within the bureaucratic machine, particularly those related to the privatization process. The most typical cases are the "free privatizations" in the early stages of economic reform, beginning with the 1988 law on socialist enterprises. Coupled with the new law on cooperative enterprises, that law provided ample opportunity for transferring the resources of public enterprises to cooperative owners; cooperatives, it will be remembered, were usually established and controlled by relatives of public enterprise managers.

Processes of this kind are an intrinsic part of current Russian economic life. Intermediary companies owned directly by managers buy products from public or private enterprises at very low prices and then resell them to customers at significant profit. In this way, the enterprise that actually produces the commodity in question is permanently kept on the threshold of bankruptcy, without the resources it needs to pay either its taxes or workers' salaries, while the owners of intermediary firms enjoy all the advantages without bearing substantial investment risks.[16]

Needless to say, a scheme like that must be protected by force. Criminal groups violate the property rights of shareholders, both public (the state often owns a considerable share in enterprises) and private. In some cases, meetings of shareholders make decisions under direct pressure from criminal groups whose members attend with submachine guns. Such things would be impossible, of course, were it not for the cooperation of local authorities with criminalized managers, out of common interests.

Another scheme, widely used in the metallurgy and textiles industries, consists of leasing an enterprise to suppliers of raw materials, who use it to transform raw materials into finished products. Such an enterprise would also be left without money to pay taxes and salaries, and the whole business would again be protected and controlled by local authorities directly or indirectly involved in the scheme.

In certain cases such activity may contradict the interests of regional governors. Then there is a public outcry, and criminal investigations are launched. One recent example is the dispatch of an investigating team from Moscow to Krasnoyarsk at the invitation of the populist governor General Alexandr Lebed, who had promised, if elected, to wage war on crime. After the election, dozens of criminal investigations began, and claims were made that numerous members of former administrations had betrayed the public interest by transferring control of state-owned shares to managers on dubious terms. Criminal accusations were brought against many individuals, including Anatoly Bykov, the director of KrAZ, a giant aluminum-producing plant.

The danger to society lies in the fact that again, as in Soviet times, criminal justice has been used for political purposes. The situation in the gray zone makes it possible to accuse and prosecute practically every decisionmaker in the field of politics or economy. The ambiguity and instability of laws obscure the criteria of criminality. Who is to be accused—this is the key question. Somebody has to be sacrificed to public discontent, something must be done to decrease the incompetence and corruption of bureaucrats and managers, but it is virtually impossible to prosecute everybody. Therefore, different, extralegal criteria must be found and applied to select the scapegoats. These criteria tend to be purely political and closely related to group interests.

In such a situation, the prosecutor's office becomes crucial. It is not difficult to understand why this office had become the focal point of political struggle in Russia by early 1999. The presidential administration attempted to dismiss Prosecutor General Yuri Skuratov in January of that year; but under the Constitution, appointments to this office are the prerogative of the Council of the Federation, the upper chamber of the Federal Assembly. The Council of the Federation twice refused to endorse Skuratov's resignation despite a sex scandal and a criminal investigation launched against Skuratov by his former subordinates. Thus, even the prosecutor general's office moved into the gray zone: Skuratov's resignation was rejected, as a result of which his office remained formally occupied although he was denied physical access to it by a presidential decree temporarily suspending him from his duties during the criminal investigation. Thus, power in present-day Russia is highly unstable, with the problem of deviant bureaucracy at the core of the ongoing political struggle.

The Alternative State

As a gray zone spreads, an alternative state is likely to emerge to secure contracts within the zone. What does this mean for contemporary Russia? A striking phenomenon of Russian economic life is the enormous number of businessmen who are murdered. In the mid-1990s, a spokesman for the prosecutor general's office stated that the number of contract murders had doubled every year since 1991. Among the more famous cases are the murders of Ivan Kivilidi—then president of the Association of Businessmen, who vigorously advocated the idea that representatives of Russian business sign a special code of behavior to exclude criminal methods from conflict settlement—and of Vlad Listiev, a well-known television personality. These and other notorious cases remain unsolved, despite repeated official claims that investigators have made notable progress and will soon apprehend the culprits.

How can we explain the rapid growth of criminal behavior in high-level business? The public is convinced that the aforementioned crimes were directly related to the victims' professional activities. Why, then, were the methods used so cruel? Why does conflict settlement entail so much violence? The answer is that in the absence of legal means to secure contracts in the gray zones of Russian economic life, alternative criminal methods will be used. In addition, there is little doubt that many such cases result from links between local administrations and criminal groups. A former member of the St. Petersburg city administration was recently arrested and accused of organizing and heading a group that specialized in dispensing "private" criminal justice.

St. Petersburg is often mentioned as a center of organized criminal penetration of political life. The St. Petersburg legislative election in December 1998 was one of the dirtiest political campaigns in recent Russian history and featured some unprecedented methods of political struggle. At the onset of the campaign, Galina Starovoitova—one of the more famous radical reformers and a deputy to the federal Duma—was murdered during a visit to the city on election business. Shortly thereafter, the public watched a television interview with the chief of a private security agency in St. Petersburg who explained the methods criminal groups use to influence political life. The journalist who set up the interview claimed that it had been extremely difficult to find a place to conduct it, and the owner of the small restaurant in which it eventually took place had to be paid a large amount of money, presumably in compensation for the risk he was running.

One of the innovations in the December 1998 St. Petersburg electoral campaign was the registration of candidates who were namesakes of the best-known contestants. The purpose of these shadow candidates was to confuse voters with multiple candidates with the same last name and first initials, thereby splitting the vote. What was required of shadow candidates in the course of the campaign was, therefore, to avoid publicity and remain unknown. This technique was used even against political parties and movements: For example, a second movement named Yabloko was registered in St. Petersburg and fielded a set of electoral candidates, in an apparent attempt to confuse regular supporters of the original Yabloko. According to some journalists, up to 50 percent of the candidates in that election were connected to criminal groups. In response, a number of democratic political parties resolved to organize an Anticriminal Political Front.

Electoral machinations of this sort are alarming because they erode the borderline between the legitimate state and the alternative state. In St. Petersburg, the alternative state in effect attempted to absorb the official state. Official policy under Yeltsin facilitated this outcome. The course that reforms have taken in Russia has proven counterproductive economically and extremely dangerous politically. The reforms have led to privatization by criminal groups in cooperation with the bureaucracy, and to political instability caused by power struggles without rules. Formal rules no longer constrain behavior, whereas alternative rules are blatantly criminal, as the St. Petersburg election demonstrated.

How, in such a situation, can the visible and the alternative states continue to coexist? Often their actions are in direct conflict. On other occasions, however, the two states merge with one another and are represented by the same people. Social stability depends upon the interaction between these institutions and the people representing them. Were there to be full and open conflict, social order might disintegrate.

What, then, are the prospects for the integration and the reemergence of a coherent society? The problem may be addressed from the perspective of social-integration theory. The way of life, sources of income, and typical behavior of ordinary individuals involved in the activities of the visible and alternative states are totally different. Those who receive their salaries from the state budget are usually very poor, whereas those who work for the alternative state have more than enough money to survive. Let us remember that the traditional social status of those people was once approximately equal. Might there therefore be an acute conflict between them, as many politicians predicted in the early years of the reforms, in 1992 and 1993?

From the perspective of integration theory, the answer depends on whether the links between these two groups and the social networks connecting them persist.[17] The fact that they belong to the same social strata, have a good deal in common in their background and social experience, and are connected by networks of friendship and social ties are important barriers to social conflict. These barriers may explain why, even in the worst days of 1992 or after August 1998, social stability remained rather high.

On the other hand, in regions where non-Russian ethnic groups dominate (as in the North Caucasus), social tensions are intense. The lack of networks uniting different ethnic groups, and the much higher involvement of non-Russians (especially North Caucasians) in the activity of the alternative state, often produce open conflict and a massive migration of Russians out of such republics (again, especially in the North Caucasus). The absence of a Russian elite in these areas prevents the formation of a social bedrock separated from but integrated through negotiation with the elite level.[18] The typical example is Karachaevo-Cherkessia during and after the 1999 elections. In this and similar cases, circumstances clearly led to social disintegration. And a striking outcome of this disintegration has been the emergence of social black holes.

Social Black Holes

Many societies in transition experience social black holes; Russia is not unique in this respect. Indeed, social infrastructures can be destroyed in many ways. Ethnic and social conflicts, unsuccessful economic reforms, and financial crises undermine traditional norms. But these difficulties do not lead necessarily to social black holes. Black holes are situations of despair in which people stop even trying to improve their status because they no longer believe that doing so is even possible. Human history is full of examples. Sometimes damage to social infrastructure is so great that individuals do not consider recovery a reasonable goal. The only possible reason for life is individual survival. And one can think of circumstances when even that disappears. Not all members of society have to share these feelings in order to produce a social implosion or black hole. But where a minority does share them, the result may be a deadly vortex of destructive thoughts and behaviors previously repressed by social controls.

The social structure that takes shape in social black holes is not clear. Hints can be drawn from the experiences of veterans of ethnic conflicts and wars like those in Vietnam and Afghanistan. This much we know: Experience obtained in black holes changes a person's worldview. In particular, a sharp distinction develops between "us" and "them" that drastically diminishes the value of human life—especially "theirs."

The political consequences of such experiences are significant. Black holes change social memory, especially institutional memory, and form internal tensions that may remain hidden for decades and then explode suddenly, as did ethnic hostilities in the former Yugoslavia. The experience of the black hole endures over a long period and is passed from one generation to another; and like any war experience, it destroys basic humanist values. War is an alternative institution, with its own rules, justifications, and heroes; but in the black hole there are no lasting rules, justifications, or heroes—only terrible losses and tragedies.

The geography of emerging black holes in Russia is relatively easy to discern. They are found in most dramatic form in three republics of the North Caucasus: Chechnya, Ingushetia, and Dagestan. Parts of the Stavropol region that adjoin Chechnya and Ingushetia are in a similar situation. In these regions, social control is usually in the hands of paramilitary organizations that belong to different ethnic groups, pitting Cossacks against Chechens, or Chechens against the many different ethnic groups of Dagestan. Social control is not exercised by formal authorities and state institutions but is realized through invisible social networks, among which interrelationships remain unclear.

Social infrastructures in these regions are in complete disarray: Children may not attend school for years, and senior citizens live without regular pensions. In countries in social decay, paramilitary organizations stage parades and publicly display their weaponry, luxury cars, electronic equipment, and wealth. People are effectively separated into two classes: the predators and the prey. This is a typical frontier situation, and it may affect human minds in a way that distorts normal social interaction for decades. Generations must pass before a frontier mentality is overcome.

Other examples of emerging black holes in Russia are the North and the Far East—in the regions of Khabarovsk, Kamchatka, Vladivostok, and Sakhalin. Each has numerous middle-sized and small towns that in many cases lack direct railroad connections to mainland Russia. Three factors seem to be of particular importance in these areas: lack of state financial support, high transportation tariffs, and high energy costs. It is impossible to survive there without heat and electricity.

Today, conditions in these areas are at a primitive level. State financial support has fallen drastically. In autumn 1999, all of Kamchatka was without fuel for several weeks. There was no heat, not even in hospitals, and schools could not open. Additional difficulties resulted from long-term arrears in salaries for employees in the social and economic infrastructure. Even hunger strikes by power station employees proved of no avail.

The outcome is the rapid growth of organized crime and the dissipation of local administrative power. In Vladivostok, a prolonged conflict between the regional governor and the former mayor continues. Numerous elections, all plagued by serious irregularities, have failed to resolve the crisis; and their results have been annulled for all kinds of reasons, including low turnout and the fact that the authorities did not approve of the outcome. Criminal activities flourish, especially in illegal trade with Japan (seafood exports and second-hand automobile imports). The situation is aggravated by the illegal immigration of ethnic Chinese into the region. It is estimated that between 1 and 2 million Chinese have recently settled on Russian territory near the Chinese-Russian border. Attempts to attract foreign investment in order to improve the economic and social situation have failed. Administrative disorder and criminal activities produce such great instability that risks are believed to outweigh the obvious economic advantages that some of the proposed projects would entail.

There is a causal relationship between the formation of black holes and the development of the shadow economy and organized crime. The existence of a shadow economy and an alternative state in regions with ethnic heterogeneity intensifies the conflicts between different groups. These conflicts produce social disorder, which in turn enhances the environment the alternative state needs to flourish. Finally, conflicts between the visible state and the alternative state lead to a further aggravation of social conditions. Chechnya is the best example of this process. The unregulated process of transition to a market economy in an ethnically mixed society is clearly much more dangerous than in a homogeneous one—a conclusion that is also supported by a comparison of the Asian and African experiences. Strong social networks within an ethnic minority, reinforced by the role of these networks in the shadow economy and in the formation of the alternative state, can prevent the development of trust between ethnic groups, thereby further undermining social stability.[19] For this reason, one cannot separate the problem of organized crime from the problem of ethnic conflict in societies in transition.

Conclusion

Today, Russia can be divided into three parts: the more or less prosperous big cities of the central region (for example, Moscow, St. Petersburg, and Nizhnii Novgorod), which show clear signs of transformation and growth despite numerous difficulties; the larger part of the national territory, which remains in deep recession; and the growing number of emerging black holes in the North Caucasus, Far East, and North. In all these areas, however, the "criminal economy" has become an integral part of the Russian economy, some 60 to 80 percent of which is "gray." The penetration by criminal elements of state bodies—especially legislatures at the regional and local level—is particularly significant. This criminal activity, as well as the deep differences in conditions among the three areas, constitutes a clear threat to political stability in Russia. With luck, apocalyptic prophecies of decay and collapse may prove unwarranted, and newly elected leaders may help mobilize popular sentiment for change. But for the time being, stability remains a distant goal.

Notes

1. See Chapters 2 and 3 in this volume for a more detailed exploration of the state's weaknesses.

2. On the "rebirth" of civil society in Russia, see Michael Urban, *The Rebirth of Politics in Russia* (Cambridge, U.K.: Cambridge University Press, 1997).

3. On the transitional situation in Russia after the decay of the USSR, see Nikolai Biryukov and Viktor Sergeyev, *Russian Politics in Transition* (Aldershot, U.K.: Ashgate, 1997).

4. For more on the "gray zone," see Viktor Sergeyev, *The Wild East: Crime and Lawlessness in Post-Communist Russia* (Armonk, N.Y.: M. E. Sharpe, 1998).

5. Concerning criminality in the period of perestroika, see Sergeyev, *The Wild East,* chapter 5.

6. V. Radaev, "Tenevaya ekonomika v Rossii: Izmenenie konturov," in *Pro et contra* 4, no. 1 (1999).

7. M. Steven Fish, "The Roots of and the Remedies for Russia's Racket Economy," in Steven Cohen, Andrew Schwartz, and John Zysman, eds., *The Tunnel at the End of the Light: Privatization, Business Networks, and Economic Transformations in Russia* (Berkeley: University of California Press, 1998).

8. R. Ryvkina, "Ot tenevoi ekonomiki k tenevomu obshchestvu," *Pro et contra* 4, no. 1 (1999).

9. D. Makarov, "Ekonomicheskie i pravovye aspekty tenevoi ekonomiki v Rossii," *Voprosy ekonomiki,* no. 3 (1998).

10. S. Glynkina, "Osobennosti tenevoi ekonomiki v Rossii," *Politekonomiia,* no. 5 (March 1998).

11. L. Kosals, "Mezhdu khaosom i sotsial'nym poriadkom," *Pro et contra* 4, no. 1 (1999).

12. Sergeyev, *The Wild East.*

13. Ibid., chapter 3. On noncooperative game theory (the prisoner's dilemma is the best-known example), see Robert Axelrod, *The Evolution of Cooperation* (New York: Basic Books, 1984); Thomas C. Schelling, *The Strategy of Conflict* (Cambridge: Harvard University Press, 1960); V. A. Lefevre, *Konfliktuiushchie struktury* (Moscow: Vysshaia shkola, 1966); A. V. Belayev and Viktor Sergeyev, "An Ensemble of Neuron-Like Automata as a Model of Social Stability" (in Russian), in *Intellektual'nye protsessy i ikh modelirovanie* [Modeling Intellectual Processes] (Moscow: Nauka, 1994).

14. See Henner Hess, *Mafia and Mafiosi: Origin, Power, and Myth* (London: C. Hurst, 1996); R. Seindal, *Mafia, Money, and Politics in Sicily: 1950–97* (Copenhagen: Museum Tusculanum Press, 1998).

15. See Harry Eckstein, "Congruence Theory Explained," in Harry Eckstein, Frederic J. Fleron, Erik P. Hoffmann, and William M. Reisinger, eds., *Can Democracy Take Root in Post-Soviet Russia?* (New York: Rowman & Littlefield, 1998).

16. About the complex relations between the state and business community, see Alexei Zudin, *Business and Politics in Post-Communist Russia* (Moscow: Center for Political Technologies, 1995); Biryukov and Sergeyev, *Russian Politics in Transition,* chapter 5 (123–132).

17. See, for example, Johann Galtung, "Pacifism from a Sociological Point of View," *Journal of Conflict Resolution* 3, no. 1 (1959): 67–84.

18. Arend Lijphart, "Multiethnic Democracy," in Seymour M. Lipset, ed. *The Encyclopedia of Democracy,* vol. 7 (London: Routledge, 1995), 863–865. See also a very stimulating

discussion in Axel Hadenius and Lauri Karvonen, *The Paradox of Integration in Intra-State Conflicts,* preprint (Uppsala: Uppsala University, 1999).

19. See Barry R. Weingast, "Constructing Trust: The Political and Economic Roots of Ethnic and Regional Conflict," in Karol Soltan, Eric M. Uslaner, and Virginia Haufer, eds., *Institutions and Social Order* (Ann Arbor: University of Michigan Press, 1998).

PART III

Society

9

Russia's New Entrepreneurs

Victoria E. Bonnell

University of California, Berkeley

Russia's new entrepreneurs[1]—originally labeled *kooperativshchiki* and later *biznesmeny* or *predprinimateli*—emerged in the second half of the 1980s, when perestroika began to undermine structures and practices of the command-administrative economy. The collapse of the Soviet Union at the end of 1991 hastened these transformations, carried out under the banner of marketization and privatization. Initiated and implemented from above by political leaders and elites, the reforms brought into existence a stratum of business people who introduced new forms of economic behavior—most notably, private entrepreneurship.[2]

In a brief period (1986 to 1999), private entrepreneurs and entrepreneurship have grown rapidly. By 1996, 77 percent of Russia's medium-sized and large enterprises were privatized, accounting for 88 percent of the total industrial output (but only about 40 percent of the total labor force).[3] There were 868,000 small enterprises registered in 1997, not counting many small firms that did not register or pay taxes (209,000 entrepreneurs in this category were reported in early 1999).[4] Before the August 1998 financial crisis, small firms accounted for 14 percent of the country's labor force and produced 12 percent of its GDP, far less than in some postcommunist countries but a substantial increase for Russia.[5]

These developments have had far-reaching consequences for the country's social and political landscape, yet many important questions remain unanswered about this remarkable social group. Who are the entrepreneurs? What is their background, demographic profile, and point of entry into the economy? In what ways have they attempted to emulate their predecessors in earlier times and other places by creating formal and informal networks capable of making their case both to political elites and to the population at large?

The new entrepreneurs—a highly variegated group—have had a mixed reception from the Russian public. Associated first with the shadow economy and then with the so-called mafia, entrepreneurs are frequently linked to crime and corruption.[6] Terms such as *nomenklatura privatization* highlight the involvement of former members of the party and state apparatus in the growing private sector and imply possible (mis)appropriations of state and public property. The wealthier stratum of entrepreneurs has often been referred to as "New Russians" *(Novye russkie)*, a complex term conveying a multitude of meanings, including "dishonest procurement of wealth, ties with privileged and criminal elements, conspicuous consumption . . . and a low cultural level."[7]

In the mid-1990s, the media began to refer to a small group of successful entrepreneurs as "oligarchs," suggesting that the economy had fallen into the hands of a few powerful men who presided over financial empires based on ill-gotten wealth.[8] This terminology has been mirrored in Western public discourse, which commonly features a rich assortment of pejorative labels including "gangster capitalists," "racketeers," "robber-barons," "crony capitalists," and "kleptocrats."

The reemergence of entrepreneurs and entrepreneurialism in Russia after many decades of ruthless suppression and relentless vilification invites historical comparison. In west European societies of an earlier era, entrepreneurs—often designated as the bourgeoisie—led the way to political reform. Historians have argued that entrepreneurial groups figured importantly among the major supporters of west European democratic institutions, a view summed up by the phrase "No bourgeois, no democracy." Sociologists and political scientists have advanced similar arguments, focusing on the proclivity of educated, urbanized, middle-class groups to support individualism, economic and political freedoms, and civic equality and participation. In social science literature, the appearance of a business class has generally been linked to the growth of civil society and a public sphere.[9]

The historical experiences of nineteenth-century western Europe offer important precedents for gauging the trajectories of postcommunist societies, but the transition in the late twentieth century from state socialism to some form of market economy nevertheless presents striking contrasts with earlier developments. Russian entrepreneurs of the 1990s confront a context that in several respects differs from the situations facing their counterparts at earlier times and places.

1. The transition we are witnessing today follows, rather than precedes, the creation of an advanced industrial economy. Russian entrepreneurs no longer need to defend the values of industrialism against agrarian interests, a conflict decisively resolved by the communist leadership. And very importantly, the process taking place in Russia after 1986 centers around the redistribution of preexisting industrial structures—that is, the transfer of existing structures from state to private control. The appropriation and not the creation of assets has been the defining feature of the Russian situation. The formation of a new group of entrepreneurs was marked, from the very inception, by this unprecedented circumstance.

2. New Russian entrepreneurs must operate within the context of an inauspicious legacy of private entrepreneurship extending back to both the Imperial and the Soviet periods.[10] This can be attributed, in large measure, to historical conditions created by a strong, centralized state. In earlier periods, the exercise of authority in industry was circumscribed because political elites viewed it as a chal-

lenge to the supreme authority of the autocratic elites or the party-state. Today, Russian entrepreneurs must contend with a relatively weak but intrusive government at the national level—a situation that contrasts sharply with a long legacy of extensive state intervention in industrial relations.

3. Since 1991, the weakness of state power at the national level has engendered two responses. First, we have seen a shift in the locus of power from the center to the regions and localities. Second, Russia has witnessed the emergence of "violent entrepreneurship" of both legal and illegal varieties. A powerful network of organizations (businesses) has taken over, to a considerable extent, functions normally performed by the state, such as enforcement of contracts and debt recovery. Vadim Volkov has identified three types of violent entrepreneurial agencies in postcommunist Russia: state and illegal (units of state police and security forces acting as private entrepreneurs); non-state (private) and legal (private protection companies); and private and illegal (organized criminal or bandit groups).[11] Recent research indicates that the mutual interpenetration of entrepreneurship and organized crime may be on the decline, but criminal networks — and violent entrepreneurship generally—remain important factors shaping the future prospects of business in Russia.[12]

4. Russian entrepreneurs must contend with widespread negative or ambivalent attitudes toward private business among certain sectors of the Russian population and the political elite. This outlook has deep roots in Russian culture, predating the Soviet era but reinforced over many decades by relentless propaganda aimed at discrediting private property and market-oriented economic activity. The reemergence of entrepreneurship as a consequence of perestroika and privatization policies has generated widespread allegations concerning the role of crime and corruption in private business. Negative public opinion about businesspeople declined for a short time after the collapse of communism; and by 1994, 49 percent of respondents were "rather positive" toward Russian entrepreneurs, and only 28 percent were "rather negative." In 1997, the numbers were nearly reversed: 49 percent viewed entrepreneurs as harmful, and only 34 percent, as beneficial.[13] This was almost certainly a response to mounting evidence of entrepreneurial wealth derived from improper acquisition of state and public assets. Since the August 1998 crisis, public opinion toward entrepreneurs has remained deeply divided.

5. New Russian entrepreneurs must contend with a global economy. The information and communication revolutions have changed the ways people do business, and in many cases, expanded their horizons to encompass global markets and an international business culture. Postcommunist Russia has been catapulted into a world economy, creating new opportunities (for example, for capital flight) as well as imposing new limitations.[14]

6. The postcommunist Russian state, for complex reasons, has been unable to create and maintain an environment suitable for private entrepreneurship.[15] Russia lacks key institutional, legal, and fiscal conditions that generally characterize economies where entrepreneurs can flourish.[16] In a recent study, Gil Eyal, Ivan

Szelenyi, and Eleanor Townsley argued that in Hungary, Poland, and the Czech lands, the demise of communism led to "capitalism without capitalists." In contrast, Russia presents a case of "capitalists without capitalism."[17] This brief but expressive formulation encapsulates a key aspect of the situation facing Russian entrepreneurs.

Four phases can be discerned in the evolution of entrepreneurs as a social group in Russia since 1986: the first, ending in 1991; the second, from 1992 to 1994; the third, from 1995 to August 1998; and the fourth, from September 1998 to Yeltsin's resignation in December 1999. We will begin our exploration of these phases with a brief comment on the situation during the Soviet period. Notwithstanding the vigorous and sometimes brutal campaign waged by the communists against private business for almost 60 years (beginning in the late 1920s), entrepreneurialism in various forms survived in the Soviet Union and ultimately contributed to the fatal weakening of the system.

Prior to perestroika, self-employed individuals (e.g., physicians, skilled workers, and engineers), managers of Soviet factories ("red directors"), and seasonal construction brigades *(shabashniki)* engaged in various forms of entrepreneurialism.[18] But it was the shadow economy, together with rampant crime and corruption, that provided the most extensive and lucrative opportunities for private entrepreneurship in late Soviet society. As Gregory Grossman has observed, "Illegal economic activity penetrated every sector and chink of the economy; assumed every conceivable shape and form; and operated on a scale ranging from the minimal or modest for the masses to the substantial for many, to the lavish and gigantic, as well as elaborately organized, for some."[19] However, soon after Gorbachev came to power, he introduced new laws that fundamentally changed the way Russians did business.

The First Phase: 1986–1991

The first phase in Russia's new entrepreneurship was set in motion by the enactment of the Law on Individual Labor Activity (1986),[20] the Law on State Enterprises (1987),[21] and the Law on Cooperatives (1988).[22] These important legal landmarks were followed by other laws regulating property rights in the USSR during 1989 and 1990. In late 1990, the Russian Supreme Soviet adopted the Law on Enterprises and Entrepreneurial Activity, sanctioning private businesses including limited partnerships, joint stock companies, general partnerships, and sole proprietorships.[23]

The evolution of Russian entrepreneurship between 1986 and 1991 has been described as "romantic," "revolutionary," and "heroic."[24] During this critical stage, new legislation and regulations and a changing economic and political environment made it possible for private business to operate within an expanding sphere of legality.[25] The circumstances that gave rise to these momentous reforms were complex and cannot be fully discussed within the confines of this chapter. Suffice it to say that by early 1987, when perestroika and glasnost were getting under way, new entrepreneurial groups had begun to appear in Russia.[26] They emerged primarily from the ranks of Komsomol leaders, intellectuals (particularly scientists), industrial managers, people in the shadow economy, state bureaucrats, and bankers.[27] Within a short period, these entrepreneurs were refashioning old organizations, such as the Komsomol, and old (but seldom utilized) forms of economic activity, such as the producers' cooperatives. The active engagement of the new groups had a profoundly corrosive effect on Soviet economic and political life and set a pattern for the subsequent evolution of entrepreneurship. The singular feature of this nascent entrepreneurialism was the large-scale transfer of public and state assets into private hands, secured in most cases by one or another form of personal access to political power.

The fascinating story of Komsomol entrepreneurship began in 1986, with reforms initiated by the newly elected first secretary of the Komsomol, Viktor Mironenko.[28] Steven Solnick's study, *Stealing the State: Control and Collapse in Soviet Institutions,* provides a detailed account of the forces that led up to these reforms and were unleashed by them. A steady decline in Komsomol enrollment since the late 1970s had cut sharply into revenues from dues, a situation exacerbated by declining subsidies from Moscow. In response, some Komsomol activists began to convert programs created in the Brezhnev era—student construction brigades, travel bureaus, youth housing complexes (MZhKs), and centers for "scientific-technical creativity of youth" (NTTMs)[29]—into new commercial ventures for the benefit of local Komsomol groups and of the activists themselves.

The rapid expansion of MZhKs and NTTMs was made possible by the exceptional (and highly lucrative) right of local Komsomol organizations to transfer funds between their own budgets and these enterprises.[30] Following the Twentieth Congress of the Komsomol in April 1987, new regulations shifted control of Komsomol finances from the Central Committee to local and primary organizations. The channeling of funds led to the creation of a wide range of businesses. According to Solnick, "Cafes, video bars, discos, and travel bureaus were founded or expanded with loans directly from Komsomol budgets; new concerns also used Komsomol printing presses and even operated out of Komsomol offices."[31] A "quiet process of 'political bourgeoisification'" was well under way by 1987, or even earlier.[32]

While local activists turned their attention to new businesses, Komsomol Central Committee officials took advantage of the vast resources of the organization (1 billion rubles in 1987) to establish the first commercial banks, tourist bureaus, and publishing operations.[33] The announcement of an Extraordinary Congress of the Komsomol to be held in April 1990 accelerated the transfers of assets out of Komsomol accounts.[34] When the Komsomol was disbanded in 1991, the flourishing "Komsomol economy" lost no momentum.

From the ranks of Komsomol entrepreneurs came some of the most successful businessmen of the 1990s, such as Mikhail Khodorkovsky and Vladimir Vinogradov.[35] Khodorkovsky, who was ranked by *Forbes* in 1997 among the top 200 richest men in the world,[36] began his business career ten years earlier, as a Komsomol deputy secretary for Moscow's Frunze district and head of the district's NTTM. Initially reselling computers, Khodorkovsky generated enough capital to start the Menatep (acronym for Inter-Branch Center for Scientific and Technological Programs) bank in 1990, which became the authorized bank for the city of Moscow three years later.[37] He made a fortune trading currency, sugar, grain, and oil. Similarly, Vladimir Vinogradov, one of the seven oligarchs of the mid-1990s, was an economist at Promstroibank in the 1980s when he became involved in Komsomol commercial activities through the Saburov Youth Construction Complex. He founded Inkombank in 1988 to service Komsomol commercial activities, with the help of the Soviet Finance Ministry and Soviet State Bank.[38]

The Komsomol entrepreneurs of the late 1980s prefigured a more extensive pattern of wealth transfers from public and state organizations into private hands. The early transfers of wealth—exemplifying the process of "power conversion"[39]—were replicated on an even grander scale when high and middle-ranking members of the party-state apparatus shifted their attention to the private sector, on the eve of privatization in 1989. By the end of 1991, "*nomenklatura* privatization"—a process that transformed authority over the economy into private ownership of property—was under way. *Privatizatsiia* (privatization) became *prikhvatizatsiia* (grabbing, swiping) because high- and middle-level party-state officials were uniquely positioned to acquire credit, real estate, export-import rights, and distribution and manufacturing firms. *Nomenklatura* privatization was concentrated in four areas: transformation of the state planning system; banking; distribution; and the privatization of existing, state-owned enterprises.[40]

Komsomol activists were not the only beneficiaries of a large-scale transfer of public and state resources. We can trace a similar pattern in the cooperative movement, which like the Komsomol, opened up new and unprecedented opportunities for entrepreneurship.[41] The cooperatives provided a legal basis for many businesses established during the final years of Soviet power and became an important vehicle for *nomenklatura* privatization. Although the Law on Cooperatives was not put into effect until July 1, 1988, various legal cooperatives had been initiated, sometimes in response to official decrees, during the preceding eighteen months.[42] By early 1988, only 14,000 cooperatives were registered in the country. One year later, however, the number had increased to 77,500; and by the beginning of 1990, 3 percent of the total Soviet labor force was employed in cooperatives.[43]

Cooperatives eventually emerged in many different contexts and took many different forms, but the most prevalent type was what Anthony Jones and William Moskoff have termed the quasi-official cooperative.[44] Typically, cooperatives of this era were initiated not by individuals but by local authorities, managers of state enterprises, or even planning ministries. The 1987 Law on State Enterprises and subsequent legislation promoted this development by introducing "self-financing" and reducing the impact of the centralized planning apparatus.[45] Another Soviet decree in 1989 permitted work collectives to lease state enterprises, which in turn stimulated the transfer of state property to the private sector.[46] By early 1990, almost 80 percent of production cooperatives were operating inside state enterprises.[47]

At the same time, a new type of firm arose for the purpose of providing protection, dispute settlement, contract enforcement, and other services to Russian entrepreneurs. As recounted by Volkov:

> The surfacing of extortion and its conversion into a regular, observable pattern of protection racket occurred in 1987–88, as the co-operative movement, the first effect of the economic liberalization, gained momentum. Initially, co-operators and petty traders became victims of those extortionists who were formerly engaged in card debt recovery and shadow business protection. Very soon new groups composed of former sportsmen emerged on the scene and began to earn money by selling protection to small entrepreneurs and traders at city markets.[48]

Violent entrepreneurship was an intrinsic part of the entrepreneurial scene from the inception of perestroika.

Individuals with access to resources and the motivation to undertake new types of entrepreneurial activity utilized cooperatives and "small businesses" (malye predpriiatiia), which were legalized in the second half of 1990,[49] as vehicles for private entrepreneurship. In this manner, enterprising industrial managers (mostly middle-level), professionals, people from the shadow economy, Komsomol activists, and state bureaucrats joined the ranks of the new entrepreneurs. The first private banks were established in 1989. Aleksandr Smolensky, founder of the country's largest commercial retail bank (Stolichny Bank of Savings-Agroprombank [SBS-Agro]) before the August 1998 crash, got his start in 1987 as head of Moskva-3, a construction cooperative. With capital accumulated from the cooperative, he opened a bank in 1989 and then went on to invest in media and oil companies.[50] Likewise, in 1987, Vladimir Gusinsky, a former theater director turned media tycoon, took advantage of the law on cooperatives to lease a glassware factory at night and produce drinking glasses. This was followed by other cooperative ventures involving office supplies, legal and business consulting services, and office renovation. Most-Bank was founded by Gusinsky in 1989 to finance these operations.[51]

Demographic surveys of perestroika-era entrepreneurs indicate that they were predominantly men with a higher or technical education. Many came from the Komsomol, science, or banking and were in their early thirties when they entered the business world. An exception to this pattern can be found among managers and some bankers, who tended to be men in their mid-forties to early fifties, holding middle- or upper-level positions. Communist party membership was widespread among bankers (nearly universal) and managers (more than 70 percent); four-fifths of Komsomol businesspeople belonged to the party, and about one-third of intellectuals. Most of the incipient entrepreneurs had withdrawn from the CPSU by 1990.[52]

Psychological profiles generally subdivide perestroika-era entrepreneurs into two "waves." Igor Bunin, author of one of the earliest empirical studies of new Russian entrepreneurs, has characterized the "first wave" of businessmen (1987–1989) as "adventurists"—that is, people who were courageous, self-made men and who entered the business world with few assets.[53] Gusinsky gave the following account of the "first wave," to which he, himself, belonged:

> Many of them tried to make some quick money and then to hide it all. They were scared of Soviet banditism. Their mentality was very closed, especially in the first years of the cooperative movement. At that time, people thought they were building something like "society with a human face". . . . These people cloaked themselves in a new ideology. . . . I would say about eighty percent of that first wave that made some money went abroad. They left because they didn't trust the state. They didn't think things could last.[54]

The "second wave" of businessmen (1989–1991) continued to draw "self-made men" but also attracted what Bunin has called "idealist entrepreneurs," who attempted "above all to realize themselves in business, [and were] not particularly concerned with economic efficiency," including physicists and engineers. Even more significant was the influx of party and state officials *(nachal'stvo)*, who drove forward the process of *nomenklatura* privatization. Their shift to the business world took place under generally favorable circumstances because they brought assets with them, unlike those in the "first wave" and the "idealist entrepreneurs." Gusinsky observed of this group: "The second wave is the toughest and most criminalized. They were people who came to the market on a wave of aggression. . . . These are tough, criminal people."[55]

During the Gorbachev era, success in business frequently depended on personal access to power and patron-client relationships. Entrepreneurs—whatever their background—could hope to succeed only if they cultivated ties with influential party and government officials. Many of these ties were forged informally, but in some cases, entrepreneurs formed unions and associations. Lobbying through voluntary associations was a novelty, although similar organizations had been formed during the late nineteenth century, only to be extinguished after the Bolshevik revolution. In the post-Stalin era, ministries represented the interests of particular industrial groups in high party and governmental deliberations. Soviet lobbying, organized along formal hierarchical lines, fell into disarray between 1989 and 1991.[56]

The first associations of entrepreneurs were formed locally in 1988, by people in the cooperative movement, followed in June 1989 by an all-union congress of cooperatives in Moscow. When delegates to this congress were asked to rank their aims, they listed first "to organize political protection for cooperators, through the nomination of people's deputies."[57] Like their predecessors in other times and places, these entrepreneurs sought to combine collectively to strengthen their political leverage.

The voluntary associations among entrepreneurs, founded between 1989 and 1991, were created by three groups. Among them were "political administrators" such as Arkadii Volsky, formerly an official on the Central Committee of the CPSU. In December 1991, Volsky founded the Scientific-Industrial Union, which was renamed the Russian Union of Industrialists and Entrepreneurs (RUIE) [Rossiiskii soiuz promyshlennikov i predprinimatelei] the following year. It became one of the most visible entrepreneurial organizations of the 1990s.[58] Other associations were established by people with a scientific background and by "political entrepreneurs."[59] Some of them, such as the Chamber of Commerce of Trade and Industry of the Russian Federation (Torgovo-promyshlennaia palata RF) (1991) and the Association of Russian Banks (Assotsiatsiia rossiiskikh bankov) (1991), remained active in the late 1990s.[60]

Phase Two: 1992–1994

In the aftermath of the August 1991 coup, President Yeltsin and his key advisers began to move in the direction of "shock therapy" and privatization—a series of reforms aimed at the rapid and radical reconfiguration of the Russian economy. The history of these reforms has been told elsewhere.[61] Suffice it to note that between November 1991 and the end of 1994, periods of reform alternated with periods of stalemate in the struggle between pro- and antireform groups. Notwithstanding the unsteady course of reform, major changes were imposed, including the lifting of price regulation; the freeing of trade; privatization; and the introduction of a voucher program. In the course of 1993–1994, 21,000 large and medium-sized enterprises—70 percent of industrial enterprises in the country—were privatized through joint stock companies.[62]

The character and impact of the reforms has been subject to considerable controversy both in Russia and in the West. For our purposes, what is important is that these years witnessed further transformations in the position of Russian entrepreneurs. The reforms drew enterprise directors into the growing private sector, transforming them from state employees into owners.[63] "The prime purpose [of the reforms]," in the words of Anders Aslund, "appears to have been to enhance privileges for the select few of the old economic nomenklatura, but this was done in the name of the market."[64] It was typical for these directors, with a higher technical education, to move up through the ranks in their enterprises and acquire high-level managerial positions in the late 1980s. When joint stock companies were formed, they often acquired substantial shares. Some of the more enterprising, clever, and corrupt directors entered the ranks of the "New Russians." Together with bankers, the directors of large former state enterprises formed the elite of Russian business.[65]

The background of the business elite in early 1993 and early 1995 is shown in Table 9.1, based on data gathered by sociologist I. V. Kukolev from a survey of 200 entrepreneurs.[66] We can see that in early 1993, perestroika-era entrepreneurs (Komsomol leaders, intellectuals, and industrial managers, but not bankers) who

TABLE 9.1 Background of Entrepreneurs, 1993–1995 (in percent)

Group	Early 1993	Early 1994	Early 1995
Komsomol	15	10	9
Physicists	24	20	19
Managers	22	14	14
Bankers	19	20	22
Enterprise directors	2	19	20
Others	18	17	16

Source: I. V. Kukolev, "Formirovanie Rossiiskoi biznes-elity," *Sotsiologicheskii zhurnal* 3 (1995):168.

entered the business world during the first phase of privatization (1986–1991) constituted 61 percent of entrepreneurs surveyed. Two years later, in early 1995, these same groups made up 42 percent of the sample. Only bankers, among the early business people, continued to increase in number between 1993 and 1995.

Several new groups entered entrepreneurial ranks during these years. Most important among them were the directors of state firms who had benefited from the privatization program. Another substantial segment—labeled "Other" in Table 9.1—consisted of several smaller subgroups: individuals (typically about 30 years of age) from privileged families, well educated, with past employment in the Komsomol or foreign trade organizations and membership in the Communist party;[67] and "superfluous" people, who were considered the most socially maladjusted in the Soviet system, generally in their early 40s, who came from educated families and often had a humanistic rather than technical education. Some of the latter group previously had eked out a living on the margins of society, finding employment as "janitors, firefighters, or stokers" in order to avoid prosecution as parasites. "Aggressive, clever, and unprincipled," they sometimes rose to high positions in financial empires.[68]

Although Russia's growing private sector was increasingly dominated by concentrations of wealth and power, this was only part of the picture. The number of legally registered small businesses, usually defined in the Russian context as enterprises with fewer than two hundred employees,[69] grew rapidly. Their proliferation provides an indicator of the vigor and prosperity of the newly privatized economy. Whereas 560,000 small businesses were registered in 1992, the number had grown to 896,000 two years later.[70] Many others were operating without registration, and therefore are not included in the statistics. By 1995, approximately 10 percent of the labor force was working part- or full-time in small enterprises—mainly in manufacturing, construction, and commerce.[71]

The accelerated pace of privatization coincided with another trend: the formation of new entrepreneurial organizations. During 1992 alone, more collective efforts were launched by entrepreneurs than during the preceding four years combined. These new associations can be divided into several categories. Some gathered together entrepreneurs from many branches of industry, such as the Association of Privatizing and Private Enterprises (Assotsiatsiia privatiziruemykh i chastnykh predpriiatii) (1993),[72] the Round Table of Russian Business (Kruglyi stol biznesa Rossii) (1993),[73] and the Society of Merchants and Industrialists (Obshchestvo kuptsov i promyshlennikov) (1992).[74] The largest group, however, consisted of organizations within specific branches of industry. Some arose on the ashes of former planning ministries; others were established in new spheres of the economy, such as private banking, advertising, and real estate.[75] Former Komsomol activists and middle-level managers from the perestroika era of entrepreneurialism often played an active role in these organizations.[76]

At the same time, the "political self-determination of business" was moving forward as entrepreneurs created new channels for exerting political influence.[77] The catalyst for these efforts was the parliamentary election of December 1993, which prompted Russian entrepreneurs to form political parties.[78] On the eve of the parliamentary election in December 1993, some of the largest banks and financial structures gave support to Yegor Gaidar's party, Our Choice Is Russia (Nash vybor—Rossii). Others (such as Viktor Gusinsky's Most-Bank) supported Yabloko and the Party of Unity and Accord (Partiia Rossiiskogo edinstva i soglasiia). Forty entrepreneurs and 32 directors of state enterprises were elected to the State Duma (which has a total of 450 seats). Not one representative of private business took a seat in the Federation Council (178 seats).[79] Generally speaking, the 1993 parliamentary election failed to bring entrepreneurs the political recognition they had sought.

Phase Three: 1995–August 1998

The appearance of a small group of extremely wealthy and influential businessmen with diversified holdings (mainly in banking, media, and natural resources) characterizes the third phase in the evolution of new Russian entrepreneurship. Their emergence was connected with several major developments—most importantly, the formation of financial-industrial groups (FIGs) and the shares-for-loans program. FIGs began to form in 1992 and 1993, led by industrial firms or banks. Legislation in 1995 gave them official standing and allowed them to register at the federal level. By May 1998, there were 80 registered FIGs, encompassing about 1,000 enterprises and 100 banks.[80] Some of the largest private banks joined together with industrial enterprises to form FIGs, which, in turn, were under the direction of the banks' founders-presidents.

The seven largest bank-led FIGs, listed in Table 9.2, are associated with entrepreneurs who collectively have come to be known as "the oligarchs" (Appendix 9.1).[81] Five of these seven (Alfa, Inkombank, Oneximbank, Rosprom, SBS-Agro), according to Donald N. Jensen, were established "with the direct political and financial support of the Komsomol or Soviet Communist Party" or of former members of the Soviet *nomenklatura*.[82] To appreciate the extent of their holdings,

TABLE 9.2   Major Russian Financial-Industrial Groups and Their Founders

Alfa Group:	Mikhail Fridman
Inkombank:	Vladimir Vinogradov
LogoVAZ:	Boris Berezovsky
Menatep/Rosprom:	Mikhail Khodorkovsky
Most Group:	Vladimir Gusinsky
Oneximbank/Interros:	Vladimir Potanin
SBS-Agro:	Aleksandr Smolensky

SOURCE: Author's compilation.

suffice it to note that in the mid-1990s the Oneximbank/Interros Group presided over seven of the 20 largest companies in Russia, accounting for 56 percent of the total industrial production and employing 400,000 people.[83]

In spring 1995, a consortium of banks put forward an ingenious proposal to ease the government deficit problem. Banks would provide loans to the Kremlin, taking shares in state-owned industrial enterprises as collateral.[84] Juliet Johnson has described what happened next:

> This idea turned into the "shares-for-loans" auctions in which several banks acquired significant stakes in key Russian export companies for rock-bottom prices. . . . The shares-for-loans auctions catalyzed the bank-led FIGs' leap from important players in the Russian economy to dominant financial-industrial conglomerates, while at the same time discrediting the privatization process in the eyes of the Russian public.[85]

Bank-led FIGs were the primary beneficiaries of this government program, and their founders-presidents became prime movers among the oligarchs. During the presidential elections in mid-1996, the oligarchs coalesced into a powerful political force backing Yeltsin's reelection.[86] Afterward, Yeltsin rewarded them with unprecedented access to the Kremlin. Several even moved into prestigious positions in the government. Potanin was appointed to high office in August 1996, as reported by the *Washington Post*:

> After the election, according to several sources, the tycoons met and decided to insert one of their own into government. They debated whom—and chose Potanin, who became deputy prime minister [for economic policy]. One reason they choose Potanin was that he is not Jewish, and most of the rest of them are, and they feared a backlash against the Jewish bankers.[87]

A few months later, Berezovsky became deputy director of the Security Council (1996–1997) and then executive secretary of the Commonwealth of Independent States (1998–1999).[88]

The political appointments of Berezovsky and Potanin marked a new stage in the interpenetration of economic and political power: the entry of the oligarchs, whose differences were temporarily subordinated to common aims, into the inner sanctum of formal power. At the same time, members of this elite group positioned themselves in the corridors of the Kremlin, whence they exerted vast influence.[89] Notwithstanding their differences on many issues, they generally played by the same ground rules: an informal, individualized, and autonomous approach to state power, which obviated formal associations among entrepreneurs. A vertical cleavage subdivided Russian entrepreneurs into three groups: an oligarchic superelite, a larger group of business people in corporate organizations, and a mass of unorganized entrepreneurs.[90]

By early 1997, all the world watched as seven men presided over far-flung economic empires (FIGs), occupied quasi-ministerial status in the government (symbolized by official government license plates and blue flashing lights on their Mercedeses and Land Cruisers),[91] and enjoyed a life style few in the world could match. In October 1996, Berezovsky publicly defended the oligarchs: "We—seven people—hired Anatoly Chubais and invested billions of dollars into Boris Yeltsin's election. We control 50 percent of the Russian economy. We should occupy the key posts in the government and benefit from the fruits of our victory."[92]

But the unified front did not last long. Deep divisions and intrigues within the group resurfaced during spring and summer 1997, in response to new ministerial appointments (creating new alliances between oligarchs and political leaders) and new auctions for state property. The sale of the telecommunication company Svyazinvest to a consortium led by Potanin's Oneximbank (and including George Soros) precipitated a "bankers' war" that decimated the facade of unity among the oligarchs. Toward the end of 1997 and in the first part of 1998, public opinion turned sharply against the oligarchs. Yeltsin lent his support to the idea of the "separation of government and capital" but did little to tamper with the power of the leading FIGs, which controlled a substantial portion of the country's GNP.[93] In March 1998, however, Yeltsin removed Prime Minister Viktor Chernomyrdin, whose policies had generally provided favorable conditions for the oligarchs.[94] In May, Sergei Kirienko, a reformer, was appointed in his place.

On August 17, a Sunday, the oligarchs rushed back to Moscow from their Mediterranean villas in anticipation of the government's impending announcement of currency devaluation and debt default.[95] What subsequently took place behind the scenes is not fully known. Shortly thereafter, Kirienko was dismissed from his post—a move perhaps prompted by Berezovsky and other oligarchs in retaliation for Kirienko's unwillingness to bail out their banks, whose massive overinvestments in lucrative short-term government bonds (GKOs) had put them at serious risk following the devaluation of the ruble.[96] The ensuing political crisis led to the appointment of Yevgenii Primakov as prime minister, who presided for eight months over a coalition of former *nomenklatura* and communists that attempted but failed to reconfigure the relationship between government and business.

Phase Four: September 1998–December 1999

The financial crisis of August 1998 plunged many bank-led FIGs into disarray, and with them, some of the leading oligarchs. By January 1999, five of Russia's ten largest banks—Inkombank, Menatep, Oneximbank, Rossiiskii Kredit, and SBS-Agro—were no longer able to meet their financial commitments. Only one of the five banks that were still solvent—the International Industrial Bank—was controlled by Russian private capital.[97] The oligarchs regrouped, but all sustained some damage. Two of the original seven faced imminent legal action (Berezovsky and Smolensky), and several others were at risk of the same (Fridman and Vinogradov).

By the end of 1999, however, the situation had changed once again. Some of the original oligarchs, such as Berezovsky, Gusinsky, and Khodorkovsky, remained powerful and highly visible in the country's economic and political life. The Primakov government and its successors did not attempt to replace the oligarchic system but instead sought to advance the fortunes of a different set of economic actors, thereby facilitating the "circulation of elites."[98] The oligarchs in ascendancy included Roman Abramovich, Vagit Alekperov, Pyotr Aven, Andrei Kazmin, and Rem Vyakhirev.

The new oligarchs traveled a road to fame and fortune that has much in common with the seven famous oligarchs who emerged in the public arena during the mid-1990s. Their informal, personalized approach to political power continues an established pattern. The new and old oligarchs have been consolidating their forces through mergers (e.g., that of Most-Bank, Menatep, and Oneximbank to form Rosbank) and agreements to undertake joint ventures (e.g., Lukoil and Gazprom). At the same time, oligarchic forms of economic organization are extending beyond the capital city to Russia's regions.[99] The regional oligarch Anatolii Bykov, head of the Krasnoyarsk Aluminum Plant, is the best-known of these provincial tycoons because of his well-publicized clashes with regional governor Aleksandr Lebed and his indictment in 1999 for money-laundering and conspiracy to commit murder.

As the Yeltsin years drew to a close, contemporary Russian entrepreneurs faced an unprecedented situation. A small but extremely powerful group at the pinnacle of the economic elite had taken possession of a great deal of wealth—a group that remains highly influential. Nevertheless, tens of thousands of entrepreneurs (in many different firms, sectors, and market contexts) carry on business in the country, without benefit of the two conditions that Max Weber considered essential for modern, rational capitalism: "a calculable legal system" and "administration in terms of formal rules."[100] The central state remains weak and has lost its monopoly on violence, yet it continues to maintain substantial interests in key industries, especially natural resource extraction. A predatory relationship has evolved between business and the state,[101] forcing Russian entrepreneurs to operate in a context of uncertainties and vagaries that discourage long-term planning and investment.

The financial collapse of August 1998 had devastating effects on a broad circle of entrepreneurs, including many start-up companies and moneymaking enterprises whose bank deposits were wiped out. Small businesses were particularly hard hit, and one-third were reported to have suspended work or gone bankrupt.[102] In Moscow alone, 30,000 small and medium-sized businesses (about 15 percent of the total) closed due to the crisis, including many merchants purchasing products abroad for resale on Moscow markets.[103] Not all businesses suffered, however. Devaluation of the ruble provided the impetus for a general shift away from foreign imports and toward domestic production.[104] Firms that fared relatively well after August 1998 include those in transit, construction, communications, natural resources, television, tires, paper, domestic food products, textiles, auditing, and consulting.[105]

Small businesses had made a strong comeback by July 1999, when 890,000 of them were officially registered. Nevertheless, this number is slightly lower than the figure for small businesses registered in 1994—a telling indication that conditions remain extremely difficult for these firms. Small businesses are still concentrated in certain cities and regions of the country. In fall 1999, about 20 percent were located in Moscow, 13 percent in St. Petersburg, and one-third in the central region as a whole. Combined they had more than 7 million employees.[106]

Entrepreneurial associations both national and regional continue to proliferate, representing the interests of specific or diverse branches of industry and geographic areas. The most prominent organization today is RUIE, with more than 2,700 institutional members representing enterprises, research organizations, commercial structures, and public organizations, including a large contingent of former "red directors."[107] Under the leadership of its president, Arkadii Volsky, RUIE has stepped up the effort to reintroduce government regulation of strategic industries, reduce taxes on business, impose government protectionism, and grant concessions to selected foreign firms.[108]

In *The Protestant Ethic and the Spirit of Capitalism,* Weber made the argument that early capitalists found "ethical foundation and justification" for their way of life in the ideas and practices of ascetic Protestantism. Eventually, however, material goods overcame religious asceticism and acquired inexorable power over people— the "iron cage"—turning them into "specialists without spirit, sensualists without heart."[109] Like their Protestant forerunners in other times and places, Russian entrepreneurs find themselves in an "iron cage." They are imprisoned by the particular mode of acquisitiveness that took form in the second half of the 1980s, with the appearance of Komsomol and cooperative businesses, and was reinforced in the 1990s by voucher privatization, loans-for-shares, and bank bailouts. Russian business culture has been shaped by a massive transfer of state and public assets into private hands. The late communist and postcommunist mode of acquisitiveness depends on personalistic ties, political influence, crime, corruption, and violent entrepreneurship. Russia's businesspeople often yearn for a "civilized" state, "civilized" business, and "civilized" laws"[110]—but they remain trapped by a different legacy of entrepreneurship at the beginning of the twenty-first century.

Appendix: Background Information on Russian Oligarchs[111]

1. ROMAN ABRAMOVICH
    Date of birth: 1966
    Education: Gubkin Institute of Oil and Gas, Moscow
    Past and present business holdings and interests:
    Natural resources: Sibneft Oil

2. VAGIT ALEKPEROV[112]
    Date of birth: 1950
    Education: Azerbaijan Oil and Chemistry Institute
    Past and present business holdings and interests:
    Media: TSN, TV6, REN TV, *Izvestiia*
    Natural resources: Lukoil (president)

3. PYOTR AVEN[113]
    Date of birth: 1955
    Education: Department of Economics, Moscow State University
    Past and present business holdings and interests:
    Banking: ALFA Bank (president)
    Financial-industrial group: ALFA Group
    Media: STS regional television network

4. BORIS BEREZOVSKY[114]
    Date of birth: 1946
    Education: School of electronics and computer technology at the Forestry
    Institute in Moscow; mechanical-mathematical faculty of Moscow State
    University; doctorate in physical-mathematical sciences; corresponding
    member, Russian Academy of Sciences (1991)
    Past and present business holdings and interests:
    Auto mfg.: LogoVAZ (founder), LADA, All-Russia Automobile Alliance
    Financial-industrial group: LogoVAZ
    Media: ORT, TV-6, *Novye izvestiia, Nezavisimaia gazeta, Ogonëk, Matador,
    Kommersant, Karavan,* Almaty TV, Channel KTV
    Natural resources: Sibneft Oil, Gazprom
    Transportation: Aeroflot, Transaero

5. ANATOLII BYKOV[115]
    Date of birth: 1960
    Education: Krasnoyarsk Teacher-Training Institute (physical education)
    Past and present business holdings and interests:
    Banking: Rossiiskii Kredit Bank; Metaleks Bank
    Financial-industrial group: Tanako Group

Natural resources: Krasnoyarsk Aluminum Plant (KrAZ) (chair of the board); Krasnoyarsk Fuel Company (controlled though Tanako), which controls Krasnoyarsk Coal Company; Achinsk Alumina Combine

6. MIKHAIL FRIDMAN[116]
Date of birth: 1964
Education: Moscow Steel and Alloys Institute
Past and present business holdings and interests:
Banking: ALFA Bank (chair of the board)
Financial-industrial group: ALFA Group
Media: ORT (part of bank consortium with Obedinennyi Bank, Menatep Bank, and SBS-Agro Bank); Alfa TV; STS
Natural resources: TNK Oil Sidenko
Other: Western Siberian Metallurgy Plant; chemicals, pharmaceuticals, food processing (tea, sugar), glass, electricity, construction, cement, art dealership, supermarket chain, oriental carpet exports, liquor imports

7. VLADIMIR GUSINSKY[117]
Date of birth: 1952
Education: Gubkin Oil Institute and Lunacharsky Theater Institute; stage director for Tula Theater before moving to Moscow in early 1980s
Past and present business holdings and interests:
Banking: Most-Bank
Financial-industrial group: Most Group (chair of the board)
Media: Media-MOST: NTV, NTV Plus, NTV International, TNT, Ekho Moskvy, Sem' dnei, *Itogi, Segodnia, Novaia gazeta, Obshchaia gazeta, Smena*, KinoMost, Central European Media Enterprises
Other: Real estate

8. ANDREI KAZMIN[118]
Date of birth: 1958
Education: Moscow Finance Institute
Past and present business holdings and interests:
Banking: Sberbank (chair of the board, president)

9. MIKHAIL KHODORKOVSKY[119]
Date of birth: 1963
Education: Mendeleev Chemistry Technology Institute, Moscow
Past and present business holdings and interests:
Banking: Menatep Bank, Rosprom holding company (chair of the board)
Financial-industrial group: Menatep/Rosprom
Media: ORT TV, *Literaturnaia gazeta*, Independent Media Group *(Moscow Times, Kapital, Playboy, Cosmopolitan)*
Natural resources: Yukos Oil Company

Other: Food processing, construction, paper, chemicals, oil, metallurgy, construction, textiles, consumer goods, and Galeriia Manezh (a new, upscale shopping mall in downtown Moscow)

10. VLADIMIR POTANIN[120]
Date of birth: 1961
Education: Moscow Institute for International Relations with specialization in economics
Past and present business holdings and interests:
Banking: MFK Renaissance Group, Oneximbank, Rosbank
Financial-industrial group: Oneximbank/Interros (president)
Media: *Komsomolskaya pravda*; *Izvestiia*; *Ekspert*; *Russkii telegraf*; regional television and radio outlets
Natural resources: Sidanko Oil, fifth-largest Russian oil producer; Gazprom; Norilsk Nickel
Other: Svyazinvest, Perm Motors, Novolipetsk Steel, ZIL autoworks, North West River shipping, Kuznetsk Aluminum, Oktyabrskaya Railroad, Lomo Precision Optics, Central Army ice hockey and basketball teams, life and health insurance companies, mutual and pension funds

11. ALEKSANDR SMOLENSKY[121]
Date of birth: 1954
Education: Dzhambul Technological Geology Institute (economics)
Past and present business holdings and interests:
Banking: SBS-Agro (Stolichny Bank of Savings—Agroprombank) (president), Finance Oil Bank, Soiuz group (chair of board)
Financial-industrial group: SBS-Agro
Media: ORT stake through consortium, *Stolitsa, Kommersant Weekly, Kommersant-Daily, Dengi, Domovoi, Segodnia* and NTV
Natural resources: Stake in Sibneft oil company

12. VLADIMIR VINOGRADOV[122]
Date of birth: 1955
Education: Moscow Aviation Institute, in space power engineering; Plekhanov National Economy Institute, in economics
Past and present business holdings and interests:
Banking: Inkombank
Financial-industrial group: Inkombank
Natural resources: Transneft
Other: Samara Aluminum, Babayev Food Processing, Magnitogorsk Steel, Nostas Pipe, Sokol Aircraft, steel, timber, metallurgy

13. REM VYAKHIREV[123]
Date of birth: 1934

Education: Kuibyshev Industrial Institute, with engineering specialty in development of oil and gas
Past and present business holdings and interests:
Media: Gazprom owns 29 regional newspapers and television stations; partial ownership of Media-MOST
Natural resources: Gazprom (chair of board), Siberia Oil company

Notes

I would like to acknowledge the able assistance of Jane Zavisca in the preparation of this chapter. I am also grateful to Vadim Radaev for his interest in the project when I was in Moscow in summer 1998. Comments and suggestions from my colleagues in the Carnegie group also were helpful in making revisions.
All dates of publication in the citations below are in American style (month/day/year).

1. I have used the word *entrepreneurs* throughout this chapter in a broad sense, interchangeably with *businesspeople,* to refer to individuals who start or direct a business; make critical decisions relating to the use of capital, labor, and other resources; and assume risk for the sake of profit.

2. *Entrepreneurialism* refers to a constellation of business practices including modes of capital accumulation, investment and marketing strategies, risk taking, innovation, ethics, contracts and mutual trust, authority relations within firms, and the creation of networks.

3. Joseph R. Blasi, Maya Kroumova, and Douglas Kruse, *Kremlin Capitalism: Privatizing the Russian Economy* (Ithaca and London, 1997), 26.

4. TASS, 2/17/99. An unknown number have eluded the authorities.

5. *Izvestiia,* 9/15/98:1; TASS, 9/13/98; Anders Aslund, "Observations on the Development of Small Private Enterprises in Russia," *Post-Soviet Geography and Economics* 38(4)(1997):191–205. One-quarter of the small enterprises were located in Moscow.

6. "Rossiiane i biznes: Dinamika obshchestvennogo mneniia," in *Obraz predprinimatelia v novoi Rossii,* ed. I. M. Bunin (Moscow, 1998), 13. In a 1991 survey, 45 percent of respondents believed that "swindle and intrigue" were typical behaviors of Russian businesspeople. The only entrepreneurial attribute that received a higher response (50 percent) was "thirst for profits." See Stephen Handelman, *Comrade Criminal: Russia's New Mafiya* (New Haven and London, 1995); and David Remnick, *Resurrection: The Struggle for a New Russia* (New York, 1997), 196–199, for accounts that highlight this phase in the public reception of new entrepreneurs.

7. "Obraz biznesa v Rossiiskom obshchestve: Vospriiatie, differentsiiatsiia, legitimatsiia," in *Obraz predprinimatelia v novoi Rossii,* ed. I. M. Bunin, 63. In 1997, British anthropologist Caroline Humphrey provided the following description of the meaning of the term within Russian parlance: "It refers to an image of people with a new and alien mentality, people who are rapacious, materialist, and shockingly economically successful. In short, New Russians are 'new' because they do not give precedence to various hoary Soviet values, which are still mostly seen in a rose hue by everyone else: the value of honest labour, of supporting the *kollektiv,* of respect for the working masses, of high-minded personal frugality, and above all the value of production of goods for the benefit of society as a whole" (Caroline Humphrey, "The villas of the 'New Russians': A sketch of consumption and cultural identity in post-Soviet landscapes," *Focaal* 30–31 [1997]:87. See also Remnick, *Resurrection,* 201.

8. It appears that the first such usage of the word *oligarch* can be traced to an article published by Thomas Graham, a U.S. diplomat in Moscow, in *Nezavisimaia gazeta,* in winter 1995 (Remnick, *Resurrection,* 177–178).

9. See, for example, Barrington Moore, Jr., *Social Origins of Dictatorship and Democracy: Lord and Peasant in the Making of the Modern World* (Boston, 1966); Reinhard Bendix, *Nation-Building and Citizenship: Studies of Our Changing Social Order* (Berkeley and Los Angeles, 1977); Seymour Martin Lipset, *Political Man: The Social Bases of Politics* (New York, 1963).

10. Gregory Guroff and Fred V. Carstensen, *Entrepreneurship in Imperial Russia and the Soviet Union* (Princeton, 1983).

11. Vadim Volkov, "Violent Entrepreneurship in Post-Communist Russia," *Europe-Asia Studies* 51(5)(1999):741.

12. Vadim Radaev, *Formirovanie novykh rossiiskikh rynkov: Transaktsionnye izderzhki, formy kontrolia "delovaia etika"* (Moscow, 1998), presents evidence for a decline. For a different view, see M. Steven Fish, "The Roots of and Remedies for Russia's Racket Economy," in *Tunnel at the End of the Light: Privatization, Business Networks, and Economic Transformation in Russia,* eds. Stephen S. Cohen, Andrew Schwartz, and John Zysman (Berkeley, 1998), 86–138.

13. "Rossiiane i biznes: Dinamika obshchestvennogo mneniia," in *Obraz predprinimatelia v novoi Rossii,* ed. Bunin, 18, 23.

14. Manuel Castells, "Paths and Problems of the Integration of Post-Communist Russia into the Global Economy: A Concept Paper," in *Tunnel at the End of the Light,* eds. Cohen, Schwartz, and Zysman, 66–85.

15. On this general point, see Fish, "The Roots of and Remedies for Russia's Racket Economy," 92.

16. What we see in postcommunist Russia is a group of businesspeople who are operating in what Barry Ickes and Clifford Gaddy have termed a "virtual economy"—that is, an economy of pretense, based on "illusion about almost every important parameter: prices, sales, wages, taxes, and budgets." The Russian economy retains distinctive features of the former Soviet system, with its subsidization of industry, and in critical respects has failed to make progress toward a market economy (Clifford G. Gaddy and Barry W. Ickes, "Russia's Virtual Economy," *Foreign Affairs* 77[5][1998]:53–67).

17. Gil Eyal, Ivan Szelenyi, and Eleanor Townsley, *Making Capitalism Without Capitalists: Class Structure and Political Economy of Post-Communism in Central Europe* (London, 1999).

18. Vladimir Gimpel'son, "New Russian Entrepreneurship: Sources of Formation and Strategy of Social Action," *Problems of Economic Transition* 36(12)(April 1994):25–26.

19. Gregory Grossman, "Subverted Sovereignty: Historic Role of the Soviet Underground," in *Tunnel at the End of the Light,* eds. Cohen, Schwartz, and Zysman, 31; Gregory Grossman, "Sub-Rosa Privatization and Marketization in the USSR," *Annals of the AAPSS* 507(January 1990):47.

20. This law, adopted on November 19, 1986, did not go into effect until May 1987. It provided a legal basis for Article 17 of the 1977 Constitution, authorizing individual labor activity. By permitting "activities and services" corresponding to local needs and traditions, the law "set in motion an evolution of private enterprise that was unstoppable" (Anthony Jones and William Moskoff, *Ko-ops: The Rebirth of Entrepreneurship in the Soviet Union* [Bloomington, Ind., 1991], 11).

21. This law, adopted on June 30, 1987, went into effect on January 1, 1988. It expanded the autonomy of enterprise directors and permitted workers to elect managers.

22. The law was adopted in May 1988 and went into effect on July 1, 1988. The original law (which was later modified) consisted of 54 articles; it placed cooperatives "on an equal footing" with state enterprises (Misha Belkindas, "Privatization of the Soviet Economy Under Gorbachev," II, 1: "The Campaign Against Unearned Income"; and 2: "The Development of Private Cooperatives," Berkeley-Duke Occasional Papers on the Second Economy in the USSR, no. 14 [April 1989], 40). See Jones and Moskoff, *Ko-ops: The Rebirth of Entrepreneurship in the Soviet Union*, 12–14, on the law itself; the remainder of the book deals with the implementation and revision of the law.

23. The law was passed on December 25, 1990.

24. Igor' V. Kukolev, "The Formation of the Business Elite," *Russian Social Science Review* 38(4)(July-August 1997):65; Ol'ga V. Kryshtanovskaia, "Transformation of the Old Nomenklatura into a New Russian Elite," *Russian Social Science Review* 37(4)(1996):31. Kukolev applied the phrase *romantic period* to the years from 1987–1988 to 1992–1993. I. Bunin (*Biznesmeny Rossii: 40 istorii uspekha* [Moscow, 1994], 394) described the period between 1986 and 1989 as "heroic."

25. For an overview of early reforms, see Jones and Moskoff, *Ko-ops*, 3–14; Anders Aslund, *How Russia Became a Market Economy* (Washington, D.C., 1995); and Blasi, Kroumova, and Kruse, *Kremlin Capitalism*.

26. The following discussion draws primarily on Bunin, *Biznesmeny Rossii*; T. I. Zaslavskaia, "Biznes-sloi rossiiskogo obshchestva: Sushchnost', struktura, status," *Obshchestvennye nauki i sovremennost'* 1(1995):17–32; Vadim Radaev, *Stanovlenie novogo Rossiiskogo predprinimatel'stva (Sotsiologicheskii aspekt)* (Moscow, 1993); Alla Chirikova, *Lidery Rossiiskogo predprinimatel'stva: Mentalitet, smysly, tsennosti* (Moscow, 1997); Kryshtanovskaia, "Transformation of the Old Nomenklatura," 18–40; Olga Kryshtanovskaia and Stephen White, "From Soviet Nomenklatura to Russian Elite," *Europe-Asia Studies* 48(5)(1996):711–733; Kukolev, "The Formation of the Business Elite"; Roy Medvedev, "A New Class in Russian Society: A New Social Experiment," *Russian Social Science Review* 39(5)(September-October 1998):55–76. For a comparison of various periodizations of resurgent entrepreneurship, see Kukolev, "The Formation of the Business Elite," 65.

27. For a discussion of these sources of recruitment, see the citations in note 24; Medvedev, "A New Class in Russian Society," 56–58; Alexei Yurchak, "Post-Soviet Entrepreneurial Culture: The State, the Subject, and the Law," unpublished paper, March 1999; Olga Yartseva, "L'entrepreneur russe depuis le début de la perestroika," *Cahiers internationaux de sociologie* 96(1994):99–112; O. V. Perepelkin, "Rossiiskii predprinimatel': Shtriki k sotsial'nomu portretu," *Sotsiologicheskie issledovaniia* 22(2)(1995):35–40.

28. The account that follows is drawn from several sources, most notably: Steven L. Solnick, *Stealing the State: Control and Collapse in Soviet Institutions* (Cambridge, Mass. and London, 1998), 108–124; Kryshtanovskaia and White, "From Soviet Nomenklatura to Russian Elite," 716–717; and Yurchak, "Post-Soviet Entrepreneurial Culture."

29. According to Kryshtanovskaia and White, a resolution of the CPSU Central Committee on July 25, 1986 "approved a proposal from the Komsomol that it establish a network of scientific and technical centres for the benefit of its members. The new centres were supposed to operate on commercial principles" ("From Soviet Nomenklatura to Russian Elite," 716).

30. Solnick, *Stealing the State,* 116. For an account of this process, based on interviews, see Yurchak, "Post-Soviet Entrepreneurial Culture."

31. Solnick, *Stealing the State,* 116.

32. Radaev, *Stanovlenie novogo Rossiiskogo predprinimatel'stva,* 57.

33. Solnick, *Stealing the State,* 112, 119.

34. Ibid., 121.

35. Kryshtanovskaia and White, "From Soviet Nomenklatura to Russian Elite,"711–733. See the Appendix, above, for details on Gusinsky, Khodorkovsky, and Vinogradov.

36. Agence France-Presse, 8/25/98.

37. RFE/RL [Radio Free Europe/Radio Liberty] Report, "Russia's Financial Empire," 1/98.

38. Ibid..

39. Akos Rona-Tas, "The First Shall Be Last? Entrepreneurship and Communist Cadres in the Transition from Socialism," *American Journal of Sociology* 100(1994):40–69.

40. Kryshtanovskaia, "Transformation of the Old Nomenklatura," 25–31; Kryshtanovskaia and White, "From Soviet Nomenklatura to Russian Elite," 716–721. Both articles are based on empirical research carried out between 1989 and 1994 by the Soviet Elites Project of the University of Glasgow (directed by Stephen White and Evan Mawdsley) and the Sector of Elite Studies, Institute of Sociology, Russian Academy of Sciences (directed by Olga V. Kryshtanovskaia).

41. Belkindas, "Privatization," 60–71. For an analysis of the role of cooperatives in Gorbachev's overall strategy, see Victoria E. Bonnell, "Voluntary Associations in Gorbachev's Reform Program," in *Can Gorbachev's Reforms Succeed?,* ed. George Breslauer (Berkeley, 1990), 63–75.

42. Belkindas, "Privatization," 60–71. Cooperatives in consumer services and banking were decreed by the Council of Ministers.

43. Jones and Moskoff, *Ko-ops,* 15. The number of cooperative employees dropped soon after by half a million.

44. Ibid., 35.

45. Solnick, *Stealing the State,* 229.

46. Aslund, *How Russia Became a Market Economy,* 225.

47. V. Zubakin, "Vtoraia ekonomika," in *Voprosy ekonomiki* 11(1994):156–157.

48. Volkov, "Violent Entrepreneurship," 742.

49. In August 1990, a Soviet law titled "Measure to Create and Develop Small Enterprises" gave new legal status to small businesses established within state enterprises (*Malyi biznes v Rossii,* ed. S. Iu. Vinokur [Moscow, 1998], 45–47).

50. See the Appendix. In 1996, the bank had 1,500 branches in 81 regions, and 1,500 corporate clients (*Washington Post,* 9/4/98).

51. Remnick, *Resurrection,* 187; RFE/RL Report, "Russia's Financial Empire," 1/98.

52. I. V. Kukolev, "Formirovanie Rossiiskoi biznes-elity," *Sotsiologicheskii zhurnal* 3 (1995):161–166; Kukolev, "The Formation of the Business Elite," 69-70, 72. A 1990 survey of organizers and directors of cooperatives from nine different Soviet cities disclosed that most were men, age 36 or older, with higher education. Twenty-five percent of those surveyed were members of the CPSU (Jones and Moskoff, *Ko-ops,* 27).

53. Bunin, *Biznesmeny Rossii,* 392–397.

54. Remnick, *Resurrection,* 207–208.

55. Bunin, *Biznesmeny Rossii,* 397–399; Remnick, *Resurrection,* 208.

56. Donald N. Jensen, "How Russia Is Ruled: 1998," RFE/RL Report.

57. Jones and Moskoff, *Ko-ops,* 111.

58. In early 1996, the organization had 4,133 members representing 2,730 enterprises and 69 regional branches (*Obshchestvennye [nekommercheskie] ob"edineniia predpriiatii i predprinimatelei Rossii: Spravochnik,* ed. N. V. Nazarova [Moscow, 1997], 75).

59. *Sistema predstavitel'stva Rossiiskogo biznesa: Formy kollektivnogo deistviia,* ed. A. Iu. Zudin (Moscow, 1997), 15–16.

60. *Obshchestvennye (nekommercheskie) ob"edineniia,* 10, 100.

61. For an overview from a neoliberal perspective, see: Aslund, *How Russia Became a Market Economy;* Blasi, Kroumova, and Kruse, *Kremlin Capitalism;* and Maxim Boycko, Andrei Schleifer, and Robert Vishny, *Privatizing Russia* (Cambridge, Mass., 1995). For an approach that emphasizes "involution" of the economy, see Michael Burawoy, "The State and Economic Involution: Russia Through a China Lens," *World Development* 24(1996):6, 1105–1117.

62. Chirikova, *Lidery Rossiiskogo predprinimatel'stva,* 15–16.

63. Kukolev, "The Formation of the Business Elite," 72–75.

64. Anders Aslund, "Observations on the Development of Small Private Enterprises in Russia," 195, 197.

65. The proportion of former *nomenklatura* has been the subject of controversy. A 1993 study of 1,000 entrepreneurs each in Russia, Hungary, and Poland concluded that 19 percent of the private business elite in Russia were former members of the *nomenklatura,* compared to 28 percent and 30 percent in Poland and Hungary, respectively (Blasi, Kroumova, and Kruse, *Kremlin Capitalism,* 61).

66. Kukolev, "Formirovanie," 168.

67. According to Kukolev, "Members of this group are not aggressive in business contacts; on the contrary, they are somewhat phlegmatic, infantile, and good-natured" ("The Formation of the Business Elite," 74).

68. Ibid., 75.

69. On the changing official Russian government definition of "small enterprise," see *Malyi biznes v Rossii,* 47–50.

70. Aslund, "Observations on the Development of Small Private Enterprises in Russia," 191–205. The number of small enterprises decreased by about 20,000 in 1995. Peak periods of increase were between 1991 and 1992, and 1992 and 1993. Growth slowed between 1993 and 1994.

71. Ibid., 196. By way of comparison, the proportion of the population employed in small firms in Estonia and the Czech Republic was 40 percent in 1994.

72. *Obshchestvennye (nekommercheskie) ob"edineniia,* 9. In 1996, the Association had 46 regional branches.

73. Ibid., 24. In 1996 this organization included 100 associations of entrepreneurs.

74. Ibid., 51. In 1996, the Society united more than 200 private firms and had more than 20,000 members, with branches in 25 Russian cities.

75. *Sistema predstavitel'stva Rossiiskogo biznesa,* 19–24.

76. Kukolev, "Formirovanie," 162, 164.

77. N. Iu. Lapina, *Biznes i politika v sovremennoi Rossii* (Moscow, 1998), 20.

78. These included the Party of Economic Freedom (Partiia ekonomicheskoi svobody), Entrepreneurs for a New Russia (Predprinimatel'i za novuyu Rossiiu), the All-Russian Union "Renewal" (Vserossiiskii soiuz "Obnovlenie"), and the Party of Democratic Initiative (Partiia demokraticheskoi initsiativy) (Ibid., 16–21).

79. Ibid., 22.

80. For the following discussion, I have drawn on Juliet Johnson, "Russia's Emerging Financial-Industrial Groups," *Post-Soviet Affairs* 13(4)(1997):333–365, table 1, 337. The state often took the initiative, encouraging state-owned enterprises to create FIGs for the purpose of building investment and ensuring state control. For 1998 data on FIGs, see Jensen, "How Russia Is Ruled: 1998."

81. Sometimes, Vitaliy Malkin of Rossiiskii Kredit, Rem Vyakhirev of Gazprom, and Vagit Alekperov of Lukoil are included (Johnson, "Russia's Emerging Financial-Industrial Groups," 333, note 2, 345, and table 3, 346–347). For more on Alekperov and Vyakhirev, see the Appendix.

82. Jensen, "How Russia Is Ruled: 1998."

83. Johnson, "Russia's Emerging Financial-Industrial Groups," 345.

84. Blasi, Kroumova, and Kruse, *Kremlin Capitalism*, 74.

85. Johnson, "Russia's Emerging Financial-Industrial Groups," 352. The program was terminated on July 25, 1997.

86. At a meeting in Davos, Switzerland, in early 1996, the major oligarchs (excluding Inkombank's Vinogradov) united to provide financial and media support for Yeltsin and bring in Anatolii Chubais to run his campaign (Ibid., 349–350).

87. *Washington Post*, 8/28/98. Of the seven oligarchs, two held political positions at an earlier time: Khodorkovsky was deputy prime minister of the fuel and energy industry in 1991, and Vinogradov was chief economist of the Presidential Council for Private Enterprise in 1992. In 1997, Potanin was declared by *Business Week* to be "the most powerful man in Russia" (Patricia Kranz, "The Most Powerful Man in Russia," *Business Week* 3554[11/24/97]:66–73).

88. *Los Angeles Times*, 8/30/98; Associated Press (AP), 6/99.

89. A. Zudin, "Gosudarstvo i biznes: Povorot vo vzaimootnosheniiakh?" *Politiia* 3(5)(1997):22–24.

90. A. Zudin, "Sotsial'naia organizatsiia rossiiskogo biznesa: Ot segmentatsii k dualizmu," *Kuda idet Rossiia? Obshchee i osobennoe v sovremennom razvitii*, T. I. Zaslavskaia, ed. (Moscow, 1997), 211–212.

91. Chrystia Freeland, "The Men Who Really Rule Russia: Oligarchs Led by Boris Berezovsky," *New Statesman* 127(4400)(8/28/98):17.

92. *Moscow Times*, 2/11/99.

93. In 1996 the eight largest FIGs may have accounted for between 25 and 30 percent of the country's GNP (Jensen, "How Russia Is Ruled: 1998").

94. Some reports indicate that Berezovsky helped convince Yeltsin to sack Chernomyrdin. Berezovsky's motive is unclear; Nemtsov attributed the move to power hunger (*Los Angeles Times*, 8/30/98).

95. Journalist Chrystia Freeland reported a few days later: "I watched the oligarchs, en masse, troop from a meeting with one deputy prime minister, to a meeting with another, to a meeting with the prime minister himself. Collectively, they have been conferring almost daily with the Central Bank chairman" (Freeland, "The Men Who Really Rule").

96. Gregory Freidin, "Yeltsin Yields to the Oligarchs," *Los Angeles Times*, 8/28/98.

97. *RFE/RL Newsline*, 3:6, Part 1 (1/11/99).

98. Ibid. According to one source in June 1999, the new big seven included Alekperov, Berezovsky, Gusinsky, Kazmin, Khodorkovsky, Smolensky, and Vyakhirev (*Russian Commerce News*, 6/14/99).

99. Donald N. Jensen, "Rumors of Oligarchs' Demise Greatly Exaggerated," *RFE/RL Newsline*, 2:234, Part 1 (12/7/98).

100. Ibid., 25.

101. Radaev, *Formirovanie novykh rossiiskikh rynkov*; Yurchak, "Post-Soviet Entrepreneurial Culture."

102. TASS, 9/23/98; ITAR-TASS, 12/23/98.

103. Agence France-Presse, 9/30/98; A. Chepurenko, "Malyi biznes posle Avgusta 1998 g.: Problemy, tendentsii, adaptatsionnye vozmozhnosti," in *Osennii krizis 1998 goda: Rossiiskoe obshchestvo do i posle* (Moscow, 1998), 109–112.

104. "Enterprise and Banking," *Russian Economic Trends Quarterly*, 1/1/99:4.

105. Production in St. Petersburg food industries increased 28 percent in 1998 compared to 1997 (ITAR-TASS, 1/19/99). The auditing and consulting sector grew by 15 to 20 percent in 1998 over 1997, according to official data. ("Russian Companies Grow As the Big Five Leave," *Russia Journal*, 3/15/99).

106. Interfax Russian News, 11/5/99.

107. Intercon Daily Report on Russia, 10/21/98.

108. TASS, 12/4/98; *Rossiiskii delovoi monitor*, 2/2/99; *Russian Business News*, 11/30/98.

109. Max Weber, *The Protestant Ethic and the Spirit of Capitalism* (New York, 1958), 75, 181–182.

110. Yurchak, "Post-Soviet Entrepreneurial Culture," 35.

111. This appendix was completed in December 1999.

112. "Russian Media IV," RFE/RL Report, 10/98; TASS, 11/24/98; Interfax, 11/23/98; *Russian Commerce News*, 1/29/99; *Moscow News*, 2/11/99; *Russian Oil and Gas Report*, 3/29/99; *Vremya MN*, 7/28/99.

113. *Moscow Times*, 11/7/98; *Moscow Times*, 1/12/99; *Kommersant-Daily*, 1/27/99; *Russian Commerce News*, 1/29/99; *Kommersant-Daily*, 2/18/99; *Moscow Times*, 2/23/99; *Neftegazovyi kompleks*, 2/27/99; *Nezavisimaia gazeta*, 3/10/99; *Moscow Times*, 6/23/99; *Moscow Times*, 6/25/99; *Moscow News*, 8/17/99.

114. *Time*, 10/20/97, 66; Jensen, "How Russia Is Ruled: 1998"; Agence France-Presse, 8/25/98; *Los Angeles Times*, 8/30/98; *Russian Commerce News*, 1/29/99; *New York Times*, 2/13/99; *Moskovskii Komsomolets*, 2/9/99; AP, 2/16/99; RFE/RL, 3/10/99; AP, 6/99; TASS, 6/9/99; RFE/RL, 6/17/99; *Vremya ORT*, 7/17/99; *Moscow Times*, 8/26/99; *Moscow Times*, 9/10/99.

115. *Moscow Times*, 2/10/98; *Kommersant-Daily*, 4/4/98; Info-NOVA Press Digest, 6/30/98; *Moscow Times*, 12/30/98; *Moscow Times*, 2/27/99; *Vek*, April 1999, 3; *Parlamentskaia gazeta*, 4/3/99, 2; *Moscow Times*, 4/9/99; *Vremya*, 8/24/99; *Izvestiia*, 8/25/99; *Russian Political Monitor*, 9/3/99; *New York Times*, 10/12/99.

116. RFE/RL Report, "Russia's Financial Empires," 1/98; *Financial Times*, 1/14/98; *Moscow Times*, 8/6/98; RFE/RL Report, "Russian Media IV," 10/98; *Moscow Times*, 11/10/98; *RFE/RL Newsline*, 12/7/98; *Financial Times*, 12/14/98; *Russian Commerce News*, 1/29/99; Interfax, 3/15/99; *Politekonomiia*, 6/99.

117. *Time*, 10/20/97; RFE/RL Report, "Russia's Financial Empires," 1/98; Interfax, 9/15/98; Interfax, 11/15/98; *Moscow Times*, 1/12/99; *Russian Commerce News*, 1/29/99; *Moscow Times*, 3/4/99; *Moscow Times*, 7/20/99; *Kommersant*, 7/31/99; *Times* (London), 8/26/98; *Intercon Daily Report on Russia*, 10/7/99; *Segodnia*, 11/13/99; *Banks and Exchanges*, 11/17/99; *Intercon Daily Report on Russia*, 12/7/99.

118. *Russian Commerce News*, 1/29/99; Reuters, 4/26/99; *Kommersant*, 7/1/99; *Vremya*, 7/1/99.

119. RFE/RL Report, "Russia's Financial Empires," 1/98; Agence France-Presse, 8/25/98; *Times* (London), 8/28/98; *International Herald Tribune*, 9/28/98; *Moscow Times*, 12/3/98;

200 *Victoria E. Bonnell*

Russian Commerce News, 1/29/99; *Moscow Times*, 5/20/99; *Moscow Times*, 6/8/99; *Business Central Europe*, 6/15/99; *Vremya*, 7/1/99; *Economist Intelligence Unit Limited*, 7/22/99.

120. RFE/RL Report, "Russia's Financial Empires," 1/98; Agence France-Presse, 8/25/98; *International Herald Tribune*, 9/28/98; *Russian Commerce News*, 1/29/99; *Financial Times*, 2/10/99; AP, 2/16/99; *Business Week*, 3/1/99; *Herald*, 3/17/99; *Business Central Europe*, 7/15/99; *Euromoney Magazine*, 9/10/99.

121. RFE/RL Report, "Russia's Financial Empires," 1/98; *Moscow Times*, 9/12/98; *Sovershenno sekretno*, 9/16/98; *Central European*, 11/10/98; *Moscow Times*, 3/5/99; AP, 2/16/99; *Russian Commerce News*, 1/29/99; *Izvestiia*, 5/14/99; *Moscow Times*, 6/23/99, 8/17/99, and 8/4/99.

122. RFE/RL Report, "Russia's Financial Empires," 1/98; Agence France-Presse, 8/25/98; *International Herald Tribune*, 9/28/98; Interfax, 10/29/98; *Financial Times*, 11/10/98; TASS, 11/12/98; *Moscow Times*, 12/15/98; *Russian Commerce News*, 1/29/99; *Kommersant*, 7/30/99; *Moscow Times*, 8/17/99.

123. *Company and Industry Information from RMG*, 11/28/97; *Russian Commerce News*, 1/29/99; *Vremya*, 7/27/99; *Moscow Times*, 8/27/99; *Moscow Times*, 8/28/99; *Intercon Daily Report on Russia*, 8/30/99.

10

The Russian
Working Class in
Times of Transition

Victor Zaslavsky

The Guido Carli Free International University of Social Sciences, Rome

The evolution of the Russian Federation during the first decade of its existence can be characterized by two parallel and interdependent processes: the
continuing decomposition of the major institutions of the Soviet system, and the
creation of a national market through deliberate state action and international
pressures for institutional isomorphism. The ongoing reforms have had a powerful impact on all strata of the Russian population, altering the fabric of social life.
In particular, the largest Russian social group—the working class—has seen profound changes in its circumstances. Reforms have proceeded at a very unequal
pace in different sectors of the economy, and the incomplete and uncertain character of the Russian transition hinders a comprehensive account of the ongoing
changes in the workers' situation. This chapter pursues the more modest goal of
analyzing several trends that have become pronounced in the first decade since
the collapse of the Soviet Union. The recent restructuring of the Russian coal industry will serve as a paradigm of radical reform that may shed light on the possible consequences of similar transitions in other sectors of the economy, affecting other segments of Russia's working class.

The Numerical Decline of the Working Class

A basic trend in the situation of the Russian working class has been its numerical
decline, which is attributable to a number of obvious factors: the general modernization trend, which favors well-developed service, public health, and information sectors over manufacturing; the fall in output and reduced demand for
industrial labor in the economies in transition; and the rapid and radical change

of the Russian social structure following the emergence of entrepreneurial, self-employed, and unemployed social groups. The precise dimensions of these phenomena are impossible to ascertain and can only be estimated.

There are several reasons for this. First of all, the state statistical service has been particularly hard hit by the financial crisis. The Russian national census, scheduled to take place in 1999 after the same ten-year interval as the previous five Soviet censuses, has been canceled for lack of funds. The Central Statistical Committee thus has to rely on self-reports by enterprises and organizations, which for a variety of reasons tend to provide the state organs with inadequate and unreliable information. The statistical categories used to describe and analyze the socioeconomic situation of the formerly planned economy have become increasingly irrelevant to the emerging market economy, complicating the socioeconomic analysis. Furthermore, there has been a complete reversal in the systematic distortion of data. Whereas enterprises during the Soviet period were prompted by the tenets of the centrally planned economy to systematically overstate their output, the current economic situation prompts the same enterprises to underreport their output and to overreport economic and social indicators in order to evade taxes, to preserve their labor force, and to gain state subsidies. The Central Statistical Committee has little experience in verifying and correcting data distorted in these ways, and it has no means of conducting control surveys. Fortunately, several research organizations, such as the Russian Center for Public Opinion Research (VTsIOM), conduct national polls and various kinds of surveys on a regular basis. These data complement and balance out the official statistics.

According to data gathered by the Russian Statistical Committee from 1992 to 1997, the share of "workers" in the category of Russian hired labor (a category that did not exist in Soviet statistics) declined from 64 percent in the early 1990s to 58.6 percent in 1997. Taking into account that in the same period the size of the hired labor group decreased from about 72 million to about 65 million, the numerical strength of the group defined in Russian statistics as "workers" had proportionally declined in the five-year period by at least 15 percent. The official statistical picture also highlights the decline in industrial workers: from 16.3 million (22.6 percent of the employed population) in 1992, to 11.0 million (17.0 percent of the employed population) in 1997, comprising about 39 percent of all workers in the Russian economy.[1] The VTsIOM data on the self-identification of respondents present a picture similar to that seen in official statistics: In 1994 the average share of respondents identifying themselves as workers was 41.5 percent; the same category in 1997 had dropped to 36.5 percent. The actual numerical decline of the working class—particularly that in industry—might well be lower, if one takes into account the Ukrainian and Byelorussian "guest workers" massively employed in Russian construction and transportation industries. These migrant workers have never been registered by official statistics, and their number cannot be established with any precision, although experts estimate that it runs into the millions. Clearly, the Russian working class has shrunk considerably since the collapse of the Soviet Union.

TABLE 10.1   Unemployment, 1992–1999

	Economically Active Population (millions)	Unemployed (millions)	Unemployed (percent of active population)	Workers Among the Unemployed (percent)
1992	75.7	3.6	4.8	59.2
1993	75.0	4.2	5.6	61.2
1994	74.0	5.5	7.4	62.8
1995	72.7	6.4	8.8	63.6
1996	73.2	7.2	9.8	64.9
1997	72.6	8.2	11.3	–
1998	72.6	8.1*	11.2	–
1999	–	9.1**	13.0	–

*July 1998 / **July 1999

SOURCES: *Rossiiskii statisticheskii ezhegodnik: Ofitsial'noe izdanie,* 1998
(Moscow: Goskomstat RF, 1998), pp. 173, 185, 189; *Voprosy statistiki* 6 (2000), p. 79.

The Russian Working Class and Unemployment

Unemployment, both as a threat and as an everyday reality, has had a major impact on labor relations in Russia. It has changed dramatically the system of stratification and power relations within enterprises and has contributed to rapid differentiation and stratification within the working class. A major rift emerged between workers and senior management as the latter took on primary responsibility for the economic direction and survival of the industrial enterprise. Whether as owners of the enterprise or as representatives of the actual owners (even in cases when the enterprise is employee-owned), management has assumed the right to hire and fire labor.

The ongoing growth of unemployment and the growing share of workers among the unemployed (by 1998, members of the working class comprised two-thirds of all unemployed; see Table 10.1) are two obvious trends in the workforce in the first years of the Russian transition. Unemployment has been the major factor determining radical changes in the situation of Russian workers.

The actual level of unemployment is higher than statistics indicate: Official figures do not account for hidden unemployment—a shortened work week, so-called "administrative vacations" at reduced pay, and unpaid leaves of absence. In 1997, between 5.5 percent and 5.8 percent of the labor force was working a reduced schedule, and 3.5 percent was on unpaid leave.[2] According to another source, in 1996 and 1997, between 10 percent and 12 percent of the workforce of large and medium-sized enterprises had a shortened work schedule.[3]

Financial pressures continue to push enterprise management to reduce manpower and to enforce labor flexibility. The rise in Russian unemployment accelerated after the August 1998 financial crisis. Unemployment in the first half of 1999 grew by 16.1 percent compared to the first half of 1998. The number of unemployed exceeded 9.5 million by early 1999, peaked around 10 million by March of that year, and then began declining toward the 9-million mark.

During the first decade of the Russian transition, all major economic indicators were uniformly negative. Although bursts of inflation and drops in economic output and in the real income of most Russians had been anticipated,[4] the severity of the crisis surprised most economists.[5] Rising unemployment had always been among the major anticipated manifestations of the crisis; the stark discrepancy between the precipitous decline both in the country's gross national product and in industrial production and the relatively slow growth of unemployment constitutes another major surprise of the Russian transition.

It should be noted that the perception of the inevitability of increasing unemployment has become deeply rooted in Russian public opinion. According to data collected by VTsIOM—which began monitoring popular attitudes toward unemployment in 1993—the fraction of respondents who considered unemployment among the most pressing and threatening social problems has been growing steadily: increasing from the initial 30 percent or so in 1993 to 45 to 48 percent in 1994–1995. By 1998, 66 percent of respondents called unemployment the most worrisome issue facing Russian society.[6] The share of gainfully employed respondents who feared losing their jobs in the near future because of staff reductions, elimination of their job, or liquidation of the enterprise remained high, fluctuating between 35 percent and 50 percent.[7] However, about 50 percent of respondents who worried about losing their jobs expressed confidence that they would be able to find another job in the same trade or profession. This figure remained stable even after the August 1998 financial crisis.

In fact, employment decline continued to lag well behind the decline in GNP until the August 1998 crisis. As a result, the Russian transition—unlike those in Poland, the Czech Republic, and Bulgaria—has been characterized by a rather slow rise in unemployment and a peculiar substitution of unemployment by wage reduction. This practice has had a major impact on the labor market and the situation of the working class.

One of the legacies of the Soviet system is a structure of production that adapts poorly to a market economy. According to Nikolai Shmelev's estimate,[8] most former Soviet enterprises—up to 70 percent of larger plants and 70 percent of state and collective farms—cannot be expected to survive in a market environment and are doomed to bankruptcy. Other analysts have come to an analogous conclusion that no more than a quarter of Russian enterprises are well positioned for market reforms, and the other three-quarters remain in need of radical and far-reaching restructuring.[9] According to estimates from the Ministry of the Economy, in 1997 the economically active population of 75 million persons included, in addition to almost 8 million unemployed, between 12 and 13 million redundant workers who were still at their jobs.[10]

TABLE 10.2   Nonmonetary Payment of Workers' Wages, 1995–1997

Share of Nonmonetary Payments in Total Wages	Enterprises Practicing Nonmonetary Payments (percent)		
	1995	*1996*	*1997*
Up to 10 percent	43.8	25.1	21.6
10–20 percent	18.8	33.1	33.3
20–30 percent	14.6	20.9	25.5
More than 30 percent	22.9	20.9	19.6

SOURCE: *Sotsial'no-trudovye otnosheniia na predpriiatiiakh: Konflikt interesov ili poisk soglasiia* (Moscow: Institut ekonomiki RAN [Rossiiskoi Akademii Nauk], 1998), p. 5.

Given the environment of general economic decline, a strict adherence to the new bankruptcy laws would have resulted in a catastrophic jump in unemployment. To prevent this, the state granted Russian enterprises a fairly long grace period during which it continued to provide subsidies. During this period, managers were expected to identify new market opportunities and respond to budget constraints in ways that generated economic value, and workers, to adapt to and learn how to survive in a new economic order. But this same grace period also made it possible for Russian managers to avoid laying off workers. These conditions predetermined the ensuing symbiosis between workers and management, based on their common interest in ensuring the enterprise's survival and maintaining their incomes.[11]

The most common entry point into market activity pursued by former Soviet enterprises was the diversion of their production to supply the "informal economy"—the modern variant of the Soviet "second economy." Enterprises became deeply involved in a range of "informal profit-seeking" activities that required "a low level of rule obedience and high level of trust in personal relations."[12] This environment created a basis for the mutual dependence between workers and management, who were united by the need to conceal these transactions from the state authorities.

The growth of nonmonetary payments to workers has been an inevitable consequence of this hidden production for the informal economy. Payments in kind—in the products of one's own enterprise, to be resold in the marketplace, or in goods received by the enterprise as a result of barter with other firms—are becoming increasingly frequent. In 1997, the machine-building industry paid as much as 24 percent of all wages in nonmonetary form, as shown in Table 10.2. In most cases, these payments amounted to a further reduction in wages, which workers accepted for lack of an alternative.

Workers generally take advantage of the informal economy by exploiting the resources of their enterprises for private gain. For instance, they spend part of their workday working on "personal projects" utilizing the equipment, electricity, and resources of the enterprise, and selling the products of their labor on the market. This production is not accounted for in statistics, nor is the income from it declared for taxation purposes. Instead, it becomes part of the shadow economy.

According to Leonid Kosals and Rosalina Ryvkina, the share of the workday devoted to private production can be estimated at about 12 to 15 percent, and the share of enterprise's resources utilized by workers for their private production totals about 8 percent.[13] The management is well aware of this practice, with about half of all managers and directors considering it "normal under the present conditions." The rest condemn it as leading to a decline of labor discipline and to the "enterprise's degradation."[14] Whatever their attitude, management normally tolerates this practice because it reinforces the symbiotic relationship between workers and managers and contributes to the enterprise's social equilibrium. This mode of adaptation to declining wages and frequent payment delays is more widespread in state and privatized enterprises than in private enterprises.

The Trade-Off Between Unemployment and Wage Reduction

A major trend in the Russian labor market during the first decade of transition has been "adaptation without restructuring," as Rostislav Kapelyushnikov put it.[15] Lacking external political support after the collapse of the party and the disintegration of ministerial structures, and facing the double uncertainty about the general direction of reforms and their own positions in view of the rapidly changing property rights, directors and top managers have been eager to avoid layoffs by reducing wages. This tendency has been exacerbated by the tradition of hoarding labor—a holdover from the centrally planned Soviet economy, with its ubiquitous shortages of labor, supplies, and equipment.[16] Afraid that they would not be able to recruit new workers should the economy recover or the state resume its subsidies, the disoriented management attempted to minimize cuts to their workforces, particularly to their skilled worker reserves. Soviet legislation that made enterprises responsible for paying three months' worth of unemployment benefits to laid-off workers also prompted administrators to look for solutions other than shedding workers outright. The solutions they found were various forms of wage reductions: a freeze on raises in an environment of increasing inflation; direct pay cuts; delays in payments; reduced working hours; temporary layoffs ("administrative vacations" with minimum pay); and unpaid leaves of absence. The proportion of the total costs of production devoted to wages has considerably decreased, making employment of superfluous workers less onerous.

The ongoing privatization initially affected the restructuring of the labor market in a contradictory fashion, simultaneously providing incentives to lay off superfluous labor and promoting the substitution of wage reduction for unemployment. The formal change from state property to private property has been one of the key developments of the period; yet privatization did not transform former state enterprises overnight into real private firms working to meet market demands and controlled by private owners who select managers capable of running efficient production. Instead, Russian privatization has been a gradual process: As many enterprises became nominally employee-owned, "the managers—in the name of all employees—continued to dominate both the formal ownership and the reins of control of the very firms the government hoped would change with privatization."[17] The first wave of privatization has resulted in the predominance of inside ownership and blurred the distinction between real and nominal owners.

The implications of the new ownership structures for the development of unemployment have been considerable. In the early phase of privatization, the key priority of senior management was to retain power and to avoid outside shareholder efforts to change the management.[18] Although the workers, as shareholders, putatively gained ultimate ownership of the privatized enterprises, their power to intervene in the day-to-day management or to share in the profits has been very limited.[19] In many cases their nominal ownership had a negative effect on the economic situation of the enterprise: Generally, the greater the share of ownership in the hands of employees, the sharper the decline in output and investment.[20]

The tendency of enterprise management to ignore the new legal provisions and rely on the paternalistic style inherited from the Soviet period has become even more pronounced. But managers can hold onto traditional paternalistic levers only to the extent that they can guarantee workers' job security. Thus, nominal ownership proved compatible with defensive restructuring that delayed the shedding of redundant employees. This process can be seen in the numerous attempts by various workers' collectives to take control over hiring and firing rules and procedures at their places of employment. Facing the problem of redundancy, management has tended to make decisions based on meritocratic principles, first laying off workers with poor disciplinary records as well as older, less skilled, auxiliary, and female workers. The workers' collectives, more concerned with maintaining "social justice," often have tried to force management to retain redundant employees who have seniority or who have greater need of employment (such as single mothers, or the parents of very young children). This practice has helped maintain social peace in the enterprise but also has damaged the prospects of younger and better-qualified workers.[21] The drunkenness on the job, absenteeism, and other violations of labor discipline that always plagued Soviet enterprises have diminished in frequency, however, since workers with poor disciplinary records were the first victims of layoffs. Another consequence has been the virtual abandonment of the external labor market by privatized enterprises, which have come to rely exclusively on the internal redistribution of labor.

What is the socioeconomic significance of the substitution of wage reduction for unemployment? As is the case with any contradictory social development, it is difficult to defend a strictly positive or negative evaluation. As Leonid Gordon and Eduard Klopov argue, this strategy essentially involves choosing the lesser evil. On the one hand, the practice of maintaining redundant employees hindered economic reforms and the rationalization of the Russian economy, in the long run contributing to the mass disillusionment in reforms and democracy. On the other hand, it dissipated the accumulated social tensions and neutralized to some extent the threat of social explosion and Weimar-like developments in Russia.[22] Some Russian analysts have also argued that by avoiding radical cuts in the workforce, the management not only reinforced the old paternalistic stereotype of defending the working collective from external threat but also increased its real control over the workforce and its ability to exercise disciplinary pressure.[23]

It might be more fruitful to consider the question from a different perspective: Was the unemployment–wage reduction trade-off a policy consciously pursued by the Russian government in preference to other options, or was it a largely inevitable result of the structural properties of the Soviet economy and of the Soviet economic culture and mind-set of the Russian population?

According to the late Ilya Zaslavsky, a longtime student of the Russian labor market, the Chernomyrdin government deliberately engineered the phenomenon of wage reduction to hinder the growth of unemployment, thus restoring the well-known Soviet practice of guaranteeing employment at the expense of efficiency.[24] Yet although wage reduction as a substitution for unemployment might have been welcomed by the Russian government, which was justifiably preoccupied with the social stresses that high unemployment would entail, it seems unlikely that the practice was consciously pursued as a matter of policy. Government control over the economy was insufficient to have supported such a large-scale, centralized policy. The case of the excess wage tax—a short-lived attempt by the government to maintain high employment levels through active intervention—can be cited as evidence of insufficient state control. This tax was predicated on the idea that the average wage at any enterprise should not exceed an amount equal to five times the minimum wage. If an enterprise's wage fund exceeded permissible levels, that enterprise paid a tax on the difference.[25] The excess wage tax did serve as an incentive to retain surplus labor; however, it proved unenforceable. Management circumvented the tax by keeping wages to redundant workers low or by sending these workers on "administrative leave" at minimum pay, which enabled managers to pay higher wages to the remaining workers as well as to themselves. In 1996, the tax was abolished.[26]

It is more realistic to assume that the practice of wage reduction as a substitution for unemployment emerged spontaneously in thousands of state and privatized enterprises facing the same economic and psychological constraints. In this respect, the habitual paternalistic policy of the directors and top managers of enterprises in small "company towns," where these enterprises represented the main or even the only source of employment, was especially important. By reducing wages or shortening the work week, or both, they avoided massive layoffs, reduced social tensions, and prevented open manifestations of protest. Pressures on the part of the regional administrations, which usually intensified in preelectoral periods, also played a significant role: Exerting negative pressure, some governors and regional administrators threatened enterprise directors with cutting off electricity and water supplies and interrupting communication lines in the case of massive layoffs. Examples of positive pressure include agreements between directors and regional administrations to maintain temporarily excessive labor in exchange for tax breaks and other concessions to enterprises.

The substitution of wage reduction for unemployment undoubtedly accorded with the values and expectations of most workers. As I have noted elsewhere, although economic reforms have disrupted the reproduction of state-dependent workers, a very considerable part of the employed population still belongs to this category.[27] From the very beginning of the transition, opinion polls invariably demonstrated that more than half of the respondents favored policies guaranteeing continued employment and minimizing individual risk over those directed at achieving higher productivity and higher wages.[28] In the same vein, the 1997 and 1998 surveys demonstrated that in the case of an economically dire situation at one's enterprise, 53 percent and 49 percent of working respondents, respectively, favored "preserving jobs" even if wages were paid irregularly, partially, or sometimes not at all, whereas only 15 percent and 18 percent preferred to be dismissed and to seek unemployment benefits.[29]

Next to the practice of wage reduction, the less-than-satisfactory performance of the state employment services and local employment centers bears considerable responsibility for the unemployment in Russia remaining much lower than expected. Only a minority of unemployed have registered with the state employment service. In the 1990s, the share of the officially registered unemployed oscillated between one-sixth and one-third of the total number (the figure for the first half of 1999 being only 16.4 percent).[30] The starvation level of unemployment benefits (20 percent to 25 percent of an average wage, largely unindexed and hence constantly eroded by inflation) obviously provides little incentive for registration. Moreover, many workers find the very procedure of registering for unemployment benefits humiliating, especially since the outcome of an application is uncertain. Lastly, the average length of time between jobs has increased steadily, from 5.8 months in 1993 to 8.8 months in 1997 and even longer.[31] The proportion of unemployed seeking a new job for more than one year increased from about 19 percent in 1993 to 33 percent in 1996 and has continued to grow.

New Divisions Within the Working Class

Rapid and profound changes in social stratification give rise to new social groups and aggregates, and widen the gap between groups in terms of economic well-being and opportunity. The fact is, political and managerial elites of Soviet-type societies have proved capable of transmuting their political positions and resources into economic capital, giving rise to "political capitalism."[32] The growing political and economic inequality between workers and managers has become one of the most pronounced characteristics of the early phase of the transition. Another feature of the evolving socioeconomic system is the growing degree of internal differentiation and stratification in the Russian working class, whose various subgroups and segments have been strongly but very unevenly affected by the ongoing social changes.

In the Soviet era, stratification was largely engineered by the party-state, which combined production priorities with internal stability considerations. The system of "organized consensus," based on the individual's dependence on the state and on bureaucratic redistribution, guaranteed job security, price stability, and a largely egalitarian income policy. A peculiar, semi-free labor market existed, in which educational and labor qualifications often correlated inversely with wage levels. Job turnover, rather than higher productivity and better skills, became the major bargaining resource of workers.[33] The system favored blue-collar workers over white-collar employees and professionals, and workers employed in heavy industry, especially in the military-industrial complex, over those in consumer goods and services. Having become increasingly dysfunctional under perestroika, this system totally unraveled after the Soviet Union collapsed.

The hardships of the economic transition have fallen very unevenly on different segments of the working class. Who are the clear winners and losers in the transition? Given the ongoing economic restructuring, the situation is too complex and fluid for any definitive conclusions; but some broad trends point to a new internal differentiation of the working class. This differentiation is based increasingly on market principles, with skills and the type of enterprise becoming crucial determinants of a worker's economic situation. The result has been a growing gap between the wages of workers employed by state enterprises and those in private enterprises. A similar gap has opened between wages and job security enjoyed by skilled workers and by medium- to low-skilled ones.

The first phase of Russian privatization resulted in the emergence of two different kinds of entities alongside the traditional state enterprises: privatized, or semi-state enterprises, and private entrepreneurial start-up firms. One of the distinguishing features of the period has been the passage of the best-skilled, most competitive workers from state and semi-state enterprises to the new private sector.[34] The number of workers employed in this fast-growing sector increased more than tenfold between 1990 and 1994 and has kept growing ever since.[35] The private sector is composed of relatively small firms that employ younger, better-skilled workers. Wages in private firms are usually one and a half to two times higher than those in the rest of the economy. Moreover, the majority of those employed in the private sector hold second jobs. According to VTsIOM data, in 1996 this group constituted only 23 percent of the total labor force; but among the category of second-job holders, 56 percent were employed by private firms.[36]

Workers employed by private firms represent a "self-selected" group that differs considerably from the rest not only in its age and skill profile, but also in terms of wages, work motivation, and work satisfaction. Skilled workers and technicians previously employed by the military-industrial complex that have made the leap to private firms are a mainstay of the new middle class. Analyzing the Russian population's evolving self-identification, Liudmila Khakhulina found that in 1998, 84 percent of respondents working in state enterprises identified themselves as lower- or working-class, and 16 percent, as middle-class, whereas in private enterprises 55 percent of respondents identified themselves as middle-class, and only 45 percent, as workers.[37]

Private firms depend on market success. In the conditions of a deepening economic crisis, they do not provide any job security. Moreover, the owners as a rule mistrust collective bargaining and firmly oppose the very idea of trade union membership among their personnel. This has not provoked any serious resistance on the part of the workers, for two interdependent reasons: First, as sociological studies have demonstrated, on the whole, "wages and working conditions in the private sector have proved to be considerably better than in the state one."[38] Second, from the very beginning of economic transition, private enterprises attracted the most productive, energetic, and enterprising workers, who valued achievement over security and were prepared to accept risk, confident of their bargaining power. The moment of collective self-organization in the private sector has not arrived yet. It will, if and when the group of privately employed workers grows numerically and loses its somewhat exclusive character.

Skilled workers who stayed on at state and semi-state enterprises have adapted differently to working in a market system. These workers try to enhance their already strong bargaining position vis-à-vis management by monopolizing their acquired occupational skills and capitalizing on their know-how and experience. Various comparative sociological studies of the situation of workers in state and in privatized enterprises—machine-building firms with relatively modern technology, and food and textile enterprises with rather obsolete technology—have demonstrated that a gap has been growing between wages, fringe benefits, and job security of skilled workers and medium- to low-skilled ones.[39] Clearly, the market is reevaluating and putting a premium on worker skills; but it would be a gross oversimplification to explain the process as the normal operation of blind market forces.

During the Soviet period, when production and employment were expanding, many factories either established their own training facilities or relied on external training institutions. In the new era of diminishing or nonexistent state subsidies, faced with growing competition, both state and privatized enterprises have been dismantling their training facilities so as to cut costs. Initially, the enterprises tried to compensate by providing on-the-job training to newly hired employees.[40] They encountered strong resistance on the part of skilled workers, who refused to transfer their specific skills to young workers and potential competitors in a time of contracting employment opportunities. Today, on-the-job training is practically dead because skilled workers will not accept apprentices or other newcomers to their work teams.

As noted already by Max Weber, the market situation of individuals and groups lacking property depends upon the value of their labor and the degree of control they are able to exercise over their working conditions and the production process.[41] Paradoxically, the value of worker skills and experience during the Russian transition has been enhanced not so much through the workers' control of technologically advanced production processes as through their specific knowledge of the obsolete and worn-out equipment that factories cannot replace because they lack investment funds. Moreover, privatized enterprises are now forced to look for one-time orders that in turn require frequent readjusting and retooling of equipment, as well as rapid learning of new operations on the part of the laborer. Skilled workers are particularly favored by such circumstances, since they adapt better to changing conditions, possess transferable skills, and are in high demand in the labor market, including that at private enterprises.

Even after the collapse of Soviet-style political control, skilled workers felt secure and independent vis-à-vis management because they were able to control the production process and limit the entry of new competitors. Their bid for drastically increased wages also has been successful, judging by the reported wage differentials: Their average wage may be 3 to 4 times higher than that of medium- or low-skilled machine operators and assembly line workers, not to mention their various fringe benefits and considerable job security.[42] This development testifies also to the high levels of solidarity achieved within the privileged group of skilled workers. There have been increasing attempts on the part of management to counteract the growing bargaining power of skilled workers by introducing fixed-term contracts. Normally such contracts increase labor market flexibility and facilitate layoffs of redundant labor. The introduction of fixed-term contracts is too recent a development in the Russian economy to discuss its full significance. The first reports indicate that Russian managers, at least initially, hope the fixed-term contracts will tie highly skilled workers to the enterprise and establish "stronger managerial control over their work."[43]

The privileges gained by highly skilled workers have been achieved at the expense of other workers and of lower management. The growing segmentation of labor is the first result of "strong" workers' ability to exploit their position for their own advantage. Conversely, unable to control the "strong" segment of labor, management increases its control over the majority of workers whose main characteristic is that they are fully replaceable. These low- to medium-skilled workers are increasingly dependent both on the administration and on skilled workers. They are especially vulnerable to production cuts, since they are first to be laid off. Such practices as unpaid leaves of absence, wage arrears, and work week reductions are particularly widespread in this group. Moreover, as these workers are deprived of a functioning system of training and promotion, they lose incentives that might induce them to acquire new skills and achieve upward social mobility. A decline in labor discipline and quality of production, and a high labor turnover among lower skilled workers, seem to be inevitable consequences of the growing segmentation of the working class. As Simon Clarke has justifiably concluded, "This development does not bode well for the development of any solidarity within the workforce as a whole, nor for the prospects of 'social partnership' between workers and management, nor for the effective development of the quality and efficiency of production."[44]

The monopoly over knowledge and skills enjoyed by the most qualified workers today is a temporary phenomenon, however. In a vibrant economy with increasing output and employment and regular investment in new technologies, particular knowledge and specific skills rapidly become obsolete. Both the state and the enterprises will eventually have to invest substantial resources in expanding vocational technical schools, colleges, and other training institutions. Skilled workers are often well aware of the temporary character of their bargaining positions and privileges, but this only adds to their determination to capitalize on their advantages in a contracting economy. Consequently, at this early stage of the transition, market reforms have already produced considerable tensions and increased open inequality in incomes, consumption, and economic opportunity among different segments of the working class.

Trade Unions in Transition

Given rampant inflation, growing unemployment, and a general fall in the workers' standard of living on one hand and broad democratization on the other, it stands to reason that independent trade unions should emerge as primary defenders of workers' rights and interests. After the collapse of the Communist party, no other organization could be expected to hear the workers' grievances over allegedly unjustified dismissals, demotions, and nonpayment of wages, and other abuses by management and owners.[45] Yet these reasonable expectations have not materialized. The reasons for the lack of trade union revival illustrate both the strength of psychological and cultural attitudes inherited from the past and the peculiar state of labor issues in the first decade of the Russian transition.

Official Soviet trade unions have never played the role of institutionalized channels for the articulation and aggregation of workers' interests and grievances. They have always been a specialized organ of the party-state, a governmental labor agency charged with administering the social insurance fund and mobilizing workers to fulfill production plans. At the factory level they played a dual role. Firstly, together with the management, they defended the "interests of the labor collective," using the limited political and bureaucratic means at their disposal to minimize the production targets imposed on the enterprise by central planners. Secondly, they functioned as representatives of the administration, inducing workers to meet established plan targets, and smoothing away tensions between the administration and the workers. In this second role, the trade union functionaries participated in "conflict commissions" and had the right to appeal on behalf of individual workers to party and union functionaries above the level of the factory management. In addition, local trade union commissions played a role in the Soviet redistributive state by supervising a wide range social services for workers, such as housing, kindergartens, sports facilities, and medical centers run by enterprises.

At least two generations of Soviet workers lived in the absence of a collective right to strike and a *de facto* prohibition on organizing true trade unions. The wave of strikes during the last years of perestroika served notice that the right of workers to form their own trade unions and engage in collective action would be one of the principal objective measures of the democratic evolution of the Russian state and society. Russian reformers understood this. Characteristically, a Yeltsin presidential decree "On Social Partnership and the Resolution of Labor Disputes" was published in November 1991, a few weeks before the formal dissolution of the Soviet Union. By 1992, the Russian Trilateral Commission for the Regulation of Social and Labor Relations, consisting of representatives of the government, employers, and trade unions, had been set up to promote a social partnership and to diminish the negative impact of market reforms on the population.[46]

The right to organize trade unions and enforce sanctions against employers by withdrawing labor was upheld by a number of laws and decrees adopted in 1995 and 1996 that regulated the activity of trade unions, labor disputes, strikes, and collective agreements. This legislation was a significant step toward the democratization of labor relations and liberation of the workforce from state domination. But these were not democratic measures for democracy's sake only. As Walter Connor aptly noted, from the very beginning the Yeltsin government was interested "in extracting itself from the owner-manager-paymaster role in the economy as the beginning of a move toward a referee role between the interests of labor and those of the yet-vague category of owners-employers."[47]

After the collapse of the Soviet system, some representatives of what Leonid Gordon termed the old "state pseudo–trade unions"[48] abandoned any pretense to independence and joined the specific managerial organs responsible for labor relations. Other functionaries of the official trade unions, having lost their particular position in the party-state system, drifted toward the defense of the interests of hired labor. One would have expected the dissolution of the Soviet Central Council of Trade Unions and its replacement by the Federation of the Independent Trade Unions of Russia to have real significance; but even though the new unions are ostensibly independent, they continue to be burdened by the Soviet legacy. They still rely on inherited welfare and distribution functions to retain their memberships, although the benefits available for distribution are dwindling rapidly even in the large, state-owned industrial plants, as enterprises drop the extensive social services they can no longer support. The fact that there has been no organizational split between management-oriented and worker-oriented factions within the corps of professional trade unionists underlines the transitional character of the present-day trade unions in Russia.

The ongoing economic crisis and the attitudes of trade unionists both contributed to the slow institutional transformation of former Soviet trade unions. Russian enterprises are desperately searching for a particular niche in the marketplace. Their starting position in market competition depends decisively on the share of the former state property the enterprise managed to privatize or control and on the ties the enterprise established with state organs, the revenue service, banks, and foreign trade organizations. These circumstances do create a commonality of interests between workers and managers-owners that paradoxically coincides with the Soviet propaganda cliché asserting a presumed commonality of interests between workers and management under socialism. Today's real commonality of interests slows the transformation of Russian official trade unions into truly independent working-class organizations. Moreover, the traditional activities and the entire life experience of the professional trade unionist cadres better suit collaboration with the enterprise administration in defending the interests of the enterprise as a whole, rather than defending the workers' interests against those of managers and administrators. The trade unionists have not yet developed a clear perception of their role as independent representatives of hired labor.

The official trade unions were so thoroughly discredited in the Soviet period that habit and inertia more than anything else explain their still considerable membership today. According to the data of a 1995 VTsIOM survey, only 24 percent of worker respondents agreed that trade unions could be trusted fully or partially, whereas 55 percent of respondents asserted that trade unions could not be trusted at all.[49] In polls ranking public organizations by the level of popular mistrust they generate, Russian trade unions have come to occupy the highest position.[50] The conclusion drawn by Joseph Blasi, Maya Kroumova, and Douglas Kruse, that "the weakness of trade unions during economic reform was predestined by their past,"[51] nevertheless requires a qualification.

The evolution of the old trade unions has been strongly affected by the emergence of true grassroots organizations of workers. Created as a rule by working-class militants and activists who participated in the strikes and other collective actions that marked the very end of the Gorbachev period, the new trade unions broke with the old Soviet tradition of lumping workers and senior management together in the same union. They act as true organizations of hired workers, articulating and defending the specific interests of certain well-defined groups of workers. A classic example is the Independent Trade Union of Miners, which became widely known during the last years of Gorbachev's rule for its steadfast defense of coal miners' interests. In their origin, traditions, and leadership, the new trade unions have no connection whatsoever with the old trade union network.

An acute competition for membership has begun between old and new trade unions. Despite the fact that new trade unions, like their Western counterparts, have a democratic structure and promise to protect the interests of their members on the national level as well as defend them against local abuses, they have had trouble making headway against the old trade unions.[52] According to a nationwide poll conducted by VTsIOM in 1994 (see Table 10.3), 77 percent of all workers considered themselves trade union members, but fewer than 10 percent had joined new trade unions, and the overwhelming majority still belonged to the old unions.

The decline of the Independent Trade Union of Miners from national visibility and enormous success in mobilizing members for collective actions to total insignificance is a particularly interesting case that is discussed separately later in

TABLE 10.3   Workers' Attitudes Toward Trade Unions, 1994
(in percent of survey respondents)

Belonging to Trade Unions

Members of old unions	68
Members of new unions	9
Not members of any union	15
Do not know	8

The Role of Unions According to Respondents' Evaluation

Unions are playing a positive role	12
Unions are playing a negative role	9
Unions do not play any serious role	64
Do not know	15

Evaluation of the Role of Traditional and New Unions

Interests of ordinary persons are better defended:	
By traditional unions	19
By new unions	15
Unions do not defend ordinary persons' interests	66

SOURCES: *Ekonomicheskie i sotsial'nye peremeny: Monitoring obshchestvennogo mneniia* 4 (1995), p. 78; Leonid Gordon, "Polozhenie naemnykh rabotnikov v Rossii 90-kh godov," *Sotsial'no-trudovye issledovaniia*, vol. 7 (Moscow: IMEMO, 1997), p. 38.

this chapter. In contrast, other new trade unions—for example, those of long-shoremen, locomotive engineers, automobile industry workers, pilots, and air traffic controllers—have noticeably strengthened the positions of these occupational groups vis-à-vis managers, owners, and the state. Characteristically, most attempts by management to pressure and intimidate trade union leaders and activists have been directed against the new unions.[53] Yet the development of new, independent trade unions that succeed in articulating the interests and grievances of their members has so far been slow and limited. An analysis of strike activity elucidates the reasons for the obvious underdevelopment of Russian trade unions.

The legalization of strikes was one of the most important achievements of Russian labor. After the collapse of the Soviet regime, strikes became a familiar way of presenting employees' demands and grievances when other available methods of pressuring employers failed. Between 1993 and 1997, the annual number of strikes grew from a few hundred to 17,000, and the number of strike participants ranged from more than 100,000 to about 900,000 annually (see Table 10.4).

TABLE 10.4   Strikes in Russia, 1991–1997

Year	Number of Strikers (thousands)	Total Number of Strikes	Strikes in Industry	Strikes in the Fuel-Energy Sector	Strikes in Higher Education
1991	238	1,755	324	–	1,177
1992	357	6,273	63	–	4,229
1993	120	264	176	163	–
1994	155	514	209	190	279
1995	489	8,856	220	190	8,555
1996	664	8,278	–	145	–
1997	887	17,007	–	–	–

SOURCES: *Rossiiskii statisticheskii ezhegodnik*, 1997, p. 127; *Rossiia v tsifrakh*, 1998, p. 54.

The available data show that the overwhelming majority of strikers belonged to such occupational categories as teachers, miners, and to a lesser extent, employees of public health service. The rest of the Russian employed population has rarely used strikes to pressure employers. Except for miners, most blue-collar workers not only have never participated in a strike but have never known any person who did.

Deeply ingrained deference to authority and unlimited faith in the strong boss remain embedded in workers' mentality, especially among the low-skilled. Sociologists conducting interviews with workers time and again encounter the old Soviet clichés—that strikes benefit only their organizers and assorted troublemakers, and that a good manager or boss can defend workers' interests far more effectively than can workers themselves. According to the 1994 survey conducted by VTsIOM, 35 percent of respondents thought strikes did more harm than good, and only 23 percent thought the opposite. Characteristically, half of all respondents in the group of low-skilled workers and only a quarter of skilled ones considered strikes more harmful than beneficial.[54] A perception of strikes as socially disruptive, counterproductive, or even illegal remains widespread among the majority of workers and state bureaucrats. Sharing this popular perception, one minister of the fuel and energy industry denied the very right of workers to strike: "The miner has no more right to leave the mine [to participate in a strike] than a soldier to drop his arms."[55]

But the Soviet legacy of popular dependence on paternalistic authority only partially explains the obvious weakness of the trade union movement and the rarity of strikes in this early stage of Russian transition. The discrepancy between the number of respondents who professed positive attitudes toward strikes and the number of strike participants is very revealing. In the regular surveys conducted by VTsIOM, even though between 10 and 15 percent of respondents expressed their personal readiness to participate in strikes, the level of actual participation remained 10 to 20 times lower than the level of willingness.[56] A realistic assessment of the impact the strike will have on the worker's personal material prospects is the likely cause of this discrepancy.

Attitudes toward trade unions, strikes, and other forms of collective action, like those toward liberal democracy in general, are not so much determined by the legacy of Soviet practice and mentality as they are a function of the postcommunist structure of economic opportunity.[57] The major obstacles to trade union activism are a contracting economy and the lack of internally generated capital accumulation for investment. For the majority of former Soviet enterprises, the foundations of self-sustained growth have not yet been laid. Instead, crisis adaptation and sheer survival of enterprises as production units represent the major preoccupations of the working population. The search for a market niche unleashes powerful competitive interests that fracture the solidarity of enterprises in the same industry and simultaneously engender overarching common interests between workers and management within the same enterprise. Although workers might have clearly defined grievances and demands, they might see no concrete economic or political actors to whom these demands may be realistically addressed.

The overwhelming objectives of organized unionism remain increasing wages and improved working conditions. Faced with economic contraction and the defensive restructuring practiced both by state and by privatized enterprises, most workers cannot participate in organizing for collective action. Only particular groups of workers and specialists that enjoy a high level of control in vitally important sectors of the economy can use unions to pursue their economic goals. But in conditions of growing unemployment and deepening economic and financial crisis, most workers have become even more dependent on management and employers than they were under the Soviet regime. As Gimpelson and Lippoldt have justifiably concluded: "The centralized system of labor administration has been largely replaced by managers' discretion. Within the evolving industrial relations, the role of trade unions has not yet been settled."[58] The paucity of strikes and the vestigial role of trade unions in contemporary Russia is ample proof, if proof be needed, that Russia's transition to the market is incomplete.[59]

The evolution of an independent trade union movement has barely begun. It is significant, however, that trade union activities in general and strikes in particular are finally receiving closer attention from the mass media and the public. Most importantly, Russian workers have acquired both legal and practical possibilities to defend their interests through collective action, to organize their trade unions, and to negotiate at least acceptable if not favorable collective agreements—agreements that go beyond formal declarations, into the uncharted territory of real labor defense.

Restructuring the Coal Industry:
The Paradox of the Miners' Movement

The rise and fall of the Russian coal miners' movement and the profound restruc-turing of the coal mine industry now underway highlight the possible course and socioeconomic consequences of truly radical reforms in the Russian economy. The miners' movements in communist Poland, in the Soviet Union, and to a lesser extent in communist Romania played an important role in the dissolution of these systems. The unique role of miners and their collective actions in precip-itating "the rapid destruction of the social order that existed for seventy years," has been acknowledged by such authoritative observers as Gorbachev and Yeltsin.[60] The trajectory of the Russian miners' movement—which started by pre-senting economic demands, then supporting democratic and market reforms, and finally demanding the renationalization of the coal industry, prohibition of private ownership of land, and resignation of the democratically elected presi-dent—continues to puzzle analysts.[61]

In the last years of perestroika, Soviet miners created the first independent trade union. In 1989, they organized the first mass industrial strike since the 1962 Novocherkassk revolt, which had been suppressed by the regime with armed force. In the 1989 strike, miners advanced broad economic demands. Two succes-sive strikes in 1991 added demands for radical political changes, including the abolition of the single-party regime and the centrally planned economy; the in-troduction of political pluralism and a market economy; and the independence of non-Russian Soviet republics. A few years later, following the ban on the Com-munist party and the dissolution the Soviet Union, democratization, liberaliza-tion of prices, privatization of state property, and other reforms, the miners shifted their support away from liberal-democratic forces and toward the regen-erated Communist party as well as other nationalist and imperialist forces. Along the way, the independent trade union lost all of its influence among the miners and in the country at large, while the miners' mass mobilization dissipated into passive acceptance of and adaptation to the hardships of restructuring.

The paradox of the miners' movements in Soviet-type societies—the "miners' move toward democracy and back"[62]—has generated a considerable literature.[63] The rapid mobilization of miners in the last years of perestroika and the radical-ization of their demands, which seemingly contradicted their immediate material interests, may be explained by a combination of factors.[64] By the 1980s, the re-sources needed to maintain the extensive growth of the economy had been de-pleted, leading to a continuous, long-term decline in rates of economic growth and labor productivity. The old social contract between the regime and the popu-lation began to crumble, as its economic and political costs could no longer be met. The fall in the standard of living was particularly hard on the miners for sev-eral reasons. The miners had been the highest-paid category of workers, in com-pensation for their arduous and dangerous work and their often appalling living conditions. The nominally high pay, however, did not provide access to foodstuffs and consumer goods that were becoming increasingly scarce in the general economic decline.

The danger inherent in mine working conditions had generated among the members of work teams an exceptionally high level of mutual dependence and a general preparedness for collective action. Already known for their exceptional ability to organize for collective action and strikes, and not only in Russia,[65] the miners were further motivated to mobilize by Gorbachev's liberalization as well as by their sense of economic deprivation. The weakening of the coercive apparatus that led to a diminishing fear of repression was accompanied by an opening up of society, which magnified "the pressures that Western material standards placed on the institutions and stability of these [Soviet-type] regimes."[66]

This last point is especially important for understanding what prompted the coal miners, working in an industry heavily dependent on state subsidies, to demand market reforms. Stephen Crowley's rejection of rational choice in favor of "cultural factors, in particular the ideological frameworks that miners constructed in order to make sense of their situation,"[67] underestimates the eagerness of Soviet citizens to join the global material civilization created by Western material progress. The opening of society during perestroika brought home the hard fact that the Soviet system was lagging hopelessly behind the West in the competition for higher standards of living. As the best-organized group in Soviet society, coal miners expressed the growing sense of relative deprivation and tremendous frustration that characterized the Soviet working population as a whole. They were motivated both by the economic expectations of selling coal for hard currency on world markets and by their quest for social justice—a fusion of economic and political demands that required mass political mobilization against the party-state.

Yet, as major supporters of marketization and liberalization of society, the miners unexpectedly found themselves among the first victims of market reforms. The miners' paradox, a sort of "jest of history," has been that the best organized, most active and united group of workers toiled in the most obsolete, wasteful, and often socially useless branch of industry. The Soviet mining industry epitomized the country's technological and organizational backwardness. For more than 30 years, it stubbornly resisted following the developmental trajectory of the coal industry in all Western industrial societies. Coal production in the old coal-producing countries, such as England, France, and Germany, had declined since the early 1960s by a factor of two to five; and the numerical decline in the mining profession was much more dramatic. By the mid-1990s, the half-million-strong group of British miners had been reduced to between 30,000 and 35,000, and France's miners, which earlier had numbered more than 300,000, had disappeared almost entirely. Unlike coal-producing countries in Europe, the United States had tripled its coal production during the same period; but thanks to technological progress and growing labor productivity, the number of miners there too had fallen—from 230,000 in 1960 to about 110,000 in the mid-1990s. In contrast, coal production in the Soviet Union experienced a moderate growth from 500 million tons in 1960 to 700 million tons in 1990, and the number of miners remained constant at 1.2–1.3 million (about 500,000, in the RSFSR).

Coal production in the Soviet Union, and even more so in Russia, required enormous and ever growing state subsidies. The operating cost of coal extraction in many mines was extremely high, even by the standards of the Soviet economy, in which raw material inputs had been severely underpriced. Moreover, the coal mining industry has always been burdened by the expense of maintaining the entire social infrastructure of isolated mining towns. This included providing employment for the female population of these towns, as labor legislation prohibited female work underground and placed various other restrictions on women working in the coal industry. The inevitable and radical restructuring of the coal industry had been discussed among specialists for about 30 years. When I graduated from the Leningrad Mining Institute in 1960, I already knew that some 50 percent of Soviet coal mines were totally unproductive and continued to exist mainly for political and social reasons. For decades the Soviet leadership avoided acting, for fear of social instability. The USSR under Brezhnev profited enormously from the world energy crisis in the 1970s but squandered its windfall profits on expanding the military-industrial complex and maintaining price stability, missing its chance to restructure the energy sector relatively painlessly.

The social costs of post-Soviet economic reform, which were predictably high for all groups of the working class, have been truly enormous for coal miners. The role of miners in the collapse of the Soviet regime, and their exceptional organizational strength, prevented the post-Soviet Russian federal government from shutting down unprofitable mines during the first two or three years of its existence. As a result of continuing state subsidies, the ranks of coal miners continued to grow—from 484,000 in 1990 to 529,000 in 1993—whereas output declined from 395 to 305 million tons.[68] Calculated according to these figures, the average Russian miner's productivity dropped to 7 percent of that of the American miner.

Meanwhile, state policy evolved toward privatization of unprofitable mines and ever diminishing subsidies that did not cover the cost of production and that arrived increasingly irregularly. In 1995–1996, due to wage arrears, miners were paid up to 20 percent less.[69] The mines, especially privatized ones, often tried to adjust by raising coal prices, only to realize that price hikes placed their product beyond the reach of potential customers.

By the second half of the 1990s, profound changes had occurred in the miners' attitudes toward market reforms and political parties as well as in the general population's attitudes toward miners. In a total reversal of their pro-market stance, the miners turned against economic reform, instead advocating the restoration of a strong state and authoritarian rule. They began supporting communists and extreme nationalists, expressing strong sympathy for such political leaders as Vladimir Zhirinovsky. As opinion studies have demonstrated, in the miners' consciousness "a Pinochet figure has appeared as the prototype of a future Russian leader."[70] Surprised by the miners' shift from supporting market and democracy to backing old communist and nationalist forces, Crowley asked, "Why was it so difficult for the miners to craft something resembling a social-democratic alternative, as workers' movements in the West had done for so long?"[71] An obvious answer, if one does not subscribe to the Leninist theory of "false consciousness," might be that a socioeconomic group lacking economic opportunity in an emerging liberal-democratic order is unlikely to support market reforms. Moreover, the workers employed by an obsolete industry with the most outdated labor process, producing unwanted goods, are the most improbable candidates to embrace and promote social democracy.

In Soviet times, miners who had led massive strikes and other collective actions were not only expressing their own grievances but also those of other workers exploited and subjugated by an economically failing and undemocratic regime. In recent years, popular attitudes toward the miners' movement have changed. The mass media in Russia began demonstrating another side of the miners' paradox: Hundreds of thousands of able-bodied, skilled workers engaged in heavy, dangerous work cannot provide for themselves, and need huge subsidies that the state can afford only at the expense of the education, pensions, and health care of the general population. These reports led to the inevitable conclusions that the closure of unprofitable mines would alleviate the burden on the economy and that the welfare and economic security of society could be undermined by collective actions of a group pursuing particular interests. The nature of the conflict between the state and the miners has profoundly changed: By penalizing the producers of useless products, the government can claim to be defending society as a whole against the selfish interests of a minority.

Encouraged by this change in popular attitudes, the Russian government began implementing a state-regulated restructuring of the coal mining industry. Since 1996, the World Bank has granted Russia a number of loans for this purpose. All of the major sociological institutes in Russia—VTsIOM, the Institute of the World Economy and International Relations (IMEMO), the Institute of Sociology of the Russian Academy of Sciences, and the Institute for Comparative Studies of Labor Relations—have been involved in monitoring the social consequences of this large-scale, government-organized program.[72] Their data provided the first empirical insights into the results of radical market reforms in the coal industry and in the Russian economy in general.

The restructuring of coal mining proved exceptionally difficult not only because many mines were located in the Far North, where they often served as the only employer in town, but especially because it coincided with the general crisis of economic transition. This crisis has drastically cut into the resources available to alleviate the hardships faced by miners and their families; in addition, the weakening of the central state has muddled the rational use of existing resources. Measures intended to counteract the negative social consequences of industrial restructuring were implemented only partially, and they did not achieve their proclaimed goals. A brief analysis helps illustrate the situation in the economically depressed regions and the emergence of the "new poor" in Russia.

The majority of miners in the six mining regions studied by Russian sociologists had worked all their lives in the same mine, with the average seniority reaching 22 years. Their mines were closed and they were laid off, with two months or less advance notice. Because of insufficient funding, the management could not pay in full the wage arrears, severance pay, and various other compensations due to laid-off workers. Thus, in 1998, in the Primorye Territory, miners received 56 percent of the total sum they were owed; in the Kuzbass, 65 percent; in the Donbass, 71 percent; in the Tula region, 47 percent; in Perm, 85 percent; and in Vorkuta, 68 percent. From 40 percent to 80 percent of miners, depending on their region, encountered considerable difficulties in trying to extract payment from management, and trade unions proved incapable of rendering any assistance. The objective lack of funds was often exacerbated by corrupt management: In a typical gambit, miners who wanted their money immediately would be told they could have half of their wage arrears and severance pay on the condition that they sign a receipt acknowledging payment in full.

The money paid out to laid-off miners, even when they received all that they were owed, was insufficient to allow them to relocate in less economically depressed regions or to radically change their way of life by starting a small business or a farm. The way miners spent their severance pay is very revealing: From 59 to 88 percent of the respondents spent this money on food and immediate necessities, and only between 7 and 11 percent of the money went toward durable goods.

According to official estimates, at least 50 percent of those employed in the mining industry will be laid off by 2003. The managers of mines remaining in operation have been carefully culling the best workers. Many of those laid off will remain permanently unemployed, since only about 25 percent to 35 percent of those looking for jobs in the mining regions have a realistic chance of landing a job. The restructuring also provoked the elimination of various small enterprises established to provide complementary employment for women in mining towns. Almost no private enterprise exists in mining regions, and the so-called programs of local development have had a very limited success, for lack of investment funds.

Attempts by the Independent Miners' Trade Union to organize collective actions focused on the miners' plight have been utterly unsuccessful. Miners are profoundly divided between those employed by the mining enterprises remaining in operation, and the unemployed. Moreover, the effects of large-scale collective actions are extremely limited and can even be counterproductive. Current demand for coal is low, and locally produced coal is often more expensive than the world market price. As for the railroad blockades initiated by small groups of miners in spring 1998, they had little effect other than to provoke public opinion against the miners.

The survival strategies of unemployed miners are familiar: They take on seasonal construction work; accept various temporary, menial jobs; and work their plots of land (except in the harsh climates of the Far North and of Vorkuta).[73] The famous "victory gardens" that existed throughout Europe in the aftermath of World War II have now arrived in Russia. The mostly middle-aged former miners, who once held down well-paid jobs, are now surviving on meager unemployment benefits and waiting for old-age pensions. They have joined the emerging group of the "newly poor." The syndrome of poverty, stagnation, and social pathology familiar from the Appalachian region, Newfoundland, and Sardinia is now being replicated in the mining regions of Russia. The only "social-democratic" solution of the miners' problem might be to redirect state coal-mining subsidies toward relocation, retraining, and a massive job-creation program. But the Russian state can no longer afford such subsidies, and the magnitude of the problem is such that no international assistance, however generous, is likely to substitute for societal self-organization.

How do miners understand, interpret, and explain the unfolding reforms of the coal mining industry and the massive closure of unprofitable mines? One widely used explanation is a blanket accusation of corruption, aimed at the various upper strata of society—from the local mining administration, to the coal industry bureaucracy, to the central government. Such social critique is of little consequence, because no specific culprits can ever be identified by respondents. Another popular explanation of restructuring is the "American conspiracy," available in two versions: the economic one, blaming American coal producers for squeezing out Russian competitors from the market; and the "military-strategic" one, explaining the closing of unprofitable mines as an attempt to undermine Russia's military-economic potential and turn the country into a source of cheap labor and raw materials.

These interpretations testify to the democratic forces' failure to reach the broad population and to the continued strength of mass media outlets managed by unreformed communists. Most importantly, these interpretations give comfort and consolation to the new poor, since they create a liberating feeling of having discovered a secret, and most importantly, an external cause of their suffering. The combination of the corruption and conspiracy theories is especially appealing to the post-Soviet mentality, turning the new poor into a mass social base of antidemocratic and antimarket political forces, and a danger for Russia's fragile democracy.

Conclusion

Economic transition has produced enormous dislocations in Russian society. These dislocations resulted from a combination of deliberate state policy, decomposition of the centrally planned Soviet economy, and the workings of market forces. The ascendance of market principles and the development of a new labor market have hit certain occupational and territorial categories within the Russian working class particularly hard—especially coal miners and workers employed by enterprises in the Far North and other unfavorable locations. As the military-industrial complex has lost the priority status it enjoyed in the former Soviet Union, workers in defense industry have experienced the greatest decline. A study of ten formerly "closed" cities that housed major production centers of the Ministry of Atomic Industry revealed that the initial transition shock was much stronger here than elsewhere and the decline in the standard of living of workers and specialists much more drastic and profound than the average for the country. These most privileged groups of Soviet society now survive on incomes close to or even below the official poverty line.[74]

The anticipated decline and relative impoverishment of workers in the military-industrial complex, Far North enterprises, and resource-extractive industries such as coal mining testify to the essential market character of the transition. But apart from groups that are experiencing an obvious downward social mobility, if we take the working class as a whole, it is too early to draw a net distinction between the winners and losers in the transition. Since the transition is far from complete, it is more productive to draw up a balance sheet of the gains and losses experienced thus far by Russian workers as a whole—especially as current variations in income and occupational mobility may be subject to change as the economic transition progresses.

In this vein, the leading experts on the Russian working class, Gordon and Klopov, would include on the positive side of the balance sheet: the creation of real labor unions, freedom to strike and take part in other forms of collective action, and a general democratization of labor relations; the end to shortages, and the possibility of consumer choice; increased market penetration of modern manufactured and technological goods, with automobile and telephone ownership becoming a mass phenomenon; steady improvement in housing; increased access to cultural and political information and foreign travel, and greater choice in entertainment and leisure pursuits. On the negative side, they would list the rise in unemployment, and the falling incomes of the majority of the population, due to decreasing real wages and the purchasing power of pensions; loss of savings accumulated prior to the early 1990s; and widespread delays in the payment of wages and pensions.[75] These empirically observable trends characterize the present Russian society, in which a market economy has not yet started to function "normally," but which is moving in this direction.

It is difficult to assess how these trends will affect long-term economic prospects of particular social groups and categories. As Harley Balzer has aptly noted, perceptions, preconceptions, and political agendas play a major role in interpreting trends in GDP and social differentiation: "Populist politicians have an interest in emphasizing if not exaggerating the differentials; those in power wish to play down the extent of stratification."[76] One can conclude, however, that even though a dominant pattern of ownership has yet to emerge, outside ownership is on the rise, and the present pattern of insider control is gradually giving way to the external control characteristic of market economies.[77] Assuming that this trend continues, the current pattern of substituting wage reductions for unemployment is likely to diminish, since outsider owners are much less inclined to engage in such practices.

For the reasons outlined above, no polarization of Russian society along class lines has yet occurred. There is insufficient evidence to decide whether the next stage of the transition will prompt the development of class-based cleavages or will facilitate the articulation of interests based on factors such as occupational groups, as has happened in postcommunist societies that have advanced farther toward a market economy.[78] The first decade of reforms in Russia has confirmed the general impression of scholars familiar with the Soviet system that the Russian transition will be a far lengthier process than that of East-Central Europe or the Baltic states.

The currency devaluation of August 1998 was a major shock for the country. On the one hand, it dealt a heavy blow to Russian consumers, whose purchasing power dwindled with the waning value of the ruble; the ranks of the poor swelled. On the other hand, the devaluation gave a considerable boost to Russian industry, protecting domestic producers from foreign competition. Russia's industrial production has since grown, and inflation has slowed. New job creation has begun to compensate for the jobs lost in the inefficient and failing, inherited industry, although much of the new jobs are "off the books," in the informal economy. Most importantly, many Russian enterprises have begun to expand, often relying on their own funds. This development resembles the Polish experience of transition from central planning.

Does this mean that the Russian transition has arrived at the turning point and has begun to exhibit the dynamics of output, employment, and labor productivity that have been observed in the East-Central European postcommunist transition?[79] Judging by the growth in output attained in 1999–2000, by the Russian population's growing confidence in and more optimistic assessment of the country's economic future,[80] and by the positive attitude of the international community toward Russia's recent economic achievements, we can answer in the affirmative. In contrast, political developments in Russia since the 1999 and 2000 elections, as well as the continuing Russian-Chechen conflict, dampen even cautious optimism. We can expect the next stage of Russia's transition, under the leadership of President Vladimir Putin, to be characterized by some form of liberal authoritarianism—the approach that the Russian political elite presently sees as most practical for addressing the country's economic and social difficulties.

Notes

I wish to express my gratitude to Professors Leonid Gordon and Lev Gudkov for their helpful comments and criticisms.

1. *Rossiiskii statisticheskii ezhegodnik: Ofitsial'noe izdanie, 1998* (Moscow: Goskomstat RF, 1998), pp. 182–185.

2. Ibid., p. 197.

3. *Obzor ekonomicheskoi politiki v Rossii za 1998* (Moscow: ROSSPEN [Rossiiskaia politicheskaia entsiklopediia], 1999), p. 261.

4. Jan Winiecki, "The Inevitability of a Fall in Output in the Early Stages of Transition," *Soviet Studies* 4 (1991), pp. 669–676.

5. Richard Ericson, "Economics and the Russian Transition," *Slavic Review* 3 (Fall 1998), pp. 609–625.

6. Aleksandr Golov, "Massovye otsenki problem rossiiskogo obshchestva: Peremeny za god," *Novaia gazeta,* March 2–8, 1998, p. 4.

7. *Ekonomicheskie i sotsial'nye peremeny: Monitoring obshchestvennogo mneniia* [hereafter, *ESP:MOM*] 7 (1993), p. 65; 4 (1994), p. 70; 6 (1994), p. 82; 1 (1995), p. 79; 3 (1995), p. 82; 2 (1997), p. 88; 5 (1997), p. 47; 6 (1997), p. 86; 3 (1998), pp. 90–91; 5 (1998), p. 57; 6 (1998), p. 68.

8. Nikolai Shmelev, *Avansy i dolgi: Vchera i zavtra rossiiskikh ekonomicheskikh reform* (Moscow: Mezhdunarodnye otnosheniia, 1996).

9. Joseph Blasi, Maya Kroumova, and Douglas Kruse, *Kremlin Capitalism: Privatizing the Russian Economy* (Ithaca, N.Y.: Cornell University Press, 1997), p. 178.

10. *Osnovnye pokazateli deiatel'nosti organov sluzhby zaniatosti za ianvar'–dekabr' 1997 god* (Moscow, 1998), p. 5.

11. See Chapter 6 in this volume.

12. Barry Ickes, Peter Murrell, and Randy Ryterman, "End of the Tunnel? The Effects of Financial Stabilization in Russia," *Post-Soviet Affairs* 2 (1997), pp. 118–119.

13. Leonid Kosals and Rosalina Ryvkina, *Sotsiologiia perekhoda k rynku v Rossii* (Moscow: Editorial, 1998), p. 97.

14. Ibid., p. 98.

15. Rostislav Kapelyushnikov, "Rossiiskii rynok truda: Adaptatsiia bez restrukturizatsii," in *Nekotorye aspekty teorii perekhodnoi ekonomiki* (Moscow: IMEMO RAN, 1999), pp. 85–161.

16. Sergei Auktsionek and Rostislav Kapelyushnikov, "Labour Hoarding in Russian Industry," *Russian Economic Barometer* 2 (1996).

17. Blasi, Kroumova, and Kruse, *Kremlin Capitalism,* p. 82.

18. Kathryn Hendley, "Legal Development in Post-Soviet Russia," *Post-Soviet Affairs* 13, 3 (July–September 1997), pp. 228–251.

19. Simon Clarke and Veronika Kabalina, "Privatisation and the Struggle for Control of the Enterprise," in David Lane, ed., *Russia in Transition* (London: Longman, 1995), pp. 142–158.

20. Kosals and Ryvkina, *Sotsiologiia perekhoda,* pp. 128–135.

21. The interviews presented in Chapter 11 of this book provide examples of this type of practice.

22. Leonid Gordon and Eduard Klopov, "Sotsiologicheskii i istoriko-sotsial'nyi vzgliad na problemu bezrabotnitsy v Rossii 90-kh godov," in *Nekotorye aspekty teorii perekhodnoi ekonomiki* (Moscow: IMEMO RAN, 1999), pp. 162–172.

23. Veronika Kabalina and Tatyana Metalina, "Sotsial'nye mekhanizmy politiki zaniatosti na rossiiskom predpriiatii," *Mirovaia ekonomika i mezhdunarodnye otnosheniia* 7 (1994).

24. Ilya Zaslavsky, "Gor'kie lekarstva, chtoby vyzdorovet'," *Chelovek i trud,* 12 (1996).

25. If the minimum wage were 140 rubles per month, the permissible average wage at an enterprise would be 700 rubles. Let us say that an enterprise employed 1,000 workers at

an average wage of 1,500 rubles per month. That enterprise's total wage fund would have been 1.5 million rubles. Because the appropriate wage fund (according to government standards) at that particular enterprise would have been 700,000 rubles, the enterprise would have had to pay a tax on the excess 800,000 rubles.

26. Vladimir Gimpelson and Douglas Lippoldt, "Labour Turnover in the Russian Economy," in *Labour Market Dynamics in the Russian Federation: OECD Proceedings* (Paris: Centre for Cooperation with the Economies in Transition, 1997), p. 33.

27. Victor Zaslavsky, "From Redistribution to Marketization: Social and Attitudinal Change in Post-Soviet Russia," in Gail Lapidus, ed., *The New Russia* (Boulder: Westview, 1994), pp. 115–142; Victor Zaslavsky, "Contemporary Russian Society and Its Legacy: The Problem of State-Dependent Workers," in Bruno Grancelli, ed., *Social Change and Modernization: Lessons from Eastern Europe* (Berlin: Walter de Gruyter, 1995), pp. 45–62.

28. See *ESP:MOM* 3 (1993), pp. 24–28; 4 (1993), p. 6.

29. See *ESP:MOM* 2 (1998), pp. 75–76; 6 (1998), p. 68.

30. Informatsiia Goskomstata RF [Rossijskoj Federatsii], as cited in *Izvestiia*, August 21, 1999, p. 1.

31. *Rossiiskii statisticheskii ezhegodnik: Ofitsial'noe izdanie, 1998*, p. 189; *Sotsial'noe polozhenie i uroven' zhizni naseleniia Rossii: Statisticheskii sbornik* (Moscow: Goskomstat, 1997), p. 52. The majority of unemployed attempt to find work on their own; only a small number register with the state unemployment agency.

32. Jadwiga Staniszkis, *The Dynamics of the Breakthrough in Eastern Europe: The Polish Experience* (Berkeley: University of California Press, 1991), pp. 38–72; Steven Solnick, *Stealing the State: Control and Collapse in Soviet Institutions* (Cambridge: Harvard University Press, 1998).

33. See Victor Zaslavsky, *The Neo-Stalinist State: Class, Ethnicity, and Consensus in Soviet Society*, 2d ed. (Armonk, N.Y.: M. E. Sharpe, 1994), chs. 1, 2, 6.

34. Gimpelson and Lippoldt, "Labour Turnover in the Russian Economy," pp. 17–50.

35. Nikolai Lapin and Liudmila Belyaeva, eds., *Dinamika tsennostei naseleniia reformiruemoi Rossii* (Moscow: Institut filosofii, RAN, 1996), pp. 103, 115.

36. *ESP:MOM* 3 (1996), pp. 26, 62, 68.

37. Liudmila Khakhulina, "Sub"ektivnyi srednii klass: Dokhody, material'noe polozhenie, tsennostnye orientatsii," *ESP:MOM* 2 (1999), pp. 20–24.

38. Kosals and Ryvkina, *Sotsiologiia perekhoda*, p. 220.

39. Galina Monousova, "Promyshlennye rabochie v Rossii: Adaptatsiia, differentsiatsiia, mobil'nost'," *Sotsiologicheskii zhurnal* 1–2 (1998), pp. 209–223.

40. Vladimir Gimpelson and Douglas Lippoldt, "Labour Restructuring in Russian Enterprises: A Case Study," *OECD Working Papers*, vol. 4, no. 69 (Paris, 1996), pp. 22–23.

41. Max Weber, *Economy and Society* (Berkeley: University of California Press, 1968), pp. 927–928.

42. Galina Monousova and Natalia Guskova, "Internal Mobility and the Restructuring of Labor," in Simon Clarke, ed., *Labour Relations in Transition: Wages, Employment, and Industrial Conflict in Russia* (Cheltenham, U.K.: Edward Elgar, 1996), pp. 82–98.

43. Vladimir Gimpelson and Douglas Lippoldt, "Labour Restructuring," p. 22.

44. Simon Clarke, "Labour Relations and Class Formation," in Clarke, ed., *Labour Relations in Transition*, p. 22.

45. Kosals and Ryvkina, *Sotsiologiia perekhoda*, p. 229.

46. On the development of the "social partnership" model, see Viktor Komarovsky, "Stanovlenie sistemy sotsial'nogo partnerstva kak sotsial'nogo instituta v Rossii," in V. Ko-

marovsky, ed., *Sotsial'noe partnerstvo v perekhodnom obshchestve: Opyt Rossii,* Sotsial'no-trudovye issledovaniia, vol. 10 (Moscow: IMEMO, 1998), pp. 5–31.

47. Walter Connor, *Tattered Banners: Labor, Conflict, and Corporatism in Postcommunist Russia* (Boulder: Westview, 1996), p. 25.

48. Leonid Gordon, *Nadezhda ili ugroza? Rabochee dvizhenie i profsoiuzy v perekhodnoi Rossii* (Moscow: IMEMO RAN, 1995), p. 4.

49. *ESP:MOM* 4 (1995), p. 78.

50. *ESP:MOM* 3 (1998), p. 6.

51. Blasi, Kroumova, and Kruse, *Kremlin Capitalism,* p. 107.

52. Andrei Isaev and Aleksandr Shubin, *Demokraticheskii sotsializm: Budushchee Rossii* (Moscow: Solidarnost', 1995); Gordon, *Nadezhda ili ugroza?*

53. Gordon, *Polozhenie,* pp. 34–36.

54. *ESP:MOM* 1 (1995), p. 78.

55. *Izvestiia,* September 3, 1996, cited in Gordon, *Polozhenie,* p. 39.

56. See *ESP:MOM* 3 (1995), p. 91; 4 (1996), p. 88; 6 (1996), p. 82; 3 (1999), p. 68.

57. Judith Kullberg and William Zimmerman, "Liberal Elites, Socialist Masses, and Problems of Russian Democracy," *World Politics* 51 (April 1999), pp. 323–358.

58. Gimpelson and Lippoldt, "Labour Restructuring," p. 24.

59. Scholars who tend to interpret the Russian transition in Marxist terms and categories discover that today's Russia is ill suited to such an analysis. As Simon Clarke has recognized, "Management does not yet confront the labor force as the representative of capital confronting a working class." Likewise, Clarke's prediction of the coming "polar confrontation between global capital and the Russian working class" has no empirical grounding (Simon Clarke, "Labour Relations and Class Formation," in Clarke, ed., *Labour Relations in Transition,* p. 13).

60. Mikhail Gorbachev, *Zhizn' i reformy* (Moscow: Novosti, 1995), p. 460; speech by Boris Yeltsin on the occasion of Kemerovo oblast's 50th anniversary, as reported in *Nasha gazeta* (Kemerovo), January 28, 1993, p. 1.

61. Aleksandr Vodolazov and Leonid Gordon, "Khozhdenie v demokratiiu i obratno, ili kuda dvizhetsia shakhterskoe dvizhenie," *Otkrytaia politika* 9–10 (1998), pp. 30–37.

62. Vodolazov and Gordon, "Khozhdenie v demokratiiu i obratno," p. 30.

63. See for example, Leonid Lopatin, *Istoriia rabochego dvizheniia Kuzbassa, 1989–1991* (Kemerovo: Plast, 1995); idem, *Rabochee dvizhenie Kuzbassa v vospominaniiakh ego uchastnikov i ochevidtsev* (Moscow: IMEMO, 1998); Vladimir Ilyin, *Vlast' i ugol': Shakhterskoe dvizhenie Vorkuty (1989–1998 gody)* (Syktyvkar: ISITO, 1998).

64. For a useful overview, see Stephen Crowley, "Barriers to Collective Action: Steelworkers and Mutual Dependence in the Former Soviet Union," *World Politics* 46 (July 1994), pp. 589–615.

65. Michael Yarrow, "The Labor Process in Coal Mining: The Struggle for Control," in Andrew Zimbalist, ed., *Case Studies in the Labor Process* (New York: Monthly Review Press, 1979).

66. Andrew Janos, *Politics and Paradigms: Changing Theories of Change in Social Science* (Stanford: Stanford University Press, 1986), p. 121.

67. Stephen Crowley, "Coal Miners and the Transformation of the USSR," *Post-Soviet Affairs* 13, 2 (1997), p. 168.

68. Leonid Gordon, Eduard Klopov, and Igor Kozhukhovsky, eds., *Krutoi plast: Shakhterskaia zhizn' na fone restrukturizatsii otrasli i obshcherossiiskikh peremen* (Moscow: Kompleks-Progress, 1999), p. 52.

69. Leonid Gordon, "Restrukturizatsiia ugol'noi promyshlennosti i sotsial'noe polozhe-nie shakhterov," *Chelovek i trud* 10 (1997), p. 27.

70. Vadim Borisov, Veronika Bizyukova, and Konstantin Burnyshev, "Conflict in a Coal-Mining Enterprise: A Case Study of Sudzhenskaya Mine," in Clarke, ed., *Labour Relations in Transition*, p. 233.

71. Crowley, "Coal Miners and the Transformation of the USSR," p. 189.

72. See Lev Gudkov, *Restrukturizatsiia ugol'noi promyshlennosti: Monitoring sotsial'nykh posledstvii* (forthcoming); Gordon, Klopov, and Kozhukhovsky, eds., *Krutoi plast*.

73. See Chapter 11 in this volume.

74. Valentin Tikhonov, *Zakrytye goroda v otkrytom obshchestve* (Moscow: INP RAN, 1996), pp. 25–26.

75. Gordon, Klopov, and Kozhukhovsky, eds., *Krutoi plast*, pp. 65–67.

76. Harley Balzer, "Russia's Middle Classes," *Post-Soviet Affairs* 14, 2 (1998), p. 167.

77. Blasi, Kroumova, and Kruse, *Kremlin Capitalism*, pp. 54–55, 193–195.

78. Mikk Titma, Nancy Brandon Tuma, and Brian Silver, "Winners and Losers in the Postcommunist Transition: New Evidence from Estonia," *Post-Soviet Affairs* 14, 2 (1998), pp. 127–128.

79. For the "standard" theoretical model of the postcommunist transition, see Olivier Blanchard, *The Economics of Post-Communist Transition* (Oxford: Oxford University Press, 1997).

80. See *ESP:MOM* 1 (2000), pp. 57–60; 2 (2000), pp. 58–59.

11

Domestic Involution

How Women Organize Survival in a North Russian City

Michael Burawoy

University of California, Berkeley

Pavel Krotov

Institute of Regional Social Research of the Komi Republic, Syktyvkar

Tatyana Lytkina

Institute of Socioeconomic and Energy Problems of the North, Syktyvkar

One of the abiding puzzles of Russian life is how to reconcile an unprecedented decline in the economy, year in, year out, with the continual survival of its populations and the absence of social disturbances. Although all figures are disputed, calculations suggest that between 1990 and 1997 the gross domestic product (GDP) and industrial output fell by some 40 percent, and capital investment fell by 75 percent. According to official figures, in 1997, 20.8 percent of the population was living in poverty. Yet at the same time we find neither massive starvation nor strikes and food riots, neither the destruction of society nor its explosion.

Many are simply not surviving: Mortality rates are increasing at all ages. By 1995, the life expectancy of men had fallen dramatically, to 58.6—the level of a century earlier. In comparison, the life expectancy of women had fallen only marginally, to 71.6. The United Nations Human Development Report for Europe and the CIS estimates the human cost of transition at 6 million male lives.[1] Between 1980 and 1995, the crude death rate increased from 11 to 15 per thousand persons. Heart attacks, cancer, infant mortality, and tuberculosis have taken an increasing toll. With birthrates falling at the same time, the Russian population is shrinking: In 1996 alone, it decreased by 5.2 percent.

Just as one can exaggerate the Russian capacity for survival, so too can one exaggerate the passivity of Russian society. There have been and continue to be outbursts of collective action, episodic demonstrations in Moscow and regional capitals as well as more widespread strikes. In recent years, teachers, miners, air traffic controllers, and municipal workers have struck effectively. But interestingly, these are occupations that still have bargaining power with local or federal governments. For the most part, the industrial workplace—the one place that organized solidarity under the old regime—has been systematically eroded and forced back into defensive postures when it has not actually disappeared. Thus, although there is some mobilization, it is ephemeral, symbolic, and scattered, and certainly not commensurate with the plight that workers face in their everyday lives. In this chapter we describe how families in one northern city make ends meet, and we explore the implications for social stability.

Involution, Strategies, and Assets

A new type of society is appearing in Russia that statistical data cannot disclose. It is a network society that is both resilient and quiescent, that adapts without mobilization. Its origin lies in Soviet society, which is where we must begin our account. The Soviet order was governed by central appropriation and redistribution of goods and services. In this order, the central place for popular self-organization was the workplace. Because the shortage economy[2] required that production have flexible autonomy, because ideology gave centrality to the interests of the working class, and because so much redistribution of goods in short supply took place through the workplace, that is where the most sustained contestation of socialism took place. It was there that the heavy apparatus of oppression and atomization had to be most effective. The party-state could blot out effervescence in all other public places but could not do so easily in the workplace. Its economic organization continually recreated both dissent and solidarity, even as party, management, and union vigilantly usurped it. Eulogized as the vanguard of society, workers regularly took up the cudgels of immanent critique, challenging the workers' state to realize its claims to efficiency, justice, and equality. And so from time to time workers went beyond skirmishes in the undergrowth, burst their chains, and exploded onto the public scene.

Still, the collapse of the old regime did not come from within the bowels of the economy but from above. Worker mobilization may have been a precipitating factor, at least in the Russian case, but the rot had begun in the higher reaches of the party-state, which could not prolong its ideological pretenses. It imploded from above, along the fault lines of its redistributive structure. Even before economic reforms began in 1992, the realm of redistribution was being conquered by a host of intermediaries, who in taking their cut of profits began to strangle production. Shock therapy initiated, in rapid succession, the liberalization of prices, so-called privatization, and stabilization. Markets flooded into the vacuum created by the crumbling planning mechanism. *But market expansion came at the expense of production.* The realm of exchange was invaded by traders, bankers, financiers, transportation monopolists, and mafia, all of whom multiplied transaction costs to bring production to its knees. It declined precipitously, leached by these intermediaries and unable to compete with cheap imports. Enterprises defended themselves against the market by retreating into barter chains, inter-enterprise debt, and wage arrears. All the time output fell. We call the process of economic regression in which exchange eats up its own productive base *economic involution.* For the purposes of this chapter, the essential point is that industrial production began to lose its centrality in everyday life both as a locus of solidarity and a source of economic survival. For many of Russia's workers, the fulcrum of economic activity has moved from workplace to family.

If *economic involution* describes how the market dissolved Soviet production, *domestic involution* is the other side of the collapse. It describes families from the working class, cut off from a living wage, focusing more and more economic activity in the household, as they combine old routines into new strategies of domestic production, entering into mutual aid exchanges across households and exploiting opportunities in wider trade.

In our analysis we distinguish between defensive and entrepreneurial strategies of survival. Each strategy has both a productive and a distributive aspect. In the realm of production, defensive households keep their feet planted simultaneously in wage labor, subsistence production, and trade. We call this the *diversification* of the household economy. In the realm of distribution, defensive households exchange resources, money, food, and labor among themselves. We call this the strategy of *sharing.*

At the same time, there are a few families whose response to involution is more proactive than reactive, more entrepreneurial than defensive. Instead of minimizing risk by diversifying their labor activities, some families devoted themselves to one particular activity—trade, petty commodity production (e.g., making garments), or even some form of service (body shop). This is what we call the *concentration* of the household economy. For such a family enterprise to succeed, however, the proceeds must *accumulate* instead of being consumed or redistributed. The goal is to reinvest resources in the focal economic activity. In short, domestic involution can take place either through diversification or through concentration of economic activity, and economic products can be shared or accumulated. Reality rarely exhibits these strategies in their pure form but as mixed and hybrid expressions of the two basic types (see Figure 11.1).

Survival strategies do not exist in a vacuum but are shaped by institutions that define rules for deploying assets. If *economic involution* spells the demise of an institutional order in which strategies are narrowly confined, *domestic involution* opens up strategies by relaxing rules and liberating assets. Just think of the multi-

FIGURE 11.1   Dimensions of Domestic Involution

	Production	Distribution
Defensive Strategy	Diversification	Sharing
Entrepereneurial Strategy	Concentration	Accumulation

ple uses of the apartment. Before, it was a place of living and entertainment; now it is an asset that can be sold and bought, easily transmitted from generation to generation. It is also a possible workshop; its balcony can be used to rear pigs and chickens; or it can become a source of rent, or a place for storing merchandise. The apartment's multifunctionality reflects the way the market has liberated the deployment of assets. There are four types of assets that are the object of wide-ranging strategies:

- material possessions (apartments, cars, dachas);
- skills (education, professional credentials, physical skills, etc.);
- social networks (the network of relatives and friends to which individuals or households can appeal for help or to which they are obligated);
- citizenship assets (claims that can be made on the state for pensions, child support, public assistance, rent subsidies).

We use this framework of involution, strategies, and assets to explore the complexity, heterogeneity, and path-dependence of survival in contemporary Russia. Throughout we underline the ways in which involution has both compelled and facilitated inventive appropriations, mobilizations, and combinations of resources, leading in most cases toward defensive strategies, and in a few, toward entrepreneurship.

From Workplace to Household

Our discussion so far has been more conceptual than historical. Strategies, however, cannot be understood outside the specific context of their enactment. However weak, there is still an institutional environment to be negotiated, and rules to be followed. The resources available are sensitive to broad context as well as to individual biography. It is one thing to survive in the tundra, another in the taiga, and quite another in the balmy climes around the Black Sea. It is important, therefore, to put flesh on the bones of economic and domestic involution—to draw out the terrain on which our twelve cases are enacted.

Our first proviso is that the shift from workplace to household, from wage labor to family labor, is rarely exclusive; generally, a balance is struck between the two realms of economic activity. To explore this changing balance, to contrast industrial with domestic involution, we chose to follow the fate of workers from two factories in Syktyvkar, capital of the Komi Republic.

The Komi Republic is a northerly republic of Russia, lying to the west of the Urals and stretching all the way to the Arctic Circle. It is the size of California, and has a population of 1.2 million. Long dominated by the gulag, its economy is based on the extraction of natural resources: oil, coal, timber, and small quantities of gas and bauxite. Syktyvkar sprang up in the 1930s as an administrative center for the archipelago of labor camps that stretched across the region. It has received successive waves of *forced migration:* the first, following the expulsion of kulaks from the rural hinterland; the second made up of ethnic Germans and Ukrainian partisans deported from the western borderlands during and after World War II; the third, of war prisoners—both returning Russians and captured Germans. Even more important was the *voluntary migration* of Russians from areas devastated by the war, and of those escaping the repressive order of collectivization. Since Soviet times there has been a continuous flow of people and resources between town and country, between Syktyvkar and rural Komi. Migrants came to the area from all over Russia, seeking the higher wages offered by the state for labor in the northern territories. Komi—especially its three major cities (Syktyvkar, Ukhta, and Vorkuta)—became the home of polyglot communities, with various national and ethnic groups living cheek by jowl. On the demand side, Syktyvkar's economy expanded rapidly around its wood-processing industries—its huge paper mill built in the 1960s, and allied industries—and then as a major administrative and educational center. Today it has a population of a quarter million.

In many ways, the two factories we have focused on—the city's garment factory and its furniture factory—are a study in contrasts. Under the old regime the garment factory, Red October, employed 650 workers, 90 percent of them women, often recent arrivals from the rural areas.[3] Workers could make up for the low basic wages with bonuses they achieved on the basis of their work performance and productivity (e.g., piecework bonuses). Red October's workers remember the factory fondly, especially the esprit de corps of its labor collective. Intense social activity centered around the work brigades—outings, celebrations, and much sharing of trials and tribulations. This was a home away from home.

The furniture factory, Polar, was a much newer enterprise, employing some 1,300 workers in its main division. Newly constituted out of a small workshop in 1982, it was housed in a single-story modern building and boasted a highly paid, young labor collective of both men and women (albeit strictly segregated occupationally by gender). It manufactured wall systems—an essential piece of furniture for all Soviet apartments. Being much newer and composed of younger workers, the Polar labor collective was not as solidary as that of Red October. There was also more competition for the jobs at Polar, because pay and fringe benefits (access to housing, dachas, kindergartens, holiday camps, and the like) were better.

Both enterprises were privatized in 1992, becoming the property of their own labor collectives, after which their economic fortunes rapidly declined. Polar's decline was particularly steep and marked, since it had been one of the most prosperous factories in the city. It was declared bankrupt and liquidated in 1998—a rare occurrence even today. Red October, meanwhile, continues to eke out an existence. Many of its machines have been sold, one floor has been bought, and another has been rented out. Two floors still house its own production facilities, and a third is occupied by the administration. About 150 workers are employed intermittently by Red October, receiving wages in the form of the garments that they produce. In this chapter we explore what has happened to employees we first interviewed in 1994 and 1995. We argue that decisions they made in those years set them on a path from which they have found it difficult to deviate.

As an aid to understanding the context, we have included a short appendix that describes some of the economic changes that have taken place in recent years— changes in wages, levels of employment, and the official poverty line. These data help us understand the real and symbolic value of the ruble at different times.[4] We also describe the types of public assistance (pensions, unemployment, and subsidies for low-income families, aid to single mothers, and so on) that often figure prominently in family strategies.

We began this project in 1994, focusing on what was happening to the workers at Polar, an enterprise we had first studied in 1991. In the twilight of communism, Polar effectively exploited its monopoly over wall system production, its easy access to raw materials, and its cozy relationship with the regional timber conglomerate. Economic reforms plunged the factory into a precipitous decline, and by the end of 1993, workers were already leaving in droves. We interviewed some of them, drawing names randomly from the enterprise register of employees. The interviews were open-ended, designed precisely to reveal the various strategies of survival that they deployed. They were all conducted by Tatyana Lytkina—often accompanied by Michael Burawoy. Lytkina's techniques of relentless probing gradually revealed the complex and multilayered realities of workers' economic lives: the multiple sources of earned revenue (wage labor, second jobs, work on the side, self-employment), and the diverse patterns of exchange between households (between relatives, neighbors, friends, and coworkers). She carried a set of interview guidelines in her head, but took along no questionnaire, no tape recorder, no pen and paper. She wrote up these interviews immediately after they took place.

In 1994 and 1995, Lytkina carried out 48 interviews with Polar employees; and in 1995 and 1996, we decided to extend the study to Red October, where she conducted a further 23 interviews. But in the latter case we did not gain access to the enterprise's list of employees, and we had to develop a snowball sample. We cannot claim that this sample is representative: At the time of our first interviews with them, 21 (44 percent) of our Polar respondents still worked at the furniture factory, whereas only six (26 percent) of Red October respondents were still employed at their facility. The garment workers were interviewed on average a year later than the furniture workers and therefore were less likely to be still working, as their enterprise was in a progressive decline. Our research strategy, therefore, was not focused on securing representativeness but on elucidating the intricacy of each individual case, with its own diachronic rhythm and specific context. From the 71 interviews, we selected 16 on the basis of their diversity, and we then interviewed these individuals a second time (in certain cases, a third and fourth time). For this chapter, we chose five of these 16 to represent the range of defensive strategies, and four to represent entrepreneurial strategies.

Since economic activity has been forced back into the household as the unit of production and reproduction, we turned to women as our interviewees. Whether due to their inherited homemaking skills or because of their devotion to their children, the burden of family survival is borne by women. As interviewees, they were more willing to talk about and better acquainted with household strategies. Exceptions notwithstanding, men have become increasingly redundant and demoralized, playing a secondary role in the family, and therefore are less informative about the workings of the household. If the changes in their life expectancy are anything to go by, working-class men have suffered more than women from economic involution. Their career possibilities have often shrunk more rapidly than those of women, most of whom occupied jobs in retail sales, banking, human services, and other sectors closer to the realm of exchange, where wages are higher and more likely to be paid.

The inheritors of the Soviet working class are enmeshed in a network society whose scattered nodes are female-dominated families, nuclei around which their husbands and other kin orbit. These demoralized men and struggling women whose goal is immediate survival do not attempt mass mobilization. Instead they draw on the elastic social networks, the resources and strategies, that remain sedimented in the working-class households of today—the legacies of the Soviet regime.

Defensive Strategies

We defined defensive strategies as the combination of diversification of economic activities within the household with the sharing of resources across households. By identifying the key assets that each family deploys, we can see how diversification and redistribution work. Each family tries to keep its foot in the labor market, having at least one member who is employed even if she or he receives no regular wage or only a minuscule one. Each family receives some government assistance, whether in the form of a pension (for disability, old age, or military service), unemployment benefits, or low-income family supplements. Of the five cases, one actively exploits a dacha; a second has a dacha but does not have the resources to grow much there; and a third has a plot of land. The other two are reliant on small but more important exchanges with kin in rural areas. Housing conditions run the gamut from a dilapidated, condemned cottage to a modern three-room apartment received as part of the Soviet government's dispensation for large families. Because economic involution has brought the loss of many jobs, workers continue to seek an outlet for their skills in occasional jobs or work on the side.

Marina: For a Roof over One's Head[5]

The stereotypic Soviet citizen often has been described as dependent, bereft of initiative, passive in the face of adversity, helpless without state handouts, and jealous of those who enrich themselves. At first sight, Marina looked as though she fit the stereotype. When we interviewed her in 1995, she was still working at Polar, hanging on in the hope of early retirement (at the age of 45), to which she would be entitled on the basis of her hazardous work. But she was denied this because her registered job classification was not designated as hazardous. Still she didn't leave—even though by 1995, wages had been irregular and falling for two years and most workers had already left. She complained a lot about all the stealing that was taking place at the enterprise, both by workers and by managers. She recently had turned down a job in retail, since such work—so she said—was immoral.

At the age of 47, in February 1998, Marina was laid off. She received 1,500 rubles in kind (a divan), half of the six months' liquidation wages owed her by law. At the time of our second interview (April 1999), she was still waiting for the remaining 1,500 rubles. When the six months were up, she registered at the Employment Agency in search of work but so far had found none. "Who wants to employ a pensioner," she says, "when there are so many young people looking for work?" So she depends on monthly unemployment compensation of 375 rubles (75 percent of her regular wages—the amount provided for by law, for the first three months of unemployment) in food, and another 310 rubles in medical assistance for her son, who has chronic asthma and gastritis.

Marina lives with her second husband, who also worked at Polar until wages became irregular. He quit in 1993 for a construction company job, which also failed to meet his expectations, after which he took a job caring for the Municipal Parks. Again he didn't last six months before turning to unemployment. That was in 1994. Now he is working for the Ministry of Internal Affairs as a joiner. He receives 300 rubles a month, more or less regularly, but again only in kind—a bus pass, food. The latest insult was 100 rubles worth of so-called Humanitarian Aid, which was, as Marina described it, only fit for their dogs. He used to do odd jobs on dachas, building stairs or bathhouses, but as Marina asked rhetorically, "Who has the money to pay for such work nowadays?"

Marina and her husband have two children, a daughter of 16 and a son of 15. Marina frequently mentions her son's disability, which often keeps him out of school. She is proud of her daughter's outstanding academic accomplishments and is hoping that through connections she may somehow go on to the university. These accomplishments are all the more amazing, given their deplorable housing conditions. The four of them live in one room of a ramshackle, frame cottage; Marina's sister, who receives the minimum unemployment benefit of 130 rubles,[6] lives with her young daughter in a smaller, adjoining room. It is difficult to comprehend how the six of them can exist together in this tiny, dark, dank space.[7] They heat their room with a small stove, carry water from an outside well, and use an outhouse.

Marina and her first husband inherited this cottage—originally, a duplex—from its owner. When they divorced, they split it equally. Her ex-husband sold his half, which lies abandoned and demolished; but Marina and her family refuse to evacuate the other half. The land has been granted to a developer who is eager to erect a new apartment building on this prime real estate near the center of town. But Marina won't budge. By law her cottage cannot be demolished until all registered there have been rehoused. At the time of the first interview, she had already turned down a modern two-room apartment, holding out for the three rooms to which she was entitled. Since then she has been offered a two-room apartment in a frame building, and most recently, space in a hostel. As the offerings of the city council have become less attractive, she has become all the more determined to hold out for her three-room fantasy, knowing that until she gets her way, she is denying some private developer sumptuous profits.

Their only other source of sustenance is their dacha, bought some 15 years ago, soon after they married. Until 1992, they used to raise chickens and pigs there, but they stopped because they didn't have the money for feed. At the first interview, they were still growing vegetables at the dacha; but by the second interview, Marina was complaining that almost everything they grew was stolen. In the realm of dacha production, as in their income and their housing conditions, their life has progressively deteriorated.

Marina considers herself a troublemaker. At Polar she protested against the ubiquitous stealing as well as her job classification. She has waged a protracted war against the municipality for many years, in the vain hope of improving her deplorable housing circumstances. Bereft of material and skill assets inherited from the past, cut off from any redistributive networks, she is reliant on the state for the little income she receives. But she is hardly passive.

Tanya: Working the Kinship Network[8]

While Marina plays her citizenship assets—unemployment benefits, sick benefits, and housing rights—for all they are worth, Tanya works on her social assets, her diverse kin networks, to keep herself afloat.

Tanya is effectively a single mother. At the age of 44, she shares a one-and-a-half-room apartment in a frame building with her daughter (20) and son (23). At the time of the first interview (1995), she still worked at Red October, but only intermittently because of her asthma and weak heart. Her pay, 200 rubles a month, was about half that of her coworkers; and during the previous year she had seen only 70 rubles a month in cash, having received the rest in kind, at the factory shop. She finally left her job in 1997 because of poor health. She now lives on her disability pension of 400 rubles. She used to do some sewing on the side, but stopped, fearing that the tax inspectors would discover this activity and take away her pension.

Tanya's first husband died by drowning. She shed no tears over it, since he was an inveterate drinker and used to beat her. Her second husband was Bulgarian, a member of Komi's Bulgarian colony.[9] When communism ended, he returned home to Bulgaria, and soon began to send Tanya money. She had even spent six months with him there. At the time of the first interview, she wanted to join him permanently with her daughter; later, she wanted to divorce him. Her life was in Komi, with her two children.

Tanya's son was wounded while serving in Chechnya. At the time of the first interview, he had recently returned, a changed person from the gentle boy she knew. When his drinking sprees made him abusive and violent, his sister and mother had to leave the apartment. He had been irregularly employed as an electrician but he rarely saw any wages. Three years later, with tears welling in her eyes, she told us that a year earlier he'd been imprisoned for petty crimes. Tanya's daughter, in contrast—even though she too had found no permanent work—brought smiles to her face. The daughter was about to deliver a baby. Its father was a policeman with no desire to marry her. They hoped he would at least pay child support.

So how does Tanya get by? Her parents in the village nearby help with food (vegetables and sometimes meat). Her mother can sometimes offer her money, since she runs a successful practice in homeopathic medicine. Tanya's eldest sister also helps her with clothes, and in an emergency, with money. As a social worker she doesn't earn much, but her husband had a lucrative job as plumber in a meat processing plant, until he had a heart attack and died the previous year, at 48. Tanya's other sister, also older than her, used to work at Red October but is now employed at a kindergarten. She can't help Tanya materially, but they have always shared their sorrows and delights.

Since the first interview, Tanya's relationship with her mother-in-law by her first marriage had taken a new turn. As grandmother to Tanya's children, she had always helped out in small ways. She was of German descent, and like so many of Komi's ethnic Germans, she had reconnected with her kin. She was now living with her brother in Berlin but continued to visit Komi, as she was employed in German automobile export. She proposed that Tanya marry her other son, the younger brother of Tanya's first husband, and that together with her daughter they move to Berlin. Tanya smiles whimsically at the thought, concluding once more that her future is here in Syktyvkar, close to her own family.

Tanya is not working. Having inherited little from the past other than her sickness, she gets by on minimal support from the state and assistance from her close-knit family (parents, sisters, and mother-in-law). She is the center and beneficiary of a redistributive kinship network. Resignation mixes with the fantasy of escape, as she contemplates her future; but the security of family ties wins the day.

Sveta: The Single Mother[10]

Tanya became a single mother, but not through her own choice—her first husband drowned and her second emigrated; but Sveta had made this a deliberate life decision. One might be surprised to discover "single mother" as a life strategy, especially as in Soviet times it was such a stigmatized status. As men become more of an economic liability, and as the distribution of public housing to families has virtually ceased, Sveta's strategy has become more acceptable and more common.

Sveta, now 37 years old, began her working life in the village as part of a construction brigade, and then retrained in a vocational college for garment workers. Upon graduating in 1985 she took up a job as a skilled "cutter" at Red October. When she began work at Red October, Sveta received a place in one of its hostels—one of the better ones in Syktyvkar, with a real community of women who worked and lived together. She roomed with two other single workers. It was in 1989 that Sveta and her two roommates collectively decided to become pregnant together. They each had a baby the following year, and in that ingenious way each obtained a separate room.

Sveta took maternity leave in 1990. She was recalled in 1992 because they so desperately needed her skills. But by the time we interviewed her in 1995, her situation had deteriorated. In the prior six months, she had received only an advance of 70 rubles out of her official wage of 320 rubles a month. She took the rest of her wages in kind, from limited offerings at the enterprise shop. As a single mother she received a little assistance from the state (78 rubles). In 1995, she was also working part-time with a friend, sewing nightgowns and men's underpants, and selling the garments through various shops in the city. But this did not bring in much (between 100 rubles and 250 rubles a month).

When we visited her again, in 1999, she said she had given up her job at Red October the previous year. But before quitting she had begun working a second job, as a cleaner in the telecommunications monopoly. Now it had become her main job. The pay was not bad, at 800 rubles a month. Until recently, she had received it in cash and regularly, but now she saw only 500 rubles a month. If worse came to worst and she was laid off, she was prepared to return to the construction sites where she had begun. Sveta had given up the idea of sewing garments on the side, as she no longer had access to machines, and more importantly, her skills were too limited to be competitive. Since her cleaning job only took up two hours a day (six days a week), she wished she had a dacha or even just a garden plot to grow food. But she never had the opportunity to obtain one, as Red October was too poor to give them out to its employees.

Sveta admitted that without help from her two brothers in the village, in the form of vegetables, meat, and eggs, she didn't know how she would survive. She regretted she couldn't help them more in return; but recently she agreed to share her room with her nephew, who is attending one of Syktyvkar's vocational colleges. Although the village is only three hours away by bus, travel is too expensive to go there often. Still, Sveta always goes in spring, to help with planting potatoes, and she takes her eight-year-old daughter there to stay a while during the summer holidays. The exchange with her native village has become more intensive as her situation has become more precarious.

Sveta is adept at exploiting her rights of access to state assistance. As the head of a low-income family, she obtains free meals for her daughter as well as a maintenance subsidy, paying only 44 rubles instead of 120 rubles for their room. In addition, as a single mother, she is entitled to another 140 rubles a month; but it's been a year since she last received it.

The two skills Sveta inherited from the old regime—sewing and construction—are of little use to her now. The one asset she has managed to claim from the old regime is her room in the hostel. She cannot diversify her economic activities, and so she makes the most of her close relationships with her brothers as well as her status as a single mother. Her decision to become a single mother, her departure for the cleaning job, and her willingness to find alternative work bespeak Sveta's energy and determination to make ends meet.

Natasha: The Two-Earner Household[11]

When we first interviewed Natasha in 1995, both she and her husband were receiving unemployment compensation, at 75 percent of their wages. Today, unemployment compensation is set at the so-called minimum wage of 87 rubles a month, except for those who lose their jobs through liquidation or restructuring. Any job would pay better than that, so we were not surprised to learn at our second interview that Natasha had found herself new employment.

Natasha began her work career in 1970, at the age of 16, in what was then a small furniture shop and later became the modern factory of Polar. She worked there 24 years. When wages became irregular and work stoppages more frequent, in 1994, she quit her job. As a worker in the hazardous lacquer shop, she might have retired if she had stayed another four years; but instead, she opted for unemployment compensation for two months, and then found a temporary job as a painter, through her husband's sister. When this job ended, she again was left unemployed. Her husband, 43 years old, had worked as a carpenter in a local construction company until pay became irregular, whereupon he too left his job for one in the municipality—thanks, again, to his sister. Like his wife, he only lasted a few months before returning to the construction industry. Again pay became so irregular that he left for unemployment, which together with his disability pension came to 500 rubles. At the time of the first interview they were both on unemployment, bringing in less than 1,000 rubles for a family of four—themselves and their 11-year-old twin daughters. Their income, therefore, was on a par with the poorest of our respondents; but their living conditions, as we shall see, were much better.

Their elder son, age 23, was living in a room in a hostel with his wife and child. He worked as a chauffeur for an enterprise director, which meant that he could use the car for private purposes. Natasha's daughter, age 21, used to work at Red October, and was living with her family in a two-room apartment (inherited from her husband's parents). Natasha would like to help her daughter but she can't even afford to feed, clothe, and buy school supplies for her two younger girls. The only plus in her circumstances is the modern, three-room apartment she received through the municipal queue for large families. They have a plot of land where they grow potatoes, but they have no dacha. They sometimes take the children to Natasha's parents' village, where Natasha grows some food, and where her 74-year-old mother helps by knitting clothes for them.

When we returned in July 1997, both husband and wife were employed: she, as a cook in a canteen, and he, with the Municipal Parks. She received a low wage of 350 rubles, with an occasional bonus of 100 or 150 rubles. His wage was much higher, at 800 rubles, but he rarely saw more than 200 rubles, with some of the difference being made up in food. Natasha said they were much better off on unemployment, but when that ran out they had to find jobs. They were desperately short of cash to pay for their children's needs.

We interviewed Natasha again in May 1999 and discovered that they were still in the same jobs. She was earning wages and bonuses of between 600 and 800 rubles a month as well as subsidized meals. He was still receiving between 800 and 1,000 rubles, on paper. Wages were usually paid in kind (food and housing maintenance). But in summer there was work on the side, which could bring in 50 rubles a day, plus a meal. On top of this her husband was receiving a disability pension of 300 rubles a month. They were still having difficulty making ends meet, and Natasha was making plans for her teenage daughters to go to technical college, where they would learn catering.

In comparison with the first three interviewees, Natasha had inherited more from the old regime. She had an extensive network of kin in town and country as well as a modern, three-room apartment. At the time of the second interview, Natasha's son was trying to exchange the three-room apartment for a two-room apartment for his parents and a separate, single-room apartment for his family. He hoped to then combine this with his hostel room in order to obtain a two-room apartment. But the plan came to naught. Even a seemingly nonfungible asset such as an apartment can be traded in and the proceeds distributed among family members. Although she appears to be better off than Marina, Tanya, and Sveta, Natasha and her husband struggle daily to meet their family's basic needs.

Irina: Working Pensioners[12]

Conventionally, pensioners are the most dependent and deprived group in society, and thus the most vulnerable to economic decline. One of the paradoxical consequences of economic involution is the relative prosperity of pensioners—at least, where the government distributes pensions on time and in cash, as it does in Komi. After they retire—men at 55 and women at 50—they often continue to work as cleaners, guards, or dishwashers, or in other menial jobs. If they economize, they can live on less than their pensions and accumulate or redistribute the rest. Thus, it is more common for pensioners to help their children than vice versa.

Irina is 67 years old. She worked at Red October for 35 years and had been chair of its Sports Club and its Trade Union Committee. She retired in 1987 with the honorific title of "personal pensioner," usually bestowed upon high party officials but sometimes on workers with distinguished careers. The title used to be accompanied by privileges such as free travel in the Komi Republic, trips to holiday resorts, and the like.

Irina lives with her second husband in a two-room apartment that he received through his workplace, having given her own apartment to her 33-year-old daughter and family. Her 35-year-old, married son also has his own apartment, where he lives with his wife and son. Irina and her husband don't receive any help from either of her children. She receives 360 rubles a month as her pension. Until 1998, she was earning a similar, additional amount as a dishwasher and cleaner at a local restaurant; but after years working there as a pensioner, she had decided that enough was enough.

Her husband receives a similar pension, plus a war veteran supplement, which together come to 500 rubles. In addition, he works as a night guard and yard cleaner at Syktyvkar Road Works. He is supposed to get 800 rubles a month for this, but he's lucky if he sees 200 rubles. He is owed 5,000 rubles in back pay. As Irina proudly announces, he is the breadwinner, paying for the apartment (electricity and maintenance) and for basic necessities such as food. "He feeds me," she says, "so why should I continue to work?" But she quickly adds, "I've never taken a single kopeck from him."

She has her own bank account, which she draws on liberally to help her children—especially her son, an electrician in the same company as his father, and his wife, who is a saleswoman. Neither of them receive their wages on a regular basis. In the space of the three years between the two interviews, Irina had given her son 8,000 rubles for a car, 5,000 rubles for a garage (also used as a pantry for her dacha produce), and 3,000 rubles to her grandson for his studies. She had received 4,000 rubles as an inheritance from an uncle, and the rest of the 12,000 rubles she had saved from her own earnings.

Not content to sit idle, both are also very active at their dacha, which they bought in 1973, initially sharing it with Irina's sister. Although it is not big—only 500 square meters—they are able to grow all varieties of vegetables and berries there, which they supplement with mushrooms that they collect in the forest and cabbage that they get from the state farm. The food gets them through the winter. With produce from the dacha, they can also help both their children economize. Irina and her husband have diversified their activities in multiple realms, and distribute what they can to their children.

Because wages in money are scarce and pensions are paid regularly, retirees seem to be almost like a labor aristocracy, free of immediate obligations yet with a monetary base from which to pursue other sources of livelihood. They can be judicious distributors of their time, their resources, and their income.

It is difficult to summarize these cases. All five households are struggling to keep their heads above the rising waters of economic involution by various methods. There is a correspondence, albeit a loose one, between the resources inherited from the old regime and strategies deployed in the new regime. It is better to think of these assets not so much as wielded instrumentally but as a field that shapes the parameters of strategies. As wage labor collapses, households are thrown back on their various material, social, and citizenship assets; the formal skills they acquired under the old regime are no longer of much use. Their defensive strategies, formed in 1994 and 1995, turned out to be amazingly stable despite the uncertain environment. A few households were more ambitious: Instead of diversifying their economic activities, they collectively concentrated their energies on one pursuit; instead of sharing across households, they attempted to accumulate resources—that is, not only to spend but also to invest. These were the aspiring entrepreneurs.

Entrepreneurial Strategies

The household strategies we have explored so far have attempted to spread risk over state assistance, household sharing, and labor diversification. However, we found a few households swimming out to sea with the involutional tide, concentrating on a single economic activity. According to involution theory, the most dynamic part of the Russian economy is in the realm of exchange; and that is what the four exceptional women whose stories follow have managed to exploit. Investing their energies in trade and petty commodity production was not something that they inherited from the past but something they developed themselves, often driven to this entrepreneurial strategy by desperate circumstances rather than disposition or desire. The narratives that follow highlight the dilemmas and risks of concentration and accumulation, explaining why some still cling to their wage labor as a form of security despite nonpayment of wages. At the same time, there is more instability and risk-taking in the life choices of the four women we discuss below, involving switches between defensive and entrepreneurial strategies. The first two women had been employed by Red October. Nina continued to work there, but she was paid in kind; she had to become an entrepreneur in order to realize a sufficient monetary income. Anna left Red October for a cleaning job but developed a dressmaking business at home. The second two women were employed at Polar, and they have been more successful. Luba has moved from one retail store to another, and Valya has created her own business in the local market. Among our interviewees, only Valya survives on self-employment without any wage labor.

Nina: Trade on the Side[13]

As mentioned earlier, the transition to the market brought wide-ranging opportunities in the sphere of exchange, from high finance to petty trade. Indeed, in the early years of the transition, Russia looked more like a flea market than a free market. Women in particular, but also teenage boys growing up in this period, were often drawn to commercial activities and the cash nexus. Our first case of entrepreneurship describes such "trade on the side"—first, on the part of the son, and then on that of the mother.

Nina is 47 years old, married, with two sons. She was recommended to us as a very popular supervisor at Red October. At the time of our first interview, in 1995, she was officially earning 400 rubles a month but saw only 70 of those in cash, receiving the rest in goods from the factory shop. Her husband did better. As a carpenter in a large grocery store, he was earning 1,000 rubles; but his wages, which he received in cash, were also being held up.

The two of them lived together with their younger son in a two-room apartment that they received from the municipality when their timber cottage was demolished. At the time of the first interview, the younger son, then 13 years old, had already embarked on an entrepreneurial career. He had begun by selling newspapers, moved on to toilet paper, and from there turned to wicker baskets. He was providing for his own monetary needs and even loaning his mother money when she was short. These precocious business activities evoked great consternation in his father, who thought his son should concentrate on his education. His mother, who had had socialist leanings all her life and was therefore ambivalent about all commercial operations, nevertheless showed a furtive pride in her younger boy, who was already helping his family.

Indeed, he helped her pay off her debts from a trip to Chechnya with the Soldiers' Mothers to look for her elder son.[14] Although suffering from the aftereffects of the war, Nina's elder son was by no means as badly off as Tanya's. Today he is an electrician, working in a commercial enterprise and living with his wife and one-year-old daughter in the apartment of his mother-in-law, who has moved out to stay with her lover.

When we returned in April 1999 to talk to Nina, we discovered that she was still working at Red October and her husband was still at the grocery store. She had not seen any alternative to staying on. She didn't want to join the army of cleaning people, ex-employees of Red October, that had occupied the city's office buildings. In any case, she would be retiring in three years and receiving a pension.

Nina described the situation at Red October as follows: There were still 150 workers there, laboring under work stoppages and irregular and pitiful payment. The month before, she had worked only nine days. With some amusement, she described her work brigade of 20 as including 10 disabled workers, three pensioners, and three who were about to retire. The piecework system existed as before, but wages were no longer paid in money but in the bras, nightgowns, and shirts they produced. Most of her coworkers were unhappy about this system, since they found the garments difficult to sell. To their complaints, management replied to the effect that they could like it or lump it. Nina, however, seemed to thrive on the system. She had been so successful at peddling her wares at enterprises and organizations around the city that she owed Red October more than it owed her. In effect, she had become a small-scale trader, selling garments that she had paid for with work hours instead of cash. Her earnings were officially 500 rubles a month, but with this petty trade, we suspected that they were much greater.

Whereas Nina had entered trade on the side, her younger son, now 17 years old, had given it up. His commercial activities led nowhere, providing him pocket money and the ability to assist his mother from time to time, but not an entrepreneurial career. He was embarrassed to continue with them, but it was too late to catch up on his schoolwork. His teachers suggested he enter a vocational college in ninth grade instead of continuing with high school. So he entered the college for construction workers. Nina now regrets that she encouraged his commercial operations, and worries about his future.

Apart from their wage labor and trade, Nina and her family were actively cultivating their dacha garden, which supplied two families—her own and her elder son's—with food through the winter. Her elder son and his family planned to spend the entire summer at the dacha that year, saving on the costs of traveling to and fro. Nina was close to her sister, from whom she used to borrow money in exchange for sewing dresses and nightgowns. But now it seemed she was not so short of cash; she was able to buy clothes for her younger son, and the previous year, even a television set. They weren't stinting on food, and she even had some left over, to help out her elder son from time to time.

Nina was running an active, diversified household economy based on two wage incomes, trade on the side, and dacha cultivation. Her situation had actually improved over the last five years: Her husband was still bringing in cash, and she had given her own job an entrepreneurial twist. She had begun to share her gains with her kin. The one major cost she regretted was the sacrifice of her younger son's education.

Anna: Between Wage Labor and Self-Employment[15]

Nina's is a transitional case: Her job compelled her to become a trader in order to realize a monetary wage. Anna's is the more usual case, of formal employment supplemented by work at home, exploiting skills acquired at Red October.

Anna was born in Syktyvkar, in 1964. After graduating from high school, she was immediately hired by Red October. Her mother, who was employed at Polar, had wanted her to go on to technical college, but Anna had already made up her mind otherwise. Anna took to Red October like a duck to water, rapidly moving up the skill hierarchy. They produced men's shirts by the piecework system. She brought home what was then the very handsome wage of 350 rubles. She would often work weekends.

She was very active in the social life of the factory, organizing tea parties, outings, collective holidays, and the like. She became a Komsomol leader, then a deputy in the City Council (1984–1987), a member of the Regional Council of

Trade Unions, and finally, a member of the Communist party in 1986, which she quit shortly thereafter, in 1989.

In 1987 she married a man who had come to the factory from the village. At one point, she even returned with him to live in the village, dreaming of owning a house and orchard there. But that was not to be. Two months later, under pressure from her mother, they returned to the city and Anna rejoined her old brigade at Red October. She took maternity leave in 1988 and again in 1991. In 1992, the enterprise was privatized to the work collective, but that event had little immediate effect on her life. In 1993, a new shop for military uniforms was opened; but soon afterward, the enterprise began to go downhill. The first work stoppages occurred in 1993, and for the first time she began to worry about her future. At the end of 1993, wage payment delays began, initially only for a few weeks. In 1994, the work stoppages became longer and longer, and in summer her department was closed for two months. The same thing happened in 1995. She quit work in July 1995.

It was not easy to leave Red October and her brigade, but there was no future in it. Managers had started to steal equipment, workers had begun to leave, and the brigades were merged and reduced in size. In 1996, after she had left, she recounted the sad story of rising debts and long delays in wages. The best workers had left, and Red October was forced to hire people without any skills, straight off the street. The only people who wanted to work there came from the unemployment office. They would work for a few months and then go back on unemployment, she said.

Before she left, Anna had taken on an extra job as a janitor at the Telecommunications Center. She had got the job through a friend. When it became clear that she would have to formally register this new job as her primary employment or lose it altogether, she left Red October, thinking she was moving into a more stable situation. She received 400 rubles a month. This was a low salary, but at least she was paid regularly and in cash. She was earning as much as at Red October and had more free time. What had once been a sideline had become her main job.

As soon as she left Red October, however, she began sewing garments at home. The first hurdle was to buy a sewing machine. Her husband opposed this enormous expenditure, but she overruled him. At the beginning of 1996, she began to take in orders, expedited by her neighbor who worked at a local tailor's artel and who was able to redirect work to Anna. Her first contract was to sew diapers for the city's maternity home. Then she began to take orders from other neighbors and friends. With the help of the same neighbor she worked out effective prices—about half the factory price—and then diversified her offerings from dresses and nightgowns to coats and suits. Since few people could pay in cash for their purchases, Anna also accepted payments in kind.

At first (in 1996), this extra work brought in much less than her "main job" as a cleaning person; but by the end of 1998, the situation was reversed. On the one side, orders continued to grow, and it became hard for her to fulfill them. On the other side, her wages at the Telecommunications Center became irregular, and her advance was lowered to a mere 60 rubles. Later there were layoffs, but she miraculously escaped them, and at the time of our last interview (April 1999), she was earning 400 rubles, paid regularly each month. Her working hours were from 5 P.M. to 10 P.M., six days a week; and although she was up to her neck in dirty rags, she couldn't give it up because her dressmaking business was not secure enough. She did not want to expand it too much, for fear of the tax inspector, who might put a stop to her business altogether, or of clients who might be too fussy or refuse to pay. She therefore took on orders only from her circle of relatives, friends, and acquaintances. Because this working-class circle itself led a tenuous economic existence, her business was all the more precarious.

Anna's husband has worked all his life at the Syktyvkar Machine-Building Factory (Syktyvkarskii Mekhanicheskii Zavod, or SMZ). His formal wage in 1999 was 1,000 rubles, but he hadn't received regular wages since 1994. Compared to workers at other factories, he was doing quite well, because he was at least receiving wages in kind. For example, in the month prior to our first interview in May 1996, he had received logs to build a dacha, and a kilo of butter. When workers protested that "they had nothing to put the butter on," management added insult to injury by giving each one 20 rubles (the equivalent of U.S.$4) out of the back pay they were owed.

There were also some complex wage transactions. For example, the accountant at SMZ agreed to "pay" Anna for garments she had ordered by installing a telephone in Anna's apartment. This would also serve as partial payment of the wages owed to Anna's husband. Because their neighbors also wanted phones installed, and installation would be cheaper for each if the phones were installed simultaneously (it would cost 8,000 rubles for three phones), Anna suggested that the accountant arrange to have the three lines installed at once, and that the neighbors pay her directly for their share of the expense. But now there was tension, because Anna's neighbors were paying up very slowly. In 1998, Anna's husband also received in lieu of wages a fridge, construction materials (again, for a dacha), and an assortment of school supplies. He has looked around for other jobs but has found nothing better. The foundry where he works is one of the few workplaces that continue to receive orders.

In 1999, the couple was living with their son (11) and daughter (seven) in a three-room apartment on the ground floor of a frame house. The building was nearly 40 years old and badly in need of repair, especially after a gas explosion in the kitchen; but Anna hadn't the money to fix it, and the municipality wouldn't do anything. Still, it was spacious. She had turned one of the rooms into a workshop, where she sewed every day. She and her husband used to live with her mother in a two-room apartment, before her mother received an apartment from Polar and moved out. They exchanged their two-room apartment for a three-room unit in the same building. The previous owners initially resisted the idea, but in the end their accumulated debts forced them to accede. Anna had to pay off a lot of bills before they could move in, but the extra room proved crucial.

Anna received a large (1,000 square meters) plot of land from Red October in 1989, through a friend who headed the manpower department *(po blatu)*. The trees were cut, the land was tilled, and over the preceding decade her husband had built a cabin with materials he received in lieu of wages. Much to the consternation of her husband, Anna insisted on reserving half of the land for flowers, the passion of her life; the other half was planted in potatoes, cucumbers, tomatoes, and other crops. Her mother and the children spend the summer holidays there. Still, Anna complains the dacha is not cost-effective, since travel back and forth is so expensive. She applies the same cash calculus to visits to her husband's family in the village. They haven't been there in two years because they have to pay not only for transportation but also for trinkets for all her nieces and nephews—all for what, a sack of potatoes?

Relations between husband and wife have shifted as she has become the major breadwinner in the family and he has to beg for humiliating handouts from his bankrupt employer. At the time of our first interview, Anna thought their relationship was better than any other, very different from that between her brother and his wife, who is always nagging him for money. At the end of the first interview, she said that although her husband had been opposed to the sewing machine at first, now he was helping her with her work. At the end of the second interview, however, she complained that he was drinking more and helping less: "When I married him in 1987, I thought I was marrying a village lad, but now I have to coerce him even to work on the dacha. Whenever I ask him to do anything, he starts bargaining, demanding cigarettes or something before he will help out. I don't know what has gotten into him."

Anna had always been an energetic leader and skilled worker. Her loyalty to Red October did not blind her to the need to seek alternative employment. With the encouragement of her neighbor and her pliant husband, she was able to slowly build up her own garment business. Depending on uncertain demand from her acquaintances, friends, and relatives, its future is precarious, which is why she continues to do what she hates—namely, to clean floors. Anna has not taken Valya's road to entrepreneurship, because she has not been forced to rely on her garment business.

Valya: The Self-Made Entrepreneur[16]

The shift from worker to entrepreneur requires more than a mobilization of assets material and social, skill- and citizenship-related. It calls for two strategic leaps: first, overcoming the disposition to play it safe by keeping one's foot in a number of niches; and second, resisting external pressures to redistribute the wealth one accumulates among poorer kin, neighbors, and friends. The shift from defensive strategies to entrepreneurial ones is not something that comes about suddenly; it emerges over a considerable period and often under the economic compulsion to survive. It was part desperation, part imagination that led Valya to become an independent trader in the local market.

Valya was born in 1968, and at our last interview she was 31 years old. Her father had died in 1973, after which her mother started to drink heavily. Her mother lost her parental rights, and Valya was taken to an orphanage at the age of five, where she stayed until she was 15. At the time, she could not forgive her mother; but looking back on those orphanage years now, she thinks she learned a great deal—especially, to be self-reliant. One of her teachers was like a second mother to her. She did well in classes, had an active social life, received rewards and trips, and even became a Komsomol leader. She recalls how freely she traveled under communism, whereas now it's too expensive.

At 15, Valya left the orphanage, returned to her mother's home, and entered a vocational college, where she received a professional certificate as a switchboard operator. She began working at the Central Telephone Exchange in 1988 but was soon forced to quit the job because customers complained about her rudeness, which Valya blamed on conflicts with her husband at home. Be that as it may, she quickly realized this work was not for her and took a job at Polar, working in the shop that lacquered the chipboard panels for the wall systems. During that time she also enrolled in courses at the commerce department of the timber industry academy, but she had to give that up when her son became sick.

In 1994, with work and wages both irregular, she left Polar to work in retail sales at an agricultural supply store—a job she found through a friend of her mother's, who happened to be the proprietor. There she met her second and current husband, who was doing some electrical work. Together they left the store in 1996 because the business was nearing bankruptcy, the conditions were poor (no sick benefits or maternity leave), and her husband was accused of stealing. Nevertheless, her two years at this store had taught her a great deal about retail trade, preparing her for her new occupation as a trader at the town market.

Another reason she had for leaving this store was that she was expecting a baby. When we interviewed her in 1997, she was living with her mother, an unemployed pensioner; her husband, aged 19, who was receiving minimal unemployment benefits; and her two children—a son of 12 and a daughter of one year. Out of desperation, in May 1997, she started her own trade in processed food, working from home. Like many of the traders at the nearby city market, she employed her own seller—a neighbor who had been a bookkeeper but had recently been laid off. She had complete confidence in her new employee, who received a nominal wage and a commission of 7 percent of the profit. Her husband transported the goods to and from the market everyday, having first collected them from the local wholesale center. He borrowed the van of a close friend, whom they paid back in gas and maintenance.

The markup on the wholesale price was much smaller, of course, than it would have been for fresh food products imported from distant cities. Many women participated in long-distance trade, going to Moscow to buy goods and then reselling them at a higher price in the north. Valya could not do this: In addition to paying her seller, she had to pay for her market space, taxes, and interest on the money she borrowed (at 10 percent per month). She also was forced to pay for protection. She nonetheless made a reasonable profit of about 2,000 rubles a month—a little more than the average wage, with the added advantage of its being actual money.

When we returned two years later, in 1999, Valya's business had expanded, but she was not living any better. She now controlled four kiosks and employed saleswomen at each of them. In order to survive, she was paying them a very low official wage (500 rubles a month), but she gave them another 700 to 1,000 rubles under the table in "bonuses." She was still borrowing money but had learned that it is best not to borrow from friends. The same rule applies to hiring: She judges potential employees on the basis of their references. Valya has her own car, a pager, and even extra storage space, but she has no ambition to open a retail store. She says if you need 15 official signatures just to open a kiosk, you can imagine how impossible it is to open a store. The previous two years had not been all clover, and she continued to live precariously on the margins. Indeed, in the second half of 1998, her child fell ill and she was forced to register on the unemployment rolls.

From the beginning, a critical asset to Valya's business was her apartment, which was situated on the ground floor of a rundown, two-story frame apartment building equipped with poorly functioning central heating. Its singular advantage was its proximity to the town market. In addition, it had three rooms (though totaling only 36 square meters of living space). Valya stored her goods in the coldest room (the poor heating turned out to be an asset). In this way she was able to minimize costs, including time spent in transportation. Valya and her family lived in the other two rooms.

When we interviewed Valya in 1997, her husband was helping her with her nascent business. Earlier his parents and two brothers had helped them out. But in 1999, Valya was fed up with her husband. She had hoped he would at least be available to transport produce, but he was arrested for drunken driving and lost his license. As far as she was concerned, the only thing he had done for her was give her a daughter. That had given him the right to avoid military service for a time; but now that their daughter was three, he had been called up. She was only too happy to see him leave. That would give her at least two years of respite. But she has not given up on men in general. She thinks back on her past, wondering whether she made a mistake in divorcing her first husband, and meanwhile has rediscovered her ex-lover, from her years at Polar.

Whereas the center of economic cooperation in the Soviet system was the labor collective, it has now entirely shifted over to the household, in Valya's case. She misses the security that came with state employment, better pensions, and holiday camps for children. But she admits that the shortage economy had its problems and is glad to be free to pursue her own line of business. She lives and works for her children. She wants them to have a good education, and she says she will do anything she can to give them a better life.

Luba: Turning Back from the Brink[17]

It was desperation that drove Valya into trade. Sitting at home with her newborn baby, she seized what opportunities were available to her—an apartment next to the marketplace, and an unemployed husband ready to work at her behest. Even now, with her business expanded, with a car and pager and several employees at her command, she still lives on the edge of poverty, knowing that moving out of her ramshackle wooden apartment is just a dream.

If Valya took the low road, Luba took the high road into retail trade. Still, like Valya, she confronted political and economic obstacles, which in the end forced her to give up the idea of developing her own, independent business. She had to contend with not one but two male-dominated worlds: that of the former *nomenklatura,* who early on had secured monopolies in trade, and that of the extortionist mobs. Luba's social connections, material assets, and organizational skills took her farther than any of the other women in our sample, but only because she led an abstemious, kopeck-pinching life, always aware of the precariousness of her family's existence.

At 42 in 1999, Luba was ten years older than Valya. She hails from a village near Syktyvkar, graduated from a culinary college, and married a local teacher who subsequently became a KGB officer. She saw him as her escape from the village and did not expect the marriage to last the ten years that it did. She took a job at Polar in 1984 with the explicit purpose of earning enough money to buy her husband a car. Then he was seconded to Usogorsk, and she went with him. There she became head of manpower in a local enterprise. When she discovered that he had been unfaithful, she left him and returned to Syktyvkar with her daughter, leaving her son behind. Her husband laughed at her, saying she'd never be able to survive without him. But she was determined. To recover her old apartment from the KGB was her first and most challenging goal, especially as KGB officers were not allowed to divorce. In the end she succeeded in recouping her former two-room apartment as well as her job at Polar. She also began receiving alimony from her ex-husband.

As in Valya's, the critical moment in Luba's career came in 1993, when Polar's fortunes began to decline, as evidenced by forced vacations, irregular pay, and disorganized work. At our first interview in July 1994, Luba expressed doubts about the enterprise's future, being critical of the way it had been privatized (passing into the hands of the collective rather than those of a single owner). She also had little sympathy for the factory's manpower policies: the elimination of managerial positions, the merging of incompatible brigades, and the layoffs of the best workers (because they were young and childless).

Luba had a precocious understanding of efficiency and markets. She could see the future of Polar as clearly as though it were written on the wall. As early as February 1994, she began experimenting with work on the side. When there was no work at the factory, she would travel to Moscow to buy goods that she could resell at home in Syktyvkar. It was through her friends that Luba joined the growing numbers of shuttle-traders, or *chelnoki*, at the same time that Valya was entering retail. As the factory was already paying workers in kind, she took one of the wall systems in lieu of wages and installed it in her own apartment, selling the one she already had. At this point, the child support she received for her daughter was her primary source of monetary income.

In July 1994, she took the critical step of leaving Polar. She saw no need to continue inhaling lacquer fumes. For what? For unstable employment? Those who stayed behind in Polar were either supported by their husbands or were waiting for early retirement. She was in neither position. Through a chance encounter, she found a job as a secretary in the Bulgarian consulate in Syktyvkar. The pay was good and in dollars, which at that time of soaring inflation was a major advantage. She lasted three months there before resigning in the face of excessive demands and insults about her lack of education. But she had developed a taste for money.

In November she took up a job in a small, poorly maintained store, where she worked until May 1995. She knew the manager as a friend from Polar. The store had no future, but she persisted nevertheless, earning money on the side and learning about the retail trade. Once more it was Luba's connections that gave her the next break. Many of her neighbors were connected to the KGB and had strong ties to local notables. It was through one such neighbor that Luba found a job in a new supermarket selling construction materials. The store was owned by the son of one of the most influential politicians in the republic. The customers were wealthy, the profits were handsome, and her wages were considerable, especially when she included the money she made on the side. Luba explained that the owner cheated the state out of its taxes, and the sales staff in turn cheated the owner of his profits. Within three months, she was able to buy a car and a television set, and she had saved up enough dollars that she could then lend them out, at interest, to friends. These early years of market expansion were indeed the golden age of retail—especially that sponsored by the old *nomenklatura*.

The owner wanted to promote her to manager at another branch, but Luba feared the resentment she would face there as an outsider. She was especially wary of any such move when she learned that her own manager, for whom she had the greatest respect, was being fired on accusations of having absconded with company funds. Instead of accepting the promotion, Luba, together with two other senior saleswomen and their manager, resigned with the intention of setting up their own shop. As she said at the end of the second interview, they were in a good position to start their own business, having the necessary protection, contacts, and money. This didn't work out, however, because the manager decided to move into the kiosk business on her own.

Luba felt betrayed. She was left without a job; so she too tried to set up a business on her own. She started her own store, selling food, but the "roof" (protection) payments to the mafia, as well as payments to the tax officers and to the fire department, were so high that she had to abandon the project after three months. Looking back on the experience, she realized that she should have been more willing to borrow money. To her that had seemed too great a risk. This is what separates her from Valya, who perhaps was more desperate but also more flexible in adapting to the new market forces.

Having given up the idea of her own business, she returned to being a saleswoman in a store. In 1997, her official salary was a meager 550 rubles; and at our most recent interview (in 1999), it was not much better, at 700 rubles. But that is beside the point, because she is able to sell her own goods on the side, without paying any of the associated costs (taxes, rent, or protection). In effect, like Nina, Luba conducts her own trade on the owner's premises, paying rent not in kind or in money but in hours of labor. On the side she also continues to lend out dollars to her friends at the standard interest rate of 10 percent per month.

Luba's relationship with her domestic partner was very different from Valya's. In 1990, soon after returning to Syktyvkar, Luba had struck up an acquaintance with a man ten years her junior. She openly conceded that theirs was more an arrangement for convenience's sake than an affair of the heart. She did not want to register the relationship, having been disillusioned by her first marriage. She provides a roof for him, while he does all the "man's work" around the apartment. In 1997, he had a job at the Municipal Water Works. Luba reported at our third interview that he used to contribute some 2,000 rubles a month to the household budget but of late had only been receiving an advance of 200 rubles. She was exasperated with his passivity. In the neighboring municipality, workers who had threatened to cut off water supplies had quickly recovered their wage arrears. Why couldn't he and his coworkers do the same in Syktyvkar? When we returned two years later, in June 1999, he had not been working for five months. He hadn't even received all the back pay owed him. He was using her car as a private taxi for hire. He had been doing this for a number of years; but since losing his job, he was making more money at it than before—some 2,000 rubles in one weekend. But they feared that he would be caught by a tax inspector traveling incognito. So he did not do his undeclared taxi-driving work during the week.

Like Valya, Luba had no time for a dacha. When we asked if she had one, she shot back, in an insulted tone, "I'm not 50 years old! Why do I need a dacha?" In her eyes a dacha was for those who had no employment potential, who were no longer active—in other words, for pensioners and others with plenty of time at their disposal. The dacha is the antithesis of the market world in which Luba lives and thrives. Whereas many of our informants could not afford a dacha, or could not afford to cultivate their dacha, Luba was the only one who dismissed the very idea of self-provisioning. Yet she does dream of returning to the village where she grew up; and going to the forest to collect mushrooms and berries is one of her greatest pleasures. The countryside to her connotes an escape from the pressures of the marketplace rather than a substitute economy.

In our first three interviews with her, Luba's aspirations were focused on her daughter, who she hoped would enter law school at the university. In 1997, the daughter entered a local community college that prepares students for university. Luba herself was planning to pay the fees, which are exorbitant in Syktyvkar University's most prestigious departments, such as law. In 1999, her daughter was working at a local photography business for a pittance of 350 rubles a month; but she was also enrolled in a correspondence course in commerce. She travels to Moscow twice a year for examinations. Luba would have preferred that her daughter transfer to the college in Moscow as a full-time student, but she could not afford to pay the tuition and living expenses there.

Her son had rejoined them from Usogorsk in 1997, and in 1999 he was in his last year of high school. Luba was already scheming to get him an exemption from military service. She thought she would be able to bribe her way through to a waiver with the help of a neighbor who worked at the local military draft center. She was unhappy with her son's progress at school, for which she blamed his stepmother in Usogorsk. But she consoled herself that at least her partner and her son were getting along well.

Luba's closest kin are her sister, brother, and father. Her sister, five years younger than herself, is married to a man who like Luba's companion, is employed in the Municipal Water Works department. Luba regularly helps her sister out financially. In 1997, Luba reported that her brother, five years older than herself, was living by himself in a hostel, divorced, and a drunkard. Rather than give him money, which he simply spends on alcohol, she gave him clothes. But she was despairing of helping him, since when he was drunk, he sold his clothes for more vodka. In 1999, Luba told us that he was now serving a three-year prison sentence.

Luba's father was still living in the village. She and her sister used to help him grow vegetables and other crops; but since he had taken up with a new partner, they rarely visited him, because of the tension between them and her. As to her relations with her own partner's relatives, Luba said, they used to be rather cool but had improved over time, as it became obvious what an effective and caring homemaker she was.

In 1997, Luba complained that she no longer had any friends, only contacts. She used to spill out her woes to her partner and her sister, both of whom had a ready ear; but they had so many problems of their own that she didn't want to overburden them with hers. In 1999, she was ruminating about the future. She had plans of buying a plot of land and building a house in her home village, so that her children could have her apartment. Despite her previous failures, Luba has not given up the idea of opening up her own shop. "The third time's a charm," she said, but she was only too aware of the very real problems she would have to overcome.

Luba did not follow Valya across the Rubicon into her own business, nor would she consider bringing her partner into some joint business. Instead she has withdrawn into a strategy of household diversification rather than concentration, deploying the managerial talents she inherited from the old regime in multiple commercial operations. Of all the women we interviewed, she is the closest to the energetic, self-reliant stereotype of the "new Russian woman." But she remains focused on the future of her children, for whom she is ready to make any sacrifice.

In comparing Nina, Anna, Valya, and Luba, we see both the risks and the imagination necessary to take the entrepreneurial road. Valya is the only one who has developed her own business. Her family is completely dependent upon it, and paradoxically, their living conditions are the worst. Nina is forced into selling manufactured garments as a means of realizing her wages. She is unusual among her coworkers in peddling Red October's bras and dressing gowns. Anna clings to her cleaning job as a source of income and an escape from home; but most importantly, it is a shield to protect her more lucrative work on the side. She could expand her business, but she fears depending upon it, because her clients are so poor, their livelihoods so uncertain. Of the four, Luba is the best equipped to develop her own business; but she has learned that the safest way is to conduct it under the "roof" of another—the owner of the shop she looks after. She is only too aware of the barriers to entrepreneurship posed by the joint conspiracy of mafia and governmental control.

As economic involution has deepened, it has driven working-class families back into defensive strategies of diversification and sharing. It has also created opportunities in the sphere of exchange; but for the workers of Polar and Red October, such opportunities are limited, being found only at the lowest rungs of a politically organized economy of trade, protection, and banking. The most enterprising women of the working class are but the fodder of a vast, male-regulated economy of transactions that occupies spaces vacated by the party-regulated, redistributive Soviet economy. Russian society is increasingly polarized between a class of marginal households retreating to subsistence and self-provisioning, largely headed by women, and a male class of merchants and regulators.

The Network Society

In accounting for the startling failure of the Russian economic transition, two social theories have assumed popular currency: cultural legacies and institutional collapse. Those who adopt the first perspective argue that the abiding legacies of communism have mired Russia in its dark past; those who adopt the second, that communism was so fragile that it collapsed like a house of cards, before Russians had a chance to create a new order to take its place, leaving an institutional vacuum and normlessness.

Our study of survival strategies suggests that there is some truth in both theories. We have shown how the inheritance of material assets, human skills, and social relations has shaped the terrain on which strategies are forged. The state continues to play a crucial redistributive role of last resort. These legacies, however, don't work in a historical vacuum; they are not the leaden weight of tradition. They are more like magnets around which poor people navigate their lives. Individuals strategize around resources—housing, occupational skills, education, relations of kinship and friendship, and state assistance—which they inherit or lose, which they create anew or dissipate. We can say that there is continuity with the Soviet order in the taken-for-granted routines that organize the deployment of resources, but these routines are combined in novel ways in response to the new circumstances.

If resources provided a certain fixity to their lives, economic involution transmits a radical uncertainty, which continually threatens to destroy the connection between means and ends. Institutions have indeed collapsed—specifically, the party and the workplace—and new institutions have yet to be consolidated. But an institutional vacuum is not the same as normlessness. People are thrown back on kin and friends, a network society that develops and sustains its own culture of diversification and reciprocity. Where before institutions homogenized and directed behavior, today their disappearance has opened up new opportunities for many-sided activities and for sharing; and for the risk-takers, concentration and accumulation. What marks Russian life today is the inventiveness of what was its working class. In the face of economic uncertainty, reactions have been remarkably stable and rational when looked at holistically, which is why we can speak of strategies at all.

At the same time, however, the process of economic involution has destroyed the grounds of collective solidarity without creating new ones; the workplace has dissolved and been replaced by the household. If the old regime could contain collective mobilization only by combining coercive strategies and individual inducements, the new regime has not created the institutional infrastructure to generate solidarities, and by the same token does not require the same repression. As Antonio Gramsci said of prerevolutionary Russia, civil society is "primordial and gelatinous," and we can say the same of postrevolutionary Russia. Instead of civil society, today we have a network society that absorbs the blows of involution but without bringing people together around visions that would propel them into collective action. Quite the opposite: Involution brings about the contraction of time and space horizons so that collective action seems more and more irrational.

Appendix: Some Poverty Statistics for Syktyvkar[18]

In order to interpret some of the ruble figures we have used in the text, the following data may be of use. The Komi Republic's statistical office regularly adjusts the cost of living for a single individual based on minimum calorific intake, interviews, and prices. We have the average annual figure for Syktyvkar, along with the percentage of the Komi Republic's population whose incomes are below this poverty line (see Table 11.1). There is an obvious arbitrariness about these figures, but they are calculated in the same way every year, so they are a good measure of change. Pensions have kept ahead of the poverty level, and in Komi, because it has a relatively young population with relatively high levels of employment, they have so far been paid regularly. We also include the average of-

TABLE 11.1   Living Standards in the Komi Republic, 1994–1998
(monthly incomes or expenditures, in new rubles)

	Dollar-Ruble Exchange Rate	Average Pension (Komi Republic)	Average Wage in Industrial Sector (Syktyvkar)	Minimum Living Standard per Individual (Syktyvkar)	%Population Below Minimum Standard of Living (Komi Republic)
1994	2.2	162.7	281	115.8	18.4
1995	4.6	311.6	730	325.3	19.2
1996	5.1	409.3	1,119	435.1	20.2
1997	5.8	472.5	1,421	430.7	16.7
1998	6/20*	481.9	1,624	479.8	20.6

*Figures are approximate exchange rates before and after August 17.

SOURCES: *Respublika Komi v tsifrakh* [The Komi Republic in Figures] (Syktyvkar: Goskomstat Komi, 1999); *Sotsial'no-ekonomicheskoe polozhenie gorodov i raionov* [Socioeconomic Conditions in Cities and Regions] (Syktyvkar: Goskomstat Komi, 1999); "Dannye sluzhby zaniatosti goroda Syktyvkara" [Data of the Employment Office of the City of Syktyvkar] (unpublished).

ficial wage in the industrial sector. It has more or less kept up with inflation, which is of less significance than the nonpayment of wages, payment in kind, and job loss.

We have managed to cull the following figures on unemployment in Syktyvkar (see Table 11.2). There is a secular increase in the number looking for work, almost twice as many as the registered unemployed. The gender composition of unemployment reflects the gender composition of employment.

Unemployment compensation fell drastically in May 1996, when an emergency situation was declared in Komi. Until that time, provided they had worked no fewer than 25 days during the preceding year, those registered as unemployed could receive: 75 percent of their average wage for the first three months of unemployment; 60 percent of their average wage for the next four months; and 45 percent of their average wage for the final five months. When the level of unemployment reached 5 percent in the towns and 6 percent in rural areas—the so-called emergency—the situation quickly changed. Only those laid off due to liquidation or restructuring had access to the old system; the rest would only receive the minimum wage, a laughable 87 rubles a month (plus 50 percent more for each child). This minimal support ends after one year, but it can be renewed for another year if after six months the individual remains unemployed.

Public assistance to low-income families is calculated on the basis of family composition, sources of income (wages, pensions, stipends, disability pay, al-

TABLE 11.2   Unemployment in Syktyvkar, 1993–1998
(figures for women are in parentheses)

	1993	1995	1996	1997	1998
Looking for Work: Total	6,416	11,716	10,946	12,104	14,873
	(3,139)	(5,511)	(5,286)	(5,792)	(7,477)
Blue collar	4,176	7,137	6,199	6,875	8,356
	(1,648)	(2,859)	(2,356)	(2,854)	(3,652)
White collar	1,736	2,433	2,072	1,908	2,755
	(1,232)	(1,728)	(1,484)	(1,340)	(2,022)
Registered Unemployed	1,300	5,711	3,807	4,178	5,937
	(738)	(2,907)	(2,007)	(2,196)	(3,462)
# Employed	125,000	124,800	123,100	122,300	106,300

SOURCE: *Dannye sluzhby zaniatosti goroda Syktyvkara* [Data of the Employment Office of the City of Syktyvkar]. These figures have not been officially published.

imony, and so on), and assets (dacha, apartment, savings, car, animals), and is correlated with the minimum standard of living. Since February 1997, the government has only guaranteed between 30 and 40 percent of the minimum standard of living, whereas before it would supplement income up to 100 percent of the minimum. Public assistance takes many forms, from cash to kind, from subsidies for housing maintenance or kindergarten to free school lunches for children.

Notes

My thanks to Jennifer Pierce, Ruth Milkman, and members of the Carnegie Conference for their comments and suggestions.

1. *Transition 1999: Human Development Report for Central and Eastern Europe and the CIS* (New York: United Nations Development Program, 1999), chapter 4.

2. The Soviet economy is conventionally understood as a "shortage economy" in which managers search, queue, and bargain for supplies, and when necessary, substitute one input for another. In this type of economy, work is continually disrupted by shortages of materials or their late arrival and by the breakdown of inadequate machinery, requiring workers continually to improvise. A capitalist economy, in contrast, is beset by "surpluses." Here the constraint is not from the side of supply but from the side of demand, which has its own distinctive effects on the organization of work.

3. The names of the two factories are fictitious, as are the names of our respondents.

4. All ruble figures are in the new denomination that was introduced January 1, 1998 (1 new ruble equals 1,000 old rubles). The exchange rates are presented in the Appendix. As a rule of thumb, one can say that before August 17, 1998, there were 5 rubles to the dollar, and after January 1, 1999, there were 25 rubles to the dollar.

5. Marina (#48): Interviews, July 9, 1995; April 1, 1999.

6. This is calculated on the basis of the minimum necessary for a single person to survive, plus 50 percent more for each child. Of course, no one can actually survive on 80 rubles (about U.S.$3) a month.

7. About 10 percent of the population live in such cottages, but most others' are in much better condition than Marina's.

8. Tanya (#69): Interviews, June 18, 1996; March 30, 1999.

9. In the Soviet days there was close diplomatic and economic cooperation between Bulgaria and Komi. Bulgarians settled in one of the richest timbering areas of Komi and promoted the local economy with their labor. Half of the timber they cut, they took for themselves, giving the other half to Komi, together with various foodstuffs imported from Bulgaria. In 1996 this arrangement was ended, the Bulgarians went home, and the Bulgarian consulate in Syktyvkar was closed.

10. Sveta (#59): Interviews, January 30, 1996; March 13, 1999.

11. Natasha (#45): Interviews, June 29, 1995; July 2, 1997; May 11, 1999.

12. Irina (#56): Interviews, January 4, 1996; April 12, 1999.

13. Nina (#72): Interviews, July 15, 1996; April 8, 1999.

14. She traveled under the auspices of the Committee of Soldiers' Mothers, an organization formed at the end of perestroika to defend the rights of soldiers who were being abused in the army. They were very active in defending the interests of those serving in the war in Chechnya, and sent delegations to retrieve war prisoners.

15. Anna (#67): Interviews, August 22, 1998; April 4, 1999.

16. Valya (#10): Interviews, July 8, 1994; July 15, 1997; June 24, 1999.

17. Luba (#4): Interviews, July 5, 1994; August 20, 1996; July 18, 1997; June 27, 1999.

18. We are grateful to Svetlana Yaroshenko for supplying the documents on which this appendix is based, and for helping us interpret them.

PART IV

The Nation

12

The Redefinition of the Russian Nation, International Security, and Stability

Igor Zevelev

George C. Marshall European Center for Security Studies

The failure to recognize the difference between nation and state has been costly for studies of contemporary world politics.[1] Nations and states have different organizational logic; they divide the global arena along different lines, and the interaction between the two structures has increasingly produced deadly conflicts. This conflictual relationship warrants an analysis linking the concepts developed by students of nationalism to the explanatory apparatus of international relations and security theory. However, the nation and the national have an astonishingly undertheorized presence among international relations theorists.[2] The most notable exception to this rule is the so-called Copenhagen School, which has made remarkable progress in attempts to reconceptualize international security as a duality of state and "societal security." Ole Waever and Barry Buzan have argued that sovereignty is the name of the game for the survival of a state, whereas survival for a society is a question of identity. They point to the replacement of military threats by concerns about the ability to survive as a viable entity as the main reason for insecurity after the end of the Cold War.[3] In their framework of analysis, the words *society* and *nation* are used almost interchangeably.[4]

This analytic framework seems to work well when applied to the Russian case, primarily for two reasons. First, many Russian political actors and intellectuals believe that there is a particularly evident discrepancy between the state and the nation in post-Soviet Russia. *Nation* has had an almost exclusively ethnic connotation in Russian theoretical and political discourse. In this discourse, the Soviet Union collapsed along false borders because Russian lands as well as 25 million people had been usurped by a new Russia. Aleksandr Solzhenitsyn, the leading Russian writer and the most consistent anticommunist, calls this development "a colossal historical defeat of Russia."[5] Second, a grave existential threat to Russia looms in nationalist discourse. The division of the Russian nation is viewed as an important component of a broader apocalyptic picture. Aleksandr Solzhenitsyn describes "the decline of Russian national consciousness,"[6] and argues: "The 'Russian question' at the end of the twentieth century stands unequivocal: Shall our people *be* or *not be*? . . . If we persist in this way, who knows if in another century the time may come to cross the word *Russian* out of the dictionary?"[7] The rhetoric of Gennadii Zyuganov, the leader of the Russian communists, is no less charged. He writes about the "possibility of losing sovereignty and spiritual and cultural assets, of the looting of sacred national objects."[8]

The official documents concerning Russian security, however, do not say a word about any discrepancy between the state and nation, nor do they express concern about the threat of extinction. The National Security Concept signed by President Boris Yeltsin on December 17, 1997 declares the crisis-like state of the economy the major threat to the national security of the Russian Federation. The solutions are seen in reform, stability, and development.[9]

Why is there such a profound discrepancy between these different visions of security threats to Russia? Does this discrepancy constitute a threat in itself? Are there any grounds for compromise or any possibility of consensus on these issues in contemporary Russia?

According to the Copenhagen School, a state must approach security as an aggregate that includes the societal sector.[10] Leaders integrate the various security sectors in their policymaking, and there is a single, integrated approach to security in political terms.[11] The Russian government does not ignore potential security threats from society: On the contrary, the governmental approach is congruent with the nationalist view in that it identifies major security threats as emanating mostly from Russian society rather than from the international system. The problem is that the government interpretation of the boundaries of Russian society and the major security threats is fundamentally different from that of the opposition.

For the Russian government, society is the totality of citizens. The state and nation are conceptually merged.[12] The definition of security threats by the government is in line with Yeltsin's general policy of state-building. Yeltsin made a commitment to democratic statehood and liberal nationhood in the early stages of his political crusade for Russian independence. He maintained this commitment more or less consistently from 1991 to 1999.[13] This choice may be explained by "personality and ideational factors"[14] or by "structural" factors (namely, weak, inarticulate Russian nationhood).[15]

For the communist and nationalist opposition, the *people* (roughly equivalent to *nation* in Russian political discourse) is detached from the state and from citizenship for two major reasons. First, a significant part of the Russian people—some 25 million—was cut off from the Russian state when the Soviet Union disintegrated. Second, Yeltsin's regime is perceived as a foreign occupation, alien to the people. Opposition in Russia bears an antisystem character (at least rhetorically), though it operates within the constitutional framework.

Theoretically, liberal institution-building may be replaced by a nationalist project quite easily. The situational and constructed aspects of national identities on both micro and macro levels facilitate such changes. As Ilya Prizel has argued, "While the redefinition of national identities is generally a gradual process, under situations of persistent stress even well-established identities can change at a remarkable rate, and a people's collective memory can be 'rearranged' quite quickly."[16] Currently, Russia is under such a condition of persistent stress, and there is no reason to believe that the people and the elite will cling indefinitely to their old supraethnic traditions and liberal project of state-building. Ethnicity could well become the cornerstone of a new Russian nation. Are there any objective factors that might facilitate the substitution of liberal state-building for ethnicized nation-building in Russia?

I would argue that different perceptions of security threats are not based on any objective incongruity between the state and the nation in post-Soviet Russia. Particular political actors construct this incongruity. It must not be taken for granted that there is an agreement within a society and between states on what exactly constitutes nations in general. There may be competing visions of nationhood in any given country and among its neighbors. There may be a dialogue or conflict over what nations are present on a given territory. Different actors may contest the boundaries of nations. Such a situation might lead to the emergence of competing interpretations of existing threats and security agendas by different theorists, political forces, and governmental agencies within a single state, and by different states and societies. If this is correct, discourse analysis, not the search for the objective boundaries of a nation or objective security threats, should be the approach used in analyzing threats and agendas. How, why, and by whom is something established as a security threat? How, why, and by whom is a nation defined? These are always political choices, not preordained realities.

This argument takes us beyond the paradigm of the Copenhagen School. Barry Buzan, Ole Waever, and Jaap de Wilde, in formulating their framework for analyzing security, defined identities as socially constructed.[17] However, they suggested that identities could petrify and become relatively constant elements to be reckoned with. Being strong security constructionists, they have admitted that they remain relatively weak social relations constructionists, close to objectivism and Waltzian neorealism. There may be two major explanations for this apparent inconsistency. The first is the legacy of artificial distinctions between the studies of identity and nationalism on the one hand and international relations and security on the other. The rapidly developing constructionist school of studies of the "national" is a natural but probably insufficiently known ally of security constructionists. The second is lack of attention from theorists to transitional societies, which is especially unjustifiable in view of the instability and insecurity inherent in the "national" redefinition of identities.

It may be natural for the Russian opposition, especially the radical opposition, to refer more to nation than to state in national security discourse, as the defense of the state and its sovereignty would tend to strengthen those in power. For the opposition, it is more effective to argue that the nation is endangered and the present leadership is doing nothing about this situation. Nationalists typically assert that they must be brought to power in order to secure the survival of the nation. "The nation, with its mixture of connection to and separation from the state, is ideal for such oppositional political maneuvers," argued the founders of the Copenhagen School.[18] The logic undergirding this assertion presupposes that there is an objective nation that has solidified and is constant. In contrast, the analysis presented in this chapter suggests that the opposition constructs its own nation, apart from the state and nation that the government is engaged in building. The opposition, through the democratic process, can place its construct and the alleged threats to its nation on the state security agenda.

There may be, however, an alternative scenario. If the opposition feels that it shares responsibility with the government for concrete policies, it may adjust its views and perceptions in order to find a common ground with the government. The defense of the state then might become a part of the opposition's security agenda. The situational and constructed nature of identity and security make such adjustments possible. It is feasible to rearrange the discourse on nation-building, whereas it is close to impossible to change the composition of an "objective" nation.

In Russia, in situations where the opposition does not feel responsible for policy, the gap between it and government often seems insurmountable. In cases where the opposition does take part in concrete policymaking, compromise is possible. In the making of foreign and security policies, an important instrument for including the opposition in decisionmaking is the ratification of international agreements by the Federal Assembly. During this process, the opposition may adopt a much more rational, pragmatic, and responsible approach than it would if its role were confined to issuing rhetorical statements on general issues. This argument is supported by an analysis of two important cases: first, the general perspectives expressed by Russian politicians on the country's identity, the aims of security policy, and internal and external threats; and second, the debates over and ratification of the strategically important Treaty on Friendship, Cooperation, and Partnership between the Russian Federation and Ukraine. The aim of the analysis is to show that shared responsibility over a vital security question can motivate seemingly opposite political forces to pull together. Concerns over international stability may cement a temporary coalition. Conversely, where low priority is given to the value of stability, a coalition of "destabilizers" is likely to emerge.

Five Worldviews

The different political actors in Russia conceptualize the state, nation, and security in various ways, and use those concepts differently, in various forms of discourse. The government develops concrete programs and official "concepts"; the opposition uses party documents and pamphlets written by their political and intellectual leaders. They have different visions of what Russia is, as well as of its major security threats and the aims and instruments of its security policies.

In this section, government documents and political programs of parliamentary and nonparliamentary parties and groups are analyzed in order to arrive at a typology of the major perspectives on nation-building and security issues. In addition, the respective political importance and evolution of each of these perspectives in the period of 1992–1999 are assessed.

The current political situation in Russia places significant limitations on research and analysis of this kind. The government is often erratic, and there are frequent personnel changes, including those in the National Security Council and other security agencies. The multiparty system is still maturing. The number of groups claiming or having the status of a political party far exceeds what might be considered optimal for informed decisionmaking on the part of voters. Forty-three electoral associations participated in the 1995 parliamentary elections. Thirty-five parties, movements, and associations were represented in the Federal Assembly between 1995 and 1999. Coalitions and associations are formed, split, and dissolve on a regular basis. Parties and movements appear and then disappear from the political arena before one can even take notice. Prominent political figures migrate between parties and groups. Duma deputies are elected on one party list and then are registered as members of another faction. The key party leaders' views might even be at odds with their parties' programs. There is no party unity on many issues.

Nevertheless, an analysis of governmental documents and political parties' positions can yield important insights for understanding the existing perspectives on nation-building and security issues, as well as political options for the Russian government. The governmental documents and parties' programs adequately reflect the approaches that have crystallized within the Russian intellectual and political elites from 1992 to 1999. Although the 1993 crisis and the subsequent adoption of the new constitution—as well as the 1993, 1995, and 1996 elections—changed the relative strength of each perspective, these events hardly led to the emergence of radically new ideas about nation-building and security policies. The framework of Russian theoretical and political debate remains basically the same even after the elections of 1999 and 2000.

The analysis of governmental documents and ideologies and the programs of various political parties, groups, and prominent politicians leads to the conclusion that there are five major perspectives, or projects, on building the state and nation in contemporary Russia, as well as five corresponding visions of interna-

TABLE 12.1 Beliefs About State, Nation, and Security in Russia: Five Perspectives

	Definition	Aims of Security Policy	Major Threats	Instruments	Outcome
State-builders (Yeltsin's government; NDR[1], Yabloko)	Russian Federation (nation-state)	preservation of state sovereignty, stability	economic crisis	economic, political, military	stability
Restorationists (KPRF[2], LDPR[3])	successor of the USSR (empire)	strengthening and enlarging the state	weakness and disintegration	political, military	instability
Ethnonationalists (intellectuals; nonparliamentary parties)	people (nation)	survival as "we"	disappearance of identity	moral (building of self-consciousness)	instability
Dominators (Otechestvo)	Eurasian power (*derzhava*)	hegemony and domination in the region	hostile neighbors	political, military, economic	instability
Integrationists (part of Yeltsin's government; most mainstream political parties)	CIS member one of the Soviet successor states	Eurasian integration	"Yugoslav scenario"	economic, political, cultural	stability

[1]NDR–Our Home Is Russia
[2]KPRF–Communist Party of the Russian Federation
[3]LDPR–Liberal Democratic Party of Russia

Source: Author's compilation.

tional security.[19] They are: new state building, ethnonationalism, restorationism, hegemony/dominance, and integrationism. The major elements of these different visions of security are presented in Table 12.1.

The concept of *new state building*, advocated by President Yeltsin and the Democratic Russia movement, dominated the official policy of the Russian government in 1991 and 1992. The theoretical foundations of this concept were laid in 1992 by Valery Tishkov, who was at that time Russian minister for nationalities as well as director of the Russian Academy of Sciences Institute of Ethnology and Anthropology.[20]

Its essence was state-building through the creation and stabilization of new state institutions within the former borders of the RSFSR. Proponents acknowledged the inviolability of the borders between the former Soviet republics and advocated the development of relations with neighboring states as fully independent entities. They considered the question of Russian ethnicity politically insignificant and instead emphasized civic patriotism. They likewise deemphasized the thorny issue of whether the Bolshevik-drawn borders of the RSFSR were "natural" or artificial (many Russians believe their national borders inaccurately reflect the real and much broader domain of Russian culture, language, religion, and traditions).

The new state-builders view Russia as a modern nation-state whose primary security policy goals are the preservation of its integrity and stability. The primary domestic security threats, in their view, are the economic crisis, organized crime, and disintegration; and in the international arena, NATO expansion, and failures of arms control.

After the breakup of the Soviet Union, several variants of *restorationism* emerged among Russians—all of them virtually indistinguishable from imperialism. The most influential party that effectively backs restorationism is the Communist Party of the Russian Federation. A less "Soviet" version of imperialism was formulated by former Russian vice president Aleksandr Rutskoy, who drifted toward a more ethnonationalist stand after 1993. The most extremist interpretation of this way of thinking in today's Russia can be found in the writings and statements of the Liberal Democratic Party's leader, Vladimir Zhirinovsky.

The essence of the restorationist project is to reestablish a state within the borders of the USSR (or in Zhirinovsky's dreams, to expand it all the way to the Indian Ocean). Until that goal is achieved, restorationists advocate that the Russian government intervene to protect the rights and status of Russians living in the "near abroad" (the non-Russian states of the former Soviet Union) by whatever means necessary, including economic sanctions and threats of military intervention.

Unlike most ethnonationalists, "imperialists" are modernizers. They favor a strong army, big cities, and industrial development. Vladimir Zhirinovsky dismissed the image of a Russia of "small villages, forests, fields, accordion player Petr, and milkmaid Marfa" as a pretty fiction put out by the Communists in collusion with the literary establishment, aimed at placating the peasants while suppressing the forces of real Russian nationalism within the elite and the urban populace.[21] His Russia is the Russia of historic might, world influence, and impressive riches. Zhirinovsky preferred the images of Russia painted by artist Ilya Glazunov: not a country of drunken peasants but an "empire, with shining palaces of Petersburg, great historical traditions and achievements, thinkers of genius, and the leading culture."[22]

The 1994–1996 war in Chechnya significantly undermined the popular appeal of imperialism. It became clear that any attempt to implement the restorationist program might lead to a war that Russians were not prepared to support.

Restorationists still see Russia as an empire. They perceive major threats to Russia in the weakness and disintegration of the state: The breakup of the Soviet Union was the first step toward the possible eventual disintegration of Russia. On the international front, the West is still the adversary.

In 1991–1993, the moderate variants of *ethnonationalism* were represented in the political arena by the Christian Democratic party, led by Viktor Aksyuchits, and the Constitutional-Democratic party, headed by Mikhail Astafiev. Later, between 1995 and 1998, Derzhava, headed by Aleksandr Rutskoy, and the extremist National Republican Party of Russia, headed by Nikolay Lysenko, became more visible in the ethnonationalist spectrum. For its theoretical underpinnings, this perspective relies on the ideas of prominent Russian writers—particularly Aleksandr Solzhenitsyn, Valentin Rasputin, and Vasilii Belov—and of mathematician and essayist Igor Shafarevich.

Many small, more extremist groups also have arisen, Pamyat being the most notorious among them. These groups are known collectively as the "Russian right," or the "Black Hundred." Like more moderate ethnonationalists, they emphasize the importance of Russian ethnicity for state- and nation-building. The basic difference between the extremists and the moderates is that the former completely reject the "Western values" of democracy, human rights, and the rule of law. The influence of the Black Hundred is thus far limited; however, in a time of social unrest their popular appeal as well as the danger they pose might well increase. Both the extremist and the moderate ethnonationalist parties and groups were significantly weakened after 1993, when some were outlawed and their newspapers were banned. This move was due to the fact that many small, militant ethnonationalist groups had played an important role in organizing the defense of the Moscow White House in September–October 1993, and had led attacks on the buildings of the Moscow mayoralty and the Ostankino television station. As the most well-organized forces of resistance to Yeltsin, they were targeted for repression.

The primary goal of the ethnonationalist political program is to unite Russia with the Russian communities in the "near abroad" and to build a Russian state within the areas of settlement of ethnic Russians and other Eastern Slavs.

The mental map of Russia held by Viktor Aksyuchits is characteristic of all ethnonationalists. According to him, the Great Russians, the Little Russians (Ukrainians), and the White Russians (Belarusians) form a united Russian people. The future Russian state envisioned by Aksyuchits includes the territories of Russia, Belarus, eastern Ukraine, and northern Kazakhstan. This state would maintain confederal relations with other areas of compact Russian settlement. The entire territory of the former Soviet Union remains a zone of Russia's vital interests.[23] Russia must assist the relocation of ethnic Russians from the "near abroad" back to Russia and meanwhile defend their interests by every available means, including military ones.[24]

Ethnonationalists define Russia as the Russian people. Russia is located wherever groups of Russians live. This perspective, in both its extremist and its moderate variants, assumes that state borders should be redrawn along ethnic lines. The major threat to security is the disappearance of Russian identity—the inevitable result of the current moral degradation of the people. The West is usually portrayed as a hostile force. Ethnonationalists do not conceive of an important global role for Russia other than that of spiritual and moral stronghold. As a rule, they argue that the country must concentrate on its internal problems. Attitudes toward the events in the former Yugoslavia have been the exception. Rhetoric of "Slavic brotherhood" and calls for assistance to Serbia intensified during the NATO air strikes in spring 1999. Most other political forces in Russia at the time were more concerned about the forceful establishment of the U.S.-led "new world order," and NATO's assuming the role of pan-European policeman, than about preserving a "Slavic brotherhood."

The *hegemony and dominance* tendency might be viewed as similar to the imperialist perspective. It is difficult to draw a clear-cut division between the two schools of thought, though the former has a number of distinctive features. Antonio Gramsci was one of the first political scientists to write about hegemony in international relations. This tradition was further developed by Robert Keohane and others.[25] According to Gramsci, a country usually becomes hegemonic because other actors either willingly or subconsciously defer to it, even if they wish to do otherwise. The followers comply because they see both the leader's policy position and its putative power as legitimate.[26]

Political scientists and international studies experts are divided on whether *hegemony* and *dominance* describe the same phenomenon. Those who believe that a distinction exists between them claim that a country might involuntarily defer to an external power without accepting the legitimacy of its policy.[27] The dominant power does not necessarily seek to create an empire by absorbing dependent political units; it may be satisfied with subjugation. Unlike a hegemonic leader, it might use more or less direct coercion to achieve compliance.

The theoretical basis for a Russian policy of hegemony and dominance over the "near abroad" was first developed by Presidential Council member Andranik Migranyan.[28] In more moderate, policy-oriented terms, this project was advocated by the former chairman of the Committee for International Affairs and Foreign Economic Relations of the Russian Supreme Soviet, Yevgenii Ambartsumov. Elements of hegemony/dominance rhetoric were also present in statements, articles, and reports by Russian foreign minister Andrey Kozyrev.[29] The essence of the project is state-building within the borders of present-day Russia, accompanied by the subjugation of other Soviet successor states and the creation of a buffer zone of protectorates and dependent countries around Russia. Russian diasporas are viewed as a convenient instrument of Russian influence and manipulation within the neighboring states.

Between 1996 and 1999, the most vocal advocate of the policy of hegemony and domination was Yurii Luzhkov, the mayor of Moscow, who relied heavily on the political expertise of Konstantin Zatulin, his adviser and the director of the Institute of Diaspora and Integration. A political alliance forged in 1999 between the Otechestvo movement, which Luzhkov heads, and Yevgenii Primakov, may lead to a softening in Luzhkov's position. Primakov shares the views of state-builders and integrationists and places an especially high value on stability. When asked what political forces he considered the most responsible, Primakov responded, "I will support any forces that advocate stability, the strengthening of Russia, the strengthening of statehood, while developing market relations, a socially oriented economy, and democracy."[30] It is noteworthy that stability was placed ahead of all other principles.

In 1997, an overt attempt was made to incorporate ideas of hegemony and domination into Russian policy on the CIS. On the eve of the May 1997 CIS summit, the institute headed by Zatulin prepared a special report for the Ministry of Foreign Affairs.[31] The ministry rejected it, and Primakov immediately disclaimed any responsibility for the report, since it did not reflect Russia's official stance. According to Zatulin, however, the report made its way from the institute directly to the president, and some of its ideas were incorporated into Yeltsin's speech behind closed doors during the summit.[32] The major message of the report's explicitly hegemonic approach was that Russia's moderate policies toward the near abroad could be replaced by more assertive ones. In order to blunt the Soviet successor states' anti-Russian policies, Russia could stir up political instability and interethnic tensions in the region. In November 1998, Zatulin was elected chairman of the Derzhava Social Patriotic Movement, founded by Rutskoy in 1994. The dominators had acquired a party base by taking over a formerly restorationist movement.

Those who subscribe to the principle of hegemony/dominance view Russia as a strong Eurasian power that should continue to dominate in the region. The major threats are seen in hostile anti-Russian neighbors. Regional groupings backed by the Western powers or by Turkey are portrayed as encircling Russia. The alliance between Georgia, Ukraine, Uzbekistan, Azerbaijan, and Moldova (the so-called GUUAM) is viewed as extremely dangerous to Russia.

Integrationism is being developed by those who call themselves political centrists. In important respects, integrationists are intellectually close to Gorbachev and his supporters—in particular, to the amorphous Civic Union and its spin-offs. Later, the All-Russian Union "Renewal," Sergey Shakhray's Party for Russian Unity and Accord, the Democratic Party of Russia, and the Congress of Russian Communities advocated similar ideas. It is important to note that the integrationist project finds wide support also outside Russia, in other successor states of the former Soviet Union. Its most active supporter is President Nursultan Nazarbayev of Kazakhstan.

The goal of the project is the economic reintegration of the former Soviet territories, and possibly their eventual military and political union. Some variants of integrationism envisioned a confederation of the former Soviet republics. The project is very pragmatic, emphasizing economy and security and downplaying more abstract components, such as identity, ethnicity, and nationhood. Supporters of this school of thought maintain that diaspora issues will become obsolete if the post-Soviet space is integrated in the economic and security realms.

Several major visions of reintegration have been advocated: Nazarbayev's Eurasian union; Shakhray's confederation of three to four countries within the Commonwealth of Independent States; and Yavlinsky's economic union. All three visions are predicated on the assumption that there is a need for supranational institutions, controlled economic reintegration, and maintenance of symbolic political sovereignty accompanied by a high degree of cooperation. Unlike the imperialist project, integrationism lays claim to a democratic program granting equal rights to all member states.

Reintegration is barred at present by the egoistic interests of the Russian political and economic elite; by non-Russian elites' fear of Russian domination disguised under democratic rhetoric; and by the U.S. policy of supporting geopolitical pluralism in Eurasia.

Integrationists believe that the major security threat to Russia is the "Yugoslav scenario," which may evolve if Eurasian countries do not cooperate on a wide range of economic, security, and humanitarian issues. The general outlook of integrationists is generally benign and peaceful.

New state-builders and imperialists were well represented in the State Duma from 1995 to 1999. Four major parliamentary parties subscribed to one of these two perspectives on nation-building: Our Home Is Russia (NDR) and Yabloko were state-builders, and the KPRF and LDPR were restorationists. It is only natural that those who represented a "new" Russia and an "old" Soviet Union were major political players: Their agendas were easily identifiable and comprehensible in election campaigns. However, it would be a vast oversimplification to reduce the nuances of political struggle to these two schools of thought. Ethnonationalists, integrationists, and dominators were poorly represented in the Duma in their "pure" form, but their influence on party politics had been significant and was increasing steadily, as their agendas were partially incorporated into the programs of the major parties.

The difficulties ethnonationalists have faced in gaining direct electoral support derive from their radicalism and exclusiveness. They cannot appeal to non-Russians, mixed ethnics, many intellectuals, or those who still identify with things Soviet. The weakness of Russian ethnonationalism was well demonstrated by its failures in the political arena. Dominators and integrationists also lacked appeal to the general public, since their ideas could not easily be wrapped up in catchy slogans. I contend that ethnonationalism, integrationism, and domination/hegemony have been gaining in influence and are taking over the intellectual leadership of the mainstream parties.

The five projects of state- and nation-building summarized above are more or less "ideal" versions. Some party programs include features from several perspectives. There is a natural affinity between some projects. On the one hand, these affinities might serve as a basis for coalition-building. On the other, parties that share similar views on nation-building and international security might be at odds with each other on economic or social policy. In addition, differences on tactical matters might part political forces with similar strategic goals.

In the next section of this chapter, I argue that concerns about nation-building and security policies—that is, about domestic and international stability—may in certain cases prevail over all other considerations among political actors, and thus may serve as a basis for coalition-building. Likewise, a shared lack of concern for stability (or in extreme cases, a common, high value attributed to destabilization) may draw other political forces closer during discussions of concrete policy issues. In sum, a confrontation between coalitions of stability-seekers and destabilizers may to a significant extent shape nation-building and security discourse in future Russian politics.

What makes a certain vision of identity and nation-building destabilizing? First of all, if current state borders are assumed to be illegitimate, then there is no place for stability. As a rule, the state borders are challenged during an attempt to achieve congruency between the state and nation. In David Laitin's words: "The boundaries of states are territorially defined, and despite border wars, remain fixed over time. Classic theories of international relations assume fixed boundaries. But the boundaries of nations are defined by the cultural stocks of people, and these boundaries are forever ambiguous."[33]

In the contemporary Russian context, state-builders and integrationists are more likely to seek stability than are restorationists, ethnonationalists, or dominators. The former do not advocate the change of borders or the use of force for solving problems with neighbors, and they have a more democratic political outlook. The implementation of their programs would bring general international stability in Eurasia in the long run. However, in the short run, the political arena may be reconfigured along unusual and unexpected lines when a disputed issue is being decided. This happened during the debates over the Russian-Ukrainian treaty in 1998–1999.

Russia and Ukraine:
Nation-Building and Bilateral Relations

Russian-Ukrainian relations are an ideal field for a constructionist exercise by Russian political actors. Malaysia, Sierra Leone, or Uruguay would be presented more or less uniformly in Russian political discourse as foreign countries, whereas Ukraine can be constructed in many different ways. It might be presented as an emerging European country, as a neighboring independent state, as a CIS member, as a culturally close Slavic country, as a part of historic Russia, as a potential member of a hostile military alliance (NATO), or as the state illegally holding a piece of land belonging to Russia (the Crimea). All of these different visions of Ukraine were present in the public and political discourse on the Treaty on Friendship, Cooperation, and Partnership between the Russian Federation and Ukraine, or the "Big Treaty," as it was called in Russia. The discussion boiled down to such basic questions as what Ukraine meant to Russia, its nation-building, and its security.

What Is Ukraine?

Ukraine never before existed as an independent state within its current borders. Today's Ukraine includes immensely divergent regions, and its new identity is a work in progress. The state faces the task of making the new nation separate and distinct from others—most of all, from Russia. There are more than 11 million Russians in Ukraine—the largest expatriate Russian population anywhere in the former Soviet Union. Eighty percent of these Russians live on the left bank of the Dnieper River, in Novorossiya, and in Crimea. However, it would be a mistake to assume that the ethnic Ukrainian-Russian cleavage is the key to understanding Russians' attitudes toward Ukraine. The situation is much more complex and multilayered. In addition to the plight of ethnic Russians, Russia's policy toward Ukraine has been shaped by such diverse issues as the difficulty of acknowledging Ukrainians as separate people; the territorial dispute over Crimea; the strategic Russian interests in Sevastopol and the Black Sea Fleet; the geostrategic importance of Ukraine as a former Soviet border region; and fear of NATO-Ukrainian rapprochement.

Russian cultural influence in the newly independent states is manifested in three forms: the presence of ethnic Russians; the partial Russification of the titular population during the Soviet period; and the Russification of non-titular, non-Russian groups. Together with ethnic Russians, the latter now serve as a barrier to ethnonationalism in the newly independent states. Given the deep-rooted and longstanding Russian influence in Ukraine, there are no unambiguous historical, cultural, or geographic boundaries separating Russians and Ukrainians.[34] Fifty-six percent of Russians in the Russian Federation consider Russians and Ukrainians one people.[35] In Ukraine, about 12–15 percent of all marriages are between Ukrainians and Russians. Many partners and children of mixed marriages shift their self-identification from census to census,[36] providing further evidence that cultural identities here are fluid. Russians in Ukraine—apart from those in Crimea and Galicia[37]—have not settled in separate, well-defined communities but as in Belarus, intermingle with other Eastern Slavs.[38] Their social conditions, culture, and political orientations closely resemble those of Ukrainians.

Regional differences have given rise to greater problems than have ethnic differences. Ethnic Russians and ethnic Ukrainians living in Eastern Ukraine, Novorossiya, and Crimea (unlike Ukrainians in Western Ukraine) are predominantly Russian-speaking, tend to vote in similar patterns, and hold positive attitudes toward Russia. According to survey data gathered by the Kiev International Institute of Sociology, in 183 cities and villages of Eastern Ukraine, between 1991 and 1994, 82 percent of the population used Russian as their language of convenience; 61 percent wanted it to have a status equal to Ukrainian as an official "state" language; 49 percent thought that Ukraine and Russia should unite to form a single state; and 72 percent of ethnic Ukrainians were Russophones.[39]

One of the many manifestations of these attitudes was a move by legislators in the Kharkiv and Donetsk oblasts to grant the Russian language the same status as Ukrainian in late 1996–early 1997, which was supported both by local Russians and by Ukrainians who spoke Russian as their first language. The local public prosecutors, however, suspended these decisions as violating the law on the Ukrainian state language. The "gray area" of intermingling Ukrainians and Russians serves as a good buffer to nationalism and smoothes away tensions in and around Ukraine.[40]

Laitin has shown that specifically Russian-speaking identity groups are taking shape in many post-Soviet states. Some of these groups are ethnically diverse and include individuals of the titular nationalities. This social formation will continue to play an important political role as newly established regimes seek to fashion nation-states within their republican boundaries. A major finding of Laitin's research is that the development of such a conglomerate identity is the principal countertrend to assimilation of Russians in the "near abroad." The interplay between the opposite trends of assimilation and the formation of "Russian-speakingness" may form an important axis of social and political life in the post-Soviet states. Paradoxically, assimilation is more problematic in culturally proximate Ukraine than in Latvia, Estonia, or Kazakhstan.[41]

It seems odd to speak of ethnic Russians living in eastern Ukraine, Novorossiya, and Crimea—where Russians have lived for centuries—as a nonindigenous people or a minority, since there are no distinguishable divisions between them and the titular groups. This situation has thus far hindered an active interventionist policy of the Russian Federation toward Ukraine in behalf of Russian diasporas there. The Ukrainian state, however, has taken a different view of matters ethnic, and has effectively launched a "nationalizing" project. The preamble to the Ukrainian constitution contains references both to "the Ukrainian nation" and to "all the Ukrainian people."[42] In the post-Soviet context, where *nation* has a decidedly ethnic connotation, this wording signifies a distinction between ethnic Ukrainians and all others. Article 11 of the constitution declares, "The state promotes consolidation and development of the Ukrainian nation, of its historical consciousness, traditions and culture; and also the development of the ethnic, cultural, linguistic and religious identity of all indigenous peoples and national minorities of Ukraine."[43] In other words, the state sees its role not only as consolidating the new civic nation but also as promoting the national consciousness of ethnic Ukrainians.

The Soviet state's longtime policy of Russifying titular nationalities prompted nationalists in many of the Soviet successor states to adopt assertive language policies that not only affect ethnic Russians living there but also Russian-speakers among the titular nationalities. Political battles have been waged over these questions in Ukraine. The status of the Russian language is still a live issue both in local and in state politics. Some local Ukrainian governments have used their authority to further decrease the legal status of Russian, while others have done the exact opposite.[44] One of Ukraine's major recent linguistic battles centered around television and radio broadcasting. On November 22, 1996, a conference was held in Kiev, with the participation of government officials, which recommended ensuring a complete switch to Ukrainian by all state- and privately owned stations, on the grounds that "the negative consequences [of using a non-state language] are no less a threat to national security than are violence, prostitution, and various forms of anti-Ukrainian propaganda."[45]

Theorist Margaret Canovan has suggested that one method of transforming a population into a nation is by "mobilizing them for struggle, preferably against their former rulers."[46] In this struggle, culture and language are the usual points of contention. From this perspective, the population of Ukraine hardly fits the definition of a modern, cohesive nation.

The situation in Crimea is different from that in other areas of Ukraine. Russians make up about two-thirds of this oblast, which was transferred to Ukraine by Nikita Khrushchev in 1954, to mark 300 years of Russian and Ukrainian unity. The legal status of Sevastopol, an important warmwater port on the Black Sea, is currently disputed by some Russian politicians. Demands for territorial autonomy were first raised in Crimea in 1990, and were quickly followed, in 1991, by demands for reunification with Russia. The presence of the Black Sea Fleet added a military dimension to the controversy. Political struggles over the status of Crimea within and between Simferopol, Kiev, and Moscow became an important part of politics in the three capitals throughout the 1990s.[47]

In sum, the nation-building project in Ukraine is not yet complete. Like many other Soviet successor states, Ukraine struggles to find a compromise between an ethnic-based justification of independence and the multicultural composition of its population. As Pal Kolsto has noted: "Structures [in the newly independent states] display 'civic' as well as 'ethnic' elements. In country after country one finds these rival conceptions of nationhood dwelling in an uneasy cohabitation."[48]

All of the former Soviet republics have adopted ethnopolitical myths[49] identifying each state as the homeland of a specific, "indigenous" people. This is reflected in the names of the new states, their flags, anthems, emblems, official histories and holidays, pantheons of national heroes, and language policies. The independence acquired in 1991 has been interpreted by most local ideologists, politicians, and intellectuals—as well as by some Western scholars specializing in a particular republic—as the establishment of the "peoples'" control over their fate. However, independence was won in the name of a particular ethnic group and not in the name of the multicultural population living in each republic. According to Pal Kolsto, "The titular ethnos is everywhere becoming 'the state-bearing' nation."[50] Intellectually, this policy has relied on the Romantic historicist tradition in its presupposition that humanity can be divided neatly into nations and its stipulation that culturally or ethnically defined nations possess sacred rights. It has thereby downplayed individual human rights and due respect for minorities.[51]

In Ukraine, the fate of ethnic Russians, the role of the Russian language, and the status of Crimea, Sevastopol, and the Black Sea Fleet represent a nexus of issues crucial to nation-building. Each of these issues is strongly related to Russia. To a certain extent, Ukrainian nation-building is shaped by the presence of Russia, even when that presence is invisible. What about Russia, then? How does it view Ukraine? How do Russian leading political forces "construct" Ukraine in the political discourse? In the next section, I show how the attitudes of the Russian political elite toward Ukraine crystallized during debates over the "Big Treaty."

What Is Ukraine to Russia?

Russian-Ukrainian relations—particularly the ratification of the Treaty on Friendship, Cooperation, and Partnership between the Russian Federation and Ukraine—were "securitized" by major political actors in Russia from 1997 to 1999. The Copenhagen School defines *securitization* as the recategorization of a policy issue as crucial to the survival of a state or nation.[52]

The leading Russian politicians used extremely charged rhetoric when commenting on the ratification of the treaty. Sergey Baburin called it a "catastrophe for strategic relations";[53] Vladimir Zhirinovsky, a "black day in Russian history";[54] and Yurii Luzhkov, a "surrender."[55] Nongovernmental organizations called for "unity and victory" and suggested that concerned citizens "rise up like a wall against the regimes."[56] Publicists wrote about a threat to the "territorial security" of Russia.[57]

What was at stake? First of all, it is important to note that Ukraine is the most important country among the Soviet successor states (and probably in all the world) for Russia's security, self-definition, and nation-building.[58] This assertion has been made by such disparate authors as Aleksandr Solzhenitsyn[59] and Zbigniew Brzezinski.[60] The preservation of the independent Ukrainian state was proclaimed crucial to the security and stability of Europe by the U.S. secretary of defense. The German chancellor declared, "No one will be able any more to dispute Ukrainian's independence and territorial integrity."[61]

The "Big Treaty" proclaimed Russia and Ukraine friendly, equal, and sovereign states whose relations are based on the principles of mutual trust and strategic partnership (Article 1) as well as respect for territorial integrity and the inviolability of existing borders (Article 2). Russia and Ukraine proclaimed that they will not use their respective territories to the detriment of the security of the other side (Article 6). The treaty interpreted the rights of ethnic minorities primarily as the rights of these persons not to be discriminated against or denied the ability to express, maintain, and develop their distinctive culture (Article 12).[62] This minimalist interpretation of the rights of minorities is in line with Article 27 of the 1966 United Nations International Covenant on Civil and Political Rights, which requires no affirmative action on the part of the state. However, in some of its other provisions, the "Big Treaty" went further, calling for the two states to create opportunities for the promotion of ethnic, cultural, linguistic, and religious distinctiveness (Article 12). The states took on obligations to create equal opportunities for studying Russian in Ukraine and Ukrainian in Russia (Article 12), and to secure television and radio broadcasting of each other's programs in their respective languages (Article 24). Generally, the treaty provided a basis for international stability and the primacy of international law.

The treaty was signed by Presidents Yeltsin and Kuchma in Kiev on May 31, 1997. It was ratified by Ukraine's Supreme Council on January 14, 1998, and by Russia's State Duma on December 25, 1998 (by a vote of 243 to 30). The Russian Council of the Federation voted to ratify the treaty on February 17, 1999 (the vote was 106 to 25, with 17 abstentions), with the stipulation that the treaty would take effect after Ukraine's parliament ratified three agreements on the Black Sea Fleet. (Prime Minister Yevgenii Primakov proffered this condition in order to ensure the treaty's passage.) The treaty came into effect on April 1, 1999, when Presidents Yeltsin and Kuchma exchanged the documents of ratification in Moscow.

Heated debates over ratification of the treaty with Ukraine in 1997–1999 splintered the Russian political arena, demonstrating that issues of identity and nation-building are intertwined with questions of policy toward the "near abroad" and of national security. Two coalitions emerged around those who were for the treaty and those who were against it. The first group included state-builders, integrationists, and surprisingly, most restorationists. The second included ethnonationalists, dominators, and some restorationists. On a personal level, it looked like a battle between the alliance of Boris Yeltsin, Yevgenii Primakov, and Igor Ivanov (the government), with Gennadii Zyuganov and Gennadii Seleznev (KPRF), against the unruly coalition of Yurii Luzhkov (Otechestvo), Sergey Baburin (Russian All-People's Union [ROS]), Vladimir Zhirinovsky (LDPR), and Aleksandr Lebed (Honor and Motherland), with numerous less important players on both sides. Analytically, the most interesting phenomenon was the split among restorationists: The KPRF found itself on one side, and the LDPR and ROS, on the other.

The Russian public seemed to be against the treaty, for the most part. According to a poll conducted by the All-Russian Public Opinion Center on February 19 through 22, 1999, 45 percent of Russians believed that the Council of the Federation should not have ratified the treaty as long as the division of the Black Sea Fleet, the status of Sevastopol, and Ukraine's debts for Russian oil and gas remained unresolved. Ratification was supported by 28 percent, and 27 percent were undecided.[63] The demographic breakdown of respondents shows a very unusual configuration of Russian public opinion toward the council's vote: Supporters were predominantly older than 55 years and residing in southern European Russia, Siberia, and the Far East (typically conservative, procommunist constituencies). Ratification was regarded as premature by the usually more liberal constituency—namely, younger people, generally residing in the cities of northern European Russia, who had voted for Boris Yeltsin in the presidential election. An astonishing 78 percent supported the view that Russia should own Sevastopol.[64]

The key governmental agency that lobbied the parliament for ratification of the treaty was the Ministry of Foreign Affairs. Its arguments were typical of state-builders: Russia must recognize an independent Ukraine as a part of the real world Russia lives in; without full and unconditional Russian recognition of Ukraine and its present borders, the two countries could never have good relations. The Ministry of Foreign Affairs was concerned with the scenario that could develop if the treaty were not ratified: Ukraine might ultimately isolate Russia physically from western Europe. The goal of the treaty was to prevent the emergence of a new, isolationist Ukrainian identity around the "Russian threat." To allay Ukrainian fears, the Russian government emphasized in its public statements that all of the issues affecting bilateral relations between the states must be resolved by political means alone, and that the treaty would open the door for a long-term lease of the Sevastopol naval base for the Russian part of the Black Sea Fleet.[65] In early 1999, on the eve of the vote at the Council of the Federation, the Ministry of Foreign Affairs warned that the rejection of the treaty would push Ukraine closer to NATO. Foreign affairs Minister Ivanov emphasized that non-ratification would evoke negative international reactions and increased tensions in Europe. He asserted that the treaty would create a favorable climate for direct economic and cultural ties between Russia and Crimea, increased trade with Ukraine, and influence over Ukrainian policy toward ethnic Russians.[66] On the crucial day of hearings and voting at the Council of the Federation, on February 17, 1999, prime minister Primakov reiterated his firm support of the Russian foreign ministry, adding his considerable political weight to the side of the pro-treaty forces. His arguments emphasized that the treaty would serve the purposes of stability and rapprochement with Ukraine.

The executive branch found allies in the parliament not only among state-builders (NDR, Yabloko) but also in many restorationists (KPRF). In the State Duma, 107 of the 243 votes for ratification of the treaty belonged to the KPRF. The arguments of the Communists differed in some respects from those of the Russian diplomats and the prime minister; but they were in agreement that instability in the region was the ultimate evil. The views of the KPRF crystallized in heated polemics with other restorationist forces.

In winter and spring 1998, a bitter struggle unfolded between the major restorationist factions—the KPRF and the ROS, headed by Sergey Baburin, the Duma's deputy speaker for CIS issues. It ended with Baburin's replacement by Svetlana Goryacheva, a Communist. Disagreement about policy toward Ukraine, other CIS countries, and Russian diasporas led to this key personnel change, which immediately affected relations between Russia and its neighbors. Baburin was opposed to the treaties that Russia had signed with Ukraine, Moldova, and Georgia, and he delayed their ratification, whereas the Communists favored immediate ratification. Baburin argued that those treaties did not sufficiently protect ethnic Russians in Crimea, the Transdniestria, and Abkhazia. Even though the KPRF and ROS are both restorationist forces, they differ significantly on tactical matters. KPRF policy contains noticeable integrationist components, whereas ROS leaders are more inclined to ethnonationalism. Though Gennadii Zyuganov is also prone to ethnonationalism, most Communists see gradual economic reintegration, and the building of close and friendly political relations with CIS countries, as a way to achieve a strategic goal: The restoration of some sort of union between some of the former Soviet republics. The Communists see any destabilization of the status quo in Eurasia as counterproductive for their long-term aims. Baburin, who shares with the Communists the strategic goal of restoration, is more inclined to stress the grievances and aspirations of ethnic Russians in the "near abroad" and is less ready to compromise their well-being for the sake of an alliance with the current regimes of CIS member countries, which he deems to be anti-Russian. This position might in part explain Baburin's evident attempt to craft a coalition of Russian ethnonationalist parties and groups. In December 1997, he participated in the Fourth Congress of Russian Nationalists, the organizers of which included a number of extremist parties, such as Russian National Unity (RNE) and the National Republican Party, and said that he would be ready to head a "united national opposition."

In his report to the CPRF congress in April 1997, Zyuganov attacked those who had raised the issue of the disputed territories—the Transdniestria, Abkhazia, and especially Sevastopol and Crimea—in bilateral relations between Russia and Ukraine, Moldova, and Georgia: "Those who deepen this division are trying to burn bridges and close the road to reunification."[67] Evidently this accusation was directed, above all, at Baburin and Luzhkov. It is telling that Zyuganov supported his position on this issue by referring to a broad vision of Russian nationhood and the boundaries of Russia: "In broad historical and cultural terms, Great Russia is the Soviet Union." On the issue of disputed areas, specifically, he said:

> After all, if you think about it, Sevastopol, and indeed Crimea as a whole, as well as such territories as, for instance, the Dniestr Region and Abkhazia, have "indefinite" status solely from the viewpoint of the Belovezhskaya Pushcha accords. From the viewpoint of the results of the 17 March referendum on the preservation of the USSR, there is nothing indefinite about it. It is necessary finally to dot the i's and cross the t's. There is historical statehood of Russia, and then there is its Belovezhskaya Pushcha statehood. What does this latter consist of? It consists of a rotten rung on a ladder leading downward—to Russia's final dismemberment into minor "principalities."[68]

This strict restorationist position, however, did not prevent Zyuganov from incorporating many ethnonationalist provisions into his vision of the boundaries and membership of the Russian nation, especially when he addressed the issue of the Russian diasporas.

Integrationism became a common ground for a coalition between statebuilders and a number of restorationists. Seleznev, the Communist speaker of the State Duma, strongly linked his political image to advocacy of a union between Russia and Belarus, eventually to be joined by Ukraine. Svetlana Goryacheva, the

Communist deputy speaker of the State Duma, argued that it was historically inevitable that Russia and Ukraine would draw closer to one another in the near future. The problems of the Crimea and Sevastopol would then be solved. If the brother peoples fought over borders now, they would be easy prey to outsiders.[69] An important role in shaping the KPRF position was played by cooperative relations between Russian and Ukrainian Communists. Ukrainians strongly encouraged Russians to ratify the treaty.

Those who opposed the treaty generally held a much more pessimistic view of the prospects for rapprochement with Ukraine. They did not believe that the treaty would stop the drift of Ukraine toward the West and NATO or strengthen pro-Russian political forces there. They also doubted that Ukraine would ever favor integration with Russia in any form. On the contrary, they believed it would try to "sell" its anti-Russian stand to the West for economic assistance, loans, and security guarantees.[70] In this context, the treaty would bring no advantages to Russia, and it would allow Ukraine to reassert its sovereignty over the disputed territories. Crimea, or at least Sevastopol, must belong to Russia, argued those who opposed the ratification of the treaty on the grounds that it would legally seal their secession. Sevastopol was portrayed as "the city of Russia's military glory" and an entity legally belonging to Russia, as it had been an independent administrative unit subordinated directly to Moscow since 1948 and was not included in the transfer of Crimea to Ukraine in 1954. The treaty's opponents also expressed awareness of NATO expansion as a security threat, but in a different way than did the treaty's advocates. The leader of the Congress of Russian Communities (KRO), Dmitrii Rogozin, argued:

> In May 1997, in Kiev, owing to the efforts of officials from Smolenskaya Square [the Russian Ministry of Foreign Affairs], Russian-Ukrainian agreements that left Kiev's way clear to [join] NATO were signed. As is known, the charter of the North Atlantic alliance closes the door to membership in this military and political bloc for those countries that have territorial disputes. Today, Russian diplomacy removed the territorial issue regarding Sevastopol and Crimea from the agenda of relations between Russia and Ukraine.[71]

Sergey Baburin argued that ratification would open the door to NATO for Ukraine and warned that NATO membership was its ultimate goal.[72]

In January 1999, opponents of the treaty achieved a temporary victory when Luzhkov persuaded the members of the Council of the Federation to postpone ratification until mid-February. Although this move did not prevent the ultimate ratification of the treaty, the cautiously worded declaration issued by the Council of the Federation upon the treaty's ratification on February 17, 1999 did reflect the main concern of Luzhkov and his supporters: "Members of the Council of the Federation express their hope that the Ukrainian side will understand that due to historic, economic, ethnic, and social factors, Russia has an objective and legitimate interest toward Crimea, where Russians constitute the majority of the population."[73]

Bitterness evoked by the perception that Ukraine has been lost forever and turned into an unfriendly country, as well as ethnonationalist sentiments and ambitions of domination, united the opposition to the treaty. This group attributed very low value to stability in the international arena. On the contrary, the antitreaty coalition saw many advantages in instability. A 1997 report issued by Konstantin Zatulin's institute (a think tank that formulates Luzhkov's positions on all CIS-related issues) argued: "In the final analysis, one ought to understand that the disintegration of Ukraine can cause problems for Russia. But it is better to contribute to this option than tolerate a constant challenge from Ukraine and the erosion of our efforts in the near abroad."[74] The report's authors did not shy away from striking historic parallels: "If we want peace with Ukraine, we must test our foreign policy. If we are afraid of tests, we will not save peace —in Munich they did not, anyway. We will kill peace by betraying our people, our positions in Sevastopol, Crimea, and Ukraine as a whole."[75]

It is interesting that Zyuganov, blaming Luzhkov's opposition to the treaty on Zatulin, characterized the latter as a quintessential destabilizer. According to Zyuganov, Zatulin spawned scandals and discord wherever he went.[76]

Conclusion

Ilya Prizel suggested that perceptions of identity shape foreign policy. In his view: "The emotional, albeit irrational, sense of nation and national identity plays a vital role in forming a society's perception of its environment and is an extremely important, if not driving, force behind the formation of its foreign policy because national identity helps to define the parameters of what a polity considers its national interests at home and abroad."[77] This perspective is illuminating in cases where a political consensus on identity issues exists; but it may be insufficient as a description of societies where competing visions of national identity are well represented in the political arena. In such societies, the opposite may be true: Foreign policy may be an important factor in the making of national identity. The postmodernist definition of foreign policy as the constant reinvention of states' self-definitions is especially applicable to countries with insecure identities.

As David Campbell has suggested, "Foreign policy is a political practice central to the constitution, production, and maintenance of political identity."[78] Campbell also has asserted: "Foreign policy (conventionally understood as the external orientation of preestablished states with secure identities) is thus to be retheorized as one of the boundary-producing practices central to the production and reproduction of the identity in whose name it operates."[79] If this theoretical framework is applicable to the case of the ratification of the "Big Treaty," then it is safe to assume that Russian Communists—though not all of them— have taken an important step in recognizing the permanence of Russia's current borders, a step that may well entail a broad rethinking of national identity and security.

Struggling through deep economic crisis, further undermined by serious social problems, and handicapped by a weakened and disorganized army, Russia can hardly afford to implement any project that would stipulate an actual redrawing of current borders. A significant part of the Russian political elite appears to agree that Russia might not survive serious instability. The sense of profound weakness in Moscow has been one of the major sources of generally cautious foreign policy. Military institutional collapse contributed significantly to this acknowledgment of real-world constraints by otherwise adventurous political forces and broadened the coalition of stability-seekers.

In sum, when addressing concrete policy issues, concerns over or disregard for stability were among the most significant factors around which political coalitions coalesced in Russia in the 1990s. Profound differences on the questions of national identity and security notwithstanding, stability-seekers found a common ground when vital security questions were at stake. Agreements among competing political actors over concrete foreign policy issues may lead to rapprochement on more fundamental questions, including the definition of national identity and of security, which in turn may provide a better basis for stability in Russia.

Notes

1. Yosef Lapid and Friedrich Kratochwil, "Revisiting the 'National': Toward an Identity Agenda in Neorealism?" in Yosef Lapid and Friedrich Kratochwil, eds., *The Return of Culture and Identity in IR Theory* (Boulder: Lynne Rienner, 1996), p. 123.

2. Daniel Deudney, "Ground Identity: Nature, Place, and Space in Nationalism," in ibid., p. 130.

3. O. Waever, B. Buzan, M. Kelstrup, and P. Lemaitre, *Identity, Migration, and the New Security Agenda in Europe* (London: Pinter, 1993), pp. 25–27.

4. Barry Buzan, Ole Waever, and Jaap de Wilde, *Security: A New Framework of Analysis* (Boulder: Lynne Rienner, 1998), p. 119. Many critics, although admitting the merits of delinking the nation from the state, have pointed to the unsatisfactory attempt of the Copenhagen School to pack "identity" and "nation" into "society." See Lapid and Kratochwil, "Revisiting the 'National': Toward an Identity Agenda in Neorealism?," p. 119.

5. See Aleksandr Solzhenitsyn, *The Russian Question at the End of the Twentieth Century* (New York: Farrar, Straus and Giroux, 1995), pp. 88–89.

6. Ibid., p. 73.

7. Ibid., pp. 106–107.

8. Gennadii Zyuganov, *Rossiya—Rodina moya: Ideologiya gosudarstvennogo patriotizma* [Russia Is My Motherland: The Ideology of State Patriotism] (Moscow: Informpechat', 1996), p. 6.

9. For the full text of the document, see "Kontseptsiya natsional'noy bezopasnosti Rossiiskoy Federatsii" [The Russian Federation's National Security Concept], *Diplomaticheskiy vestnik* 1, January 1998, pp. 3–18.

10. See Buzan, Waever, and de Wilde, *Security*, pp. 170–171.

11. Ibid., p. 196.

12. This framework relies theoretically on the writings of Valery Tishkov, former minister of nationalities of the Russian Federation. Tishkov broke the Soviet tradition of defining a nation in ethnocultural terms and outlined it as a purely civic, political entity. See Valery Tishkov, *Ethnicity, Nationalism and Conflict in and after the Soviet Union* (London: PRIO/UNRISD/Sage, 1997), especially pp. 3, 33–35, 230, 250, 260–261, 275–276.

13. See George Breslauer and Catherine Dale, "Boris Yel'tsin and the Invention of a Russian Nation-State," *Post-Soviet Affairs* 4, vol. 13, October-December 1997, p. 321.

14. Ibid., note 42.

15. See Igor Zevelev, "The Russian Quest for a New Identity: Implications for Security in Eurasia," in Sharyl Cross, Igor Zevelev, Victor Kremenyuk, and Vagan Gevorgian, eds., *Global Security Beyond the Millennium: American and Russian Perspectives* (London: Macmillan, 1999), pp. 116–120.

16. Ilya Prizel, *National Identity and Foreign Policy: Nationalism and Leadership in Poland, Russia, and Ukraine* (Cambridge: Cambridge University Press, 1998), p. 8.

17. Buzan, Waever, and de Wilde, *Security*, p. 205.

18. Ibid., p. 124.

19. For the texts of political parties' programs, see V. A. Oleshchuk, V. V. Pribylovsky, M. N. Reitblat, *Parlamentskie partii, dvizheniya, ob"edineniya: Istoriya, ideologiya, sostav rukovodyashchikh organov, deputaty parlamenta, programmnye dokumenty* [Parliamentary Parties, Movements, Associations: History, Ideology, Members of Governing Bodies, Parliamentary Deputies, Program Documents) (Moscow: Panorama, 1996); Vladimir Pribylovsky, *Russkie natsionalisticheskie i pravo-radikal'nye organizatsii, 1989–1995: Dokumenty i teksty* [Russian Nationalist and Right-Wing Radical Organizations, 1989–1995: Documents and Texts], vol. 1 (Moscow: Panorama, 1995).

20. Tishkov was not pushing for the disintegration of the Soviet Union as was Gennady Burbulis; he was merely trying to deal with post-Soviet Russian reality.

21. *Trud*, January 1, 1995.

22. Ibid.

23. Interview with Viktor Aksyuchits, leader of the Russian Christian Democratic Movement, in *Etnograficheskoe obozrenie* 4, 1996, pp. 125–126.

24. Ibid., p. 129.

25. See Robert Keohane, *After Hegemony: Cooperation and Discord in the World Political Economy* (Princeton: Princeton University Press, 1984).

26. David Forsythe, *The Internationalization of Human Rights* (Lexington, Mass.: Lexington Books, 1991), p. 90.

27. Ibid., p. 91.

28. *Nezavisimaya gazeta*, January 12 and 15, 1994.

29. *Izvestiia*, January 2, 1992; *Mezhdunarodnaya zhizn'*, March-April 1992.

30. *Komsomol'skaya pravda*, May 5, 1999.

31. *SNG: Nachalo ili konets istorii* [The CIS: The Beginning, or the End of History] (Moscow: Institut diaspory i integratsii, 1997).

32. Author's interview with Konstantin Zatulin, summer 1997.

33. David Laitin, *Identity in Formation: The Russian-Speaking Populations in the Near Abroad* (Ithaca and London: Cornell University Press, 1998), p. 340.

34. For an analysis of various trends in historiography on this issue, see Hugh Seton-Watson, "Russian Nationalism in Historical Perspective," in Robert Conquest, ed., *The Last Empire: Nationality and the Soviet Future* (Stanford: Hoover Institution Press, 1986), pp. 15–17.

35. The responses to the public opinion polls carried out by the Center for the Study of Public Opinion, cited in Interfax, October 27, 1997.

36. See Vladimir Malinkovich, "Russkii vopros v Ukraine" [The Russian Question in Ukraine], *Otkrytaya politika*, no. 9-10, 1996, p. 77.

37. Russians do constitute a separate community in Western Ukraine. Here, the attitudes of local authorities and of politically active Ukrainian nationalists toward Russians are often hostile, leading to further differentiation between Ukrainians and Russians. For examples of the numerous media reports of harassment of Russians in Galicia, see *Nezavisimaya gazeta*, April 4, 1997; *Rossiyskaya gazeta*, April 29, 1997. For overviews of the situation of Russians in Belarus and Ukraine by Russian scholars, see R. A. Grigorieva and M. Yu. Martynova, "Russkoye naseleniye Belarusi: Etnokul'turnaya situatsiya" [The Russian Population of Belarus: Ethnic and Cultural Situation], in V. I. Kozlov and Ye. A. Shervud, eds., *Russkie v blizhnem zarubezhye* [Russians in the Near Abroad] (Moscow: Institut etnologii i antropologii, 1994), pp. 10–37; V. I. Kozlov and M. V. Kozlov, "Russkie i russkoyazychnye v Belarusi i na Ukraine" [Russians and Russian-speakers in Belarus and Ukraine], in ibid., pp. 38–52; and N. M. Lebedeva, "Russkaya diaspora ili chast' russkogo naroda? K probleme samoopredeleniya russkikh na Ukraine" [Russian Diaspora, or Part of the Russian People? On the Problem of Self-Determination of Russians in Ukraine], in ibid., pp. 53–59.

38. I have borrowed from Anatol Lieven in using the word *intermingling* to describe the ethnic situation in Eastern Ukraine (see Lieven, "Restraining NATO: Ukraine, Russia, and the West," *Washington Quarterly*, Autumn 1997, p. 65).

39. Dominique Arel and Valerii Khmelko, "The Russian Factor and Territorial Polarization in Ukraine," *Harriman Review* 9, Spring 1996, pp. 81, 83, 85, 86.

40. See Lieven, "Restraining NATO," p. 65.

41. See Laitin, *Identity in Formation.*

42. Ibid., p. 508.

43. Ibid., p. 510.

44. See Dominique Arel, "Language Politics in Independent Ukraine: Towards One or Two State Languages?," *Nationalities Papers* 23, no. 3, September 1995, pp. 613–614.

45. *Nezavisimaya gazeta*, April 4, 1997, p. 5.

46. Margaret Canovan, *Nationhood and Political Theory* (Cheltenham, U.K.: Edward Elgar, 1996), p. 105.

47. For a more detailed discussion of the Crimean question, see Jeff Chinn and Robert Kaiser, *Russians As the New Minority* (Boulder: Westview, 1996), pp. 148–151; Anatol Lieven, *Chechnya: Tombstone of Russian Power* (New Haven: Yale University Press, 1998).

48. Pal Kolsto, "Nation-Building in the Former USSR," *Journal of Democracy*, no. 1, January 1996, p. 120.

49. This term is used by Walker Connor in his "The Impact of Homelands Upon Diasporas," in Gabriel Sheffer, ed., *Modern Diasporas in International Politics* (New York: St. Martin's, 1986).

50. Kolsto, "Nation-Building in the Former USSR," p. 131.

51. For more on Romantic views of nationhood, see Canovan, *Nationhood and Political Theory*, pp. 6–9.

52. See Buzan, Waever, and de Wilde, *Security*, pp. 23–24, 204.

53. Sergey Baburin, "Dogovor s Ukrainoy nel'zya ratifitsirovat' lyuboy tsenoy" [The Treaty with Ukraine Must Not Be Ratified At Any Price], *Nezavisimaya gazeta*, January 14, 1999, p. 3.

54. *RFE/RL Newsline* 29, vol. 3, pt. 2, February 18, 1999.

55. Ibid.

56. Leaflet of the Patriotic Women's Union.

57. Aleksey Plotnikov, "Chto ostalos' za tekstom: Dogovor s Ukrainoy i territorial'naya bezopasnost' RF" [What Was Left Out of the Text: The Treaty with Ukraine and the Territorial Security of the RF], *Nezavisimaya gazeta*, March 4, 1999, p. 5.

58. A brilliant analysis of Russian-Ukrainian relations with a focus on the issues of national identities is Anatol Lieven's *Ukraine and Russia: A Fraternal Rivalry* (Washington, D.C.: United States Institute of Peace Press, 1999).

59. See Solzhenitsyn, *The Russian Question at the End of the Twentieth Century*, pp. 90–92; and idem, *Rossiya v obvale* [Russia in the Abyss] (Moscow: Russky put', 1998), pp. 75–83.

60. See Zbigniew Brzezinski, *The Grand Chessboard: American Primacy and Its Geostrategic Imperatives* (New York: Basic Books, 1997), pp. 92, 113, 121.

61. As quoted in Brzezinski, *The Grand Chessboard*, p. 113.

62. See "Dogovor o druzhbe, sotrudnichestve i partnerstve mezhdu Rossiiskoy Federatsiey i Ukrainoy" [Treaty of Friendship, Cooperation, and Partnership Between the Russian Federation and Ukraine], *Diplomaticheskiy vestnik* 7, July 1997, pp. 35–43.

63. Interfax, February 26, 1999.

64. Ibid.

65. See the speech by Deputy Minister of Foreign Affairs V. S. Sidorov in parliamentary hearings before the State Duma Committee on CIS Affairs and Relations with Compatriots, in *Diplomaticheskiy vestnik* 5, May 1997, p. 43.

66. Igor Ivanov, "Moskva i Kiev dolzhny byt' uvereny drug v druge" [Moscow and Kiev Must Have Confidence in Each Other], *Nezavisimaya gazeta*, January 23, 1999, p. 3.

67. Johnson's Russia List, April 25, 1997.

68. Ibid.

69. Interview with Aleksandr Sevastyanov, editor in chief, *Natsional'naya gazeta* 2, no. 14 (1998).

70. Alexey Pushkov, "Korennoy proschet storonnikov dogovora Moskvy i Kieva" [A Basic Miscalculation By Supporters of the Treaty Between Moscow and Kiev], *Nezavisimaya gazeta*, February 17, 1999, p. 8.

71. Dmitrii Rogozin, *Formula raspada* [Recipe for Disaster] (Moscow: Forum, 1998), p. 40.

72. Baburin, "Dogovor s Ukrainoy nel'zya ratifitsirovat'."

73. Zayavlenie Soveta Federatsii v svyazi s ratifikatsiey Dogovora o druzhbe, sotrudnichestve i partnerstve mezhdu Rossiiskoy Federatsiey i Ukrainoy [Declaration of the Federal Council in Connection with the Ratification of the Treaty on Friendship, Cooperation, and Partnership Between the Russian Federation and Ukraine], *Diplomaticheskiy vestnik* 3, March 1999, p. 18.

74. *SNG: Nachalo ili konets istorii*, p. 14.

75. Ibid., p. 16.

76. Julie Corwin and Jan Maksymiuk, "Sparring over Sevastopol," *RFE/RL Newsline* 29, vol. 3, pt. 1, February 1999.

77. Prizel, *National Identity and Foreign Policy*, p. 14.

78. David Campbell, *Writing Security: United States Foreign Policy and the Politics of Identity* (Minneapolis: University of Minnesota Press, 1998), p. 8.

79. Ibid., p. 68.

13

Serving Mother Russia

The Communist Left and Nationalist Right in the Struggle for Power, 1991–1998

Veljko Vujačić,

Oberlin College

By unifying the "red" ideal of social justice, which is in its own way, the earthly substantiation of a "heavenly truth"—namely, that "all are equal before God"—with the "white" ideal of nationally conceived statehood, understood as the form of existence of the centuries-old, sacred ideals of the people, Russia will at last obtain the social consensus of all strata and classes that it has long yearned for, as well as restore supreme state power, bequeathed to it by tens of generations of ancestors, acquired through their suffering and courage, and sanctified by the grief of the heroic history of the Fatherland!

—**Gennadii Zyuganov**[1]

Internationalism is the idea of mixing. Nationalism is the idea of qualitative difference [ideia kachestva]. Nationalism is a separate apartment—not a communal apartment or a dormitory. Living in this apartment, you will visit your neighbors with pleasure, and also have them as guests, but you will not share their dining table or toilet.... In my apartment I am the boss. And I alone will decide whom I will invite, and whom I will not even open the door to. As a human being I might feel sorry for the homeless or those who had their homes burnt down, but I am not obliged to let them stay overnight. Especially since there are many of them and I only have a two-room apartment. The same is true in a national state. The Southerners have filled up all of Moscow, and then there are the Vietnamese, the Chinese, the Kurds. . . . Moscow and other Russian cities should not be dormitories.

—Vladimir Zhirinovsky[2]

Before the August Coup:
Origins, Personalities, Forces

On a spring day in Moscow, in 1991, the ideological secretary of the newly formed Communist Party of the Russian Federation—Gennadii Zyuganov—stopped by the offices of the new right-wing weekly *Den'* in order to meet with its editor, Aleksandr Prokhanov. Prokhanov, a journalist and a writer of military novels celebrating the combat achievements of the Soviet armed forces in Afghanistan, had launched *Den'* in January of that year.[3] The purpose of his new weekly was to provide a forum for the elaboration of nationalist ideology and to unify all "patriotic forces" toward the common cause of state preservation. Officially an organ of the USSR Union of Writers—an organization known for its conservative stance in the epoch of glasnost—*Den'* was published in a well-equipped building of the Moscow garrison.[4] Eight months later, in August 1991, its military sponsors—Marshall Dmitrii Yazov and General Valentin Varennikov—became participants in the unsuccessful coup against Mikhail Gorbachev.

Zyuganov's visit to the offices of Prokhanov's *Den'* on that spring day in 1991 was hardly an accident. The two had met before, on Moscow's Old Square, in the offices of the Central Committee apparat, where Zyuganov had worked since 1989 as the deputy head of the propaganda department.[5] Prokhanov's meeting with Zyuganov turned into a political "love at first sight." On that day, claimed Prokhanov, he saw a different kind of Communist official—not the familiar "gray product" of the Soviet cadre machine.[6] Unlike many of his colleagues, wrote Prokhanov, Zyuganov had not lost touch with the Russian people. Neither corrupt nor obsessed with his career and the material privileges routinely bestowed upon Communist officials, Zyuganov was a "simple, village type of man" who had spent his life "with nature" instead of "things"; metaphorically, if not actually, a "gardener" and a "beekeeper"—in other words, a cultivator, a creator and founder *(sozidatel')*. To someone other than Prokhanov, Zyuganov's strange imperviousness to the temptation of "commodity fetishism," that widespread disease of late Soviet officialdom, would have been a sign of an uncommon degree of dogmatic ideological commitment; to a right-wing ideologist like Prokhanov, it was a clear indication that Zyuganov was "one of us," a representative of the *narod,* the simple Russian folk.

Zyuganov's visit to Prokhanov was marked by a sense of urgency. The party and state were falling apart, stated Zyuganov. Gorbachev was destroying the country, and unless something was done immediately, collapse was inevitable. It was necessary to draft a direct appeal to Russian patriots of all social classes, from peasants to workers, specialists and intellectuals, soldiers, officers and war veterans—all those for whom the word *Fatherland* was not just an empty phrase but a living reality. *Otechestvo v opasnosti!* (The Fatherland is in danger!) By 1991, this familiar phrase, which had hitherto been reserved for the pages of right-wing tabloids or the official newspapers and thick journals of the conservative Union of Writers— *Literaturnaia Rossiia* and *Nash sovremennik*—had become common currency in conservative party circles. As the class enemy increasingly appeared in the forms of Baltic, Moldavian, Georgian, and Armenian separatists and internal traitors of suspiciously "cosmopolitan" background, the perennial class struggle increasingly gave way to a famous Jacobin slogan: The Fatherland is in danger!

Such was the main message of Zyuganov's and Prokhanov's "Slovo k narodu" (A Word to the People), a direct appeal to the Soviet and Russian people, published in *Sovetskaia Rossiia* on July 23, 1991.[7] Widely seen as an ideological prelude to the August 1991 coup, "Slovo k narodu," according to Prokhanov, was in fact devoid of ideology. Leaving no place for the "mystique of power," placing no trust in official institutions, whether of the KGB or the party, its content reminded Prokhanov of Stalin's famous address to the Russian people at the beginning of World War II. Just as before—when every conceivable state institution had collapsed in front of the Nazi onslaught—now there was no longer any room for anyone but "brothers and sisters."[8]

Brat'ia i sestry! Brothers and sisters! We can forgive Prokhanov his pathetic, hyperbolic style, his romantic turns of phrase: They were and remain an integral part of his characteristically right-wing appeal to emotions, not reason. But as far as reasoning is concerned, and despite Prokhanov's protestations to the contrary, we must not fail to observe that a profound ideological change was in the making. On that day, the working class, the proletariat as the main agent of historical change, was relegated once and for all to the dustbin of history; in its place stood the simple, suffering, and overly patient Russian people *(terpelivyi russkii narod).*

By mid-1991, however, neither Prokhanov and his writers nor the newly patriotic Russian Communists held a monopoly on political expressions of Russian nationalism. Unexpectedly, in the course of the first direct elections for the Russian presidency, a new and powerful contender for the nationalist vote appeared: the scandal-mongering demagogue Vladimir Zhirinovsky. At first derisively dismissed as a political "buffoon," Zhirinovsky would demonstrate the appeal of openly anticommunist and aggressively imperial Russian nationalism during successive parliamentary and presidential elections. Less interested in vindicating the Soviet-Russian past than his Communist rivals, or in elaborating a new Russian idea, like many intellectuals and writers, and more adept at appealing to the masses, Zhirinovsky became the most successful, most calculating champion of those who had suffered under the Soviet system and were about to suffer in the new and chaotic world of market reforms. In that peculiarly Slavic art—the art of suffering and its public display—as his apocalyptic political autobiography would testify,[9] he was unmatched. His choreography suited the purpose of the moment: Here, the stern *vozhd'* (leader) admonishing his army and people to challenge the aggressive foreigner and restore the mighty empire; there, the understanding and compassionate protector of that quintessential symbol of the simple people *(prostoi narod)*—the overworked and downtrodden Russian grandma, the proverbial *babushka;*[10] finally, the unsurpassed artist of political scandal and humor—the proverbial "holy fool" who held the key to the real Russian truth and would never compromise it, even if that meant dousing his opponent with a glass of water in front of television cameras or arm-twisting a female deputy on the floor of the Duma.

In the newly created Russian parliament, too, new forces had appeared that despite their willingness to collaborate with conservative officialdom in its attempts to prevent the disintegration of the state, increasingly strove for an independent, distinctly Russian, albeit not necessarily ethnically exclusive way out of the crisis of the state. The first incarnation of this new parliamentary right was the Rossiia club of deputies, whose most talented representative was a young politician from Omsk—Sergey Baburin.[11] Its main cause—the placing of Russia's state interests above all other considerations and the elaboration of a "third way" between the socialism of the past and the seemingly inescapable capitalism of the future—placed the group squarely in the new political right.[12] However, its preference for statist considerations in the determination of Russia's national interests distinguished it from the ethnic, anti-Semitic, and frequently openly fascist right. The influence of these new *gosudarstvenniki* (statists) was, for most part, indirect. Neither as successful in elections as Zyuganov's Communists or Zhirinovsky's "liberal democrats" nor as impressive on the street level as Viktor Anpilov's Working Russia (Trudovaia Rossiia) movement[13] or the trained storm troopers of the extreme right, these parliamentary deputies still played an important role. By providing the right with a much-needed aura of respectability at the highest levels of state and by influencing the political thinking of more "centrist" forces, they were instrumental in changing the discourse of the political elite and pushing it in the direction of a new, state-oriented, Russian patriotism.

Then there was the extreme, neofascist Russian right, which openly laid claim to the legacy of its historical predecessors, the Black Hundreds and the Union of the Russian People.[14] This latter force—or more precisely, set of numerous interconnected yet fragmented and frequently minuscule groups—was the first to be associated with Russian nationalism in the epoch of glasnost. It all began with the notorious movement Pamyat (Memory) and its demagogic speaker Dmitrii Vasilev, whose diatribes about the disproportionate number of Jews in the early Bolshevik leadership and their suspiciously large role in various unexplained conspiracies and catastrophes were accompanied by demands for the restoration of "ethnic proportionality" in state and cultural institutions (i.e., their Russification) and for the salvation of Russia through a return to its Orthodox traditions. Vasilev's Moscow-based Pamyat soon found its counterparts in other major Russian cities, from Leningrad to Novosibirsk, all of them increasingly open in their anti-Semitism.[15] By 1990–1991, however, the various black shirts of the early Pamyat had parted ways, and the movement dissipated. The only group that would leave a more permanent mark was Aleksandr Barkashov's small but disciplined Russian National Unity, whose pagan symbolism, uniformed, armed storm troopers, and swastikas unmistakably evoked its Nazi prototype.[16]

These were the four pillars of the new Russian nationalism in its many varieties: on the "left," the conservative wing of the newly formed Communist Party of the Russian Federation (KPRF) and the even more radical neo-Stalinists of the Trudovaia Rossiia movement led by Anpilov; on the neo-imperial, anticommunist right, Zhirinovsky and his Liberal Democratic Party of Russia (LDPR); on the more respectable right, the parliamentary statists of Sergey Baburin's Rossiia; and lastly, on the extreme right, the various openly fascist groups, with their numerous pamphlets and tabloids full of conspiracies, pagan and orthodox warrior symbolism, and the ugliest anti-Semitic and racist propaganda imaginable. All of them fought, in their own way, for a united, great, and indivisible Russia and against the hated democrats, "traitors," and cosmopolitans. And all of them would, from time to time, be brought together in temporary coalitions that could not withstand the many ideological divisions and interests that separated them.

Finally, a fifth force should be mentioned: the various intellectuals and nationalist ideologists who tirelessly worked on producing new variants of the celebrated Russian idea, whether in the old, thick literary journals such as *Nash sovremennik* or in completely new publications by the extreme right, such as Aleksandr Dugin's *Elementy* and Eduard Limonov's openly National-Bolshevik and "left fascist" newspaper *Limonka.*[17] Towering over all of them was the most tireless of them all, the "nightingale of the General Staff" and the editor of *Den'* (after October 1993, retitled *Zavtra*)—Aleksandr Prokhanov.[18] Prokhanov's *Den'* was intended to be the *Action Française* of the Russian right: a journal that served as a forum for discussion and for the elaboration of a distinct patriotic language and style of thought. If he had not succeeded in saving the empire in this editorial endeavor, at least Prokhanov had indeed "fulfilled the plan."

The United Left and Right Opposition, 1991–1993

The story of contemporary Russian nationalism, whether that of the Communist left or the Russian right, is one of many beginnings and no end. Were it not for the limited space available to us here, it could well begin with the emergence of Pamyat in 1986, or the publication of Nina Andreeva's notorious open letter headed "I Cannot Forsake My Principles"—a neo-Stalinist manifesto of antiperestroika forces published in *Sovetskaia Rossiia* in March 1988;[19] or alternatively, with Shafarevich's *Russofobia*—the manifesto of all patriotic forces—published in two installments in *Nash sovremennik* in 1989;[20] or perhaps with the ill-famed "Letter of 74," published by the members of the Union of Writers in *Literaturnaia Rossiia* on the eve of the 1990 elections to the RSFSR Congress of People's Deputies;[21] or with the convocation of a conference of patriotic forces for a "great, united Russia" held under the auspices of the CP RSFSR in February 1991.[22] Each and any of these dates would be, in its own way, a good starting point for the story of contemporary Russian nationalism and, indeed, several others could be taken as well.[23]

Yet there is a good reason for beginning the story in the aftermath of the August 1991 coup and the formal dissolution of the Soviet state in December of the same year. These two events—the final defeat of the CPSU and the formal dissolution of the Soviet state—profoundly changed not only the correlation of existing political forces but also the ideological and territorial framework within which the political battle was taking place. Before the August coup many patriots had placed their trust in official institutions, hoping that the conservative wing of the party would contain the much-hated democrats and prevent the disintegration of the Soviet state with the help of the army and the KGB. In December 1991, when the Belovezh agreement formally dissolved the union, all such hopes dissipated. The tremendous sense of disappointment at the failure of the sterile party apparatus, and especially of the newly organized CP RSFSR, to fully embrace the nationalist cause was accompanied by the sober realization that the nationalist right could now stand on its own feet without having to make ideological concessions to "Soviet patriotism" or to depend on the discredited Communist party structures for organizational support.[24]

Paradoxically, even as the dissolution of the Soviet state constituted a major political defeat for the nationalist right, it also provided it with new causes and opportunities. The first political advantage that unexpectedly accrued to the right was purely "negative," and fit very well into the politics of hatred. Its clearest and earliest formulation came from the pen of right-wing litterateur Eduard Limonov, who in the immediate aftermath of the August coup observed that a profound ideological and political change was in the making. In Limonov's words: "The democrats have taken all responsibility for the tragedy. From now on, only they will be responsible for the disintegration of the state, for all the blood spilled in our country."[25] And yet, it was these same democrats who provided the rightists with the freedom to engage in their own, independent agit-prop and street mobilization, and who would spare their leaders and activists on several critical occasions (e.g., when the unsuccessful October 1993 coup attempt threatened to erase them from the political scene).[26]

Disassociated from the detested Communist officialdom and the ideological baggage of Sovietism and empowered by the new democratic freedoms that it would do its best to subvert, the right could blame the ruling democrats for all the real and imaginary transgressions of the new regime. At the same time, in line with the well-known tactics of all such movements, right-wing activists would provoke street fights with the forces of order, and then play the role of victim of a new "democratic fascism" that was beating up the simple Russian people and their patriotic vanguard.[27]

This largely "negative" advantage of the new situation was accompanied by several positive ones. First and foremost among them was the very fact that the dissolution of the Soviet state had taken place under the auspices of the new de-mocratic regime, with the highly problematic consequence of leaving some 25 million ethnic Russians and an additional 5 million Russian-speakers on the wrong side of Russia's borders. The loss of Ukraine, Belarus, and Northern Kaza-khstan had cut off the large, compactly settled Russian populations there from their national homeland.[28] From early 1992 on, the question of the status of the new Russian minorities in the Soviet successor states provided the political right with practically endless causes for mobilization, and simultaneously served to put the democratic authorities on the defensive. Not surprisingly, the question of Russian minorities in the so-called near abroad soon found itself high on the agenda of Yeltsin's administration, due in large part to repeated accusations of treason from the nationalist right.

A second, if ultimately short-lived political advantage that accrued to the right was related to the ban on the CPSU. Deprived of their offices and of the right to organize, what could millions of genuinely patriotic Communists do but join a new national party? So reasoned the head of the Rossiia group of deputies in the parliament, Sergey Baburin, whose new party—the Russian All-People's Union (ROS)—was specifically designed to attract this group.[29] Many patriots, however different in their ideological orientations, agreed with Baburin, basing their con-fidence on the assumption that both Communists and nationalists were united by their common hatred of cosmopolitanism, democracy, and bourgeois culture. "One of my basic convictions is disgust with capitalism and the bourgeois race," declared Eduard Limonov. The traditionalist neo-Slavophile publicist Mikhail Antonov agreed: Russia was turning into a colony of the West with the help of an indigenous "comprador, antinational, internationalist-cosmopolitan class," which all patriots, Communist or not, had a responsibility to fight.[30]

For their part, patriotic Communists wholeheartedly agreed, as evidenced by the reaction of the early proponent of the transformation of the Russian Com-munist party into a party of "patriots"—Gennadii Zyuganov. In an early post-coup interview with Prokhanov's *Den'*, Zyuganov argued that thenceforth, no party would enjoy mass support if it remained indifferent to the national idea. The CP RSFSR had been fully cognizant of the fact that the party was the insti-tutional foundation of Soviet-Russian statehood. Zyuganov crudely sketched the continuity between the Russian and Soviet periods: Tsarist Russia had rested on the tripartite foundation of God, tsar, and Fatherland; and its Soviet counter-part relied on the trinity of communist ideology, the General Secretary, and the socialist fatherland.[31] Only a few months later, Zyuganov would demonstrate how far he was from classical communist orthodoxy: The struggle we are waging today, he said, addressing patriots of all colors, was not one "for communism or capitalism, democracy or plutocracy, but for the rebirth of our state. In this struggle, communists and monarchists, nationalists and democrats should all be united."[32]

Other, more dogmatic Communists did not come out so straightforwardly on the nationalist side. Characteristic in this respect was the new street leader of the

Moscow proletariat, Anpilov, whose Working Russia movement was the first to organize rallies in the post-coup period. Anpilov's focus was on the social question—the hungry people standing in lines for basic necessities (he called his proletarian street processions *marsh golodnykh ocheredei*), and the many others who were bound to suffer under conditions of sudden price liberalization and the traumatic beginnings of shock therapy. Egalitarianism, social justice, and the growing poverty of unprotected social strata were the main themes of Anpilov's incessant mobilization efforts: Bread and cheese should be available to all strata of the population, with the larger goal of preventing "a capitalist restoration."[33]

It was in this context of state collapse and the social disorientation caused by the sudden liberalization of prices that the first joint mass rallies of Communists, monarchists, and nationalists took place under both Soviet and Russian imperial banners. On February 23, 1992, various Communist and nationalist groups marched through the streets of Moscow in celebration of the Day of the Soviet Army, an organization that had been unceremoniously disbanded only a month before. On its way to Manezh Square, the procession encountered heavily armed police cordons. The most determined activists broke through four police cordons but were nevertheless unable to reach the well-protected area around the Kremlin. The heavy police casualties were a clear indication that the organizers of the rally had provoked much of the violence.[34] In the patriotic camp, however, this eruption of violence was taken as a confirmation of the antinational character of the democratic regime as well as an excellent opportunity for renewed mobilization efforts. *Den'* referred to the events of February 23 as "Bloody Sunday," in a rather pathetic attempt to evoke the tragic event that preceded the revolution of 1905.[35]

The wave of street activity resumed on March 17, 1992—the anniversary of Gorbachev's ill-fated referendum on the preservation of the Soviet Union. It was an occasion that brought together many of the democrats' main enemies and almost 60,000 of their followers both from the Communist left and the nationalist right, marching under the red Soviet and the old imperial black, yellow, and white banners. There they all were: former members of the USSR Congress of People's Deputies Sazhi Umalatova and the "black colonel" Viktor Alksnis,[36] television journalist Aleksandr Nevzorov, General Makashov, Zyuganov and Anpilov, Limonov, and Baburin. The strange amalgam of communist and nationalist slogans, choreography, and political traditions was unprecedented: on the one hand, the singing of the Soviet anthem with "all power to the Soviets"; on the other, references to the rally as an ancient Russian "all-people's assembly" *(vsenarodnoe veche)*, accompanied by attacks on the government of "cosmopolitans." A new, Russian-style national socialism was clearly in the making.[37]

The rallies of February 23 and March 17 served as a catalyst for unifying Communists and nationalists. The first joint declaration of the leftist and rightist opposition was written in response to the violence of February 23. It called for an investigation of the causes of the violence, made an appeal to army officers, and waged an attack on the "Russophobic" mass media.[38] This declaration was soon followed by another, which appealed for national reconciliation and announced the unification of the opposition of left and right. The common front of the "red" and the "white" that Prokhanov and Zyuganov had long advocated was becoming a reality.[39]

In June 1992, this unity found a new if short-lived organizational embodiment in the Russkii Natsional'nyi Sobor (RNS; in English, Russian National Union), a new organization of the right, led by former KGB major-general Aleksandr Sterligov.[40] The RNS defined itself as both anticommunist and antidemocratic. The democrats in power were "false democrats"—in reality, former "partocrats" who had masked themselves first as perestroika liberals and later as democratic reformers. The language of RNS proclamations was full of scorn for these traitors to the homeland, who cleverly substituted anti-Russian sentiments for anti-Soviet ones, thus producing a wave of Russophobia that had resulted in "discrimination, humiliation, and in many cases terror of the Russian population."[41]

In a special declaration addressed to all compatriots, the RNS warned that Russians in the Baltic states were becoming second-class citizens; in Central Asia, hostages and white slaves; in the Caucasus, victims of local interethnic conflicts; and in Moldova, targets for bullets. "And we—a great nation—knowing all this, keep silent."[42] This mysterious Russian silence was explained by the informational and psychological warfare being waged by the democratic mass media and Yeltsin's "occupation government," who were working in collusion with international forces in order to transform Russia into a source of raw materials for "transnational capital."[43]

The RNS's founding congress formulated the most pressing tasks of the patriotic movement: the unification of all patriotic organizations, with the purpose of restoring a unified Russian state; the organization of a mass patriotic movement in all regions of Russia; the creation of regional Russian professional associations and other organizations; the restoration of state control over the economy, with the parallel development of national Russian entrepreneurship; an end to "genocide by hunger"; the creation of patriotic informational structures and mass media; proportional representation for Russians in state and cultural organizations; support for the Orthodox church; and lastly, the prevention of the selling of Russian national wealth. Most of these themes found their way into the resolutions of the first official congress of the new party, held on June 11 and 12, 1992—significantly coinciding with Russia's new Independence Day.[44] It was an occasion that brought together virtually the whole patriotic elite, from academician Igor Shafarevich, to village prose writers Valentin Rasputin and Vasilii Belov, General Makashov, Zyuganov, select Cossack groups, and the fascist Barkashev.

If the formation of the RNS was the first serious attempt to bring together patriots of the right, its more centrist counterpart—Rossiisskoe Narodnoe Sobranie—was founded in the hope of reconciling Russian nationalism with democracy. Its founders—Ilia Konstantinov, Viktor Aksyuchits, and Mikhail Astafiev—had all left Democratic Russia in protest against the breakup of the Soviet state.[45] Mainly envisaged as an organization of national-democrats committed to a territorial *(rossiiskii)* rather than an ethnic *(russkii)* self-definition of Russian nationhood, Rossiiskoe Narodnoe Sobranie never developed a mass base; but its significance cannot be gauged by that criterion alone. At a time when the ban on the Russian Communist party had not yet been lifted and the various forces of the extreme right were attracting only a marginal following, these patriotic deputies could ensure that nationalist ideas would be voiced from the elevated stage of the Congress of People's Deputies. Henceforth, no one could claim that Pamyat extremists were the only representatives of Russian patriotism.

And yet, the connections between this respectable parliamentary right and its more extreme rightist counterparts were in evidence as early as February 1992, when the Congress of Civic and Patriotic Forces first brought the new democratic patriots together with the nationalist right. The respectability of the February meeting was significantly enhanced by the participation of Russia's vice president, Aleksandr Rutskoy, whose speech to the congress was one of the first manifestations of his dissent from the course of reform being pursued by the Gaidar government.[46]

An unprecedented "democratic" experiment, Rutskoy stated, [47] was taking place in Russia, leading to "economic genocide" against the Russian population, pensioners standing in lines for milk, and hungry children in Russian schools. Russia as an "organic civilization" was being destroyed, and Russians in the republics were being left to sink or swim. At the national level, a criminalized black market was being developed by businessmen eager to make a profit without investing work and productive energy. Instead, the vice president stated, Russia should develop economic reforms centered on production and stimulated by adequate tax policies; sponsor the rebirth of its glorious army and the Cossack movement; restore specifically Russian entrepreneurial traditions *(kupechestvo)* and prevent the brain-drain of specialists to the West; defend the rights of Russians in the republics; and form a multiparty system with distinct national colors. Rutskoy purposefully distanced himself from various neocommunist forces, arguing for an "enlightened patriotism" within the framework of the democratic order; but he left room for an alliance among various "centrists," the parliamentary right, and the more extreme forces lurking in the background.[48]

The prospect of just such a coalition emerged in the aftermath of the Sixth Congress of People's Deputies (April 1992), whose participants witnessed the first serious confrontation between Yeltsin's government and the opposition.[49] By September 1992, the opposition had formed a coordinating body—the Political Council of the United Opposition. All interparty differences were to be suppressed in the name of saving Russia.[50] On October 24, the long process of ideological and organizational unification culminated in the formation of the National Salvation Front (FNS), a new umbrella organization for many nationalist and neocommunist groups.[51] The president of its political council, Ilia Konstantinov, indicated that the projected social base of the FNS was among army officers, state security personnel, managers and patriotic entrepreneurs, Cossacks, and workers.[52]

The program of the FNS was in line with its projected social base as well as with the programs of its historical national-socialist predecessors. Thus, in the economic sphere, the FNS proposed a new "statist-corporatist" course: the "profit motive" was to be rejected in the name of increasing national wealth; unemployment was to be kept at 2 percent; an end would be put to speculative privatization and comprador capital; inter-branch corporations would be formed in industry and agriculture; the domestic producer would be defended from foreign competition; the state would finance science and culture; and salaries would be based on productivity.[53]

However, the FNS could not realistically count on the support of more than 6 percent of the population in Moscow (the majority were unskilled workers, pensioners, and men over 45), and possibly even less in provincial Russia, where the patriots were poorly organized. Nor was the FNS's cause greatly helped by the many conflicts among its leaders and its dependence on communist organizations for support.[54] Nevertheless, the right's potential for creating trouble in alliance with such masters of street activity as Anpilov, and Stanislav Terekhov,[55] became visible on May 1, 1993, in the immediate aftermath of the opposition's defeat in the April 1993 referendum. Frustrated by their failure to undermine the still popular president, the activists of Trudovaia Rossiia and Terekhov's Officers' Union engaged in a veritable orgy of violence directed against the "democratic forces of order."[56] Anticipating more battles in the future, FNS leader Konstantinov asserted that the May events showed that only the "street opposition" could stop Yeltsin from violating the constitution and disbanding the parliament.[57]

Developments in the Russian parliament created a new political space for cooperation between the center and the extreme right: Vice President Rutskoy and parliamentary speaker Ruslan Khasbulatov increasingly depended on the nationalist and neocommunist parliamentary factions for votes; and the latter groups, to maintain their seats in parliament, needed to give an aura of democratic respectability and constitutionalism to their extremist agendas. This Weimar-like dynamic—especially given the unwillingness of the Constitutional Court to prosecute the August 1991 coup leaders, and its lifting of Yeltsin's ban on the National Salvation Front and the Russian Communist party (restored in February 1993)—led to an increasingly bitter conflict between the president and the parliament. Both in their speeches and in their actions, Rutskoy and Khasbulatov were moving closer to the agenda of the nationalists. If Rutskoy was repeatedly accusing the government of corruption, he was also moving ever more clearly in the direction of the "Russian idea," underscoring his background as a patriotic Russian officer, protesting the treatment of Russians in Moldova and Ukraine, and mocking the customary democratic attacks on "Russian chauvinism."[58] Khasbulatov, for his part, mostly restricted himself to "defending the constitution"; but he, too, could not reconcile himself to Russia's role as a source of raw materials for the developed West and expressed his concern about this development in an interview published in *Den'*. One month previous to that article, Prokhanov's journal had published an interview with the president of Russia's Constitutional Court, Valerii Zorkin, also defending constitutionalism.[59]

When the final confrontation took place between president and parliament, toward the end of September 1993, the sudden dependence of the "parliamentary forces" on the activists of Anpilov's Trudovaia Rossiia, Barkashev's Russian National Unity, Terekhov's Union of Officers, and select Cossack groups and volunteers from Trans-Dniestria and Abkhazia, was no mere accident.[60] Even if both Rutskoy and Khasbulatov were far from ideological extremism,[61] their reliance on these new "defenders of constitutionalism" proved fatal to their cause. The fate of the "respectable" parliamentary right was sealed by General Albert Makashov,[62] who lived up to his heroic reputation by smashing the doors of the detested *Tel-Aviv-denie*[63] with the help of a rocket-launched grenade. All this effort was to no avail: On October 4, 1993, the first "march on Moscow" ended in dismal, bloody failure.

Paradoxically, the main winners of October turned out to be those who were never taken very seriously either by the right or by the overly confident democrats: the "buffoon" Zhirinovsky, and the revamped Russian Communist party (now the Communist Party of the Russian Federation) led by Zyuganov. Together they would monopolize the patriotic vote, marginalizing their rivals from both the parliamentary right and the extreme right, as well as those from Anpilov's neo-Stalinist left.

Mastering the Politics of Resentment

Vladimir Zhirinovsky and the Liberal Democratic Party of Russia

The remarkable political autobiography of Russia's most successful right-wing populist begins with these words:

> I was born on April 26, 1946, in the city of Alma-Ata. It was Thursday evening, eleven o'clock. It was raining. This was the first spring after the war. We lived in a two-story building on Duganskaia street, in a city that used to be called Vernyi and that was founded by Russian Cossacks in 1854. Russian people founded that city. That is why I can always rightfully say that I was born in Russia and among Russians. Only later would Stalinist ukases first create a Kazakh ASSR, then a Kazakh SSR, and in these CIS [Commonwealth of Independent States] times, even an independent state of Kazakhstan. As if Russians were just fertilizer for the soil from which someone else's states should spring, while the Russians themselves need no state of their own. For some reason, Russians should not have their state where they were born and live, where their ancestors died, where they founded cities—as a rule, not as conquerors, for there was no state where the Russian Cossacks settled.[64]

Zhirinovsky's fate, this paragraph suggests, was from the first day tied to that of the Russian people, a people now deprived of its territory and statehood through a combination of Stalin's arbitrary decisions about national borders; democratic treason; and republican nationalism.

At first glance, Zhirinovsky's *Last Thrust to the South* is a long record of personal suffering. Deprived of his father at an early age, living in a crowded communal apartment, watching his mother toil to her deathbed for some extra scraps from the cafeteria that she cleaned, competing for her attention and these scraps of food with his lazy stepfather, never happy in love, a victim of discriminatory policies that favored local Kazakhs over ethnic Russians in Kazakhstan, rejected as a provincial Russian by the children of the privileged Moscow *nomenklatura*, many of them today's democrats—this is but a short list of the personal grievances of the self-proclaimed leader of the Russian nation.[65] And yet, these are not solely personal grievances. After all, did not millions of Russians live in crowded communal apartments with overworked mothers and lazy stepfathers, with little food on the table, rejected as socially uncouth provincial youths by the children of the privileged? Did not everyone suffer in some way from the indignities of Soviet existence?

Zhirinovsky's appeal must be understood in terms of his uncanny ability to connect his own personal and political experiences to those of his audience; to provide visible targets for the latter's social grievances; and to incorporate them into an aggressive national-imperialist program, whose fictional elements (Russian soldiers washing their feet in the Indian Ocean) give it the character of a fantasy of national redemption. In this sense, Zhirinovsky's language and message offer a classic illustration of the politics of ressentiment, which as Liah Greenfeld has argued, has provided the emotional foundation of nationalist ideologies in all historical latecomers, including Russia.[66] In all such cases, the intensity of personal experiences of deprivation and marginality is directly related to the need for compensation and identification with the nation, and further strengthened by insecurity about the purity of one's ethnic background.[67] Therefore, when Zhirinovsky says, "I am just like you," the meaning of his phrase goes well beyond pure demagogic populism. It is a reaffirmation of his belonging to a national fraternity of us, me and you, the simple Russian people—who are better than those others—whether they be foreigners, Americans, Kazakhs, Jews, persons of "Caucasian nationality," or the sundry political and social forces who are truly responsible for our suffering—the evil Communists, the treasonable democrats, the snobbish Muscovites, the know-it-all *intelligenty*.

To dismiss the Zhirinovsky phenomenon as the temporary and insignificant success of a populist demagogue and scandalous buffoon is not only to refuse to analyze the sources of his appeal among different social constituencies but also to overlook a major factor in contemporary Russian politics: the sheer political weight of the country's external political defeat and economic collapse, with all of their social and psychological consequences—first and foremost, the ubiquitous sense of national humiliation. The politics of identity is supposed to result in the empowerment of the oppressed; and this is exactly what Zhirinovsky was the first to do in the Russian context, sensing the potential gain to be had from mobilizing the downtrodden and humiliated (not necessarily in an exclusively economic sense), giving them a sense of status-superiority on the basis of national belonging, and promising redemption or revenge in the not-too-distant future. In this sense, Zhirinovsky has fulfilled an objective social-psychological need, and if he disappears from the political scene, someone will inevitably fill the space he leaves behind.

Zhirinovsky's first political success came a year after the formation of his Liberal-Democratic Party of Russia, when he sought the approval of the RSFSR Congress of People's Deputies for his nomination as a contender in Russia's upcoming presidential elections. His speech was a stunning success: Defying all expectations, Zhirinovsky won the support of 477 parliamentary deputies—more than twice the requisite number (213). In the brief campaign that followed, Zhirinovsky traveled everywhere, attracting the common people and tirelessly repeating that he alone of all candidates could not be accused of destroying Russia; he was not of the *nomenklatura,* but neither did he support the democrats' plans to destroy the country. To a strongly pro-Yeltsin audience in Chelyabinsk he stated prophetically: "Vote for him. . . . Five years from now there will be new elections, and I will be back. And they [the democrats]will not, for they will have nothing to say to you."[68] Five years later he retracted, warning friends and opponents alike not to underestimate Boris Nikolaevich: for the President was a completely "mystical figure," not guided by "the schemes of Friedman but by political intuition," and for that reason could not be defeated "by logic alone." Unlike some "village schoolteachers" (Zyuganov) and "little boys from the capital's special schools" (Gaidar and others), he and Boris Nikolaevich were political "mystics": Reason alone could not explain their political personae.[69]

And, indeed, reason is hard pressed to explain how the totally unknown Zhirinovsky won 6.2 million votes (5.8 percent of the total) in the 1991 elections, coming in third, after Yeltsin and Ryzhkov. The next two years of his career were fraught with difficulties. In August 1991 he supported the coup leaders, in the hope that they would save the state—a move that could not have brought him popularity, although at least he could say that he was consistent in defending the empire. Between 1991 and 1993, the rest of the political right did its best to ignore and humiliate him. He often had to speak from a small truck, while Baburin, Makashov, Zyuganov and others occupied center stage. They would not even let him into the National Salvation Front, although the organization was supposed to be open to all patriots. Prokhanov's *Den'* also ignored him. Zhirinovsky's own small newspapers—*Liberal, Sokol Zhirinovskogo, Pravda Zhirinovskogo,* and *Iuridicheskaia gazeta*—in which he published his speeches and programs, were read only by a few followers. In this time of trouble, Zhirinovsky traveled and spoke wherever and whenever he could, at home and abroad, in Moscow and in the regions, just in order to stay in the limelight. His "politics of permanent elections" and the occasional scandal were well calculated, albeit signs of desperation.[70] After the elections of October 1993, he finally had a good laugh at his rivals' expense. While the "heroes of October" were staring at their prison bars or failing to collect signatures,[71] he was busy appearing on television, campaigning for the Duma, and—much to the shock of Moscow intellectuals and democrats—celebrating his unexpected victory. No one could ignore him any longer.

Zhirinovsky's stunning success in the December 1993 Duma elections (22.92 percent of the party-list vote, but none in single-member districts, underscoring the dependence of LDPR candidates on their leader) has been attributed to a variety of factors: his unabashed demagogic promises and personal appeal in a crisis-ridden environment; the effectiveness of his media campaign among undecided and disoriented voters; his Russian chauvinism and political authoritarianism;[72] the sheer fallout of the October 1993 events, which effectively discredited his nationalist rivals or prohibited them from competing in the Duma elections; and lastly, the "protest vote" of those who wished a pox on both houses—the Kremlin as well as the House of Soviets.

In empirical terms, the protest vote interpretation has carried the greatest weight: Only 35 percent of Zhirinovsky's voters identified with his party or its program; relatively few had much use for his nationalism; and most blamed the democratic government (not the communist past) for their economic difficulties. On the more positive side, Zhirinovsky's voters were predominantly less-educated, middle-aged men with strong authoritarian values, and disproportionately from medium-sized or smaller cities, the working class in the defense sector, or the unemployed—in other words, from the geographical, social, and sometimes "ethnic" periphery (for example, the Far East and the Pskov region).[73] Hard hit by the economic reforms and prone to seek an iron hand to resolve political problems, these were voters who for the most part distrusted the Communists and did not wish to see a return to the past, even if they preferred some of its aspects to the present.[74] Zhirinovsky repeatedly stressed that he represented a "third force"[75] between the discredited Communists and the new democrats, somewhat outrageously appropriating the labels "centrist" and "liberal" in the process, and his voters had received the message.

However, the conclusion that Zhirinovsky represented only the most "marginal" segments of the population, hostile to markets and democracy, is not entirely borne out by the facts. His voters' economic attitudes were not very different from those of the average Russian, and were significantly more favorable to the market economy than those of the average supporter of the KPRF or the Agrarian party. Nor were Zhirinovsky's followers entirely hostile to the idea of democracy, although a full 31 percent among them thought that "a strong leader should not be restricted by the law" (as opposed to 21 percent of all Russians, 26 percent of KPRF followers, and 18 percent of Agrarian party voters). Finally, the social-educational profile of the LDPR demonstrated that a significant proportion of engineers, clerical workers, and skilled workers were attracted to the party.[76] A cursory glance at LDPR party candidates—i.e., the leadership—shows a distinctly middle-class profile, with engineers, doctors, jurists, and professors predominating over the occasional officer or worker.[77]

The view that Zhirinovsky's 1993 success can be attributed in part to a "protest vote" seems to have been borne out by his losses in the 1995 parliamentary elections. When the electoral campaign was longer and was conducted in a calmer atmosphere, giving rivals time to consolidate, Zhirinovsky's party lost about half of its electoral support, gaining "only" 11 percent of the Duma seats chosen according to party lists, and only one seat in a single-member district race. But we should not forget that the LDPR competed successfully against the much better financed "parties of power," such as Gaidar's Russia's Choice and Chernomyrdin's Our Home Is Russia, and beat a direct rival for the nationalist vote, Aleksandr Lebed's Congress of Russian Communities, which failed to pass the 5 percent threshold. As a result, the LDPR faction held 51 seats (11 percent of the total) in the Second Duma, slightly more than Yavlinsky's Yabloko. The LDPR also made strides in party-building, and advanced its candidates in 83 percent of the single-member districts—even more than the best-organized party, the KPRF.[78]

Alone among candidates of the far right, Zhirinovsky successfully competed in the 1996 presidential elections, coming in fifth and winning a respectable 5.7 percent of the total vote. He undoubtedly would have won a greater share were it not for Lebed, whom Zhirinovsky accused of stealing votes from him. Still, Zhirinovsky's share of the vote was weighty enough that Zyuganov briefly thought of courting him between the two rounds of the presidential contest, before deciding to try his luck elsewhere. In response, Zhirinovsky made a few strong anticommunist statements, which along with Lebed's more important endorsement of Yeltsin, certainly had an impact on the election results.[79]

Zhirinovsky's successes are hardly a matter of luck. He has tapped into the sense of national humiliation more successfully than anyone from the right; appealed to distinct social constituencies; built a party organization; and projected a personal leadership style and a media profile, even if one not taken too seriously by most Western analysts, who had little to say about him, and as is usual in such cases, largely ignored him. Zhirinovsky's greatest weakness was and remains not so much his proverbial extremism (arguably, media attention brought him more votes than he might have lost on account of his extremism) as the organizational dependence of his party on its leader. The Fifth Congress of the LDPR, in April 1994, cemented his authority, making him the party's president for the next ten years (through 2004) and giving him the right to make all of the important party appointments.[80]

Under these conditions, the leader has felt compelled to continue drawing attention by printing endless books with ever more apocalyptic titles, as well as a monthly bulletin about the work of his faction in the Duma.[81] His tactics there have remained unchanged: In one speech, delivered in June 1995, he managed to insult practically the whole establishment, from the president to Gaidar, the army generals, and Yavlinsky—whom he accused of arranging the murder of Boris Pugo (one of the August 1991 coup leaders)—and referred to Rybkin, Luzhkov, and Nemtsov as agents of a "Zionist, American-Israeli conspiracy" against Russia.[82]

Should Zhirinovsky's relative success be explained by his strong and consistent ideological commitment, as Stephen Hanson has argued in an interesting article that compares his and Zyuganov's party-building efforts?[83] Perhaps, insofar as initial party building is concerned. But if one pays closer attention to his ideology, Zhirinovsky has been anything but consistent. In his programmatic statements, genuinely liberal elements are mixed with frank endorsements of *vozhdizm* (the cult of the leader); ethnic slurs, with statements that Russia was always an empire in which ethnicity did not and will not really matter; anticommunism, with support for the August 1991 putschists; and the emphasis on the market, with promises to protect all the poor, downtrodden, humiliated people of Russia. When it does not take the form of apocalyptic proto-fascist fantasies about "last thrusts to the South" or "last battles for Russia," his nationalism is mundane, even banal: Nationalism is like having your own apartment, as opposed to being forced to live in an internationalist communal apartment. Yet this banal metaphor is understandable to all, and even brilliant, for it resonates with the experience of millions of Russians: After all, who wants to live in a *kommunalka* and share his toilet and dining table with strangers?

Limonov the litterateur and therefore the ideologist par excellence, who spent a lot of time with Zhirinovsky, was repelled by this ideological hodgepodge and left his shadow cabinet early on; but as a keen if eccentric observer, he found Zhirinovsky to be a genius of political entrepreneurship and a brilliant provincial demagogue—a Russian Huey Long. Aside from that, Limonov identified as one of Zhirinovsky's main strengths his willingness to culturally and aesthetically embrace the modern, in contrast to the hopeless traditionalism of Russian nationalists and Communists.[84]

Zhirinovsky, who grew up in the *kommunalka*, takes it for granted that "being determines consciousness" and knows that the "Russian soul" alone cannot move the world; consequently, he left the deadly combination of collectivism and the "Russian soul" to the Communists, their pensioners, and the village prose writers. In contrast, having spent some time in the discothèque, Zhirinovsky has attracted some angry young people and a few rock-and-roll bands, the political equivalent of a million pensioners, with more dividends to be had in the future.

Finally, let us never forget or underestimate the power of ressentiment: One of the most surprising conclusions of an in-depth study of the self-identification of ethnic Russians, conducted by eminent Russian sociologists in 1995, found that the majority of respondents (61 percent) deemed Russians' "readiness to suffer through difficulties and ordeals" the most important trait distinguishing them from other ethnic groups. In contrast, many fewer thought Russians were the carriers of a "special historical mission" (12 percent) or had a "distinctly Russian" insight into "truth and higher meaning" (20 percent).[85] The very fact that the sociologists decided to offer the first response as an option (a response, incidentally, that a Western sociologist investigating the ethnic self-identification of Russians would never have thought of) speaks volumes; and the response says even more. In the Soviet Union, everyone had to "suffer through difficulties and ordeals" for at least several hours every day. If you need a reminder of what life was like, read Zhirinovsky's autobiography, but remember: There is only one short step between being an expert at suffering and inflicting it upon others.

Gennadii Zyuganov and the Rise of "Russian Communism"

The lessons that the political right and the neocommunist movement derived from the October 1993 events were far from uniform. For those gathered around Prokhanov's *Den'*, October provided the pretext for creating a new nationalist "martyrology": The patriots who had laid down their lives "for Russia" had been the first to sow the seeds of that revolt that would lead, sooner or later, to the triumph of the just, patriotic cause.[86] Others, like the defeated Rutskoy and Khasbulatov, tried to rebuild under changed circumstances or at least to justify their positions, albeit with little effect. Those on the very extreme left and right, Anpilov and Barkashov, in particular, would never openly challenge the regime again.

And yet, in some sense, the extremists even made gains. For instance, Barkashov's currency rose among potential fellow-travelers, who admired his heroism. At first, in hiding, he was almost killed; subsequently he was arrested, and his organization was banned. Once the ban was lifted and Barkashov was freed as part of the general amnesty in February 1994, his newly won notoriety and patience at organization-building won him more followers, making Russian National Unity by far the largest fascist movement in Russia, with 53 regional branches and perhaps as many as 10,000 to 12,000 members by the end of 1996.[87]

Others grew more suspicious of him, especially the Communists: Having previously treated him as Russia's heroic son, they quickly distanced themselves from this provocateur bent on discrediting the Russian idea.[88] Barkashov, for his part, despised the "compromiser" Zyuganov and "the Jew" Zhirinovsky: His criteria of "Russianness" were strict. Nevertheless, he indirectly supported Yeltsin in the 1996 elections: Let the democrats ruin the country till the end, and then it will be ours, he reasoned; Zyuganov would only mix things up.[89] His attitude did not bring him many friends among more respectable patriots, but he never sought them anyway, instead preferring companions in arms *(soratniki)*—the official term used to describe the highest-ranked members of his movement.[90] His black shirts defiantly paraded through the streets of a Moscow suburb at the beginning of 1999, apparently with the help of some connections in the Russian interior ministry (MVD)—a disturbing sign of where the sympathies of some officials lay.[91] By that time, the recruitment of "sympathizers" or "sponsors" in coercive state institutions had become an integral part of Barkashov's tactics.[92]

The former parliamentary right, too, was amnestied and released after October, an event much celebrated by Prokhanov: Rutskoy and Makashov in particular became regular guests in the pages of *Zavtra*. Khasbulatov, Zorkin, Achalov, and the others were not left out; but all of them had lost their reputations and would never again reemerge as fully credible actors on the national level. Not that they did not try; almost as soon as they left their prison cells, they formed a new movement, Concord for Russia (Soglasie vo imia Rossii). But how could anyone trust those who had brought such havoc to the streets of Moscow to suddenly bring about "concord"?[93] In comparison with its predecessor, the National Salvation Front, Soglasie was a truly harmless society of former judges, vice presidents, and parliamentarians in search of new sinecures. Not surprisingly, the new organization quickly faded, and its leaders dispersed.[94]

After an unsuccessful bid for parliament as the head of a still-new bloc with the pompous title Derzhava (Great Power), Rutskoy settled for a provincial governorship in fall 1996, withdrawing to his native Kursk—not bad, for someone who might well have spent the rest of his life strolling in the prison courtyard. Only Baburin and Makashov remained truly active in the new Duma after 1995: Baburin, posing as a figure of national stature, the deputy speaker of the Duma, presidential material;[95] and Makashov, making openly anti-Semitic comments and thereby discrediting the KPRF just when it was becoming an almost respectable parliamentary party. Naturally, whatever he might have lost among the "parliamentary communists," Makashov gained among members of the extreme left-right coalition, who hailed him as a true "patriot" and awarded him the "Star of Stalin."[96]

The ones who really profited from the October events were Zyuganov and his reconstituted KPRF. The outcome is somewhat surprising, given just how involved Zyuganov had been in the formation of the united left and right opposition and the patriotic struggle against "the occupation regime." Yet his search for a modicum of respectability was observable early on. Anpilov's street radicalism repelled Zyuganov, and the two never got along, although Zyuganov never minded taking an opportunity to address the masses that Anpilov had brought out into the agora. For all his hatred for democracy, Zyuganov realized that the regime still had a strong reservoir of credibility, in contrast to his own Communists, who had barely been legalized by the Constitutional Court in November 1992. His organizational and agitprop skills, acquired through years of ideological work on all levels of the partocracy, served him well; his conviction in the rightness of the cause, immense energy, and self-confidence, even better.

Zyuganov's real ambition was to combine the cadre organization of his party of the "left" with the values of the "right." The new party, he stated on the eve of its reconstitution in February 1993, would be a "party of the people," not just the proletariat. Those comrades who clung doggedly to the "class approach" failed to appreciate the necessity of a "broad platform" based on a fusion of ideas of social justice with national-state interests, and they would fall by the wayside. This was because the main struggle in contemporary Russia was between the "liberal cosmopolitans" and the "party of national statehood." Social justice, popular rule, the priority of state interests, and patriotism were the common cornerstones of the Russian and the Soviet traditions and would help bridge the gap between the Communist left and the nationalist right.[97] Yet, just when the realization of these ideals seemed closer than ever, with Anpilov's proletarians of the left and Barkashev's troopers of the right united in their desire to "uphold the constitution," Zyuganov publicly backed down, calling on his supporters to refrain from provocations.[98] Neither the extreme left nor the extreme right forgave him this "cowardice." They supported his presidential candidacy in 1996 with great reluctance, if at all; Zyuganov, for his part, correctly thought that the extremists he had courted in 1991 and 1992 would only damage his reputation, whereas many nationalists would vote for him anyway.[99]

Zyuganov's stature as the new general secretary rose further after his party was restored to parliamentary respectability, with a significant 12.4 percent of the vote and 14.2 percent of the seats in the new Duma.[100] During the next three years he tirelessly toiled on both the ideological and the organizational fronts, writing endless articles for *Sovetskaia Rossiia*, publishing several books on the Russian idea,[101] disciplining his party comrades in the Duma, and courting voters and legislators. The ideological influences of the political right on his thinking were more than obvious: He borrowed from the fascist Aleksandr Dugin the idea of a "mondialist conspiracy" against Russia, and argued along lines reminiscent of one of Mussolini's teachers, the Italian nationalist Enrico Corradini, that the world was divided into "capitalist" and "proletarian nations," not classes. The ideas of Toynbee and Spengler, and even Huntington's "clash of civilizations," liberally coexisted alongside those of Lenin in his writings; and the Soviet-Russian past was glorified alongside "Orthodoxy, Autocracy, Nationality." The history of the CPSU was rewritten as well, with the "heroic party" of Stalin, Zhukov, Stakhanov, Gagarin, and other Soviet-Russian "patriots" confronting the "party of treason" represented by Trotsky, Mekhlis, Kaganovich, and other cadres of suspiciously "cosmopolitan" background. From the last KGB director Kryuchkov, Zyuganov borrowed the idea that the destruction of the Soviet Union had been planned years beforehand by Western intelligence services, which had infiltrated the CPSU with "agents of influence" at the highest levels: Gorbachev, Yakovlev, and others might not have worked for the CIA literally, yet they were somehow "programmed" from the outside to weaken the party-state. How the omnipotent and evil West achieved this feat was never explained; but conspiracy theories, in any case, were never meant to demystify social reality.[102]

The KPRF, however, was not Zhirinovsky's LDPR: Zyuganov had to struggle hard to refashion himself as primus inter pares. Disturbingly, many of his comrades either showed marked reformist tendencies or "dogmatically clung to the class approach." His second in command, Valentin Kuptsov, for instance, who represented the more pragmatic current in the party, pointedly attacked "unthinking discipline" and "bureaucratic centralism" at the first KPRF congress in February 1993; he also spoke about the "creative adaptation of Marxism" to new circumstances, and underscored the need for collaboration with various "centrist" forces.[103] In contrast, the more orthodox wing wanted to remain within the framework of traditional Leninism, rejecting Zyuganov's "nationalist deviation."[104]

As a consequence, early KPRF programs represented an uneasy compromise between orthodox Leninist, reformist, and nationalist values and ideals, reflecting

the various tendencies in the party. Thus, the theses for the new KPRF party program claimed the Leninist heritage but simultaneously conceded that the CPSU
had become corrupt, failing to adapt to the demands of the technological revolution; the KPRF itself was defined as a party of "state patriotism, internationalism,
social justice, and Communist ideals." The short-term collaboration with all patriotic forces, the program promised, would lead to the formation of a government of national salvation; the long-term goal was the restoration of socialism.[105]

Nevertheless, the nationalist influence was evident: An April 1994 KPRF congress resolution sharply attacked the "cosmopolitans in power," who were trying to
mask themselves as "false patriots"; called for the unification of all patriotic forces;
and denounced the Belovezh agreement.[106] Zyuganov, for his part, tried to appease
the orthodox wing by summoning Lenin as a witness. The "bourgeois abuse of the
notion of the people," the great leader apparently stated, did not mean that the
working class should isolate itself from the *narod* as a whole but rather lead it. In
short, the focus of mobilization should not be on the proletariat but on the Russian people and its struggle to restore the thousand-year-old state.[107]

The official KPRF program, adopted at the party's Third Congress (January
22, 1995), represented a compromise between the different currents in the party.
Still, nationalist motifs were hardly absent. Thus, the attack on Western-style
consumer capitalism was not waged from the point of view of the exploited
working class but from that of the exploited periphery held hostage by a predatory "new world order." The only way out of this impasse was to "activate the national liberation struggle of the Russian people," which in turn presupposed cooperation with various "centrist, truly democratic, and patriotic" forces, a
deliberately vague formulation. In any case, the important point was that "the defense of Russia's national-state interests organically flows into the struggle against
colonial enslavement and counterrevolution, and for socialism and Soviet forms
of popular power." For these and similar reasons, Russia should choose its own
developmental path—one compatible with such traditional values as collectivism
(obshchinnost', sobornost'); patriotism, or "the closest mutual tie between the individual, society, and state" *(derzhavnost');* striving to embody the higher ideals of
truth, good, and justice *(dukhovnost');* and the equality and equal value of all citizens, independent of national, religious, and other differences *(narodnost').*[108]

In September 1995, when the KPRF electoral platform was drafted, most references to Marxism-Leninism were dropped. Under the title "For Our Soviet
Homeland," the platform promised that the party would repudiate the Belovezh
treaty and restore the "illegally dissolved" Soviet state; strengthen the country's
defenses by rebuilding the military-industrial complex; replace the government
of "national treason" with a coalition government of "national trust," led by
popular-patriotic forces; and end Russia's subservience to the West. The platform
did not envisage a return to state socialism. Although promising a crackdown on
speculative capital and crime, as well as a much stronger role for the state in social policy, the KPRF pledged to respect private property and rejected old-style
equalization policies *(uravnilovka).* Lastly, in a clear sign that the party was

counting on the nationalist vote, the platform lambasted Zhirinovsky, who, it stated, had supported Yeltsin and Chernomyrdin on all key issues, failing to fulfill his electoral promises.[109]

Zyuganov, for his part, underscored that the party had rejected its earlier atheism and was open to all believers, particularly Russian Orthodox ones.[110] In line with this shift in the direction of nationalist values, a KPRF appeal on the very eve of the Duma elections called on all compatriots, "brothers and sisters," to vote for the party of the people: Neither the working class nor the vanguard was mentioned, although the party slogan—*trud, narodovlastie, sotsializm* (labor, popular power, socialism)—signaled a continued commitment to some of the basic tenets of socialism.[111]

The KPRF's new national-populist course, coupled with its distinct door-to-door campaign style, was an immense success: In the December 1995 elections, the party won 22.3 percent of the total vote, and 157 seats in the Second Duma (a full 50 of them in single-member districts), emerging as the largest parliamentary party (with a total of 34.9 percent of the seats). Yet even this was not a full indication of Communist strength, as Viktor Anpilov's Trudovaia Rossiia bloc won an additional 4.5 percent of the vote, almost passing the 5 percent threshold for entrance to the Duma.[112] More impressive still, the combined communist-nationalist vote represented more than half of the total vote, opening up the prospect of a common candidate sponsored by all patriotic forces in the upcoming presidential elections.

As Yitzhak Brudny has demonstrated, it was precisely such considerations that determined the KPRF's strategy in the presidential race that followed, although Zyuganov was aware of the limitations of the procommunist vote.[113] Not surprisingly, when it was officially announced in February 1996, Zyuganov's candidacy was endorsed in the name of the Popular-Patriotic Forces of Russia, although there was little doubt that Communists would occupy the "commanding heights" in the new coalition.[114] In order to underscore its nationalist credentials, the communist faction in the Duma voted to renounce the Belovezh agreement—its most controversial move in the Russian parliament.

Consequently, in Zyuganov's electoral platform all references to labor and socialism were dropped in favor of a set of broader nationalist ideals: *Rossiia, rodina, narod* (Russia, homeland, nation). Evidencing the priority he gave to nationalist considerations, Zyuganov emphasized that he was a Russian "both by blood and in spirit," who had joined the Communist party because he was convinced that the "two-thousand-year-old Communist idea" was in harmony with distinctly collectivist and egalitarian Russian traditions as well as with the true interests of the homeland. Were it not for his association with the KPRF, Zyuganov's platform would be read as the manifesto of a conservative nationalist party candidate: the fatherland; the 25 million Russians left beyond Russia's borders; the traditional family (the right of women to childbearing and a "peaceful motherhood"); the importance of preserving distinct Russian traditions, culture, and language; the endorsement of a mixed economy, with various forms of property; the priority given to questions of external security—where in all of this was communism? The only real trace of communist values lay in the broad emphasis on social justice and the struggle against the comprador bourgeoisie that was robbing Russia of its resources and its people of their income.[115]

Not for nothing did Prokhanov write in his characteristically high-flown style that "the iconographic image of two horses, one white and one red, on which (the Russian saints) Boris and Gleb sat, has become the metaphor of contemporary Russia, in which social and national energy are flowing into each other, giving birth to absolutely new political movements, the largest one of which is destined to be Russian communism."[116] His view was seconded by the head of the Spiritual Heritage (Dukhovnoe Nasledie) think tank, Aleksei Podberezkin, who was in charge of elaborating a new state-patriotic ideology for the KPRF.[117] The contemporary Russian idea, argued Podberezkin in a pamphlet explicitly endorsing Zyuganov's candidacy, was encapsulated in the formula "socialism + spirituality + contemporary scientific and technological achievements." This new emphasis on spirituality, added Podberezkin, in no way contradicted traditional communist ideals, for the simple reason that communism and Christianity had sprung from the same roots and shared the same values.[118]

But what about the *kolbasnyi vopros,* the famous "sausage question"? Was not one of the main strengths of the Communists their social appeal at a time of rapidly growing social polarization? Paradoxically, it was in answering the pressing questions of the "material base" that the communist campaign showed its greatest weakness: The spiritualization of socialism had progressed to such a point that the party's economic program had been forgotten. It remained unformulated until a couple of weeks before the first round of elections.[119] By that time Zyuganov somewhat comically turned his attention to "Russian youth," being fully aware of the generational limitations of his electorate.[120] He also courted the patriots in a last bid for support at the first congress of his electoral coalition—Narodno-Patrioticheskii Soiuz Rossii (NPSR; in English, the Popular-Patriotic Union of Russia).[121]

Yet it was not enough. When the votes of the first round were counted, Zyuganov came in second, with 32 percent of the vote—little more than the combined vote of Communists and agrarians in the 1995 Duma elections. Despite his attempt to combine nationalism with appeals for a mixed economy, Zyuganov was still perceived as too "red" by most voters: A full 45 percent of Yeltsin's voters stated that their first motive was to defeat Zyuganov. Tellingly, Zyuganov failed to attract the critical segments of the population—the younger and better-educated urban strata. The stereotypical view of the Communist party, as a party of "pensioners" with a strong base in the rural areas and among the uneducated, was confirmed. In only two categories—people over 55 years of age, and those without high-school education—did Zyuganov fare better than Yeltsin. Finally, the Zyuganov vote was regionally limited: In addition to his failure to carry large urban centers, in the second round Zyuganov failed to capture even the majority of regions in which the nationalist vote was traditionally strong. However Russian his new communism might be, the red flag was too negative a symbol for many nationalist sympathizers.[122]

When measured by another standard, however, Zyuganov was tremendously successful: Only five years after the August coup, he had made the KPRF the largest opposition party in the new Duma and had emerged as the most serious opposition contender in the race for the presidency, winning 40.2 percent of the vote in the second round. Aside from controlling a number of parliamentary committees, the KPRF had captured the chairmanship of the Second Duma; and Zyuganov successfully monopolized the role of leader of the communist-nationalist opposition. As one unsympathetic nationalist bitterly noted, Zyuganov had waged a much more successful struggle for the commanding post in the opposition than he had against Yeltsin's "occupation government."[123]

That this was indeed one of Zyuganov's main goals became clear in August 1996, as he presided over the institutionalization of his electoral coalition, the NPSR, which was designed to further the transformation of the KPRF into a "party of patriots." Not surprisingly, the guiding idea of the new movement was to combine social justice with Russian patriotism.[124] Zyuganov, for his part, advocated a "parliamentary road to socialism," stating that the party should turn itself into a "constructive and responsible opposition." Realizing that the KPRF was predominantly a party of "cultural traditionalists" and needed to expand its electoral base by moving toward the center, Zyuganov argued that "constructive conservatism" should be the main ethos animating the party's future activity.[125]

Just what this meant in practice became evident only a few days later, when the Communist faction in the Duma voted in its archenemy, Viktor Chernomyrdin, as the new prime minister, provoking the first divisions in the NPSR. Baburin, for one, would have none of it, calling the communist action a "shameful act"; and Viktor Tiulkin, Anpilov's rival for leadership of the far left, asked Zyuganov to remove the word *communist* from the name of his party.[126] The KPRF's relations with Rutskoy were also far from idyllic, especially after the Communists advanced their own candidate in the Kursk gubernatorial election, only to backtrack at the last moment, letting the former vice president take the field.[127]

Nor was the party's reputation among patriots enhanced by its further slide into "unprincipled compromise" over the government budget in December 1996. Satisfied with the results of the fall 1996 gubernatorial races, in which the NPSR claimed victory in 25 regions, Zyuganov saw little reason to call for new Duma elections.[128] In reality, as Steven Solnick has shown, the elections produced a mixed result from the standpoint of nationwide parties and blocs, with regional considerations playing the most important role.[129] Worse still, the dependence of the governors on the central government—especially those in the poorer regions, in which the Communists were more likely to triumph—gave them a strong incentive for cooperation rather than confrontation with the "party of power."[130] For these reasons, the KPRF's December 1996 compromise with the government was widely understood either as a form of capitulation or as the first sign that the Communists were becoming a loyal opposition.

By April 1997, the parliamentary road chosen by the KPRF risked alienating so many of its supporters that the Fourth Congress of the KPRF felt obliged to underscore the "irreconcilable" albeit still "responsible" character of its opposition to the government. Thus, the future of Russia would be both "great" and "socialist," twin goals that would be achieved in a presumably peaceful fashion.[131] The collection of signatures on a petition demanding Yeltsin's resignation, which animated KPRF members in yet one more quasi-electoral campaign in summer 1997, resulted in another compromise, further disappointing radicals both inside and outside the KPRF. Zyuganov somewhat unconvincingly justified the KPRF's new accommodation with the Chernomyrdin government on the grounds that Gazprom (which was headed by Chernomyrdin) was one of the few large enterprises in the country that still functioned and that maintained a bond between Russia and Ukraine (the latter being dependent on Russian natural gas supplies). At the same time, Zyuganov emphasized, the KPRF's new, centrist image would attract younger people to the party. "Veterans" could carry the movement no longer, and the Communists would have to show more flexibility in their treatment of urban youth subcultures, although retaining their commitment to traditional Russian values.[132] But none of these justifications appeased grassroots Communists, especially after the indecisiveness of parliamentary Communists resulted in the nomination of the archliberal Sergei Kirienko as prime minister in spring 1998.[133]

When the second congress of the NPSR convened in November 1998, it once more raised the specter of a final "national-liberation struggle" of the Russian people against colonial oppression, somewhat pompously comparing its efforts to those of Gandhi, Martin Luther King, and the Palestinian *intifada*. Yet, upon closer inspection, the manifesto of "popular-patriotic" forces reveals a somewhat different picture: Behind the high-flown rhetoric of national liberation, one finds that the rebuilding of a "great Russia, which will inevitably begin after the failure of the liberal revanche" (i.e., after Kirienko's dismissal and replacement with Primakov), could not be achieved in the absence of "stable, civic peace, or a social contract." It was the purpose of such a contract to end the tragic divisions of the Russian people into "mutually hostile groups." Lest it be thought that this was a way of giving in to the democratic enemy, the NPSR proclaimed that the achievement of civic peace could not occur until all those who had brought Russia to the verge of catastrophe underwent a sort of Nuremberg trial. In the new, civic, patriotic Russia, there would no longer be a place for various extremists of the "right," such as Chubais, Chernomyrdin, and Zhirinovsky.[134] And what would be the fate in this patriotic Russia of the various putschists, the officer Terekhov, the "heroic" General Makashov, the Nazi Barkashev, the proletarian tribune Anpilov, the "nightingale of the general staff" Prokhanov, the sundry heroes of the October uprising, and all those who had made a profession out of their hatred of "civic peace"? Predictably, to this question the NPSR manifesto offered no answer.

Conclusion

In the aftermath of the August 1991 coup, the communist-nationalist opposition went through several distinct stages. In the first and most radical stage, between 1991 and October 1993, the united opposition of left and right political forces mounted a consistent but unsuccessful effort to subvert the regime through a combination of parliamentary pressure and violent street activity. The failure of the first "march on Moscow" in October 1993 significantly altered the equation, even if it simultaneously damaged the reputation of the regime. The high cost of violence was a lesson that both the Communist left and the nationalist right took seriously, with the consequence that the "revolutionary road" to power was largely abandoned.

In the second stage, from October 1993 to the June 1996 presidential elections, Zyuganov's Communists and Zhirinovsky's nationalists pursued the parliamentary path to power while remaining firmly committed to a change of regime. Both had their moments of success—first Zhirinovsky, and then the Communists. Together they demonstrated that the sympathies of a good half of the electorate lay outside a ruling regime that had deprived them of their incomes and basic security and threatened their Soviet and/or Russian identity as well. Yet the parliamentary road to power came at the price of institutionalization and the acceptance of the enemy's rules of play.

This became particularly evident in the third stage, which extended from 1996 through mid-1999. The transformation of an antisystem party into an electoral machine, as Richard Sakwa has argued,[135] posed a classic Michelsian problem for Zyuganov's Communists. Whereas the KPRF's rhetoric was often revolutionary, its deeds were parliamentary, and its electorate traditionalist and conservative in the classic sense of the words. Yet, from time to time, the Communists had to prove that they were indeed the party of opposition, threatening votes of no-confidence, collecting signatures for Yeltsin's resignation, and even copying the much-hated American model by impeaching the president in 1999. Their failure on almost all scores, however, only further alienated their radical constituency, as the "moderates" among them looked for ways to retain their Duma seats and privileges by advocating statesmanship, "civic peace," and collaboration with centrist forces.

Does this mean that the 1996 election indeed marked the end of polarized politics, as Michael McFaul has argued?[136] Yes, insofar as this event legitimized elections in general as the only acceptable means of acquiring power; led to the institutionalization of the opposition; and demonstrated the potential appeal of strongman centrism. Nevertheless, one should not underestimate the many sources of instability, from the dissatisfaction of the disenfranchised social strata to the dramatic economic situation, the ineffectiveness of state authority, and the ambivalent attitude of the army and coercive state institutions toward democracy. To these internal factors must be added the widespread resentment over NATO's expansion, not to mention its spring 1999 bombing campaign over Yugoslavia, which provoked an intense, negative reaction across the Russian political spectrum.

Under these conditions, Russian politics will inevitably move in a more nationalist direction, even as more credible political actors marginalize the most extreme nationalists and Communists. In this respect, the most important contribution of the communist and nationalist opposition over the past decade is the development of a distinctive, nationalist rhetoric that relates Russia's internal economic and social problems to its external humiliation at the hands of the West. The widespread sense of humiliation is a problem that all contemporary Russian politicians must address if they are to remain credible actors on the political scene. Only within this broader ideological and political context can Vladimir Putin's recent political campaigns and hard-line rhetoric be fully understood.

On a deeper historical and sociological level, Russia's current plight can perhaps best be understood in light of a recurring dilemma posed by Western-style modernization. Many decades ago, Karl Deutsch described this dilemma in his characteristically lucid fashion:

> Western political theorists have seen the essence of the "rule of law" in its power to make life predictable. Yet, time and again, the Western world has been surprised that its "rule of law" seems to be rejected by large numbers of people outside the West, despite the obvious benefits of predictability which it seemed to bring to them. Perhaps now we can resolve this seeming paradox. Populations may have rejected the Western-style "rule of law" quite often because it did not predict their future, or because it predicted for them a future of poverty, insecurity, or subordination which they could not accept. . . . Yet, where predictability from contract failed or became unpalatable, for whatever reason, men might still choose another road to make life predictable. They might fall back on predictability from identification and from introspection. Instead of contracting freely for prices, wages, or employment conditions on rigid abstract terms, they might prefer to have these terms set and manipulated "arbitrarily" by an authority which to them did not seem arbitrary because it seemed to them an authority "of their own kind," run by persons like themselves.[137]

Notes

I would like to thank all the participants of the Carnegie conference on "Russian Politics: Stability of Disorder" held at UC Berkeley on May 15–16, 1999, for their useful comments and suggestions. I would also like to thank my research assistant from Oberlin College, Sarah Scannell, for helping me collect and organize material for this chapter, as well as Andreas Umland of Stanford University for supplying me with critical sources and taking an interest in my work on Russian nationalism.

1. Gennadii Zyuganov, *Derzhava* (Moscow: Informpechat', 1994), p. 33.
2. Vladimir Zhirinovsky, *Poslednii vagon na sever* (Moscow, 1996), pp. 12–14.

3. *Den',* it is less well known, was also the name of a Slavophile newspaper founded by Ivan Aksakov in 1861. For Aksakov's contribution to the development of Russian nationalist ideology, see Stephen Lukasevich, *Ivan Aksakov, 1823–1886: A Study in Russian Thought and Politics* (Cambridge: Harvard University Press, 1965).

4. The full story behind the publication of *Den'* was revealed in the aftermath of the August 1991 coup. See *Literaturnaia gazeta,* August 28, 1991.

5. For a brief biographical profile of Zyuganov, see Joan Barth Urban and Valerii D. Solovei, *Russia's Communists at the Crossroads* (Boulder: Westview, 1997), pp. 43–45. An interesting source on Zyuganov's early days in Orel is Alessandra Stanley, "Red Scare," *New York Times Magazine,* May 26, 1996.

6. Aleksandr Prokhanov, "Nosha russkoi sud'by," *Sovetskaia Rossiia,* September 21, 1995.

7. "Slovo k narodu," *Sovetskaia Rossiia,* July 23, 1991; *Den',* no. 15, July 1991. For a concise review and analysis of "Slovo k narodu," see John B. Dunlop, *The Rise of Russia and the Fall of the Soviet Empire* (Princeton: Princeton University Press, 1993), pp. 163–165.

8. Prokhanov, "Nosha russkoi sud'by."

9. Vladimir Zhirinovsky, *Poslednii brosok na iug* (Moscow: LDP, 1993).

10. See, for example, the outside cover of Zhirinovsky's *Poslednii udar po Rossii* (Moscow, 1996), where the leader is depicted holding a crying *babushka* in his arms, in contrast to the inside cover of the same book, where he is pictured in an officer's uniform, seated under the seal of the double-headed eagle, gazing sternly into the camera lens.

11. Characteristically, Baburin's book of speeches and programmatic statements is entitled *Rossiiskii put'* (Moscow: ANKO, 1995), and his party is called Rossiiskii Obshchenarodnyi Soiuz. Both titles, as well as the name of the parliamentary faction (Rossiia) clearly point to a territorial *(rossiiskii)* rather than an ethnic *(russkii)* self-definition among this group of Russian nationalists.

12. The idea of a "third way," between laissez-faire capitalism and Marxian socialism, was present in many currents of the early-twentieth-century European right, including fascism. See George L. Mosse, ed., *International Fascism* (London and Beverly Hills: Sage, 1979), pp. 1–45. For a Russian version of "third way" ideology, see Igor Shafarevich, "Dve dorogi k odnomu obryvu," *Novyi mir,* no. 7, 1989.

13. Viktor Anpilov's Trudovaia Rossiia movement grew out of several orthodox communist currents whose members were brought together in the many street demonstrations that took place in Moscow in 1992 and 1993. For a brief history of Trudovaia Rossiia and a short biography of Anpilov, see Aleksandr Verkhovskii, Anatolii Papp, and Vladimir Pribylovskii, *Politicheskii ekstremizm v Rossii* (Moscow: Panorama, 1996), pp. 198–203, 223–225.

14. For more on the emergence of proto-fascist organizations at the turn of the century, see Hans Rogger, *Jewish Policies and Right-Wing Politics in Imperial Russia* (Berkeley: University of California Press, 1986), especially pp. 188–233; Don C. Rawson, *Russian Rightists and the Revolution of 1905* (Cambridge, U.K.: Cambridge University Press, 1995); and O. T. Vite, V. M. Voronkov, and R. Sh. Ganelin, *Natsional'naia pravaia prezhde i teper',* vol. 1 (St. Petersburg: Institut sotsiologii Rossiiskoi Akademii Nauk [RAN], 1992). The legacy of the Black Hundreds was defended in a pamphlet by V. Ostrevtsev, *Chernaia sotnia i krasnaia sotnia* (Moscow, 1991), and was openly promoted by patriotic circles in the Soviet military on the eve of the August 1991 putsch.

15. For a good, brief history of Pamyat as well as a selection of representative documents, see V. D. Solovei and I. A. Erunov, *Russkoe delo segodnia*, vol. 1: *Pamiat'* (Moscow: Institut etnologii i antropologii RAN, 1991), as well as V. Pribylovskii, *Pamiat': Dokumenty i teksty* (Moscow: Panorama, 1991). For the rise of early patriotic movements in Leningrad, see the excellent empirical contribution of O. N. Ansberg, I. A. Levinskaia, Io. M. Lesman, and V. G. Uzunova, "Natsional-patrioticheskoe dvizhenie v Leningrade," in *Natsional'naia pravaia prezhde i teper'*, vol. 2 (St. Petersburg: Institut sotsiologii Rossiiskoi Akademii Nauk, 1992), pp. 97–151. Semyon Reznik, *The Nazification of Russia* (Washington, D.C.: Challenge, 1996), is especially good on early anti-Semitic ideology and in providing a sense of the atmosphere prevalent in extreme right-wing circles.

16. Barkashov joined Vasilev's Pamyat in 1985, and was in charge of the military training of cadres. Dissatisfied with Vasilev's passivity, in 1990 he formed his own organization, Russian National Unity (Russkoe Natsional'noe Edinstvo) (V. Pribylovskii, *Vozhdi* [Moscow: Panorama, 1995]), pp. 26–28).

17. Eduard Limonov, an émigré writer best known for his sexually charged autobiographical novel *Eto ia—Edichka*, returned to Russia in 1990. He soon became a regular contributor to *Sovetskaia Rossiia*, which published a number of his important programmatic articles in 1991 and 1992. A proponent of "direct action," he took a liking to the dynamic street leader of the Moscow downtrodden, Viktor Anpilov, as well as to Vladimir Zhirinovsky. He later recorded his dissatisfaction with the latter in a political memoir entitled *Limonov protiv Zhirinovskogo* (Moscow: Konets veka, 1994), which remains a valuable source of information on the left-right opposition in its formative period. Limonov formed his National-Bolshevik Party in late 1993 and began printing his paper *Limonka* in 1994 (a pun on his name; the Russian word means "lemon-shaped grenade," an image of which decorates the front page of his paper). Aleksandr Dugin was a member of Pamyat who in the 1990s became inspired by contemporary European right-wing and anti-American thought. In his many contributions to *Den'*, he singled out the ideology of *mondializm* (liberal universalism and cosmopolitanism) as the worldview of the "Atlanticist" secret order bent on world domination, to which he opposed the ideology of Eurasianism. Dugin began publishing *Elementy* in 1992.

18. For a useful portrait of Prokhanov as "the last soldier of the empire," see Sven Gunnar Simonsen, *Politics and Personalities: Key Actors in the Russian Opposition* (Oslo: International Peace Research Institute, 1996), pp. 91–109. For a brief biography, see Pribylovskii, *Vozhdi*, pp. 84–86.

19. Nina Andreeva, "Ne mogu postupat'sia printsipami," *Sovetskaia Rossiia*, March 13, 1988. The story of Andreeva's letter and its sponsorship by Yegor Ligachev is well told in David Remnick, *Lenin's Tomb* (New York: Random House, 1993), pp. 70–86.

20. Written in the early 1980s, Shafarevich's *Russofobia* first gained notoriety with its publication in *Nash sovremennik*, nos. 6 and 11, 1989. The last, "anti-Zionist" part of the treatise was too sensitive to be published in June 1989; hence the five-month delay. For a brief analysis of Shafarevich's manifesto and its influence on subsequent right-wing thought in Russia, see Veljko Vujacic, "Gennadii Zyuganov and the Third Road," *Post-Soviet Affairs*, vol. 12, no. 2, April-June 1996, pp. 118–154.

21. "Pis'mo pisatelei Rossii," *Literaturnaia Rossiia*, March 2, 1990. The "Letter of 74" was a sharply worded indictment of the wave of "Russophobia" spread by the "cosmopolitan-democratic media" with the purpose of discrediting every manifestation of Russian patriotism as fascism and undermining the unity of the Soviet state. Instead, according to the writers, "Zionism" was the main problem.

22. The conference brought together 26 procommunist and patriotic organizations, from the far left to the far right. In Prokhanov's words, the main goal of the conference was to save the "thousand-year-old Russian state" from destruction. To further this goal, the conference established the Coordinating Council of Patriotic Forces, headed by Eduard Volodin and the ideological secretary of the CP RSFSR, Gennadii Zyuganov. See Ivan Antonovich, "Patrioticheskie sily Rossii: Vozmozhnost' ob"edineniia," *Izvestiia TsK KPSS,* no. 7, July 1991; and B. Koval' et al., eds., *Rossiia segodnia: Politicheskii portret v dokumentakh* (Moscow: Mezhdunarodnye otnosheniia, 1991), pp. 316–318.

23. For more on Russian nationalism as an ideological current before perestroika, see Yitzhak Brudny, *Reinventing Russia: Russian Nationalism and the Soviet State, 1953–1991* (Cambridge: Harvard University Press, 1988). Alexander Yanov, in *The Russian New Right* (Berkeley: University of California, Institute of International Studies, 1978), anticipated the merger of orthodox communism and extreme nationalism in contemporary Russia some 20 years before it took definitive shape.

24. For two characteristic reactions from the right, see Nikolai Anysin, "Plach' po kozlu otpushcheniia," *Den',* no. 20, October 10, 1991; and Aleksandr Prokhanov, "Chetvertaia plata," *Den',* no. 21, October 25–November 8, 1991.

25. Eduard Limonov, "Fal'shivaia demokraticheskaia, fal'shivaia revoliutsiia," *Literaturnaia gazeta,* October 16, 1991.

26. One of the most striking features of post-1991 developments in Russia has been the relative weakness of the state in dealing with political extremism, despite the existence of legislation prohibiting the open propagation of "national and racial hatred." Most striking has been the release of the 1991 coup plotters, and the amnesty of those responsible for the violence of October 1993. On March 23, 1995, Boris Yeltsin signed a presidential order aimed at coordinating the work of all government organs in the struggle against fascism and political extremism, and simultaneously instructed the Russian Academy of Sciences to come up with a working definition of fascism; both initiatives have proven ineffective. For an excellent overview of the legislative, judicial, and broader political problems of the struggle against extremism, see the introductory essay in Verkhovskii, Papp, and Pribylovskii, *Politicheskii ekstremizm v Rossii,* pp. 7–68.

27. A characteristic attempt to counter the democratic attacks on the right as a fascist force was undertaken by Sergey Baburin. On May 4, 1995, Baburin and a group of "concerned citizens" announced the formation of their own Anti-fascist Patriotic Center with the aim of saving Russia from the threat of fascism, which was defined by Baburin as "a form of international Russophobia." Accordingly, Baburin continued his definitional exercise: Fascists are all those who oppress Russians and are "carrying out a genocide of the Russian people," including the ruling authorities, a number of democratic organizations, and certain media outlets. See the bulletin *Politicheskii ekstremizm v Rossii* (Moscow: Fond "Grazhdanskoe obshchestvo," 1995), no. 1, pp. 1–2.

28. The minimal historical borders of Russia, from the standpoint of a nonimperial Russian nationalist, were outlined clearly by Aleksandr Solzhenitsyn in his pamphlet *Kak nam obustroit' Rossiiu* (Leningrad: Sovetskii pisatel', 1990), translated as *Rebuilding Russia* (New York: Farrar, Straus and Giroux, 1991).

29. *Sankt-Peterburgskie vedomosti,* September 7, 1991. For the history of the formation of Baburin's Rossiiskii Obshchenarodnyi Soiuz and its programmatic documents, see *Za velikuiu, edinuiu Rossiiu: Istoriia ROS v dokumentakh* (Moscow: Novator, 1995).

30. Eduard Limonov, *Literaturnaia gazeta,* October 16, 1991; Mikhail Antonov, *Literaturnaia Rossiia,* October 10, 1991.

31. *Den'*, no. 23, November 17–23, 1991.

32. *Den'*, no. 10, March 8–14, 1992.

33. Anpilov organized his first rally on November 7, 1991, the day of the October revolution, and subsequent ones in December 1991 and in January, February, and May–June 1992. For Anpilov's early goals, see the interview with him in *Den'*, no. 6, February 9–15, 1992.

34. See *Izvestiia,* February 24, 1992, for a good description of the violent rally. For a eulogy of Anpilov as the leader of the Moscow proletariat, see the brochure *Viktor Anpilov* (Moscow: Paleia, 1992).

35. "Krovavoe voskresen'e," *Den'*, no. 9, March 1–7, 1992.

36. Colonel Viktor Alksnis was the leader of the Soiuz group of deputies in the USSR Congress of People's Deputies and a key advocate of the introduction of a state of emergency in late 1990 and 1991. Sazhi Umalatova was notorious for having proposed that Gorbachev resign at the Fourth USSR Congress of People's Deputies. She was also instrumental in organizing the Sixth Extraordinary Congress of People's Deputies on the eve of the March 17 rally, attended by deputies who refused to accept the Belovezh agreements. See the pamphlets *Zapreshchenyi s"ezd* and *Sazhi Umalatova* (Moscow: Paleia, 1992).

37. *Sovetskaia Rossiia,* March 19 and 21, 1992; *Literaturnaia Rossiia,* March 20, 1992; *Den'*, no. 12, March 22–28, 1992.

38. *Sovetskaia Rossiia,* February 29, 1992; *Den'*, no. 9, March 1–7, 1992. The letter was signed by virtually the entire elite of the patriotic and neocommunist camps.

39. "Deklaratsiia o sozdanii ob"edinennoi oppozitsii," *Den'*, March 15–21, 1992.

40. For more on Aleksandr Sterligov, see Vladimir Pribylovskii, *Vozhdi,* pp. 99–102. His own views are summarized in Aleksandr Sterligov, *Opal'nyi general svidetel'stvuet* (Moscow: Paleia, 1992), and in the newspaper *Russkii Sobor,* which he launched in early 1993.

41. "Materialy uchreditel'nogo s"ezda Russkogo Natsional'nogo Sobora" (unpublished document, Nizhnii Novgorod, February, 1992).

42. Ibid.

43. "Osnovnye neotlozhnye deistviia Russkogo Natsional'nogo Sobora," in Ibid.

44. "Preobrazhenie Rossii: Programma deistviia Russkogo Natsional'nogo Sobora po spaseniiu otechestva" (unpublished document, Moscow, June 1992).

45. Ilia Konstantinov was a former leader of the Leningrad Popular Front; Viktor Aksyuchits was the head of the small Russian Christian Democratic Movement; Mikhail Astafiev was the leader of the equally small Constitutional-Democratic party.

46. Rutskoy's dissent from the government first became observable in late fall 1991, when he distanced himself from the economic reform program proposed by the Gaidar government. By early 1992, Rutskoy was sharply attacking the imminent "Americanization" of Russia in an article titled "Prichastie u MekDonaldsa" (*Izvestiia,* February 1, 1992).

47. Rutskoy's speech as well as the programmatic statements of "civic and patriotic forces" can be found in *Obozrevatel'*, no. 2-3, February 1992.

48. Extreme rightists, however, remained unhappy with Rutskoy's wavering between Yeltsin and the opposition. See Vladislav Shurygin, "Vtoroe litso," *Den'*, no. 29, July 19–25, 1992.

49. For more on the meeting of various branches of the opposition, see *Den'*, no. 26, June 28–July 4, 1992.

50. For the explicit defense of the constitutional struggle against Yeltsin's regime, see "My—russkoe soprotivlenie," *Den'*, no. 39, September 27–October 3, 1992. For more on

the political council and the aims of the united opposition, see "Radi spaseniia Rossii," *Sovetskaia Rossiia*, September 19 and 22, 1992.

51. *Sovetskaia Rossiia*, October 27, 1992; "Vestnik FNS," *Nasha Rossiia*, no. 21, 1992; *Den'*, no. 41, October 11–17, 1992.

52. *Sovetskaia Rossiia*, October 17, 1992.

53. *Sovetskaia Rossiia*, November 19, 1992.

54. For a good analysis of the FNS, see L. I. Dadiani, *O popytkakh sozdaniia v Rossii levo-pravogo bloka oppozitsionnykh sil, 1989–1996* (Moscow: Institut sotsiologii RAN, 1997). The most important leadership conflict involved the struggle between Aleksandr Sterligov and Gennadii Zyuganov, which ended in Sterligov's removal from the leadership of the FNS.

55. Stanislav Terekhov founded the Union of Officers in December 1991. His organization took active part in most mass protests of the united opposition, as well as the war in Trans-Dniestria. By spring 1993, Terekhov was a member of the political council of the FNS and one of its main organizers in Moscow. For Terekhov's worldview, see his speech to the officers, "Idet tret'ia mirovaia voina," *Sovetskaia Rossiia*, June 23, 1993.

56. According to press reports, more than 400 policemen were injured in the fighting, 21 of them critically. See *Moscow News*, May 9, 1993. For reactions from the "left-right" on this "democratic provocation," see *Sovetskaia Rossiia*, May 4 and May 6, 1993.

57. *Narodnaia pravda*, no. 19, May 1993.

58. Rutskoy's collected speeches and articles from the period can be found in *Neizvestnyi Rutskoi: Politicheskii portret* (Moscow: Obozrevatel', 1994). For his attacks on corruption, see pp. 43–97, 209–237; for his reflections on the Russian idea, see pp. 275–305. For his mockery of the democrats, see "Ia—shovinist," pp. 283–284. Rutskoy's full conversion to nationalism occurred in the aftermath of the October events (see Aleksandr Rutskoy, *Obretenie very* [Moscow, 1995]).

59. Khasbulatov's speeches can be found in *El'tsin—Khasbulatov: Edinstvo, kompromiss, bor'ba* (Moscow: Terra, 1994). For his commentary on Russia as a source of raw materials for the West, see his speech from July 28, 1993 (in Ibid., pp. 465–467). For his interview in *Den'*, see no. 35 (September 5–11, 1993). Prokhanov's interview with Zorkin can be found in *Den'*, no. 30 (August 1–7, 1993).

60. For a general collection of documents on the October events, see *Moskva: Osen'-93: Khronika protivostoianiia*, 2d ed. (Moscow: Respublika, 1995). For Terekhov's unsuccessful attempt to take over the Unified Command of the Forces on the night of September 23, see *Izvestiia*, September 28 and 29, 1993. Terekhov's own report on the events is in *Sovetskaia Rossiia*, March 29, 1994. A good sense of the mentality of the defenders can be gathered from B. Belenkin and Elena Strukhova, *Listovki Belogo doma: Moskovskie letuchie izdaniia, 22 sentiabria–4 oktiabria 1993* (Moscow: Logos, 1993). See also the first issue of the "banned" *Den'*, October 1–7, 1993.

61. Rutskoy's version of events is presented in his *Krovavaia osen': Dnevnik sobytii 21 sentiabria–4 oktiabria 1993 goda* (Moscow, 1995).

62. General Albert Makashov of the Ural-Volga Military District emerged as one of the most outspoken opponents of Gorbachev's perestroika in 1990. For his vicious attack on the democrats at the founding congress of the CP RSFSR, see *Uchreditel'nyi s"ezd Kommunisticheskoi partii RSFSR: Stenograficheskii otchet* (Moscow: Politizdat, 1991), vol. 1, pp. 120–122. A year later, he unsuccessfully ran for the Russian presidency, garnering only 3.74 percent of the vote. His extremism found new venues in 1992–1993, when he participated in the war in Transdniestria, joined several oppositional organizations, and made an ap-

pearance at many street protests. The culmination of his activity was the storming of the Russian Central Television station in Moscow, Ostankino, on October 3, 1993. After this attack failed, he took part in the defense of the White House (the Russian parliamentary building). Miraculously, he was later amnestied and released, and was even elected a deputy to the Duma on the KPRF ticket in 1995. For a brief biography of Makashov, see Verkhovskii, Papp, and Pribylovskii, *Politicheskii ekstremizm v Rossii*, pp. 267–270.

63. During their two-week siege of Ostankino in June 1992 (which ended with the intervention of government forces), the activists of Anpilov's Trudovaia Rossiia routinely used this epithet in reference to Russian Central Television. The epithet is an obvious anti-Semitic play on the Russian word for "television" *(televidenie)*. Makashov's attempt to forcibly regain the mass media "for the Russian people" occurred on the night of October 3. For a more detailed account of these events, see *Moskva: Osen'-93*, pp. 383–415.

64. Zhirinovsky, *Poslednii brosok na iug*, p. 6.

65. Ibid., pp. 5–64.

66. Liah Greenfeld, *Nationalism: Five Roads to Modernity* (Cambridge: Harvard University Press, 1992).

67. Zhirinovsky addresses the theme of his Jewish background in the first few pages of *Poslednii brosok*, where he tries to demonstrate his "pure Russian roots." For a discussion of the influence of this personal background on Zhirinovsky's politics, see Vladimir Solovyov and Elena Klepikova, *Zhirinovsky: Russian Fascism and the Making of a Dictator* (Reading, Pa.: Addison-Wesley, 1995), pp. 23–52. For more on his early political career, see the collection of documents *Neizvestnyi Zhirinovskii* (Moscow: Panorama, April 1995).

68. For a hagiographic, albeit interesting description of Zhirinovsky's 1991 campaign, see I. S. Kulikova and S. N. Plekhanov, *Fenomen Zhirinovskogo* (Moscow: Kontrolling, 1992).

69. Zhirinovsky, *Poslednii vagon na sever*, pp. 28–29.

70. A good sense of these two critical years of his activity can be gathered from Limonov, *Limonov protiv Zhirinovskogo*, and his official biography by Sergei Plekhanov, *Zhirinovsky: Kto on?* (Moscow: Evraziia-Nord, 1994).

71. Chief among these rival parties was Baburin's ROS, which had not collected the required number of signatures. Some signatures mysteriously disappeared when the special police, allegedly searching for the fascist Aleksandr Barkashev in the aftermath of the October showdown, paid a visit to the headquarters of Baburin's party. For the ROS point of view, see *Za edinuiu, velikuiu Rossiiu*, pp. 224–231. Baburin nevertheless won a seat in a single-member district and continued to figure prominently in the Duma.

72. Both the demagogic and nationalist components of Zhirinovsky's appeal are strongly stressed in Solovyov and Klepikova, *Zhirinovsky*. A somewhat sensationalist, although fairly representative selection of Zhirinovsky's outrageous statements is Graham Frazer and George Lancels, *Absolute Zhirinovsky* (Harmondsworth, U.K.: Penguin, 1994).

73. Mathew Wyman, Bill Miller, Stephen White, and Paul Heywood, "Parties and Voters in the Elections," in Peter Lentini, ed., *Elections and the Political Order in Russia* (Budapest: Central European University, 1995), pp. 124–142.

74. Stephen White, Richard Rose, and Ian McAllister, *How Russia Votes* (Chatham, New Jersey: Chatham House, 1997), especially pp. 141–153.

75. "Eto my—tret'ia politicheskaia sila," *Krasnoiarskaia gazeta*, April 14, 1992.

76. Wyman et al., "Parties and Voters in the Elections," p. 128.

77. For the list of LDPR candidates as well as the party slogans and program, see *Iuridicheskaia gazeta*, no. 40-41, 1993.

78. White, Rose, and McAllister, *How Russia Votes*, p. 203.

79. See Yitzhak Brudny, "In Pursuit of the Russian Presidency: Why and How Yeltsin Won the 1996 Presidential Election," *Communist and Post-Communist Studies*, vol. 30, no. 3, 1997, pp. 255–275. In fact, as Brudny demonstrates, Zhirinovsky's voters were more likely to vote for Zyuganov than for Yeltsin, although they did vote for both. More importantly, Zyuganov was still unable to win the overall nationalist vote.

80. V. V. Zhirinovsky, *Politicheskaia klassika* (Moscow, 1996), pp. 61–62; *LDPR: Ideologiia i politika* (Moscow, 1995), pp. 3–21.

81. Vladimir Zhirinovsky, *Poslednii udar po Rossii*; *Posledniaia bitva Rossii* (Moscow, 1996); *My vozrodim Velikuiu Rossiiu* (Moscow: LDPR, 1997); *Esli ne my, to kto?* (Moscow: LDPR, 1998).

82. Speech to the Duma, June 21, 1995, under the title "My dolzhnyi imet' ob"edinennuiu oppozitsiiu," *Pravda Zhirinovskogo*, no. 11, 1995.

83. Stephen Hanson, "Ideology, Uncertainty, and the Rise of Anti-System Parties in Post-Communist Russia," in John Löwenhardt, ed., *Party Politics in Post-Communist Russia* (London and Portland, Ore.: Frank Cass, 1998), pp. 98–128.

84. *Limonov protiv Zhirinovskogo*, pp. 126–127.

85. I. M. Kliamkin and V. V. Lapkin, "Russkii vopros v Rossii," *Polis*, no. 5, 1995, pp. 78–95. See table 3, p. 84.

86. See, for example, Shamil' Sultanov, "Nashie mertvye s nami v stroiu," *My i vremia*, no. 48, November 1, 1993; Ivan Ivanov [pseudonym], "Oni srazhalis' za rodinu: Zapiski razvedchika," *Zavtra*, nos. 2 and 3, 1993.

87. For more on the development of Barkashov's movement, see V. Likhachev and V. Pribylovskii, *Russkoe Natsional'noe Edinstvo* (Moscow: Panorama, April 1997).

88. For examples of the initially positive reporting on Barkashov in the communist camp, see *Sovetskaia Rossiia*, January 4, February 12, March 5, 1994. For a change in tune, see the article "Order na edinstvo," *Sovetskaia Rossiia*, October 25, 1994. For Barkashov's own explanation of the October events, see *Zavtra*, no. 2, December 1993, and no. 12, March 1994; and Aleksandr Barkashov, "Ob uchastii dvizheniia Russkoe Natsional'noe Edinstvo v sobytiiakh 21 sentiabria–4 oktiabria 1993 goda," *Russkii Vostok*, no. 17, 1993.

89. See his interview with Prokhanov under the title "Rossiia—imperiia dukha," *Zavtra*, no. 45, November 1998.

90. For Barkashov's ideology and a description of the structure of his movement, see his brochure *Azbuka russkogo natsionalista* (Moscow, 1994).

91. "Virtual'nye voiny s real'nym natsizmom," *Itogi*, February 9, 1999.

92. See Stephen D. Shenfield, "The Weimar-Russia Comparison: Reflections on Hanson and Kopstein," *Post-Soviet Affairs*, vol. 14, no. 4, pp. 355–368.

93. "Soglasie vo imia Rossii: Obrashchenie k grazhdanam RF levotsentristskoi oppozitsii," *Sovetskaia Rossiia*, March 19, 1994; *Zavtra*, no. 20, May 1994.

94. For a brief history of Soglasie, see Dadiani, *O popytkakh sozdaniia v Rossii levopravogo bloka oppozitsionnykh sil*, pp. 97–110.

95. See Sergei Baburin, "Ia idu v boi," *Zavtra*, no. 9, March 1998, an interview in which he announced his intention to seek a nomination for the Russian presidency.

96. In October 1998, Makashov openly accused the "kikes" of destroying Russia by "sucking the blood of indigenous peoples," destroying their "industry, agriculture, the army, fleet, and strategic nuclear forces." His status as a Duma deputy added weight to his comments, discrediting the KPRF leadership. For the integral text, see Al'bert Makashov, "K rostovshchikam Rossii," *Zavtra*, no. 42, 1998. For right-wing eulogies and the "Stalin medal"

awarded to him by Prokhanov, see *Zavtra*, no. 44, November 1998; and no. 52, December 1998. For the democratic point of view, see *Itogi*, November 17 and December 22, 1998.

97. Interview with Aleksandr Prokhanov under the title "Partiia naroda," *Den'*, January 10–16, 1993.

98. On the night of October 1, Zyuganov volunteered to appear on Russian television, speaking out against public violence and the parties and movements that advocated it (Urban and Solovei, *Russia's Communists at the Crossroads*, pp. 89–90).

99. For Zyuganov's critique of extremism, see *Sovetskaia Rossiia*, June 23, 1994.

100. The figures are from White, Rose, and McAllister, *How Russia Votes*, p. 123.

101. Gennadii Zyuganov, *Drama vlasti* (Moscow: Paleia, 1993); idem, *Derzhava* (Moscow: Informpechat', 1994); idem, *Za gorizontom* (Moscow: Informpechat', 1995); idem, *Rossiia i sovremennyi mir* (Moscow: Obozrevatel', 1995). For his articles and interviews from this period, see *Veriu v Rossiiu* (Voronezh, 1995) and *G. A. Ziuganov o G. A. Ziuganove* (Perm, 1995).

102. For a more detailed analysis of Zyuganov the ideologist, see Veljko Vujačić, "Gennadii Ziuganov and the Third Road"; and Urban and Solovei, *Russia's Communists at the Crossroads*, pp. 97–121.

103. For the Kuptsov line, see Urban and Solovei, *Russia's Communists at the Crossroads*, pp. 50–51.

104. M. R. Kholmskaia, *Kommunisty Rossii: Fakty, idei, tendentsii* (Moscow, 1998), p. 40.

105. "Ot krizisa—k ustoichivomu razvitiiu, narodovlastiiu, i sotsializmu," *Sovetskaia Rossiia*, May 21, 1994.

106. *Sovetskaia Rossiia*, April 28, 1994.

107. "Za delo naroda, vo imia otechestva," *Sovetskaia Rossiia*, April 26, 1994.

108. "Programma KPRF," *Sovetskaia Rossiia*, February 2, 1995.

109. "Za nashu Sovetskuiu rodinu," *Pravda Rossii*, September 7, 1995; "Sindrom Zhirinovskogo," *Sovetskaia Rossiia*, September 30, 1995.

110. Interview in *Sovetskaia Rossiia*, October 24, 1995.

111. *Sovetskaia Rossiia*, December 16, 1995.

112. White, Rose, and McAllister, *How Russia Votes*, pp. 224–225.

113. Brudny, "In Pursuit of the Russian Presidency," pp. 264–270; Gennadii Zyuganov, "Ispytanie doveriem," *Sovetskaia Rossiia*, January 16, 1996.

114. *Sovetskaia Rossiia*, February 17, 1996.

115. *Rossiia, Rodina, Narod: Predvybornaia platforma kandidata na dolzhnost' Prezidenta Rossiiskoi federatsii Ziuganova Gennadiia Andreevicha* (Moscow, March 1996). Also in *Sovetskaia Rossiia*, March 19, 1996.

116. Aleksandr Prokhanov, "Nosha russkoi sud'by," *Sovetskaia Rossiia*, September 21, 1995.

117. For more on Podberezkin, see the interview with him in *Sovetskaia Rossiia*, July 22, 1995.

118. *Chto takoe dukhovnoe nasledie i pochemu ono podderzhivaet na prezidentskikh vyborakh G. A. Ziuganova* (Moscow: Obozrevatel', 1996), pp. 47–87.

119. "Ot razrusheniia k sozidaniiu," *Sovetskaia Rossiia*, May 28, 1996; "Eto mozhno sdelat' segodnia," *Sovetskaia Rossiia*, June 6, 1996.

120. "Gennadii Ziuganov—prezident molodezhi," *Sovetskaia Rossiia*, June 8, 1996. For the comical aspect, see "Molodezh' za Ziuganova," *Ogonek*, no. 16, April 1996.

121. *Sovetskaia Rossiia*, June 11, 1996. For the endorsement of nationalists, see *Zavtra*, nos. 19, 22, May 1996; *Al's-Kods*, no. 1 68), June 1996; *Russkaia gazeta*, no. 5, 1996; *Russkie vedomosti*, no. 25, 1996; *Rodnye prostory*, no. 2 (29), 1996; and undoubtedly many others of patriotic tendency. The more traditionalist *Russkii vestnik* (nos. 18-20, 1996), however, endorsed Lebed.

122. See Brudny, "In Pursuit of the Russian Presidency," pp. 264–273.

123. See A. N. Tarasov, G. Iu. Cherkasova, and T. V. Shavshukova, *Levye v Rossii: Ot umerennykh do ekstremistov* (Moscow: Institut eksperimental'noi sotsiologii, 1997), p. 163.

124. See *Sovetskaia Rossiia*, August 10, 1996, for the NPSR program and Nikolai Ryzhkov's endorsement of "Russian patriotism + social justice" as the guiding principle of the new coalition.

125. "Litsom k narodnym boliam," *Sovetskaia Rossiia*, August 8, 1996.

126. Tarasov, Cherkasova, and Shavshukova, *Levye v Rossii*, p. 163.

127. Ibid., pp. 171–172.

128. Ibid., pp. 166–167.

129. Steven L. Solnick, "Gubernatorial Elections in Russia: 1996–1997," *Post-Soviet Affairs*, vol. 14, no. 1, 1998, pp. 48–80.

130. Kholmskaia, *Kommunisty Rossii*, p. 54.

131. G. A. Zyuganov, "Rossiia budet velikoi i sotsialisticheskoi," *Sovetskaia Rossiia*, April 22, 1997.

132. Interview with Aleksandr Prokhanov in *Sovetskaia Rossiia*, May 12, 1998.

133. For reactions from the communist grass roots, see *Sovetskaia Rossiia*, May 21, 1998.

134. "Manifest NPSR," *Sovetskaia Rossiia*, November 24, 1998.

135. Richard Sakwa, "Left or Right? The CPRF and the Problem of Democratic Consolidation in Russia," in John Löwenhardt, ed., *Party Politics in Post-Communist Russia*, pp. 128–159.

136. Michael McFaul, *Russia's 1996 Presidential Election: The End of Polarized Politics* (Stanford: Hoover Institution Press, 1997).

137. Karl Deutsch, *Nationalism and Social Communication* (Cambridge, Mass.: MIT Press, 1966), pp. 113–114.

14

Dagestan and the Stability of Instability in the North Caucasus

Edward W. Walker

University of California, Berkeley

I n the first week of August 1999, some 1,000 to 2,000 armed militants entered the Republic of Dagestan from the breakaway Russian region of Chechnya (Ichkeria) to "liberate" Dagestan from "Russian occupation." Several days later, a spokesman for the militants in Grozny (Dzhokhar), the Chechen capital, announced the establishment of an "independent Islamic Dagestan." Apparently comprised of a mix of Chechens, Dagestanis, and Islamic militants from Central Asia, the Middle East, and possibly elsewhere, the Chechen-based insurgents were commanded by the radical Chechen "field commander" Shamil Basayev and his ally, a mysterious Jordanian or Saudi citizen of unknown ethnic background, who goes by the name Khattab.[1] A year earlier, Basayev had been instrumental in forming the political party Congress of Peoples of Chechnya and Dagestan (CPCD), the main platform of which was the unification of Chechnya and Dagestan in an independent Islamic state. He and his allies apparently believed that the insurgents would be welcomed by the predominantly Avar population in the Tsumadin and Botlikh *raions* (districts) of Dagestan, where the initial incursion took place.[2] Having established a base in western Dagestan, their apparent intent was to force the withdrawal of Russian troops from the rest of the republic and overthrow the republic's pro-Moscow elite.

The August incursion seemed to confirm Moscow's worst fears about instability in the North Caucasus. Dagestan, Moscow commentators had long argued, was the key to Russia's presence in the region and the most likely target of Chechen irredentist aspirations. Territorially the largest republic in the North Caucasus (50,370 sq km, roughly the size of West Virginia), it is also the largest in population (an estimated 2.1 million in 1996). The highly mountainous republic (*Dagestan* is a Turkic word meaning "land of mountains") lies at the eastern edge of the Caucasus range, on the Caspian Sea. For millennia, Dagestan's narrow littoral plain has been the principal transportation route between the Eurasian steppes, which border it to the north, and the Transcaucasus and fertile, warmer lands in the south.[3] The only railroad connecting Russia to the South Caucasus today passes through Dagestan.[4] Even more importantly, at least in the minds of Moscow officials, is the oil pipeline from Azerbaijan that passes through Dagestan on its way to the Russian Black Sea port of Novorossiisk. Because the existing pipeline has limited capacity, the Russian government has pressed the Azerbaijan government and Western oil companies to construct a "main export pipeline" along the same route, to carry much larger flows of oil when Caspian oil production increases over the next five to ten years.[5]

Accordingly, Dagestan is considered of major strategic importance in Moscow. It is also considered highly unstable. Even before the events of August 1999, federal officials were obsessed with a perceived threat from "Wahhabism," or fundamentalist and politicized Islam in general, in the republic. These concerns were heightened when three highlander villages in central Dagestan, some thirty kilometers southwest of Makhachkala, announced in August 1998 the formation of an independent "Islamic territory."[6] Dagestan is also the most ethnically diverse of all the former Soviet autonomous republics, and many of its 34 officially recognized "nationalities" have territorial and other grievances against others. And with the exception of war-torn Chechnya and perhaps Ingushetia, Dagestan is the poorest of Russia's "subjects of the federation," and it has a reputation for widespread corruption and violent crime.[7]

There have been frequent reminders of the potential for large-scale violence in the republic, including repeated kidnappings, assassinations, and terrorist bombings. The region first captured world attention in early 1996, when, in the midst of the war in Chechnya, Chechen militants took over a hospital in the town of Kizlyar, leading to the deaths of scores of Dagestani civilians. In early 1998, armed supporters of an opposition leader seized and vandalized the main government building in Makhachkala during a confrontation with the republic's militia. Earlier that year, sixty people had been killed by a bomb that destroyed an entire apartment building; and another eighteen people were killed by a bomb in Makhachkala in September 1998. There have reportedly been ten attempts on the life of the second most influential politician in the republic, the mayor of Makhachkala, Said Amirov. In August 1998, the mufti of Dagestan, Said Muhammed-Hadji Abubakarov, was assassinated by a remote-controlled bomb that also killed his brother and driver. Attacks on federal and republic troops in Dagestan also have been common: In July 1997, a bomb blast in the town of Khasavyurt killed nine policemen and wounded six. A Russian army base in Buinaksk was attacked in December 1997, allegedly by a group of between 100 and 120 Wahhabi militants. Clashes along the border with Chechen-based militants increased over the course of 1999, to the point where early that summer, for the first time since the end of the 1994–1996 war, Russian forces began carrying out retaliatory strikes against alleged terrorist bases inside Chechen territory.

Nevertheless, Dagestan has managed to avoid all-out anarchy and civil war. To the surprise of Basayev and his allies, the August 1999 insurgents were met by overwhelming popular hostility; even Dagestan's ethnic Chechens publicly expressed their opposition.[8] Local Dagestanis demanded that government authorities allow them to form volunteer brigades to defend their homes against the invaders. As a result, the joint federal and Dagestani operation to resist the incursion was supported by the great majority of the Russian public. For the first time since World War II, Russians could credibly claim that their military was fighting on the side of "the people."

After three weeks of fighting, federal forces, Dagestani interior ministry troops, and local self-defense units managed to force the guerrillas to withdraw to Chechnya. Federal forces followed up by launching air strikes against the Chechen towns of Vedeno and Urus Martan, where the militants were allegedly regrouping, which prompted Basayev to announce that his fighters "reserved the right to retaliate throughout Russia."[9] Moscow ignored the threat and went on to attack the "Wahhabi" villages in central Dagestan, using artillery and air strikes to empty the villages of both civilians and armed oppositionists. As this operation was coming to an end, some 1,000 to 2,000 militants from Chechnya entered Dagestan's Kazbek and Novolaksky *raions*, where the majority of Dagestan's Chechen-Akkins reside.[10] Again, however, the militants received little local support, with Russian and Dagestani forces driving them back into Chechnya by mid-September. Tragically, after a series of terrorist bombings in the Dagestani city of Buinaksk, in Moscow, and in Volgodonsk, Rostov oblast (in southern Russia) killed almost 300 Russian citizens, the escalating violence turned into a full-scale war. With federal officials blaming "terrorists" and "bandits" based in Chechnya for the bombings, the public mood in Russia changed from righteous indignation at the "Chechen invasion" of Dagestan to fear and fury. The Russian government, which had faced widespread popular opposition to the war in Chechnya from 1994 to 1996, was under considerable pressure this time to resolve the "Chechen problem" decisively. The result was another invasion of Chechnya by Russian forces, which began in late September 1999.

The fighting in the republic in August and September 1999 and the subsequent renewal of war in Chechnya contributed to a further deterioration of social conditions in Dagestan. Authorities in the republic had to cope with another flood of refugees, this time from western and central Dagestan as well as from Chechnya. The fighting also aggravated inter-nationality relations in the republic, above all because of increased hostility toward local Chechens from many of Dagestan's other national minorities. Nevertheless, the republic's "stable instability" has survived: There has been no general revolt against Moscow or Makhachkala, and the current Dagestani regime still retains the support of a majority of its citizens.

My objective in this chapter is to explain why, despite all the sources of instability, large-scale and sustained violence has not come to Dagestan, and to assess whether Dagestan's stable instability will last.[11] My focus on Dagestan is predicated on the conviction that Moscow's concerns about the republic are well founded. Excluding Chechnya, Dagestan is indeed the region of Russia where the risk of large-scale political violence is greatest. It is also the key to Moscow's position in the North Caucasus. If intercommunal violence in this strategic republic is avoided, and if Dagestan's political elite remains reasonably loyal to Moscow, then organized resistance in Chechnya will almost certainly be contained within Chechnya's traditional borders, making another decisive military victory by the Chechens unlikely. If so, Moscow may eventually work out a mutually acceptable arrangement on Chechnya's legal status with some kind of authoritative Chechen government. If Dagestan implodes, however, Moscow's military and political objectives in Chechnya will become even more difficult to attain, and the generalized economic and humanitarian crisis in the North Caucasus will become even more intractable.

This chapter is organized as follows: I first assess the *general risk* of large-scale, sustained political violence by focusing on broad structural factors, stressing in particular socioeconomic considerations, the nature of political cleavages in the republic, and regime type (consociationalism) and elite incentives. I then identify the *issues* that are the most likely to provoke large-scale sustained violence if it does break out, as well as the likely *participants,* by focusing on concrete political grievances and assessing whether those grievances are tractable or likely to intensify. Finally, I identify some *early warning indicators and triggers* of violence that are most likely to apply in the Dagestan case.[12] I conclude that although Dagestan will remain vulnerable to episodic acts of political violence, the structure of the republic's political cleavages makes it unlikely that there will be any general mobilization of the Dagestani population in the form of internal war between Dagestanis, a war of national liberation against Moscow, or an Islamic holy war led by forces based in Chechnya.

Assessing Risks: Structural and Background Factors

The Economy

Dagestan (after postwar Chechnya and Ingushetia) is the Russian Federation's poorest republic. In 1996, per capita income there was one-third the average for Russia as a whole. Dagestan had the highest ratio of rural to urban population of all of Russia's regions and republics: In 1989, only 44.0 percent of its population was urbanized.[13] Its highland peoples were even more rural—74.6 percent of Avars, 76.8 percent of Dargins, and 83.3 of Lezgins.[14] Like other regions of Russia, Dagestan has suffered from the inevitable pain of transition from central planning to a market economy; but its peak-to-trough economic decline has been particularly acute, in part because the republic's industry was heavily weighted toward military production. Virtually no large or medium-sized industrial enterprises are operational in the republic today.[15] Real unemployment is estimated at over 30 percent, and youth unemployment, at 80 percent. The economy has also been hurt by the out-migration of Slavs, particularly Russians, who had been overrepresented in management and other skilled positions. In addition, the republic's external economic links were interrupted during the war in Chechnya by the temporary closure of its border with Azerbaijan and by the interruption of railroad service, telephone links, and on occasion even automobile traffic to the north.

Dagestan's economic prospects are poor. Its only significant economic advantages are its access to maritime trade on the Caspian; its rich fisheries (particularly in sturgeon); its location as a transit corridor for trade between Russia and the South Caucasus; and the pipeline bringing oil from Baku to the Russian port of Novorossiisk.[16] However, its fisheries have been depleted by widespread poaching and industrial pollution, to the point where environmentalists are concerned about the viability of the Caspian sturgeon population and its derivative caviar industry; and its role as a transportation link has been undermined by the turmoil in Chechnya. The war in Chechnya, as well as predictions of an impending breakdown of public order, will continue to deter foreign investment—for which there is relatively little incentive in any case, given that the republic has no significant hydrocarbon reserves or other potentially lucrative natural resources. Finally, and perhaps most importantly in the long run, Dagestan is very distant from international markets.

As is the case elsewhere in the Russian Federation, agriculture here is handicapped by inadequate investment in equipment and fertilization, poor storage and processing capacity, and an inferior distribution system. More fundamentally, the climate and pervasive land scarcity make a substantial revival of agricultural production unlikely. Land hunger in the republic has been aggravated by the high natural rate of population growth, as the republic's population almost doubled between 1959 and 1989. The forests and the small terraces laboriously constructed in the past for growing fruits, vegetables, and grain were destroyed long ago, during tsarist military campaigns against the highlanders; and Soviet-era collectivization again disrupted traditional highlander agriculture, driving many farmers to migrate to towns and cities in search of another livelihood.

Dagestan's economic difficulties have conflicting implications for political violence in the republic. On the one hand, the shrinking economic pie makes distributional conflicts more intense, aggravating housing shortages and raising the stakes of inter-group conflicts over land. Economic hardship also make it difficult for state authorities to appease aggrieved parties; and it contributes to the spread of organized crime, which tends to emerge in urban areas, along clan *(tukhum)* and lineage *(jin)* lines, thereby reinforcing inter-clan and in some cases inter-nationality enmity. On the other hand, Dagestan's poverty makes it highly dependent on financial support from Moscow: Some 80 percent of Dagestan's government budget is covered by subventions from the federal government.[17] As a result, separatists cannot credibly claim that the republic would be better off economically were it to become independent.

The Structure of Political Cleavages

Dagestan's extreme ethnic heterogeneity, and the impracticality of creating sep-arate administrative territories for each ethnic group, help account for the fact that it was one of the few autonomous areas in the USSR not to bear the name of one or two nationalities. Rather than "belonging" to a particular eponymous (titular) nationality, the republic was treated as a form of collective property that more or less "belonged" to the republic's ten major "indigenous" *(korennye)* nationalities: Avars, Aguls, Dargins, Kumyks, Laks, Lezgins, Nogais, Rutuls, Tabasarans, and Tsakhurs. According to the Soviet system of ethnic classification (which underwent frequent changes), however, an additional twenty-four na-tionalities resided in the republic in 1989, the year of the last Soviet census. Sev-eral of these were considered indigenous but had their own "homelands" else-where in the North Caucasus—most notably, the Chechens. The rest had external homelands outside the region, including Russians (9.2 percent, then the lowest figure for all autonomous republics and autonomous oblasts in the RS-FSR) and Azeris (4.2 percent). Finally, the republic is also home to numerous ethnolinguistic groups that were too small to receive recognition as "nationali-ties" by Soviet ethnographers but instead were treated as part of the dominant nationality in their region of residence.[18]

Linguistically, Dagestan's ethnic groups fall into three broad groups. The Northeast Caucasian language group (Nakh-Dagestani) forms one of three branches of the Paleocaucasian language family, which linguists consider among the oldest in the world (between 5,000 and 6,000 years old, in the case of Nakh-Dagestani).[19] The many Nakh-Dagestani languages are spoken mostly in the in-terior highlands and are completely unrelated to other languages in the republic, or indeed, anywhere else. Roughly two-thirds of Dagestan's citizens were mem-bers of Paleocaucasian ethnolinguistic groups in 1989. Most of the remaining one-third spoke either an Altaic-Turkic language (Kumyk, Nogai, Azeri) or a Slavic language (mostly Russian). There was also a small community of Jews who spoke Tat, an Indo-European language related to Persian that has its own literary tradition.

With the exception of several tiny ethnolinguistic groups facing linguistic as-similation, it does not appear that Dagestani nationality and subnationality iden-tities were weakening in the late Soviet period. Native language retention—a crit-ical indicator of the survival of minority cultures—remained high for Dagestan's major nationalities. Among Avars, Dargins, Kumyks, and Lezgins, it was above 98 percent in 1989, showing virtually no decline from 1959.[20] In addition, intermar-riage among nationalities within Dagestan was relatively infrequent, particularly between Slavs, Altaic peoples, and Paleocaucasians.[21]

Despite the extreme ethnic heterogeneity of the republic, there has been very limited nationality-based political mobilization there since 1991. Many other lines of cleavage are at least as salient as that of ethnicity. At the broadest level, residents of the republic in the Soviet period clearly had a measure of loyalty to the USSR, as suggested by the fact that Dagestan voted overwhelming for the preservation of the USSR in the Gorbachev-sponsored referendum in March 1991. While political identification with the more "Russian" Russian Federation today is much weaker, Dagestanis typically claim that their fellow citizens to some extent identify with Dagestan as a multinational political entity.

Below these "civic" orientations are at least three cultural clusters. First and largest is the cluster of peoples of highland origin (e.g., Avars and Dargins) who speak various Paleocaucasian languages referred to collectively as *Nakh-Dagestani*. Many of these groups have migrated over time and now live in low-land areas. Islam is an important part of their life, although it is a form of Islam that has been modified by traditional laws and practices. Political appeals rooted in highlander, North Caucasian, pan-Caucasian, or Islamic loyalties have had greater resonance among the highlanders than among other peoples of the re-public. The second-largest group is made up of lowland, Turkic-speaking, Altaic peoples—Kumyks, Azeris, and Nogais (18.7 percent of the population in 1989).[22] Typically referred to as "Tatars" by Russians before the Bolshevik revolution, the Kumyks, Azeris, and Nogais are culturally very different from Dagestan's high-landers, despite being traditionally Muslim. Except for the traditionally nomadic Nogais, they tend to be more urbanized and secularized; and rather than identi-fying strongly with other North Caucasian peoples, they are oriented more to-ward "fellow Turks" in Azerbaijan, Central Asia, and even Turkey, with their ex-plicitly secular regimes. Despite the fact that Kumyks have been present in the republic since at least the thirteenth century and were politically and culturally dominant prior to the October 1917 revolution, highlanders generally do not consider Kumyks, Nogais, and Azeris as having a claim to being true Dagestanis equal to that of the "indigenous" highlanders. Lastly, the republic's Slavs (9.2 per-cent of the total population in 1989) naturally have a Russian cultural orienta-tion.

Religious cleavages are also important. In 1989, some 90 percent of the popu-lation belonged to traditionally Muslim ethnic groups—a figure that has proba-bly grown as a result of the in-migration of Dagestan's non-Slavic diaspora and the out-migration of Slavs. Islam arrived in the republic between the seventh and eighth centuries but moved only gradually from the lowlands into the highland areas, spreading in the mid-eighteenth century into what is today Chechnya and then on to the central and western North Caucasus.[23] Most Dagestanis were tradi-tionally Sunni Muslims of the Shafi'i school.[24] Sufism was widely practiced, and the Naqshbandi and Qadirii Sufi brotherhoods (*wierds*) were particularly influ-ential, as in Chechnya. The Nogais, however, were traditionally Khanafi Sunnis,[25] and many Lezgins and some Dargins were Shia, as were most of the republic's Azeris. Russians and other Slavic minorities were typically Orthodox Christians. Lastly, there is a small population of Jews, including the "Mountain Jews"/Tats.[26]

The extent to which these religious traditions survived seventy years of Soviet official atheism and repression of religious beliefs and practices is difficult to as-sess. In the Soviet period, the urbanized and better-educated lowlanders were typically more Sovietized and more secular than the rural highlanders. Nevertheless, like Muslims elsewhere in the former Soviet Union, many Dagestanis adapted Islamic beliefs and practices to Soviet conditions. Clerics found ways to represent Islam as politically nonthreatening, and lay believers engaged in nonpoliticized practices of prayer and visiting of shrines.[27] Moreover, although most mosques were destroyed in the Soviet period, the Muslim Religious Board for the North Caucasus—one of four such institutions in the former Soviet Union—was located in the republic, which had been one of the Russian empire's centers of Islamic learning prior to the Bolshevik revolution. Although the North Caucasus Muslim Religious Board was penetrated and closely monitored by the Soviet political police, its location in the republic gave Islam a visible presence and institutional infrastructure that was absent in most other traditionally Muslim urban areas.

As the Soviet regime grew more tolerant of religion in the late 1980s, Dagestan experienced a dramatic Muslim revival that was arguably unmatched in the former Soviet Union and that is still in progress at present. At the beginning of 1999, there were an estimated 1,670 mosques in the republic (most villages now have their own mosques), 25 *medresses* (Islamic schools), and nine Islamic schools of higher learning in the republic. The number of Dagestanis making the *hadj* to Mecca each year is reportedly in the tens of thousands. The republic now is home to some 3,500 imams and mullahs, and more than 1,000 Dagestanis are enrolled in Islamic schools abroad.[28]

By most accounts, it is not religion but clan, lineage, and family that constitute the most important lines of political cleavage in the republic. Dagestan's many ethnic groups are variously organized. Clans (*tukhums*, or *teips* in the case of the Chechen-Akkins) typically consist of between sixty and eighty families related by blood. Male members are honor-bound to defend fellow clan members and avenge wrongs, including by killing. Many nationalities also have sub-clan or "lineage" affiliations (*jin* or *khel*), members of which are usually from a single family with an identifiable, if sometimes mythical, progenitor and a common family name. The *jamaats*, on the other hand, are town-based (hence, territorialized—unlike the *tukhums* or the Chechen *teips*) political communities with their own customary laws and leaders. *Jamaats*, or village councils of elders that regulate relations between clans and sub-clans, are the most immediate and visible authoritative body in the everyday lives of most highlanders as well as of many lowlanders (particularly recent migrants from the highlands). Usually a *jamaat's* jurisdiction is confined to a single large village or two to three smaller villages. (It is interesting to note that much of the political conflict taking place in the republic is between *jamaats* rather than nationalities.)[29] The *tukhums* likewise have their own elders for regulating intra-clan conflicts. The rules and norms governing intra- and inter-clan disputes are informed by traditional laws and practices (*adat*), to a certain extent by Islamic law (*sharia*), and when necessary, by civil (formerly Soviet, now Russian) law and the courts.

Lastly, there is a consciousness of difference between highlanders and lowlanders, between urban and rural residents—in 1989, 56 percent of the population lived in rural areas[30]—and even, on occasion, between classes (especially between educated people in the professional and managerial classes on the one hand, and less-educated unskilled labor and the rural dwellers on the other).

Dagestani society is thus characterized by a dense complex of cleavages, most of which are not coterminous—unlike those that divided Armenians from Azeris in Nagorno-Karabakh, for example. A few lines of cleavage are crosscutting, simultaneously incorporating different segments of the population: for example, that of citizenship in multinational Dagestan; class identity; urban identity; or the occasionally strong identity of being a Muslim.[31] But most are nested one within the other, like a Russian *matrioshka* doll—Muslim, highlander, nationality, sub-nationality, *jamaat,* clan, village, and family—with political loyalties intensifying as the unit of identification gets smaller. As a leading Dagestani sociologist explained:

> I am from (the village) of Akhty. . . . [Someone from] Akhty would never identify himself as a Lezgin. One could say the same thing about Avars and Dargins. The population of villages that have become known in connection with the recent standoff with Wahhabis—Kadar, Karamakhi, and Chabanmakhi—never identified themselves as Dargins. They belonged to the *jamaat* of Kadar and Karamakhi and Chabanmakhi. . . . Magomedali Magomedov, Chairman of the State Council, is a Dargin, but he can't do anything with the Dargin villages of Kadar, Karamakhi, and Chabanmakhi.[32]

This complex of nested cleavages, and the intensity of local loyalties, make it very difficult to mobilize entire nationalities in the republic, let alone all of Dagestani society. Even in the nineteenth century, the charismatic leader Imam Shamil, who used a combination of religious messianism and coercion to mobilize the highlanders, had to overcome *jamaat,* clan, and village loyalties as well as opposition from feudal principalities (*shamkalate*s and khanates) during his thirty-year struggle with the tsar's armies. Villages, *jamaat*s, and principalities would go over to the Russians, although many would later return to Shamil, depending upon the course of the war, the ability of tsarist generals to coerce or bribe local leaders, and the credibility of Shamil's threats against traitors.[33] Today, the political salience of these village and *jamaat* loyalties is reinforced by the remoteness of many village communities, the relative ease with which isolated highland villages can be defended, and poor communication and transportation infrastructures within the republic.

Consociationalism and Elite Incentives

A complicated and largely informal system of distributing privileges and official positions according to nationality evolved in Dagestan during the Soviet period. These practices, which drew on prerevolutionary political customs, were reinforced and legitimated by the Soviet system of ethnic federalism and by Soviet nationality policy. The use of informal ethnic quotas and balancing was more widespread in Dagestan than in any other region of the Soviet Union. Informal understandings arose about the ethnic distribution of appointments of mayors, procurators, chiefs of police, judges, and so on, at the levels of the republic, city/town, and district *(raion)*.[34]

These practices have become more explicit and formalized in the post-Soviet period. In 1992, 1993, and again in 1999, referendums on the establishment of a directly elected president were rejected in the republic, with the opposition asserting that a winner-take-all electoral system would render ethnic power-sharing impossible. Instead, Dagestan's first postcommunist constitution, adopted in 1994, established a collective presidency in the form of a State Council comprising representatives of fourteen nationalities—the ten "Dagestani" nationalities, plus Russians, Azeris, Chechen-Akkins, and Tats.[35] In an effort to encourage cross-nationality voting and to discourage the election of candidates with appeal to single ethnic constituencies, parliamentary deputies from the fourteen constitutionally recognized nationalities were to nominate three candidates from their own nationality as their representative on the State Council; the legislature as a whole would then vote on those three candidates. The assumption was that radical nationalists would be unable to win support from the assembly as a whole, even if they managed to win nomination by deputies from their own nationality. In addition, the chair of the State Council—in effect, the republic's president—could serve for only a single two-year term, after which he or she would be replaced by someone of a different nationality. The chair of the State Council and the prime minister were not allowed to be of the same nationality. In the wake of the constitution's ratification, Magomedali Magomedov, a Dargin who had chaired the republic's Supreme Soviet in the late perestroika era, became the first leader of the State Council in 1994 and the republic's de facto president. However, Dagestan's first prime minister (Abdurazak Mirzabekov) was a Kumyk, and the leader of parliament (Mukhu Aliev) was an Avar.

Measures were also adopted to ensure a balance among the nationalities in parliamentary seats. However, the drafters of the 1994 constitution rejected the Soviet model of ethnic federalism, in which the lines of electoral districts were drawn on the basis of national homogeneity, and each nationality coincided with a particular administrative territory. Instead, they redrew electoral district lines to divide national groupings among many districts, thus preventing political consolidation and mobilization on the basis of nationality. Deputies from certain districts were elected on the basis of a standard majoritarian system requiring a second round in the event that no candidate received a first-round majority. The remaining districts were designated as "multinational" and were permanently assigned to particular nationalities in order to ensure balanced ethnic representation. Only a representative of the designated nationality could run in those districts. Therefore, to win an election, candidates would have to win support from nationalities other than their own.[36] The allocation of particular districts to particular nationalities was accepted by the Dagestani electorate as a means of avoiding inter-nationality conflict, and the specific allocation arrangement was likewise regarded as reasonable.[37] The outcome of the first parliamentary elections under the new constitution, which took place in early 1995, was parliamentary representation that almost exactly matched the share of nationality groups in society. A second election was held in March 1999, with similar results.

As others have suggested, Dagestan's regime generally fits the model of "consociationalism" elaborated by Arend Lijphart to describe nonmajoritarian democracies with formal and informal rules for power-sharing among ethnic groups, such as those in the Netherlands, Belgium, and arguably, Switzerland.[38] However, despite the international community's embrace of consociationalism as a remedy for ethnic conflict, a growing body of social science literature suggests that consociationalism can be as much a *source* of interethnic conflict as a solution.[39] Consociationalism tends to politicize ethnicity, creating permanent political interests along ethnic lines of cleavage and prejudicing ethnic cleavages over others (such as those of class, religion, region, and gender). In addition, there is inevitably an arbitrary quality to what qualifies as a recognized group, which can lead to disaffection among nonrecognized groups. The sustainability of consociational regimes is also tied to a popular and elite perception that the allocation system it provides for is fair and effective—a perception that can dissipate very rapidly, particularly where the relative share of different ethnic groups in the total population changes.[40]

Many of the more negative consequences of consociationalism have been evident in Dagestan. Twenty of the thirty-four nationalities identified in the 1989 census are not represented in the State Council, and many of Dagestan's myriad ethnolinguistic groups are not constitutionally recognized. Critics have argued that the regime is an oligarchic and authoritarian arrangement that protects the position of incumbents while masquerading as a means to ensure harmony among nationalities.[41] Critics also have noted that ethnic balancing violates Russia's constitution and the supposedly democratic principle of "one-person, one vote." They advocate instead a directly elected president and a bicameral legislature.[42] Finally, as discussed in greater detail below, Magomedov has already managed to revise the constitution to allow him to remain head of the State Council, thereby undermining the republic's consociational bargain.

Informal Mechanisms for Conflict Resolution

Dagestan's formal state institutions are complemented by informal conflict resolution mechanisms employed by village, clan, and *jamaat* leaders, often with support from government officials, to maintain public order. By some reckonings, these informal mechanisms are rooted in the republic's mountainous topography and land scarcity and are thus typical of highlander cultures throughout the world.[43] Dagestan's highlanders traditionally grazed their sheep in highland pastures in the summer, moving to lowland areas during Dagestan's harsh winters.

As a result, they would frequently cross territory that belonged to other *jamaats* or nationalities, which would lead to occasional disputes. Procedures to resolve these disputes became deeply entrenched in local cultures.[44]

As noted earlier, each clan and *jamaat* has its own council of elders responsible for resolving internal and external disputes. Typically, crimes are punished by compensation to victims, with families, clans, or *jamaats* being obligated to pay on behalf of the guilty. If compensation is not forthcoming, then members of the victim's family are honor-bound to retaliate against the perpetrator and his family. There is also the well-known highlander tradition of the *kunak*, or "loyal friend/host," who is honor-bound to protect a friend or guest and revenge any wrongs. These "blood feud" traditions generally act as a powerful disincentive to violence and help ensure that compensation rulings by elders are complied with. In some cases, however, they have contributed to a prolonged sequence of retaliatory violence.

State Capacity: Elite Coherence and State Resources

Dagestan was the last autonomous republic in Russia to declare sovereignty, doing so only in April 1991. At the time, reformers in Moscow viewed Dagestan as among the most conservative regions of the RSFSR—anti-perestroika, antidemocratic, antimarket, pro-Communist, and pro-Union. This impression was reinforced by returns from the March 1989 elections to the USSR Congress of People's Deputies and from elections to the RSFSR Congress of People's Deputies a year later, when Dagestanis voted overwhelmingly for Communist party candidates. In the referendum on the preservation of the USSR in March 1991, 83 percent of Dagestan's electorate voted in favor of the Union, compared to 71 percent in the RSFSR and 76 percent USSR-wide. During the attempted coup in Moscow, in August 1991, Dagestan's political leaders indicated that they would abide by the decrees of the Emergency Committee and ignore the counterdecrees of Yeltsin and his allies.

Despite being on the losing side in August 1991, the republic's political elite managed to survive the USSR's dissolution. They made clear that although they were suspicious of the Yeltsin government in Moscow and generally hostile to its reform program, they would not insist on independence or greater autonomy, as were the Chechens and the Tatars. Accordingly, Dagestan signed the Federation Treaty sponsored by Yeltsin in March 1991—a treaty that both Tatarstan and Chechnya rejected. Under Magomedov's leadership, the elite represented itself, with notable success, as the sole guarantor of stability and interethnic harmony in Dagestan, championing "multinationalism" *(mnogonatsional'nost')* and opposing rapid democratization and marketization on the grounds that radical reforms would upset the republic's traditional power-sharing mechanisms. The Dagestani elite also appealed to the legacy of Soviet multinationalism (as distinct from internationalism), which observers claim resonated effectively with the public and helped explain Dagestanis' preference for Communist (hence, traditional) candidates. Accordingly, the republic has retained many Communist symbols from the Soviet period, including a massive statue of Lenin on the central square in Makhachkala.

The pragmatism of Dagestan's political elite, and above all Makhachkala's repeatedly expressed backing for the territorial integrity of the Russian Federation, helps explains why Dagestan has received not only economic but also consistent political support from federal authorities in Moscow. Notably, even before the buildup that followed the fighting in August and September 1999, there were some 15,000–30,000 federal troops (mostly from the Russian interior ministry and border guards) in the republic.[45] Although their primary mission has been to police the border with Chechnya and Azerbaijan, they can be called upon by Magomedov to defend the capital—as indeed happened, after some delay, in the standoff with oppositionists in Makhachkala in early 1998.[46]

Dagestan thus has a reasonably unified political elite, with some coercive capacity and financial resources at its disposal to co-opt or repress challengers.[47] In moments of crisis, the republic's elite has responded effectively, including for the most part during the August 1999 incursion by Basayev and his allies.[48] It has also been supported for the most part by the republic's religious establishment, which along with its counterparts in North Ossetia, Chechnya, Karachay-Cherkessia, Kabardino-Balkaria, and Ingushetia formed a "Coordinating Council of the Muslims of the North Caucasus" in August 1998, with the mission of promoting Islam while combating Wahhabism.[49]

On the other hand, state capacity in Dagestan is clearly limited by the republic's economic problems and by Moscow's financial difficulties, which limit the amount of direct aid federal authorities can provide. Makhachkala is, however, in no position to improve its financial position without Moscow's help. It is almost entirely unable to extract resources from the local economy given the collapse of industry, the size of the republic's informal sector, the pervasiveness of subsistence agriculture, and the importance of small-scale commodity trading. State autonomy is also limited: Clan, nationality, and organized criminal interests are well represented at all levels of government.[50]

Challengers and the Capacity to Engage in Collective Political Violence

Nationality-Based Political Organizations

National movements formed late in Dagestan and failed to mobilize a significant portion of their national constituencies. The earliest to form was the Kumyk movement, Tenglik (Equality), which agitated for the formation of a separate Kumyk union republic or autonomous region within the RSFSR. Tenglik helped spawn a countermovement by the Avars, who accused the Kumyks of trying to reestablish the political dominance they had enjoyed before the October 1917 revolution. Makhachkala made some concessions to the Kumyks, appointing several to prominent government posts, including Abdurazak Mirzabekov, who became the republic's first prime minister under its new constitution. Kumyk demands for autonomy subsequently abated. Other national movements formed in 1990 and 1991, the period of "nationalist romanticism" in the USSR: The Avars formed the Imam Shamil People's Front; the Dargins, Sadesh; the Nogais, Birlik; and the Laks, Tsubars. None, however, were able to win sustained support from their national constituencies, and only a handful of their candidates have won parliamentary seats.

A partial exception has been the Lezgin national movement, Sadval, which has organized several large demonstrations in opposition to the closing of the Dagestani-Azerbaijani border. The border issue is of immediate concern to the Lezgins, who traditionally herded sheep across the border and maintained close ties to Lezgin communities across the Samur river. The border issue thus provides Sadval with an effective mobilizing theme that other national movements lack. Its continued political prominence also results from the tense relationship between Russia and Azerbaijan and from Baku's oft-repeated claim that Sadval is being used by Moscow to promote the secession of Lezgin communities in Azerbaijan. Nevertheless, Sadval has been unable to win enthusiastic support from Lezgins on either side of the border for the unification with Lezgin territories in Dagestan and Azerbaijan or for the establishment of a separate Lezgin autonomy within Russia, and it has limited influence in Makhachkala.

Congress of Peoples of Chechnya and Dagestan (CPCD)

Created in April 1998 by then Acting Chechen Prime Minister Shamil Basayev, the CPCD actively sought the unification of Chechnya and Dagestan in a single Islamic state.[51] It formed an early alliance with an organization known as the Islamic Shura [Council] of Dagestan, led by an Islamic militant from Dagestan, Magomed Tagayev—reputedly an ideologue of radical Islam in the North Caucasus. Prior to the incursion into Dagestan in August 1999, however, Chechnya's president Aslan Maskhadov repeatedly rejected the CPCD's program, announcing several weeks after its formation that he "deeply respects the choice of the peoples of Dagestan and Ingushetia" to remain within the Russian Federation.[52] This statement contributed to a falling-out between Maskhadov and Basayev, who resigned as acting prime minister in early July 1998.

The CPCD is opposed by the political elite in Dagestan. In mid-May 1998, the leaders of twenty political and public organizations signed a statement condemning the organization, and Dagestani authorities arrested a Basayev deputy in July 1998 on the Dagestani-Chechen border on charges of carrying an illegal weapon (he was released several days later). Even before the CPCD-sponsored incursion into Dagestan in August 1999, the organization had little popular support within the republic. When Basayev announced in late summer 1998 that

CPCD *boeviki* (resistance fighters) would move into Dagestan to defend the three Wahhabi villages if they were attacked, a leader from one of the villages reportedly stated that Basayev's statement was a "provocation" designed to encourage violence.[53]

Wahhabis

To officials in Moscow and Makhachkala, the most serious threat to stability in Dagestan comes from radical politicized Islam and so-called Wahhabism. As noted earlier, most Dagestanis were traditionally adherents of Sufism, a mystical branch of Sunni Islam that entails the "journeying" of a disciple (the *murid*) under the tutelage of an adept (*sheikh, murshid, pir, ustad,* or *orsha*) toward God.[54] Sufis partially reject *sharia* law and are typically tolerant of local practices and customary law *(adat).* Wahhabism, in contrast, is new to the North Caucasus. An Islamic puritan movement that emerged in the early eighteenth century on the Arabian peninsula, Wahhabism was adopted by the Saudi royal family in 1744. It began to establish a foothold in the North Caucasus only after large numbers of Muslims began to make the *hadj* to Mecca in the Gorbachev era. Later, missionaries and mullahs from Islamic countries arrived in Dagestan, some of whom may have been practicing Wahhabis.

During the 1994–1996 war in Chechnya, a limited number of militant Wahhabis and Islamic mujahideen, many of whom had fought in the Afghan war against the Soviets, made their way to Chechnya to help the *boeviki.* It is doubtful that they numbered more than several hundred.[55] After the 1994–1996 war, militant Wahhabis managed to establish guerrilla training camps in Chechnya and western Dagestan, and according to officials in Moscow and Makhachkala, began planning a *jihad* (holy war) against Russia. There were also frequent reports that Wahhabi militants were receiving financial aid and weapons from abroad, particularly from Kuwait, Saudi Arabia, and Afghanistan. Wahhabis were also reportedly recruiting additional mujahideen in Central Asia (particularly among Uzbeks), Afghanistan, and elsewhere—claims that were substantiated by Western journalists who returned to Chechnya in fall 1999 and reported a significant number of non-Chechens among Chechen resistance forces.

Nevertheless, government officials in Makhachkala assert that no more than 5 percent of Dagestanis consider themselves Wahhabi.[56] It is, however, unclear just what is meant by *Wahhabism* when the word is used by officials to describe certain Muslims, or even by self-described Wahhabis.[57] Until the recent crackdown, their stronghold was in the Buinaksk *raion* in central Dagestan, including the three Dargin villages mentioned earlier (Karamakhi, Chabanmakhi, and Kadar).[58] A journalist visiting the area in early 1998 reported that most men, in accordance with Wahhabi teaching, were fully bearded, and that most women went about veiled in public.[59] It is rumored, however, that these three villages embraced "Wahhabism" only because Khattab is married to the sister of the leader of the local *jamaat*.

To the extent that Wahhabism is finding a significant base of social support elsewhere, it appears to be among unemployed young males, particularly those who fought in the 1994–1996 war in Chechnya and who remain loyal to their field commanders and militia units. Wahhabism is, however, opposed by both the political elite and the Dagestani (and Chechen) Muslim-educated *ulema*, who view Wahhabism as a threat to their influence and position. The Wahhabis also must overcome seventy years of assertive Soviet atheism and official pressure on religious beliefs and practices. Although, as noted earlier, Islamic beliefs and practices survived in the Soviet period,[60] most Dagestani men at that time drank alcohol, smoked cigarettes, and prayed intermittently at best (although few ate pork); and Dagestani women rarely covered their faces in public (although they would typically cover their head with a scarf, particularly in rural areas). Urban Dagestanis still find the asceticism of Islamic fundamentalism difficult to accept (particularly its proscription of alcohol); and highlanders are reluctant to abandon *adat* in favor of rigid *sharia* law, or to forswear their pre-Islamic traditions and beliefs.

Proliferation of Weapons

In the Soviet period, highlanders typically carried long knives (*kinjal*), possessed swords handed down by their ancestors, and owned hunting rifles. They also prided themselves on wielding weapons with skill. Today, automatic weapons, grenades, antipersonnel mines, and heavy machine guns are readily available for purchase on the black market, and local militants and criminal organizations are typically well armed.[61] Soviet weapons made their way into private and semiprivate hands in 1990 and 1991 and in the early post-Soviet period, when the armories of the Soviet forces were raided and looted by irregular forces in Chechnya, Georgia, Abkhazia, and elsewhere in the region. The Russian defense ministry actually agreed to distribute arms to the Chechens as part of a deal allowing Russian forces to withdraw safely from the republic. Later, impoverished Russian soldiers regularly sold weapons for profit, and many more were captured by the Chechen *boeviki* in the 1994–1996 war. The Chechen government also reportedly purchased weapons from abroad. More recently, after the August 1999 incursions into Dagestan by forces from Chechnya, firearms were distributed by government authorities to volunteer Dagestani "self-defense" units.

These events have contributed to a substantial arming of the Dagestani population. Supporters of various oppositionists regularly carry automatic rifles in public. During their confrontation with Dagestani troops in March 1998, the Khachilayev brothers were able to marshal some 2,000 armed individuals with automatic weapons and grenade launchers.[62] Likewise, the "Wahhabis" in Karamakhi, Chabanmakhi, and Kadar mounted a vigorous defense of their villages both in May 1998 and again in September 1999.

External Support

The ability of foreign powers (other than Chechnya) to interfere in Dagestan's internal affairs is limited by various factors. The government in Baku, for example, is disliked even more by the Lezgins in the border region than is the government in Moscow or in Makhachkala. Moreover, even though the Azerbaijani government has reason to fear that instability could spread across the border from Dagestan, it has to beware of taking steps that will make its powerful northern neighbor even more hostile toward it. Georgia has similar cause to oppose a destabilization of Dagestan, although the Georgian-Dagestani border is largely impassable to wheeled transport, particularly motor vehicles. As for Moscow, it continues to support Magomedov, as it, too, has every reason to prevent violence and disorder in the republic.

The key source of external support for antisystem challengers in Dagestan is Chechnya. In fact, the peoples of Dagestan gave little support to the Chechens during the 1994–1996 war, although some attempts were made (mostly by Chechen-Akkins) to block Russian military units moving into Chechnya from Dagestan in December 1994. There was little sympathy in Dagestan for Dzhokhar Dudayev, the militant Chechen president, or for Chechen radical nationalism, which at the time had little religious content and was primarily directed against Chechen incorporation into the Russian Federation. Moreover, Dagestanis had been frequent victims of robberies and kidnappings at the hands of Chechens in the years prior to the invasion, particularly on the vital railroad linking Dagestan and Stavropol, which Dagestanis and Azerbaijanis use to bring vegetables and fruits to market in Moscow and other Russian cities.

Nevertheless, Dagestani officials were cautious in their response to the 1994–1996 war. Makhachkala took the position that although the war was deeply regrettable, Moscow's decision to invade was understandable; and it quietly allowed Russian troops to use Dagestani territory to carry out operations in Chechnya without objection. It also took steps to muzzle Dagestanis who advocated support for the Chechens, arresting the parliamentary leader of the Congress of Mountain Peoples and his deputy, and suspending publication of the journal *Islamic Way* for reprinting Dudayev's statements.[63] After the war, relations between Makhachkala and the Chechen government improved when Maskhadov made clear that his government had no territorial claims on Dagestan, opposed Wahhabism and the CPCD, and sought a dialogue with Magomedov and other leaders of the North Caucasus. Nevertheless, anti-Chechen feelings in Dagestan persisted, thanks to terrorist incidents and kidnappings blamed on Chechnya-based militants. The August 1999 incursions only intensified these feelings. Accordingly, the Chechens can expect little help from Dagestan in their conflict with Moscow.

Political Grievances, Issues, and Organizations

Historical Memories and Traditional Enmities

With the exception of Chechen hostility to Moscow and traditional enmity between Cossacks and highlanders, historical animosities between nationalities in Dagestan are limited.[64] Prior to the Russian conquest, conflict was common, but typically it was between *jamaats*, *shamkalates*, or khanates, not between nationalities. Accordingly, the "ancient hatreds" between Dagestan's nationalities (often alluded to by political scientists)—even between highlanders and Turkic-speaking lowlanders—are not effective mobilizers of inter-nationality violence in the republic. Traditional enmity toward Russia and Russians is also limited. Even the legend of Shamil and the nineteenth-century highlander resistance to Russian occupation has an ambiguous legacy today. Shamil was an Avar who managed to unite most of the highlanders in the eastern North Caucasus (and briefly, Circassians and other highlanders in the western North Caucasus as well) in a war against Russian penetration from 1834 to 1859. His methods of rule, however, were harsh, and he encountered significant popular resistance to his introduction of ascetic Sufism. As noted earlier, he also had to deal with opposition from the traditional feudal aristocracy and with frequent defections of individual villages, *jamaats*, and clans to the Russians. Thus, although Shamil's struggle provides the Avars and the Chechens—many of whose ancestors were among Shamil's *murids* (warriors)—with a potent mythology of resistance to foreign domination, multiple Shamil myths exist today that can be, and are being, appropriated by different political actors in the North Caucasus. Even official Makhachkala has used the legend of Shamil, claiming he was tolerant of national differences and at heart a democrat, to legitimate its consociational practices.[65]

Territorial and Border Disputes

During the Russian civil war (1918–1921), the highland peoples of the North Caucasus took advantage of Moscow's weakness to establish a weak, territorially ill-defined, but putatively independent state, the Mountain Republic (Gorskaia Respublika).[66] Soon after the defeat of the Whites by the Red Army in 1921, the Gorskaia Respublika was dissolved and the Dagestan ASSR was established. Initially, the ASSR comprised most of the territory of the Imperial-era gubernia of Dagestan as well as the Kumyk district of what had been Terskaia gubernia. In 1922, traditionally Cossack and Nogai lands in what had been Stavropol *krai* and Astrakhan oblast were added to the republic. Some of this territory was returned to Astrakhan in 1938, but some 40,000 Cossacks still live along the left (northern) bank of the Terek River in the north-central region of Dagestan. Accordingly, when highlander radicals began to agitate for an independent Dagestan at the end of the Gorbachev era, Cossack communities responded by threatening to secede from the republic.[67]

Other territorial disputes are results of the 1944 deportation of the Chechens, Ingush, and other North Caucasus nationalities, allegedly for collaborating with the Germans. Among those deported were approximately 30,000 Chechen-Akkins from Aukhovsky (since renamed Novolaksky) *raion* in Dagestan. The deportations were followed by the dissolution of the Chechen-Ingush ASSR, when traditionally Chechen lands were made a part of Dagestan. Much of this land was restored to Checheno-Ingushetia after its reestablishment in 1957, but Novolaksky and Khasavyurtsky *raions* were not. Moreover, when the rehabilitated Chechens returned to their villages in Novolaksky *raion* after 1957, they discovered their homes occupied by Laks, many of whose villages had been burned by Soviet authorities, who had then forcibly resettled them there. Predictably, the resettled Laks were unwilling to leave, having no homes to return to. The Chechens were therefore forced to find new homes in neighboring Khasavyurtsky and Khazbekov *raions*, where most Dagestani Chechens are now concentrated. Thousands of Avars subsequently moved into Novolaksky *raion* in the 1970s, after their homes were destroyed by a powerful earthquake.

Encouraged by the 1990 USSR Law on Repressed Peoples, Chechen communities began insisting in the late Gorbachev period that they be allowed to return to their traditional villages. In 1992, thousands of Chechens moved into Novolaksky *raion* without official permission, and the local media claimed they were intent upon driving the Laks and Avars out. Violent clashes took place between Laks and Chechens that fall, which prompted Makhachkala to declare martial law in the district and to call in federal troops to restore order. Tensions abated after the Dagestani government promised to ease restrictions on residency permits for Chechens, to compensate the Chechens for financial losses, and to finance the resettlement of the Laks. However, little if any of the promised financial support was forthcoming, and the plan to resettle the Laks was resisted by Kumyks, who claimed the Laks were being resettled on traditional Kumyk lands. Accordingly, there are still significant tensions between Chechens and Laks and Avars, which were rekindled when Basayev's forces entered the region in September 1999.[68]

A number of other territorial disputes cut across Dagestan's borders. Most notably, traditional Lezgin lands have been bifurcated by the republic's border with Azerbaijan. According to the 1989 census, there were some 205,000 Lezgins in Dagestan and 171,000 in Azerbaijan. However, Lezgin leaders have claimed that the Soviet census substantially underreported the total number of Lezgins, particularly in Azerbaijan, where Lezgins faced discrimination by Azerbaijani authorities and accordingly identified themselves as Azeris. The actual number of ethnic Lezgins, they assert, may be as high as 600,000.[69] As noted earlier, the Lezgin nationalist group Sadval began calling for the establishment of a united "Lezginistan" shortly after its formation in 1991. Convinced that Sadval was being supported by Soviet—and later, Russian—secret services, Azerbaijani officials helped create an Azerbaijani counterpart in mid-1991, which was called "Samur" (the name of the river running along the Dagestani-Azerbaijani border). The group immediately declared its opposition to any border revisions.[70] Nevertheless, most Lezgins remain suspicious of Baku, particularly after it attempted to draft Lezgins to fight in the war over Karabakh.

Relations between Dagestan and Azerbaijan are also complicated by the presence of some 45,000 Avars in northern Azerbaijan. On occasion, Avar leaders have demanded that Avar-inhabited areas of Azerbaijan be united with Avar districts in Dagestan, or even that a distinct, autonomous Avar territory be established within Russia. Again, authorities in Baku claim that Moscow is encouraging these irredentist aspirations. A minor clash took place between Azerbaijani troops and Avars in July 1994, heightening tensions and raising fears in Azerbaijan that Russia would attempt to seize Lezgin or Avar lands by force.

The fact that Lezgins, along with Avars, Dargins, Azeris, and other nationalities, have traditionally passed unencumbered across the border between Dagestan and Azerbaijan has exacerbated tensions along the Samur River. The Russian government attempted to establish full border control in late 1992; but after Sadval organized protest demonstrations in Dagestan and Azerbaijan, Moscow backed down, instead establishing a loose customs regimen by which locals could cross the border without visas. However, as relations between Moscow and Grozny deteriorated in 1994 and concerns grew in Moscow about alleged smuggling of drugs and weapons across the border, the Russian government attempted to limit cross-border traffic, which led to clashes between Lezgins, Azeris, and the Dagestani police. When the war in Chechnya broke out later that year, Moscow tried, albeit with limited success, to close the border entirely. These restrictions were later partially lifted; but Lezgins and other peoples in the region continue to resent the disruption caused by what they consider an artificial border, and some have begun to agitate for the establishment of a separate, autonomous republic within Russia, uniting all the peoples of southern Dagestan.[71] Meanwhile, on the other side of the border, Azeri merchants and truck drivers have objected to the need to bribe officials from each of the many Russian organizations involved in monitoring cross-border traffic. Moreover, they resent the fact that Azeri citizens, regardless of their nationality, are charged higher customs duties than Russian citizens. Lastly, Moscow and Baku have been at loggerheads over the management of the water resources of the Samur River. Tensions along the border reached a high point in late 1998, and the Russian media began to speculate about a possible border war with Azerbaijan.[72]

Demographic Pressures

Overall population growth in Dagestan has been high but with considerable variation among nationalities, due to out- and in-migration and to differences in birthrates and morbidity. Most notably, between 1959 and 1989, the Russian share of the population fell by more than half, from 20.2 percent to 9.2 percent.[73] By 1989, Dagestan was one of only four ASSRs in the RSFSR that did not have a Russian majority in their major cities.[74] In the period since, there has been a steady out-migration of Russians and other Slavs from the republic, particularly of skilled workers, enterprise managers, and technicians. There has also been a

significant inflow of "Dagestani" peoples, in part because of discriminatory treatment of "Caucasians" in the rest of Russia. Slavs who remain feel increasingly
marginalized.

Demographic change has affected interethnic relations in rural areas in particular ways. The traditional economy of the highland peoples, with its intense cultivation of very small land plots, was disrupted by forced collectivization under
Stalin, which drove many into collective and state farms in lowland areas. The
movement of highlanders to lowland areas increased at the end of the 1950s, particularly among Avars and Dargins. Soviet authorities encouraged this internal
migration because official doctrine held that traditional highlander ways of life
were incompatible with "developed socialism."

The settlement patterns of Dagestan's internal migrants were not conducive to
assimilation or cultural amalgamation. Highlanders relocating to lowland rural
areas tended to remain compactly settled, often dominating entire kolkhozy (collective farms) or reconstituting entire village communities. Those who did not
relocate have typically maintained close ties with their family villages. They have
thus retained their highland traditions, including intensive cultivation, which has
threatened the agricultural practices of the sheep- and cattle-herding Nogais and
Kumyks. Moreover, because "indigenous" Avars and Dargins were the particular
beneficiaries of Soviet affirmative action policies—in contrast to nonindigenous
"Tatars," such as the Kumyks—the former dominated official positions even in
traditionally Kumyk territories. The Kumyks have thus resented their loss of political control, which helps explain why Tenglik pressed in 1990–1991 for the establishment of a separate Kumyk autonomy.[75] Similarly, the Nogais became a
small minority in their traditional steppe grazing lands in the north.[76] The fact
that the Kumyks and Nogais constituted such small minorities in these areas,
however, undermined both the legitimacy and the practicality of their autonomy
aspirations, which have since abated.

The most significant destabilizing demographic factor in recent years has been
the influx of internally displaced persons (IDPs) into Dagestan from Chechnya.
The number of Chechens in the republic increased rapidly, from some 13,000 in
1959 to 58,000 in 1989. To this were added 150,000 Chechen IDPs by mid-1995.
Many later returned to their homeland; but an estimated 50,000–60,000 remain,
which has contributed to housing shortages and inadequate social services and
made Chechen demands to return to their pre-1944 homes in Novolaksky *raion*
more urgent. To date, however, most IDPs from the renewed warfare in Chechnya
have fled to Ingushetia, not Dagestan—in part, because the border with Dagestan
has been sealed off by Russian and Dagestani troops, and in part because the
Dagestani population is less willing to accept another influx of Chechen IDPs in
the wake of the violence in August and September.

Demographic changes have complicated relations with other neighbors. Land
scarcity and population growth, along with the republic's dismal economy, have
driven many Dagestanis into Stavropol *krai* in recent years.[77] The strain this has
placed on the Stavropol economy and government budget, along with frequent

cattle- and sheep-rustling and kidnappings by Chechen raiders, has contributed to deepening anti-highlander sentiments among Russians in the region, which helps account for the popularity of conservative nationalism and indeed outright fascism in Stavropol *krai* as well as farther west, in Krasnodar *krai*.[78]

Ethnic and Class Inequalities

Economically, Russians, Kumyks, and Nogais have suffered disproportionately in recent decades. However, they constitute a weak and divided minority and thus pose little threat to public order. The most politically significant tensions over group inequalities are between Dargins on the one hand and Avars and Lezgins on the other. The Dargins are disproportionately represented in the republic's executive organs, which is where key decisions are made about appointments and the allocation of government benefits. Magomedov is a Dargin, and so too is Said Amirov, the mayor of Makhachkala. The Dargins are, however, less numerous than the Avars, and both Avars and Lezgins resent Dargin political domination of the republic. Avar parliamentary deputies therefore took the lead in opposing the amendments to the constitution that allowed Magomedov to prolong his term of office.

Early Warning Signs and Likely Triggers

Political Succession

Magomedov has been a skillful political leader. Like other former communist *apparatchiki* in the Soviet successor states, he has used his *nomenklatura* ties to good effect. He has been particularly adept in co-opting much of the opposition by handing out official posts and state subsidies. However, his second and final (at least, according to the current constitution) term will end in 2002; or he might be assassinated or die of natural causes in the interim. At some point, he will have to be replaced, which will immediately raise issues of ethnic balancing and fairness. Replacing him with someone of a different nationality, as the constitution prescribes, risks unsettling the elite and might require a new pact on the ethnic distribution of power. Replacing him with another Dargin, on the other hand, would be a clear violation of consociational norms and would be resented by Avars and Lezgins in particular. If the elite manages to reach an agreement on a successor and a shuffling of portfolios, the Dagestani people will likely accept it. If not, elite conflict could lead to violence and regime breakdown.

Violation of Consociational Rules and Practices By the Dagestani Elite

As the end of Magomedov's two-year term as head of the State Council approached in June 1996, he managed to convince two-thirds of parliament to

amend the constitution and extend his term of office to four years. He again lobbied successfully for a constitutional amendment, in March 1998, that allowed
him to serve a second four-year term. Oppositionists vigorously objected to these
maneuvers, claiming that Magomedov headed a corrupt and exploitative elite
and had been ineffective in overcoming the republic's problems. Prior to the
events of August and September 1999, there were signs that Magomedov's grip
on power was weakening, including episodic anti-Magomedov demonstrations
and marches on Makhachkala to demand his resignation.[79] The renewed warfare
in Chechnya, however, will probably boost his popular support, as Dagestanis
conclude that any political instability in Makhachkala is undesirable. Nevertheless, Magomedov may again violate the informal norms of consociational
democracy when his term ends in 2002 by engineering another constitutional
amendment; or he may even attempt to remain in office illegally, which could
end the consensus among Makhachkala's elite.

Ill-Considered Policy Changes in Makhachkala and Moscow

Until September 1999, the Dagestani government had been circumspect in dealing with the highlander communities that challenged its authority. For example,
in 1998, it struck a compromise with the "Wahhabis" in Karamakhi, Kadar, and
Chabanmakhi. Makhachkala has also redirected revenue from Moscow to local
governments and *jamaat* councils.[80] One result of this policy of accommodation
and compromise has been to undermine Makhachkala's control over local governments and to make it more difficult to implement an effective economic reform program. However, reaching out to local elites has at the same time made it
less likely that a unified opposition will emerge. Magomedov's policy of compromise and co-optation will likely persist despite the federal government's assault
on the Wahhabi villages in September 1999. However, if Makhachkala changes
course and is seen as clearly favoring one nationality over another, then inter-
nationality relations in the republic could deteriorate.

Moscow's policy toward Dagestan has been driven above all by its desire to
keep the Chechen conflict from spreading. For this reason, the suspicion felt by
pro-Yeltsin politicians in Moscow toward the *nomenklatura* elite in Makhachkala
quickly gave way to appreciation for Magomedov and his conservative and pro-
federation policies. Accordingly, Moscow continued to subsidize the Dagestani
government and repeatedly made clear its political support for Magomedov.[81]
Since early 1998, it has supplemented this approach with a growing stress on "law
and order."[82] In May of that year, Moscow established a special headquarters in
Stavropol to coordinate federal law enforcement agencies in the North Caucasus.
It also placed the region's interior ministry troops, army units, border guards,
and all other federal forces in the North Caucasus under the command of a "special administration." Two months later, this special administration oversaw military exercises in Dagestan that included the participation of federal interior min-

istry troops as well as units from the Ministry for Emergency Situations, the Federal Security Service (FSB), the Federal Agency for Government Communications and Information, border guards, railroad troops, and defense ministry troops.[83] The intelligence services were also encouraged to become more active in gathering intelligence in the region.[84] At the same time, the showdown with the Khachilayev brothers in May 1998 prompted federal authorities to launch a much-publicized crackdown on crime and corruption in the republic.[85] A special investigative team was sent to Makhachkala, which ordered the arrest of Magomed Khachilayev for his role in the May events and for illegal weapons possession.[86] Other prominent Dagestani officials, including Nadir Khachilayev, were also placed under investigation.[87] The investigation of Nadir led the Russian State Duma for the first time to lift the immunity of one of its deputies. Nadir fled to Chechnya, and after expressing his opposition to the August 1999 incursion by Basayev's forces, reportedly participated in the defense of the Wahhabi villages in September, was wounded, fled to his native Lak region, and was finally arrested by federal authorities.[88]

Accompanying these "firm hand" measures by Moscow were renewed efforts to ameliorate the republic's economic crisis and humanitarian suffering. A "Program for the Economic, Social, and Political Development of the North Caucasus Region up to 2005" was drafted in Moscow in 1998; and in the summer of that year, the Security Council announced the formation of a special federal agency for coordinating federal social and economic programs in the region. These plans suffered a setback due to Russia's August 1998 financial crisis, which also affected Dagestan's economy, aggravating the shortage of medical supplies and leading to predictions of inadequate food supplies over the winter.[89] Despite the crisis, however, the federal government continued to provide Makhachkala with substantial financial support.

Moscow's policy toward Dagestan could change if Russia is either decisively defeated or is decisively victorious in Chechnya, or if extreme rightists or extreme leftists come to power in Moscow. Advocates of a "firm hand" might then attempt to limit Makhachkala's autonomy, thereby undermining the fragile political balance in the republic. They might also reduce federal subsidies to the region or redraw Russia's internal borders in an effort to eliminate the ethnic republics altogether.[90] A further deterioration of the federal government's fiscal balance could also force Moscow to reduce or even end its financial support for Makhachkala. Such changes, particularly if rapid and obvious, might induce the Dagestani elite to defend their prerogatives by becoming openly defiant of Moscow, even to the point of armed resistance to Russia's presence in the republic.

Conclusion

At best, Dagestan's stable instability will persist for years, if not decades, and Russia will have to cope with unrest on its southern border regardless of the outcome of the current conflict in Chechnya. The Dagestani economy is deeply depressed and is unlikely to recover substantially in the foreseeable future. Economic hardship will make it very difficult to reduce organized crime. High and variable birthrates will strain the Dagestani government's ability to provide adequate public services and minimal social protections, and they will intensify inter-nationality disputes and put pressure on Dagestan's consociational practices. Finally, the republic's extreme heterogeneity multiplies the potential conflicts between nationalities, sub-nationalities, clans and sub-clans, *jamaats*, villages, religious groups, criminal organizations, and other political actors in the republic.

The capacity of the Dagestani government to ameliorate these problems will be limited by its difficulties in collecting taxes; its financial dependency on an impoverished federal government in Moscow; and the poor professional standards and inadequate resources of the local police and federal and republican troops on Dagestani territory. Political extremists will continue to have ready access to highly destructive weapons. Moreover, it is very unlikely that Moscow will able to restore order in Chechnya in the foreseeable future. As a result, Dagestanis will likely continue to suffer from episodic terrorist incidents, kidnappings, armed robberies, and sheep- and cattle-rustling.

Nor will Dagestan's consociational practices guarantee stability in the republic. On the contrary, they will ensure that disputes between nationalities over representation in central institutions remain on the republic's political agenda, and they will inhibit the development of a Dagestan-wide civic consciousness. This is not to suggest, however, that some other institutional order would significantly ameliorate inter-nationality tensions or reduce of the risk of political violence. Dagestan's consociational practices have been inherited from its pre-Soviet and Soviet past, and they have acquired considerable popular legitimacy. Abandoning them now would be unpopular and might well precipitate civil war. Moreover, no institutional arrangement, whether it be affirmative action, ethnic federalism, cultural or territorial autonomy, or consociationalism, can guarantee interethnic harmony in plural societies. Inevitably, elites have to manage intercommunal conflicts that arise over the distribution of valued goods and symbols; and effective management requires responsiveness to changing social norms, demographic conditions, and political preferences.

In general, then, it is extremely unlikely that the republic's economic and political problems will be significantly ameliorated for the foreseeable future. On the other hand, sustained large-scale political violence is also unlikely. The republic's great variety of national and sub-national groups, as well as the strength of clan, village, *jamaat*, and religious identities, make it very difficult for pan-highlander, pan-Caucasian, or pan-Islamic appeals to resonate with the Dagestani population. Nor do the Dagestanis wish to see the death and destruction visited upon Chechnya come to Dagestan. Even more unlikely is the emergence of a politically potent ideology of Dagestani nationalism directed at the establishment of an independent, multinational Dagestani state. Ten (or at best fourteen) nationalities, not one, are considered the primary "owners" of the republic, and collective ownership by multiple groups creates significant collective action problems and makes legitimation on the basis of "self-determination" very problematic. Nor is it likely that one national group will be able to mobilize its constituency and establish political hegemony. Were such an effort to be made, there would be a countervailing mobilization and balancing alliances among others. As in India, the great multiplicity of ethnic and religious cleavages therefore contributes to the resilience of an otherwise brittle consociational system.

Nevertheless, if the best case for Dagestan is stable instability, the worst—a complete breakdown of public order, and sustained large-scale violence—cannot be ruled out. I have identified a number of possible triggers of violence: political succession; a violation of the formal rules or informal practices of consociationalism; a renewed attack, this time more successful, by militants from Chechnya; a sudden and substantial cutback in federal subsidies; an unsuccessful use of force to impose Moscow's writ on recalcitrant regions; or a decision by Moscow to revoke Dagestan's autonomy. Any of these could provoke large-scale violence. But if the elite in Makhachkala remains unified and plays by the rules of the consociational game, and if the governments in Makhachkala and Moscow continue to express their commitment to multinationalism and interethnic cooperation, then the republic's stable instability will very likely persist.

Notes

1. Khattab is usually described ethnically as an Arab, but there has been speculation that he may be of Chechen or Circassian ancestry. Like radical Muslims elsewhere, however, he considers himself a member of the Islamic community (the *umma*) and above national or ethnic identity, and he accordingly refuses to disclose his ethnic background.

2. More specifically, most residents of the region are members of the Andi and Dido subgroups of the Avars.

3. The only other significant transportation arteries between the North and South Caucasus are the Georgian Military Highway, built by the Russians in the nineteenth century through the Daryal gorge and over the Krestovyi pass in the central Caucasus range; and the Black Sea coastline of Abkhazia, which is even less negotiable than the coastal plain of Dagestan. Both corridors have been interrupted by the conflicts in South Ossetia and Abkhazia, and the railroad line through Abkhazia joining Russia and Georgia is no longer operational.

4. In July 1997, the federal government completed a 78-kilometer railroad spur between the town of Karlan-Yurt in Stavropol *krai* and the Dagestani town of Kizlyar. As a result, trains from elsewhere in Russia can now enter Dagestan without first passing through Chechnya.

5. In 1997, the Russian and Chechen governments, along with the Russian pipeline company Transneft, entered into an agreement to restore the flow of oil through the pipeline and to give Grozny a share of the transit fees. However, the inability of the Chechen government to prevent illegal thefts of oil from the pipeline or to provide effective security for Russian maintenance and repair crews meant that the pipeline operated only intermittently. It was shut down for most of 1999.

6. *Nezavisimaia gazeta*, August 20, 1998; *Current Digest of the Post-Soviet Press* (henceforth, *Current Digest*) 50, no. 33 (1998), 14.

7. Separate "mafia" groups reportedly control different parts of the Dagestani economy: For example, the Dagestani press refers regularly to a "caviar mafia," a "customs mafia," and an "oil mafia."

8. See the statement of the National Council of the Chechen-Akkins (ITAR-TASS, August 11, 1999).

9. *RFE/RL Newsline,* August 27, 1999.

10. According to local reports, the militants involved in the first incursion were more ethnically mixed than those of the second, with the former including larger numbers of Dagestanis and men from outside the Caucasus, and the latter being primarily Chechens.

11. I follow much of the literature on collective political violence in defining large-scale violence as more than 1,000 deaths per annum for two consecutive years. For those doing quantitative analysis on violence who need an operationalizable dependent variable, 1,000 deaths per annum is generally a reasonable, albeit arbitrary, threshold. It fails, however, to account for the size of the groups involved; 1,000 deaths a year in conflicts between very large ethnic groups is not the same as 1,000 deaths for small ethnic groups, in terms of threats to group survival or the extent of ethnic mobilization.

12. My approach in what follows is generally informed by the work of Barbara Harff and Ted Robert Gurr under the "Minorities at Risk" and "Failed States" projects at the University of Maryland. See Ted Robert Gurr and Michael Haxton, "Minorities Report (1): Ethnopolitical Conflict in the 1990s: Patterns and Trends" (College Park, Md.: University of Maryland, Center for International Development and Conflict Management, Minorities at Risk Project, 1996); and Barbara Harff and Ted Robert Gurr, "Systematic Early Warning of Humanitarian Emergencies" (College Park, Md.: University of Maryland, Center for International Development and Conflict Management, Minorities at Risk Project, 1997).

13. Robert J. Kaiser, *The Geography of Nationalism in Russia and the USSR* (Princeton: Princeton University Press, 1994), 203.

14. Ibid., 212.

15. *Finansovye izvestiia,* 30 January 1997; *Current Digest* 29, no. 5 (1997), 16.

16. The symbolic importance of the pipeline, and its perceived implications for Russia's presence in the Caucasus, far exceed its financial importance, which is likely to be meager.

17. In 1994, 88 percent of the republic's budget revenues were covered by transfers from the federal treasury—a higher percentage than for any other subject of the federation other than Ingushetia (*Segodnia,* June 7, 1995; *FBIS-SOV-125-S,* June 29, 1995, p. 53).

18. For example, there are at least 14 mutually unintelligible languages related to "Avar"—Andi, Akhvakh, Archi, Bagulal, Beshti/Kaputchi, Botlikh, Chamala, Ghinukh, Godoberi, Gunzbi, Khvarshin, Karati, Tindi, and Tsezi/Dido—the speakers of which were required to identify themselves as "Avar" in their internal passports. Likewise, the republic's second largest nationality, the Dargins, can in turn be divided into Dargins proper, Kubachins, and Kaitags. In other cases, Soviet ethnographers were accused of creating ethnic cleavages where none existed. For example, Lezgin nationalists claim that Aguls, Rutuls, Tabasarans, and Tsakhurs are in fact all Lezgins and that the languages they speak are no more different from Lezgin than, for example, Andi is from Avar (Robert Bruce Ware and Enver Kisriev, "Political Stability and Ethnic Parity: Why Is There Peace in Dagestan?," paper presented at the American Political Science Association conference, Washington, D.C., August 30, 1997).

19. Johanna Nichols, "War and the Politics of Non-Natural Language Endangerment in the Caucasus" (paper presented at the conference "Institutions, Identity, and Ethnic Con-

flict: International Experience and Its Implications for the Caucasus," University of California at Berkeley, May 2–3, 1997), 54–61.

20. Kaiser, *The Geography of Nationalism*, 273.

21. Ibid., 313.

22. The republic's Turkic-speaking people could in fact be treated as members of separate "civilizations": The Nogais were traditionally nomadic peoples of the steppe, like the Kyrgyz or Bashkirs, whereas the Kumyks and Azeris were sedentary and more urbanized, with relatively well-established feudal political systems prior to the Russian conquest. See Sergei Arutiunov, "Explaining the Absence of Ethnic Conflict in Russia's Republic of Dagestan," paper presented at the conference on the "Politics of Identity," University of California at Berkeley, March 4, 1996. One could also treat the Cossacks, with their free frontier traditions and long-standing presence in the republic on the one hand, and more recent Slavic immigrants on the other, as members of separate civilizational clusters, despite the fact that both are Slavic and traditionally Orthodox.

23. Paul B. Henze, "Islam in the North Caucasus: The Example of Chechnya" (Santa Monica, Calif.: RAND, 1995).

24. Alexandre Bennigsen and S. Enders Wimbush, *Mystics and Commissars: Sufism in the Soviet Union* (Berkeley: University of California Press, 1985).

25. There are four main legal branches of Sunni Islam: Shafi'i (which is traditionally more accepting of Sufism), Khanafi'i, Khanbali'i, and Maliki'i.

26. Ronald Wixman, *The Peoples of the USSR: An Ethnographic Handbook* (London: Macmillan, 1984). The Mountain Jews and Tats were treated as a single nationality in the 1989 census.

27. Mark Saroyan, *Minorities, Mullahs, and Modernity: Reshaping Community in the Former Soviet Union*, ed. Edward W. Walker (Berkeley: University of California, International and Area Studies, 1997).

28. *Nezavisimaia gazeta regiony*, April 27, 1999.

29. Enver Kisriev, "The Historical and Anthropological Roots of Negotiation Culture in Dagestan and Chechnya," paper presented at the Conflict Management Group Lecture Series, Cambridge, Mass., September 3, 1998.

30. Kaiser, *The Geography of Nationalism*, 203.

31. In general, the tendency is for those still resident in highland and rural areas to have greater loyalty to territorialized political communities (the *jamaat* and village), whereas highlanders who have migrated to cities and towns tend to be organized along clan and family lines (Sergei Arutiunov, personal communication, University of California at Berkeley, April 28, 1999).

32. Kisriev, "The Historical and Anthropological Roots," 4.

33. Moshe Gammer, "Competing Historical Narratives in Dagestan and Chechnya and Their Use of a 'National Hero'," paper presented at the Fourth Annual Convention of the Association for the Study of Nationalities, New York, April 17, 1999.

34. Sergei Arutiunov, "Explaining the Absence of Ethnic Conflict in Russia's Republic of Dagestan"; and Robert Chenciner, *Daghestan: Tradition and Survival, Caucasus World* (New York: St. Martin's, 1997).

35. Anna Matveeva, "Dagestan," *Former Soviet South Briefing, The Royal Institute of International Affairs: Russia and Eurasia Programme* May 13, 1997.

36. Robert Bruce Ware and Enver Kisriev, "Dagestan's Ethnic Electoral System: The Selection of the Second People's Assembly," unpublished paper, 1999.

37. Matveeva, "Dagestan."

38. Arend Lijphart, *Democracy in Plural Societies: A Comparative Exploration* (New Haven: Yale University Press, 1977); Ware and Kisriev, "Political Stability"; and Robert Bruce Ware and Enver Kisriev, "Ethnic Parity and Democratic Pluralism in Dagestan: A Consociational Approach," paper presented at the Fourth Annual Convention of the Association for the Study of Nationalities, New York, April 15–17, 1999.

39. Ian Lustick, "Stability in Deeply Divided Societies: Consociationalism Versus Control," *World Politics* 31, no. 3 (1979):225–244; Brian Barry, "The Consociational Model and Its Dangers," *European Journal of Political Research* 3, no. 4 (December 1975):393–411; Paul R. Brass, "Ethnic Conflict in Multiethnic Societies: The Consociational Solution and Its Critics," in *Ethnicity and Nationalism: Theory and Comparison,* ed. Paul R. Brass (London: Sage, 1991), 333–348; and Steven Ian Wilkinson, "Consociational Theory and Ethnic Violence," paper presented at the Fourth Annual Convention of the Association for the Study of Nationalities, New York, April 15–17, 1999.

40. Indeed, changing demographics and the strain they placed on consociational practices was one of the factors behind the breakdown of Lebanese consociationalism.

41. Muhammed-Arif Sadyki, "Will the Russian South Explode This Summer?," *NG Stsenarii,* May 13, 1998, 1–3.

42. *Segodnia,* June 26, 1998; *Current Digest* 50, no. 26 (1998), 13.

43. Arutiunov, "Explaining the Absence."

44. Kisriev, "The Historical and Anthropological Roots," 6.

45. The precise number of federal troops has been difficult to determine because federal officials are understandably less than forthcoming with such information. An article in *Trud* in early 1998 asserted that there were about 20,000 federal troops and 15,000 Dagestani militiamen *(militsii)* in the republic *(Trud,* January 9, 1998; *Current Digest* 50, no. 2 (1998), 13). Other sources, however, give lower figures. Moreover, Moscow beefed up its troop deployments in the North Caucasus in late 1998 and the first half of 1999, and then dramatically increased them after the events of August and September 1999 and the renewed fighting in Chechnya.

46. Interior ministry troops, including members of the elite Alpha unit, took up positions around the city during and after the crisis, securing governmental buildings, main roads, and bridges *(Kommersant-Daily,* May 23, 1998; *Current Digest* 50, no. 21 (1998), 3.

47. I do not mean to deny the considerable tensions between political factions in Makhachkala, as highlighted by the conflict with the Khachilayev brothers and by resistance from various political factions to Moscow's efforts to crack down on crime and corruption over the past year. But Magomedov has been careful not to directly threaten the privileges and interests of political clans: For example, he has allowed the Russian prosecutor general's office and interior ministry to take the lead in the recent anticorruption campaign.

48. For example, Makhachkala officials were generally credited with having played a constructive role in trying to end the hostage crisis in Kizlyar in 1996, and they managed to defuse both the takeover of the parliament building in spring 1998 (see Enver Kisriev, "Seizure of the House of Government," *Bulletin: Network on Ethnological Monitoring and Early Warning of Conflict* [Cambridge, Mass., Conflict Management Group, September 1998], 19–26) and the confrontation with the three "Wahhabi" villages several months later without resort to large-scale violence (*Nezavisimaia gazeta,* September 3, 1998; *Current Digest* 50, no. 35 [1998], 17).

49. *Izvestiia,* August 19, 1998; *Current Digest* 50, no. 33 (1998), 14. However, prior to his assassination in mid-1998, Dagestan's head mufti, Said Muhammed-Hadji Abubakarov,

openly expressed reservations about Magomedov, which led some of his supporters to accuse the Dagestani government of having ordered the assassination.

50. Matveeva, "Dagestan."

51. An earlier organization, the Confederation of Mountain Peoples (Highlanders) of the Caucasus, later renamed the Confederation of the Peoples of the Caucasus, played an important role in Dagestani and North Caucasian politics in the early post-Soviet period but has since become essentially irrelevant.

52. *RFE/RL Newsline,* May 12, 1998.

53. *Nezavisimaia gazeta,* August 27, 1998.

54. Bennigsen and Wimbush, *Mystics and Commissars.*

55. Carlotta Gall and Thomas de Waal, *Calamity in the Caucasus* (New York: New York University Press, 1998).

56. *RFE/RL Newsline,* May 12, 1998.

57. Dagestanis typically refer to Wahhabis using the Russian word *Vakhabiti,* which is used throughout the former Soviet Union to refer to any kind of politicized Islam.

58. Dargins and Laks are reportedly more committed to Islamic practices than are Avars or their related groups (Andis, Tsezi, and others) (interview with Sergei Arutiunov, University of California at Berkeley, May 13, 1999).

59. Igor Rotar, "Islamic Radicals in Dagestan," *Jamestown Foundation Prism,* no. 6, part 2 (March 20, 1998).

60. Mark Saroyan, *Minorities, Mullahs, and Modernity.*

61. *Kommersant-Daily,* September 24, 1998; *Current Digest* 50, no. 38 (1998):21.

62. *Izvestiia,* May 22, 1998; *Current Digest* 50, no. 21 (1998):1.

63. Sebastian Smith, *Allah's Mountains: Politics and War in the Russian Caucasus* (New York: I. B. Tauris, 1998).

64. Although highlanders and lowlanders, including Cossacks, cooperated intermittently during the war, there was also significant fighting between them, with highlanders generally supporting the Bolsheviks, and the Cossacks siding with the Whites. After the Whites were defeated, harsh reprisals were carried out by the Bolsheviks against allies of the Whites and other "class enemies" in the North Caucasus, particularly the Cossacks, and in many cases the highlanders participated in these reprisals. The result was a reinforcement of the highlander-Cossack perception of themselves as enemies and the loss of Cossack lands.

65. Gammer, "Competing Historical Narratives."

66. The Mountain Republic survived for a brief period under Soviet rule as the Mountain Republic ASSR, but it was subsequently broken up into ethnically defined, autonomous republics and oblasts.

67. Ebert Wesselink, *Dagestan (Daghestan): Comprehensive Report* (WRITENET [U.K.], 1998), available at http://www.caspian.net/daginfo.html (March 23, 1999).

68. Ibid.

69. Elizabeth Fuller, "Caucasus: The Lezgin Campaign for Autonomy," *RFE/RL Research Report* 1, no. 41 (1992):30–32.

70. *Nezavisimaia gazeta,* July 21, 1992; *Current Digest* 44, no. 29 (1992):24.

71. *Nezavisimaia gazeta,* October 6, 1998; and *TV i Radio monitoring, Politika,* October 4, 1998.

72. Nabi Abdullaev, "Azerbaijan and Dagestan Clash Over Border Issues," *Institute of East-West Studies Regional Report,* December 8, 1998.

73. Until the early 1980s, there was net in-migration of ethnic Russians to the North Caucasus, in large part because of the climate and resorts on both the Caspian and the Black seas. Many migrants were retired military officers attracted by the climate, excellent and cheap food, and beaches. The rapid outflow of Russians from the region began during perestroika and accelerated as the region became increasingly crime-ridden and impoverished with the Soviet collapse and the 1994–1996 Chechen war.

74. Kaiser, *The Geography of Nationalism,* 222–223.

75. From constituting close to half the population in Kumyk *raions* in the early 1960s, Kumyks fell to 20 percent by the early 1990s. See Wesselink, *Dagestan.*

76. By 1989, only some 28,000 Nogais were still resident in the republic. Although they constitute a substantial majority in the Nogai *raion,* they have become a tiny minority in other districts that they consider part of their ancestral territory.

77. *Segodnia,* June 6, 1998; *Current Digest* 30, no. 25 (1998):14.

78. Some Moscow analysts have suggested that the influx of migrants from the North Caucasus is helping foster fascism throughout Russia, and that the North Caucasus republics should be forcibly expelled from the Russian Federation and the border closed (see, for example, Mikhail Chulaki, "The Swastika and Nationalism," *Izvestiia,* August 11, 1998; *Current Digest* 50, no. 32 [1998]:6–7).

79. See, for example, *Kommersant-Daily* (September 24, 1998) and *Current Digest* (50, no. 38 [1998]:21) for an account of a march on Makhachkala by supporters of the Khachilayev brothers. When Magomedov was reelected president in 1998 by the Constitutional Assembly, his opponent, who received 78 votes to Magomedov's 168, was Sharafutdin Musayev, reportedly a close political ally of Nadir Khachilayev.

80. *Itogi,* August 31, 1998.

81. There were signs of intragovernmental disagreement in Moscow over Dagestan policy when Anatolii Kulikov, widely considered a hard-liner on Russian internal security policy, was head of the Russian interior ministry. Supporters of the use of mainly "economic levers" in Dagestan, who were particularly well represented in the Ministry of Nationalities and parts of the presidential administration, were pitted against supporters of a "firm hand" in the interior ministry. Intragovernmental tensions over federal policy toward Dagestan seem to have abated after Sergei Stepashin became interior minister in April 1998, and further abated after he was appointed prime minister in May 1999. Stepashin argued that Moscow should not only provide financial and political support to regional leaders but also take the lead in attacking crime in Dagestan.

82. The secretary of the Russian Security Council explained Russia's policy toward Dagestan in early 1998 as follows: "A settlement in the North Caucasus will be pursued through social and economic measures, combined with a determination to use all the manpower and resources at the state's disposal to safeguard law and order in the North Caucasus and in Dagestan in particular" (*Segodnia,* May 26, 1998; *Current Digest* 50, no. 21 [1998]:4).

83. *Izvestiia,* July 28, 1998; *Current Digest* 50, no. 30 (1998):10.

84. *Izvestiia,* May 20, 1999; *Current Digest* 51, no. 20 (1999):16.

85. There was speculation in Dagestan that the confrontation with the Khachilayevs was deliberately provoked by Moscow in order to provide an excuse to launch an anticorruption campaign, which of course served the dual purpose of shoring up Magomedov politically (Nabi Abdullaev, "Dagestani Regime Uses Feds to Undermine Opposition, Faces Protests," *Institute of East-West Studies Regional Report,* September 17, 1998; and idem,

"Federal Crackdown in Dagestan Continues," *Institute of East-West Studies Regional Report*, February 11, 1999).

86. Nabi Abdullaev, "Ethnic Leader's Arrest in Dagestan Causes Popular Disturbance," *Institute of East-West Studies Regional Report,* September 10, 1998. Nadir was not arrested, because the Russian constitution affords immunity to deputies of the federal parliament. Supporters of Magomed, who was a deputy in the Dagestani parliament, subsequently appealed to the Dagestani constitutional court, arguing that the Russian federal constitution afforded immunity to deputies of republic parliaments as well. The court rejected the argument. Demonstrations in Makhachkala and elsewhere prompted Kolesnikov to remove his prisoner from Makhachkala to Pyatigorsk, in Stavropol *krai.*

87. These include Gadzhi Makhachev, the republic's vice prime minister and a leader of the Avar national movement; Ruslan Gadzhibekov, the mayor of the city of Kaspiisk, near Makhachkala, and an ally of the Khachilayevs; Esenbolat Magomedov, the director of the Dagestani branch of the Western Caspian Committee on the Fishing Industry; and Sharafutdin Musayev, then head of the republic's Pension Fund. Musayev, however, managed to escape arrest by fleeing Makhachkala for his family village.

88. Nabi Abdullaev, "Nadir and Magomed Khachilaev: Politicians for the New Russia," *Jamestown Foundation Prism,* October 1999, no. 18, part 2.

89. Radoslav K. Petkov and Natan M. Shklar, "Russian Regions After the Crisis: Coping with Economic Troubles, Governors Reap Political Rewards" (paper presented at the Fourth Annual Convention of the Association for the Study of Nationalities, New York, 15-17 April 1999), 7.

90. I believe that these outcomes are unlikely, however. Whatever government is in office in Moscow will probably try to work with whomever is in power in Makhachkala.

About the Contributors

Victoria E. Bonnell is professor of sociology and director of the Institute of Slavic, East European, and Eurasian Studies at the University of California, Berkeley. She is the author of *Iconography of Power: Soviet Political Posters Under Lenin and Stalin* (1997) and coeditor (with Lynn Hunt) of *Beyond the Cultural Turn: New Directions in the Study of Society and History* (1999). She is currently working on a study of Russian entrepreneurial culture.

George W. Breslauer is Chancellor's Professor of Political Science and Dean of the Social Sciences, at the University of California, Berkeley. He is the author or editor of eleven books about Soviet and post-Soviet politics and foreign relations, including *Khrushchev and Brezhnev as Leaders* (1982) and the forthcoming *Gorbachev and Yeltsin as Leaders*.

Michael Burawoy is professor and chair of the department of sociology at the University of California, Berkeley. He is the coauthor (with Janos Lukacs) of *The Radiant Past: Ideology and Reality in Hungary's Road to Capitalism* (1992) and coeditor (with Kathryn Verdery) of *Uncertain Transition: Ethnographies of Change in the PostSocialist World* (1998). For the last decade he has been studying Russia's descent into the market.

Manuel Castells is professor of city and regional planning and professor of sociology, University of California, Berkeley. Between 1989 and 1999 he conducted research in various areas of Russia on issues of technological modernization and economic development. He is the author of twenty books, including the trilogy *The Information Age: Economy, Society, and Culture* (Blackwell, 1996/2000), translated into Russian by the Higher School of Economics Press.

M. Steven Fish is associate professor of political science at the University of California, Berkeley. He is the author of *Democracy from Scratch: Opposition and Regime in the New Russian Revolution* (Princeton, 1995). He has published articles in *Comparative Political Studies*, *East European Politics and Societies*, the *Journal of Democracy*, *Post-Soviet Affairs*, *Slavic Review*, and other journals. His research interests include comparative politics, regime change, political parties, social movements, and electoral politics.

Clifford G. Gaddy is a fellow at the Brookings Institution, with a joint appointment in the Foreign Policy Studies program and the Center on Social and Economic Dynamics. He is the co-author, with Barry W. Ickes, of *Russia's Virtual Economy* (forthcoming) and the author of *The Price of the Past: Russia's Struggle with the Legacy of a Militarized Economy* (1997).

Barry W. Ickes is a professor of economics at the Pennsylvania State University, director of research at the New Economic School in Moscow, and chairman of the board of the National Council for Eurasian and East European Research. He is the co-author, with Clifford G. Gaddy, of *Russia's Virtual Economy* (forthcoming). His articles have appeared in the *American Economic Review, Rand Journal of Economics,* and *Foreign Affairs.*

Emma Kiselyova is a research associate at the Institute of Slavic Studies and at the Institute of Urban and Regional Development, University of California, Berkeley. Formerly, she was assistant director of the Institute of Economics and Industrial Engineering, Russian Academy of Sciences, Novosibirsk, and deputy director of the Siberian International Center on Regional Development. Among other publications, she is co-author of *The collapse of the Soviet Union: the View from the Information Society* (University of California, 1995) and of *The Missing Link: Siberian Oil and Gas and the Pacific Economy* (Institute of Urban and Regional Development, University of California, Berkeley, 1996).

Pavel Krotov is director of the Institute of Regional Social Research of the Komi Republic, Syktyvkar, Russia. He is also a doctoral candidate at the University of Wisconsin at Madison. His research interests include the fate of Russia's natural resource industry and its effect on economic development, changing political attitudes, and strategies of survival. His latest publication is "Symptoms of 'Dutch Disease' in Russia: Is There Any Remedy? Possibilities of Sustainable Development of a Resource Abundant Region," Institute for East European Studies, Berlin, Germany, 2000.

Tatyana Lytkina is a research associate of the Institute of Socio-Economic and Energy Problems of the North, Komi Science Center, Syktyvkar, Russia. She is the author, with Svetlana Yaroshenko, of "Life Strategies in the Transition Period," in *Mechanisms of Market Adaptation in the Economy of the North,* edited by V.I. Spiryagin and S. Yaroshenko. Syktyvkar: Komi Scientific Center, 1998.

Victor M. Sergeyev is professor of comparative politics and Director of the Centre for International Studies MGIMO-University of the Ministry for Foreign Affairs of the Russian Federation. He is the author of many books and articles, including *Russia's Road to Democracy* (with N. Biryukov) (1993), *Russian Politics in Transition* (with N. Biryukov) (1997), and *The Wild East* (1998). His current interest include comparative studies of political culture, globalization processes in international relations, analysis of decisionmaking, and cognitive studies.

Robert Sharlet, Chauncey Winters Professor of Political Science at Union College, has published extensively on the nexus between Soviet and now Russian law and politics. He is at work on a book on Russian constitutional politics and law.

Veljko Vujačić is assistant professor of sociology at Oberlin College. His publications include "Historical Legacies, Nationalist Mobilization and Political Outcomes in Russia and Serbia: A Weberian View," *Theory and Society* (December 1996); "Gennadii Ziuganov and the Third Road," *Post-Soviet Affairs* (April-June 1996); "Sociology and Nationalism," Alexander Motyl, ed., *Encyclopedia of Nationalism* (Academic Press, 2000) He is currently working on a book manuscript "From Class to Nation: Communism and Nationalism in Russia and Serbia."

Edward W. Walker is executive director of the Berkeley program in Soviet and Post-Soviet Studies at the University of California, Berkeley, where he teaches in the department of political science. He is the author of articles on politics, nationalism, and ethnic conflict in the former Soviet Union and is completing a book entitled *Dissolution: Sovereignty and the Breakup of the Soviet Union.*

Victor Zaslavsky is professor of political sociology at Guido Carli Free International University of Social Sciences, Rome, Italy. He previously taught at the University of Leningrad, Memorial University (St. John's, Canada), University of Florence, University of Venice, University of California Berkeley, and Stanford University. Among his recent publications are *Togliatti e Stalin: Il Partito comunista italiano e la politica estera sovietica* (with E. Agarossi), the winner of the 1998 "stiria" prize, Italy; *La Russia senza Soviet*, Rome, Ideazione, 1996; and *The Neo-Stalinist State: Class, Ethnicity, and Consensus in Soviet Society*, 2nd ed., Armonk, Sharpe, 1994.

Igor Zevelev is professor of Russian studies at the George C. Marshall European Center for Security Studies. Prior to joining the Marshall Center, Zevelev was head research associate at the Institute of World Economy and International Relations of the Russian Academy of Sciences, where he also served as head of department and deputy director of the Center for Developing Countries. He is the author of *Russia and the New Russian Diasporas* (forthcoming); *Global Security Beyond the Millennium: American and Russian Perspectives* (co-edited with Sharyl Cross, 1999); *Urbanization and Development in Asia* (1989); *Southeast Asia: Urbanization and Problems of Social Development* (1985) and numerous articles on Asia, Russia, human rights, international relations, and security issues.

Kimberly Marten Zisk is associate professor of political science at Barnard College, Columbia University. She is the author of *Engaging the Enemy: Organization Theory and Soviet Military Innovation, 1955–1991* (Princeton University Press, 1993), which received the Marshall Shulman Prize from the American Association for the Advancement of Slavic Studies; *Weapons, Culture, and Self-Interest: Soviet Defense Managers in the New Russia* (Columbia University Press, 1998); and numerous articles and book chapters on related themes. She was a post-doctoral fellow at Stanford's Center for International Security and Arms Control and a visiting scholar at Harvard's Olin Institute for Strategic Studies. Her current research focuses on the U.N. Security Council and the politics of peacekeeping.

Index

Abramovich, Roman, 188, 190
Akaev, Askar, 29–30, 41
Aksyuchitis, Viktor, 272
Alekperov, Vagit, 188, 190
Alfa Group, 185–186
Aliev, Mukhu, 335
alternative states, 160, 162–163
Ambartsumov, Yevgenii, 273
Amirov, Said, 347
Andreeva, Nina, 294
Angstrem, 127–128
Anpilov, Viktor
    Gennadii Zyuganov vs., 308
    mass rallies and, 297
    Russian nationalism and, 294
    Working Russia movement and, 293
anti-institutional personalism, 24
AO-RELCOM network, 136
Armeiskii sbornik (journal), 83
ASSR (autonomous Soviet socialist
    republic), 343, 344
Astafiev, Mikhail, 272
Astrakan, 343
August 1991 coup, 295
autonomous Soviet socialist republic
    (ASSR), 343, 344
Avars, 345, 346, 347
Aven, Pyotr, 188, 190
Azerbaijan, 327, 344–345
Azeris, 345

Baburin, Sergey
    deputy speaker of the Duma, 292–293,
    308
    formation of ROS and, 296
    restorationism and, 283
    treaty with Ukraine and, 281, 282, 284
Baglai, Chief Justice Marat
    classification of cases of, 71–73
    on constitutional jurisdiction, 64
    extrajudicial behavior of, 70–71

influence on RCC, 74–75
    judicial experience of, 69
Baglai-Tumanov Court, 71–73
Baku, 345
bankruptcy, 115
banks
    associations of oligarchs with, 185–186
    background of oligarchs and, 190–192
    bankers war and, 187
    December 1993 election and, 185
    financial collapse of August 1998 and,
    188
    financial-industrial groups (FIGs) and,
    185–186
    mergers and joint ventures of, 188
    political power of oligarchs and,
    186–187
    shares-for-loans auctions and, 186
Baranets, Viktor, 40
Barany, Zoltan, 24
Barkashov, Aleksandr, 95, 307
Basayev, Shamil, 326, 327, 339
Belovezh Agreement, 295
Berezovsky, Boris, 186, 186–187, 188,
    190
binding interpretations, 63
Black Hundred, 272, 293
Black Sea Fleet, 279, 280, 282
Blankenagel, Alexander, 65–66
Bonnell, Victoria E., 3–12, 175–200
Bosnia, 94
bourgeoisie, 176
Breslauer, George W., 3–12, 24, 35–58
budgetary constraint reforms, 106–109
Bulgaria, 21
Bunin, Igor, 182
Burawoy, Michael, 9, 231–261
bureaucracy, deviant, 160, 163–165
Business Network, 138–139
Buzan, Barry, 265
Bykov, Anatolii, 188, 190